BEOWULF

broadview editions
series editor: L.W. Conolly

BEOWULF

second edition

Facing page translation by R.M. Liuzza

broadview editions

Library and Archives Canada Cataloguing in Publication

Beowulf. English
    Beowulf / facing page translation by R.M. Liuzza. — 2nd ed.

(Broadview editions)
Includes bibliographical references.
ISBN 978-1-55481-113-7

    I. Liuzza, R. M II. Series: Broadview editions.

PR1583.L58 2012   829'.3   C2012-904206-4

Broadview Editions
The Broadview Editions series represents the ever-changing canon of literature in English by bringing together texts long regarded as classics with valuable lesser-known works.

Advisory editor for this volume: Martin Boyne

Broadview Press is an independent, international publishing house, incorporated in 1985.

We welcome comments and suggestions regarding any aspect of our publications—please feel free to contact us at the addresses below or at broadview@broadviewpress.com.

North America
Post Office Box 1243, Peterborough, Ontario, Canada K9J 7H5
2215 Kenmore Avenue, Buffalo, NY, USA 14207
Tel: (705) 743-8990; Fax: (705) 743-8353
email: customerservice@broadviewpress.com

UK, Europe, Central Asia, Middle East, Africa, India, and Southeast Asia
Eurospan Group, 3 Henrietta St., London WC2E 8LU, United Kingdom
Tel: 44 (0) 1767 604972; Fax: 44 (0) 1767 601640
email: eurospan@turpin-distribution.com

Australia and New Zealand
NewSouth Books
c/o TL Distribution, 15-23 Helles Ave., Moorebank, NSW, Australia 2170
Tel: (02) 8778 9999; Fax: (02) 8778 9944
email: orders@tldistribution.com.au

www.broadviewpress.com

This book is printed on paper containing 100% post-consumer fibre.

Typesetting and assembly: True to Type Inc., Claremont, Canada.

PRINTED IN CANADA

Contents

Acknowledgements

My thanks are due to David Johnson, J.R. Hall, Molly Rothenberg, and Myra Seaman for their generous assistance during the writing of the introduction. I am grateful to my students at Tulane University for their reading of the text during several semesters; to Broadview Press for its exceptional encouragement, advice, and support; and to the many friends, students, colleagues, and readers who have offered suggestions and corrections for this second edition.

Permission has been granted for the following:

Selections from Saxo Grammaticus, *The History of the Danes*, translated by Peter Fisher and edited by H. Ellis Davidson, copyright © 1979 D.S. Brewer, are reprinted with the permission of Boydell and Brewer Ltd. Selections from *Bede's Ecclesiastical History of the English People*, edited and translated by Bertram Colgrave and R.A.B. Mynors, copyright © 1992 Oxford University Press, are reprinted with the permission of Oxford University Press. Letter 46, c. 738, and Letter 73, c. 746, from *The Letters of Saint Boniface*, translated by Ephraim Emerton, copyright © 1940 Columbia University Press, are reprinted with permission of the publisher. Selections from *Beowulf: A Dual-Language Edition*, edited and translated by Howell D. Chickering, copyright © 1977 Anchor Books, are reprinted by permission of Random House, Inc. and Howell D. Chickering. Selections from *Beowulf*, translated by Kevin Crossley-Holland, are from *The Anglo-Saxon World: An Anthology*, copyright © 1982 Boydell Press, and are reprinted with the permission of Boydell and Brewer Ltd. Selections from *A Readable Beowulf: The Old English Epic Newly Translated* by Stanley B. Greenfield, copyright © 1982 by the Board of Trustees, Southern Illinois University Press, are reprinted by permission of Southern Illinois University Press. Selections from *Beowulf* by Marc Hudson, copyright © 1990 Bucknell University Press, are reprinted by permission of Associated University Presses. Selections from *Beowulf: The Oldest English Epic*, translated by Charles W. Kennedy, translation copyright © 1940 by Oxford University Press Inc., renewed 1968 by Charles W. Kennedy, are used by permission of Oxford University Press USA. Selections from *Beowulf: An Imitative Translation*, translated by Ruth P.M. Lehmann, copyright © 1988, appear courtesy of the University of Texas Press. Selections from *Beowulf*, translated by Edwin Morgan, copyright © 1962, the University of California Press, have been reprinted by permission of Carcanet

Preface

Adeo sanctum est vetus omne poema.—Horace.

Beowulf is one of the earliest full-scale works of English literature and is still sometimes regarded as a straightforward heroic poem, an uncomplicated point of origin (for good or ill) of the "English Literary Tradition." But most serious readers of the poem have come to recognize that *Beowulf* is a complex product of Anglo-Saxon cultural tensions, itself a work of long gestation and mixed heritage born of melancholy and nostalgia. Fueled by these relatively new readings of a classic text, interest in *Beowulf* continues unabated: student editions by Jack, Alexander, and Mitchell and Robinson; publications such as Bjork and Niles's *Beowulf Handbook*, an updated reprint of Colin Chase's collection *The Dating of Beowulf*, and a reissue of Kevin Kiernan's groundbreaking *"Beowulf" and the "Beowulf" Manuscript*; book-length studies by Davis, Deskis, Earl, and Hill, and new anthologies of *Beowulf* criticism by Baker and Fulk all indicate that scholars and students are still intrigued by the poem, still active in its interpretation, and still struggling toward some understanding. The years since this translation was first published have seen hundreds of articles, dozens of books, a new standard edition, and several collections, notably Joy and Ramsey's groundbreaking *Postmodern 'Beowulf'* in 2006. These new works offer a depth of study and breadth of context not formerly available to the non-specialist reader, and I hope that a new translation that has benefited from their influence may not be an unworthy companion to them.

The present work is intended to bring together a readable and reliable translation with adequate notes, a collection of supporting texts and commentary, and an introduction that situates the poem in a literary history. This revised edition includes the Old English text facing each page of the translation. For those who do not wish to learn Old English, I believe I have provided a fluent and accurate text; for those who already know *Beowulf* in its original language, I hope I can offer a reading of the poem at close range in the form of a translation, a record of the poem's effect on me, and an account of my sense of its context and meaning. Like most readers of *Beowulf*, I have often been struck by the many ways in which translations of the poem fail to capture its peculiar beauty. My own work, I know well, does little better, but I hope that my love for the poem has not been entirely unrequited, and that some sense of the *Beowulf* I have read and continue to read with such pleasure is conveyed in my work.

The supporting texts were chosen to illustrate the poem's background and context, but since the date and place of composition of *Beowulf* are unknown and the subject of much debate, and the critical history of the poem has linked it to both pagan Germanic and Latin Christian sources, I have felt free to include works of various kinds and dates: analogues from Old Norse and Latin, poems in Old English, references in Latin chronicles to characters appearing in the poem, letters from an eighth-century English missionary saint, and sermons from the turn of the millennium. All are meant to suggest, sometimes obliquely, the richness of the cultural milieu in which *Beowulf*, the story and the text, circulated.

Louisville, KY / Knoxville, TN

Introduction

Only one copy of the Old English poem that modern editors call *Beowulf* has survived, and it is likely that it has survived only by accident. A manuscript containing *Beowulf* and a small collection of other texts—a poetic treatment of the deuterocanonical Old Testament story of Judith, a prose life of St Christopher, and two treatises of fantastical geography now known as *The Wonders of the East* and *Alexander's Letter to Aristotle*—was copied by two scribes, probably in the decade after 1000, in a monastic center somewhere in the south of England. It is an eclectic anthology containing prose and verse, hagiography and secular heroism, oriental and biblical and Germanic lore; its contents baffle our modern expectations of genre. The texts are from different sources, and the prose pieces are all translations of Latin works. What unites them, apparently, is an interest in monsters and marvels, faraway places and long-distant ages, and fantastic beings of extraordinary size; in his 1995 book, Orchard described its contents as "Pride and Prodigies." Whatever its original purpose or audience, the book fell into obscurity in the centuries after the Norman Conquest in 1066, and its later history is unknown until 1563, when the English antiquary Laurence Nowell (c. 1515-c. 1571) signed his name on the first page of *St. Christopher*. The Nowell Codex, as it is sometimes called, later came into the library of the collector Sir Robert Cotton (1571-1631); the present-day shelfmark of the manuscript (British Library MS Cotton Vitellius A. xv) recalls the arrangement of Cotton's library, in which books were stored in shelves surmounted by busts of Roman emperors. Cotton bound the manuscript with an unrelated twelfth-century copy of Augustine's *Soliloquies* and other works. In 1731, while Cotton's collection was stored at Ashburnham House in Westminster awaiting donation to the future British Museum, a disastrous fire damaged or destroyed hundreds of volumes and nearly consumed the *Beowulf* manuscript as well.[1]

Apart from a notice in an early manuscript catalogue by Humphrey Wanley in 1705, it was not until the end of the eighteenth century that scholars began to appreciate the contents of this scorched and charred manuscript. The romantic nationalism of the time expected—indeed, more or less required—that at the beginning of every great nation's literature would stand a national epic analogous to the Greek *Iliad*. The French had the *Chanson de Roland*, the Germans the *Nibelungenlied*;

---

1   The damage to the library is surveyed by Prescott, "The Ghost of Asser" and "Their Present Miserable State."

Beowulf, the earliest full-length heroic poem in any Germanic language, was claimed by the English (because of its language), the Danes (because of its subject), and the Germans (because of its setting in the pre-Christian north). The first printed notice of the poem, along with some badly translated passages, was in Sharon Turner's second edition of his *History of the Anglo-Saxons* (1805), where it is called "a composition most curious and important.... [I]t may be called an Anglo-Saxon epic poem." In 1787 a copyist who was probably commissioned by the scholar Grímur Thorkelin (1752-1829), an Icelander in the service of Denmark, made a transcription of the poem; later Thorkelin himself went to the British Museum to make another (see Kiernan, *Thorkelin Transcripts*). Like Turner, Thorkelin's inability to read Old English did not prevent him from admiring *Beowulf.* He was convinced that the poem was originally composed in Danish, even though it survived in an English translation, and that its author had been an eyewitness to the funeral of the hero Beowulf, which he placed in the year 340 (Bjork, "Thorkelin's Preface"). These theories are nonsense, but Thorkelin's transcripts are still invaluable evidence for many readings now lost from the crumbling edges of the manuscript's pages. His first edition of the poem (with a Latin translation) in 1815, however, was a task somewhat beyond his powers, and it was quickly superseded by other and better editions, including that of J.M. Kemble in 1833, Benjamin Thorpe in 1855, and C.W.M. Grein in 1857. The poem was translated into Danish verse by N.F.S. Gruntvig in 1820, and long passages appeared in English in J.J. Conybeare's *Illustrations of Anglo-Saxon Poetry* in 1826; a full English prose translation was produced by Kemble in 1837. In this way the poem gradually reached a wider audience; eventually more reliable scholarly editions and more accurate translations became available. The standard modern edition of the poem, which appeared in several revisions between 1922 and 1950, is that of Friedrich Klaeber; a new standard edition appeared under Klaeber's name, edited by Fulk, Bjork, and Niles, in 2008.

Beowulf between Myth and History

> *If all time is eternally present*
> *All time is unredeemable.*[1]

Although, like other Old English poems, *Beowulf* is copied on its manuscript pages from margin to margin like prose, the poem consists of 3,182 extant lines of alliterative verse, divided into 43 numbered sec-

---

1   All epigraphs in this Introduction are from T.S. Eliot, "Burnt Norton," *Four Quartets* (London: Faber & Faber, 1943).

tions of varying length with an unnumbered prologue. Its language is allusive and embellished and its plot complex and digressive, but its story is relatively straightforward. The Danish king Hrothgar, descendant of the legendary Scyld, has built a magnificent hall Heorot, but the hall is invaded night after night by a marauding beast named Grendel (sec. I-II). A young warrior of the tribe of the Geats named Beowulf hears of Hrothgar's troubles and comes to his rescue; after a series of challenges and boasts he faces Grendel unarmed, and tears off the monster's arm in a wild wrestling match (III-XII). Celebration is lively but short-lived; the next night the monster's mother attacks the hall in revenge for the death of her son, killing one of Hrothgar's most trusted retainers (XIII-XIX). Undaunted, Beowulf follows her tracks to an underwater lair and, after a difficult fight, kills her with an extraordinary sword that he finds in her cave (XX-XXIII). He returns to the Danish hall to much praise, celebration, and gift-giving; soon he returns to his native land and recounts his adventures to his own king and uncle Hygelac (XXIV-XXXI).

Fifty years are passed over in a few verses, and Beowulf is now himself an aged king. His kingdom is attacked by a dragon who has been roused from his underground barrow when his hoard of ancient treasure is plundered (XXXII-XXXIII). Beowulf, although old, ventures forth to fight the dragon, armed with a fireproof shield and accompanied by a troop of men. His companions flee in terror, but a young warrior named Wiglaf comes to the king's aid; together they kill the dragon, but in the fight Beowulf is mortally wounded (XXXIV-XXXVIII). He dies beside the heap of treasure he has won for his nation; amid gloomy predictions of the impending downfall of the Geats, he is buried with mourning and sad ceremony (XXXIX-XLIII).

In such bare outline, the story has an almost archetypal symmetry and simplicity, and scholars have not failed to notice parallels between the hero's combats and various elements of northern folklore and world mythology.[1] The story of Beowulf in Denmark—a young man of great strength who kills a monster in single combat without the aid of weapons—conforms to the pattern of a traditional folktale identified by Friedrich Panzer in 1910 as the "Bear's Son Tale" or "The Three Stolen Princesses" (see also Stitt). Although Grendel is described by the narrator as a demonic descendant of the biblical figure Cain, his closest narrative relatives are the trolls that inhabit Scandinavian folktales (see Appendix B1) such as the *draugr*, a kind of restless and

---

1 Good examples of this approach can be found in Page and Cassidy, Nagler, Damico, Barnes (with a response by Rosenberg); general reflections may be found in Niles, "Myth and History."

violent zombie. The dragon, on the other hand, may serve as an emblem of Satan in the biblical Book of Revelation, but in this poem he seems more like a creature of the natural world, malevolent but not necessarily demonic; he is not called the "foe of mankind" (164) or the "ancient adversary" (1776), as Grendel is. The *Cotton Maxims*, a collection of Old English proverbs about the nature of the world, state that "A dragon will be in his barrow, ancient and proud in his treasures" (Dobbie 55-57, line 26). A similar sort of dragon appears in the narrative of Danish historian Saxo Grammaticus (Appendix B2), and the slaying of a dragon is an ancient motif (though adapted in *Beowulf* to a particular and tragic purpose) of which the poem's own account of Sigemund (875-98) is both analogue and foreshadowing. The story of Beowulf follows the narrative patterns of a folktale: a hero who quests and fights in isolation from friends and family, fabulous battles against monstrous foes, the theme of a young man who was thought to be lazy (lines 2183-89) but later becomes a mighty hero, even the concatenation of three challenges in ascending order of difficulty. The fabulous outlines of the story equally recall the broad brushstrokes of myth: the mighty Beowulf may be a distant echo of Thor (Lerer); his descent into the mere may dimly depict a shamanistic initiation (Glosecki 152-210); his death may contain a hint of Ragnarok, the northern apocalypse (Dronke). *Beowulf*, then, appears to be a reflex of an ancient and universal plot.

Certainly the ultimate roots of the story, unknown and probably unknowable, are deep in the common soil of all storytelling, in the archetypal story Joseph Campbell (using a term borrowed from James Joyce) has called the "monomyth" (30).[1] Joseph Fontenrose has pointed out that the hero's struggles have something in common even with the battles of Hercules or Theseus or Apollo. Such mythic and folkloric analogues are generally strongest, however, in inverse proportion to the clarity with which the details of the story are remembered; in the mythopoeic night, all cats are gray. Whatever its underlying structural patterns, *Beowulf* is neither myth nor folktale; its stories of dragon-slaying and nocturnal struggles are set against a complex background of legendary history. The action of the poem unfolds on a roughly recognizable map of Scandinavia: Hrothgar's hall Heorot has been plausibly placed in the village of Lejre on the Danish island of Zealand, and we may tentatively identify Beowulf's

---

1   Campbell's description of "the nuclear unit of the monomyth" might well be applied to much of the story line of *Beowulf*: "A hero ventures forth from the world of common day into a region of supernatural wonder: fabulous forces are there encountered and a decisive victory is won: the hero comes back from this mysterious adventure with the power to bestow boons on his fellow man."

tribe of Geats with the historical Gautar of southern Sweden.[1] The mythical figure of Scyld soon yields to the historical figure of Hrothgar, and a number of the poem's characters—among them Heremod, Hrothgar, Ingeld, and Hygelac—are mentioned in other sources and were certainly regarded as figures of history rather than fable. The Frankish historian Gregory of Tours (d. 594) mentions the disastrous raid of Hygelac (whom he calls Chlochilaicus and describes as a Danish king) and dates it around the year 520 (see Appendix A1). And, like its characters and setting, the concerns of the poem are historical. Behind the drama of isolated hand-to-hand encounters against monstrous adversaries, *Beowulf* is an intensely political poem; the poet is as intrigued by Danish diplomacy and the bitter feud between the Geats and Swedes as he is by the hero's battles. Kingdoms and successions, alliances and truces, loyalties and the tragically transient stability of heroic society are the poem's somber subtext, a theme traced less in the clashes of the battlefield than in the patterns of marriage and kin, in stories remembered and retold, in allusion and digression and pointed foreshadowing.

Whatever historical interests may be found in *Beowulf,* however, it is difficult to read the poem with anything like a modern expectation of historical accuracy. Like many medieval works, *Beowulf* is frustratingly ambivalent—it is not quite mythical enough to be read apart from the history it purports to contain, nor historical enough to furnish clear evidence for the past it poetically recreates. The action of the poem is set in a somewhat vague heroic *geardagum* ("bygone days," line 1), an age not meant to be counted on a calendar, nor its kingdoms and tribes marked on a map; nor, undoubtedly, were the monstrous races of Grendels and dragons so clearly distinct in the poet's mind from the real dangers of the real world just beyond the margins of the known. While medieval authors certainly made distinctions between *historia* and *fabula,* the boundaries between these terms are not nearly as impermeable as those of our modern categories "history" and "fable"; this unruly poem, like the manuscript in which it survives, does not stay within the framework of our generic expectations. Moreover, the poem itself is a monumental exercise of the historical imagination, poetically re-creating a past that is itself multilayered and temporally complex. Inside the story a sense of time past and time passing is evoked by reference to earlier events such as the reign of

---

1   On Lejre, see Niles, *Beowulf and Lejre.* Historical background may be found in Chambers; the identity of the Geats is discussed in Malone, "King Alfred's Geatas," and in Farrell, but Leake argues that they are instead to be identified with the legendary Getae, a tribe of no fixed geographical abode.

Heremod and the death of Herebeald, and by forecast of future ones such as the burning of Heorot or the conquest of the Geats (the scene in which Wealhtheow gives Beowulf a necklace, lines 1192-1214, is a striking instance of the poem's historical depth of field), and by the carefully allusive interweaving of historical and political concerns into the main plot, suggesting the context in which the hero's exploits occur and the consequences they entail.[1] In many respects the poem already contains its own background and foreground, a fictionalized matrix of past and present within the text; our modern efforts to explain Beowulf's origins or context or even to place the hero's actions into some perspective can only mimic or mirror the poem's own contextualizing impulses. Fred C. Robinson has noted that

> the average reader of English literature often comes to *Beowulf* with the naive expectation that reading this early poem will bring him face to face with the collective unconscious of English culture, will allow him to experience at first hand what is primordial, elemental and primitively powerful in it. But the experience is more complex than that, for the Anglo-Saxons who wrote and read *Beowulf* were themselves exploring the unconscious of their culture by returning to dark beginnings in an age long antecedent to theirs. If reading *Beowulf* is an exploration of our primal selves, we are led on that exploration by a refined, reflective, Christian Anglo-Saxon poet whose curiosity about the remote origins of his people is perhaps not unlike our own. (*"Beowulf"* 142-43)

The poet looks back on a world long vanished, imaginatively bringing its textures and values to life; his own complex sense of the past prevents us from reading his work either as a transhistorical and transcultural fragment of primordial myth or as a transparent window onto the cultural or material conditions of a lost heroic age.

This interweaving of legendary history and fabulous tales in *Beowulf*, the combination of the political intrigues of battles, feuds, marriages, and successions, and the archetypal combat of a solitary hero against a supernatural foe has caused much critical anxiety throughout the history of *Beowulf* studies. Klaeber echoed the sentiments of most of his contemporaries when he lamented that the poet's poor taste had caused him to spend so much time on childish matters like monsters and dragons and less on the more interesting and dignified subjects of wars and alliances: "we may well regret that those sub-

---

1   The poem's historical interests are examined by Hanning; Frank, "Sense of History"; Dean; and Helterman.

jects of intensely absorbing interest play only a minor part in our epic, having to serve as a foil to a story which in itself is of decidedly inferior weight" (*Beowulf and the Fight at Finnsburg*, 3rd ed., lv). J.R.R. Tolkien's 1936 essay "*Beowulf*: The Monsters and the Critics" is usually credited with re-establishing the fabulous elements and heroic combats at the center of the modern reader's appreciation of the poem. In many respects, however, the separation of the poem into "mythical" and "historical" elements is a false dichotomy. If, as many modern scholars maintain, it is the business of myth to condense and contain the most fundamental sources of cultural tension—those areas in which the self and the world are in greatest friction—and to validate current ideologies by dramatizing them and retrojecting their contours into the past, then the hero's "mythic" combats equally reflect an interest in the social order, an authorization of certain cultural conditions and practices; the placing of these combats in a context of legendary history indicates a desire to examine these cultural tensions in relation to the passage of time. Beowulf's fabulous adversaries perform strenuous cultural work: Grendel can be regarded as a monstrous embodiment of the principle of fratricide, his mother a manifestation of the harsh economy of revenge and the even darker powers of the primal claims of tribal kinship against the masculine world of the warrior band or *comitatus*, and the dragon a kind of perverse king hoarding his wealth in a morbid anti-hall. Without detracting from the poet's delight in the physical reality of Beowulf's battles—his depictions are richly textured, from the terror of Grendel's fiery eyes to the coiling and belching of the dragon—each combat can be read as a dramatized locus of cultural anxiety, pitting the hero against some aspect of his own society drawn in grotesque caricature. The monsters outside the hall are projections of the evils within the hall—the implied treachery of Hrothulf (hinted at in lines 1013-19 and 1163-65, though not all scholars have read them so), the remembered treachery of Unferth, the predicted treachery of Ingeld, the fatal treachery of Beowulf's cowardly retainers. These battles against the inhuman forces of destruction outside the hall, no matter how praiseworthy and heroic, however, do nothing to prevent the blossoming and flourishing of all-too-human evil within the hall. The order that is restored by the slaying of Grendel and his mother is not permanent, and the destruction of the dragon requires the death of Beowulf himself, a loss that appears to inaugurate the destruction of his whole nation. As Joyce Lionarons has noted, the "mythical" elements of *Beowulf* portray the labor required to create and sustain a civilized social order, threatened within and without by a culture of violence; its monsters are narrative manifestations of the forces of disorder and chaos that an orderly society must hold at bay but which will, in the dark world of the poem, inevitably triumph. This sad triumph is made possible by the debilitating effects of the passage of time and the failure of the social order to channel the human passions successfully. In this sense the poem springs, quite precisely, from the intersection of myth and history, the individual psyche and its cultural milieu, the desire to authorize the present by means of the past— in effect denying the passage of time—and the necessity of accepting the inevitable contingency and loss that such passing brings.

Beowulf between Song and Text

> *Words, after speech, reach*
> *Into the silence. Only by the form, the pattern,*
> *Can words or music reach*
> *The stillness, as a Chinese jar still*
> *Moves perpetually in its stillness.*

Both the ultimate and the proximate origins of *Beowulf* are unknown. Most scholars assume that the surviving manuscript is a copy of an earlier written text and is probably the last in a long chain of copies.[1] Moreover, the poem begins with the assumption that we are hearing a familiar story, or a least a story from a familiar milieu: "We have heard of the glory ... of the folk-kings of the spear-Danes" (*We Gar-Dena ... þeodcyninga þrym gefrunon*), the poet asserts, and his cryptic allusions throughout the poem suggest that his audience was already familiar with a larger repertoire of songs and stories of kings and heroes. A poem such as *Widsith* (Appendix A6) assumes that heroic history was considered a fit subject for secular entertainment, and a surviving fragment of a poem about the fight at Finnsburh (Appendix A5; the battle is also recounted in sections XVI and XVII of *Beowulf*) proves that at least some Anglo-Saxons had heard stories like the ones in *Beowulf*; the complaint of Alcuin (Appendix A3) indicates that even churchmen enjoyed stories about the adventures of ancient heroes like Ingeld. In the poem itself we are given several scenes of poetic entertainment— a poet sings of the wonders of creation (90-98), Beowulf is praised by songs about Sigemund (867-915), the Danes are entertained by a story of Finn and Hengest (1065-1160). It is often assumed that such scenes reflect the actual circumstances of the composition and reception of *Beowulf*: the poem originated as an oral performance rather than a text. The poem begins *Hwæt, we ... gefrunon* (in the present translation,

---

1   A notable dissenter from this scholarly consensus is Kiernan, *"Beowulf" and the "Beowulf" Manuscript.*

"*Listen*! We have *heard*"—the opening word is a call for attention), and always remains firmly in the realm of listening and hearing rather than reading and writing. When the narrator affirms the truth of his story he uses expressions such as "I have never heard" (38, 1011, etc.) or "as I have heard" (74, 838, etc.), rather than, as later medieval narrators might say, "as books tell us" or "as my *auctor* alleges"; this is a poem of fame and familiar story, with no indication that the narrator relies on written documents or regards books as the bearers of truth about the past.

The practice of oral poetry in early medieval cultures is naturally invisible; all surviving evidence for literary history is in writing. Scholars have analyzed the repetitions in Homeric and other bodies of early verse, however, and made field studies of oral-traditional poetry performed by singers of traditional poetry in the early twentieth century, and these have offered models and analogies for imagining the practice of the Anglo-Saxon *scop* or singer-poet. They suggest that he would have worked from a collection of traditional stories improvised in performance from a repertoire of formulaic elements, groups of words that met the demands of meter and sense and could be used and reused according to the needs of the poem.[1] Traditional phrases and descriptive tags would make it easier to sketch a character or action in song, and recurring scenes and motifs (approaching the hall, donning armor, crossing the sea, preparing for battle, etc.) could be added in variable combinations at each performance; the core of the story and the elements of poetic style remained the same, but the surface changed with each new telling. Such a traditional method of oral composition, employing a collection of metrical formulae, stock scenes, and narrative patterns, probably existed as part of the common heritage of the Germanic peoples, and the Angles and Saxons may have brought songs of kings and heroes to Britain from their continental homeland. Such traditional stories, told and retold over centuries, may have contributed to both the narrative form and the diction of *Beowulf* as it survives today.

Metrical formulae and narrative set-pieces were the building-blocks of traditional poetry, a highly patterned language for a highly formal narrative style; the expectation of striking originality from a work of art is a modern phenomenon. A delight in recurrence-with-variation in language and story is one of the deepest aesthetic principles of Old

---

1 The literature on the "oral-formulaic" theory is vast: among the most useful introductions to methods and problems are Lord; Magoun "Oral-Formulaic Character"; Creed; Calder; and the many works of John Miles Foley, including "Tradition and the Collective Talent," *Theory of Oral Composition*, *Oral-Formulaic Theory and Research*, and "Texts That Speak."

English poetry, and many of the individual lines of *Beowulf* can be found repeated in other Old English poems and within the poem itself. The expression *weox under wolcnum* "grew under heaven" (literally, "under the clouds") in line 8 appears, with variations, in other poems and elsewhere in *Beowulf* (Grendel comes *wan under wolcnum* "pale under the clouds" in line 651; later we are told he *wod under wolcnum* "went under the clouds" 714; Hrothgar says that he *weold under wolcnum* "ruled under the clouds" in 1770). We can assume, then, that the formula "*X under wolcnum*" was one of the poet's ready-made metrical packages. Likewise the expression *ofer hronrade* "over the whale's-riding" (10) formed a metrically correct periphrasis for "the sea," and it is found elsewhere in expressions such as *ofer swanrade* "over the swan's-riding" (200) and *on seglrade* "over the sail-road" (1429)—the formula might be expressed as "*ofer X-rad*," with "X" variable according to mood, tone, and the needs of alliteration. The line introducing the hero's speech, *Beowulf maþelode, bearn Ecgþeowes* ("Beowulf spoke, son of Ecgtheow") is repeated in lines 529, 631, 957, 1383, 1473, 1651, 1817, 1999, and 2425, and a similar formula is used to introduce speeches of other characters (e.g., *Wiglaf maðelode, Weohstanes sunu* "Wiglaf spoke, son of Weohstan," lines 2862 and 3076). A modern reader must learn to hear such outright repetitions not as stylistic defects—failures to "make it new"—but rather as aspects of the traditional craft of the singer; in the hands of a good poet like the author of *Beowulf*, such repeated formulae are not deployed unfeelingly or automatically according to some principle of compositional thrift but are used to enhance and elaborate the poem's stately formal art.

Recurring narrative moments such as sea-voyages, arrival at a hall, arming, or funeral obsequies could be crafted out of a stock of appropriate formulae and built according to a pattern of expected elements; these "themes"—the equivalent on the level of narrative of the formula on the level of diction—are used to produce an artful interaction between a particular moment in the poem and an audience's expectations.[1] Speech situations that are parallel in organization and narrative function, such as Beowulf's three introductory boasts in Denmark, are characterized by elaborate variation and differences in detail and effect; their recurrence establishes a kind of motif, elaborated in a slightly different register at each retelling. Francelia Clark has drawn attention to the fact that each recurrence of a repeated element in

---

1   Two classic studies of the theme in Old English (OE) poetry are Greenfield, "Formulaic Expression," and Magoun, "Theme of the Beasts of Battle"; and see, more recently, Amodio.

Beowulf such as the mention of Hygelac's ill-fated raid on Frisia (reference to it appears in lines 1202-14, 2200-02, 2354-60, 2910-21, and possibly 2499-2507) generally offers new information and new emphasis in each retelling; the amount of direct verbal repetition is dramatically small. Even Beowulf's recounting of his own adventures (1999-2151) offers a number of striking new perspectives on the events we have already witnessed: we learn of Grendel's strange glove and Ingeld's predicted attack, and interestingly enough we do *not* hear anything about Unferth's verbal challenge to Beowulf. The whole structure of the poem offers a large-scale example of such a repeated motif, in which an old king is supported by a young champion; here too it is recurrence-with-variation, the tension between structural similarity and narrative difference, that drives the poem's art and meaning.

The formulaic diction and narrative style of traditional poetry was "an instrument of enormous, and absolutely singular, sensitivity" (Foley, *Immanent Art* 193) that was employed even by thoroughly literate poets such as the author of the OE *Phoenix* (a verse translation of a Latin original) and the translators of the OE *Metrical Psalms*. The fact that such traditional diction is masterfully used in *Beowulf* is no certain indication of its origins as an oral performance—though the highly polished craft of the poem is no argument against it either.[1] And while a theory of oral formulaic composition may help us appreciate the artistry of a work like *Beowulf*, it also has interesting consequences for the scholar who seeks the origins, context, and meaning of the poem. The concept of "traditional poetry" tends to encourage a sense of a body of "folk" verse without individual authorship or historical roots; it minimizes the role of individual intention and artistry in the creation of a given work. By blurring the boundary between tradition and the individual talent, the idea of oral composition complicates, if it does not altogether preclude, the discovery of a particular place and specific time for the production of a given work. It moves the reader away from the idea of an "implied author" for a work of Old English poetry and toward what Carol Braun Pasternak has called the "implied tradition." If *Beowulf* is simply condensed from the always-already present tradition of oral Old English poetry, composed in pre-existing formulae and inherited narrative building-blocks, then the specific circumstances of its creation are all but irrecoverable. A literary work in oral circulation is always new, recreated at each performance; in effect it has no history, no matter how ancient its traditional narrative or style may be.

Even if the ultimate roots of *Beowulf* are in performance and tradition, however, we should still consider the origins of the surviving text.

---

1   For discussion of this topic see Benson, "Literary Character," and Russom.

Writing fixes a literary work in a particular form—relatively speaking, for manuscript copies are subject to scribal alteration in the course of their transmission[1]—and this form should bear the marks of its context, whether linguistic or historical. Earlier critical opinion on the date of *Beowulf* placed the genesis of the poem in the late seventh or early eighth century, relatively early in Anglo-Saxon literary history. In 1982 a volume of essays on *The Dating of Beowulf* (edited by Colin Chase) offered a series of vigorous challenges to this received opinion, and since then many scholars have drifted away from their earlier consensus and toward a later date (ninth or tenth century) for the poem's composition. Others, notably R.D. Fulk in the 2008 revision of *Klaeber's Beowulf*, have restated and reinforced arguments for the traditional earlier date. The range of current opinion on the question is limited only by the absolute limits of the poem's possible date, c. 520 (when Gregory of Tours says the raid of Hygelac took place) and c. 1000 (when the surviving manuscript was written). The dialect of the poem offers no indication of its origins: like most surviving works of Old English poetry, the language of *Beowulf* is largely late West-Saxon, with some element of Anglian (northern) vocabulary, a kind of poetic mixture not easily traced to one time or place. Moreover, Old English orthographic habits were somewhat fluid, and scribes might well have modernized and altered the dialect of an older poem in the course of their copying. The poem's meter, even if it derived from an inherited traditional practice, would have been relatively fixed when the poem was committed to writing, and various metrical-linguistic features (the use or avoidance of definite articles with certain forms of adjectives, the use of contracted or uncontracted forms of some words, and the distribution of certain metrical patterns) have been analyzed, most thoroughly in R.D. Fulk's *History of Old English Meter*, in the hopes of correlating their appearance in *Beowulf* to some chronology outside the poem. Such efforts have been strenuous but remain inconclusive. As Ashley Crandell Amos argued in 1981, the reliance of formal poetic language on traditional diction and phrase, the uncertain nature of linguistic and metrical tests, and the limits of our knowledge of Old English dialect chronology all preclude certainty.[2]

Details of story and scene that might have been relatively fluid in performance would have been relatively fixed when the poem was

---

1 This fundamental fact of manuscript textuality is discussed by Sisam, "Authority of Old English Poetical Manuscripts," and O'Brien O'Keeffe, *Visible Song.*

2 Janet Bately also offers an important discussion of this topic. A general overview of the issues at stake in the controversy over the dating of *Beowulf* can be found in Liuzza, "On the Dating of *Beowulf*."

written down, and these too might offer clues to the poem's context. Archaeological and sociological approaches to the dating of the poem, however, have been scarcely more fruitful than metrical and linguistic ones. The poem's material culture—its cups and swords and ships and halls—appears to reflect sixth- or seventh-century reality, but this may be deliberate archaism or poetic license on the part of the poet; in *Beowulf*, the antiquity of heirloom weapons is a large part of their value. Moreover, the poet's sense of material reality, unlike his sense of the social and moral order, is not particularly historical. He makes no distinction between the antique artifacts unearthed from the dragon's hoard—the poem's most ancient event—and the trappings of warriors like Beowulf himself. When it comes to material objects, everything for the poet is old: either old and bright, or old and rusty. From this we may infer that his descriptions of material objects are not to be trusted as a criterion for dating the poem. Similarly, the forms of social organization found in the poem are those, more or less, of all heroic poetry—a generous warrior-chief surrounded by a band of both loyal and treacherous retainers who fight for gold and glory; the poem's "lived reality" offers only vague indications of a particular historical origin. Most other aspects of the social world—economic dependency, law and justice, labor and service, and perhaps most strikingly to the modern reader, romantic love—are outside the poet's interest.

Historical allusions in *Beowulf* have also been mined for possible clues to the poem's context. An apparently gratuitous passage of praise for the continental king Offa (1931-62) was regarded by Dorothy Whitelock as possible evidence that the poem was composed in the late-eighth-century court of the Mercian king of the same name (*Audience* 58-64); Sam Newton revives the theory that the poem's Wylfings (461) are a reference to the East Anglian royal line of Wuffings. The spectacular seventh-century ship burial found at Sutton Hoo in East Anglia in 1939 has often been linked to *Beowulf*, not just for the richness of its artifacts and its apparent blending of Christian and pagan symbols and customs, but also for the connections it suggests between eastern England and southern Sweden.[1] It may be argued that the casual nature of the poem's historical allusions implies a poet who expects his audience to recognize a whole array of characters, large and small, from northern legend, and may thus argue for a relatively

---

1 A general review of archaeological approaches to the poem is found in Hills. On Sutton Hoo in particular see A.C. Evans, Bruce-Mitford, Carver, and the essays in Farrell and Neuman de Vegvar; an elegant caution is sounded by Frank, "*Beowulf* and Sutton Hoo."

earlier date, but the extent of Anglo-Saxon knowledge of such matters is not really known. Indeed the general setting and interest of the poem need some explanation: any opinion on the date of *Beowulf* must account for the oddity of an English poem so peculiarly sympathetic to the Danes and their history, and so intimately interested in the details of the feuds of a pack of dark-age Scandinavian Hatfields and McCoys. Why did an English poet feel drawn to work this old material into such a powerful story?

Relations between the Anglo-Saxons and the northern continent were complex at all periods in early English history. On the one hand the English endured a devastating century of Viking raids, beginning spectacularly with the sacking of the monastery of Lindisfarne in 793 and becoming earnest and incessant after 830. These raids destroyed churches, farms, and villages, disrupted ecclesiastical and intellectual life, and brought down nearly all the kings of England until peace was reached in the reign of Alfred the Great, king of Wessex, in the 890s; a later reminiscence of the terror of this period can be found in Ælfric's account of the martyrdom of King Edmund of East Anglia (Appendix D2), who was killed in a Viking attack in 869 or 870. A century later the utter demoralization of the nation in the face of another wave of northern invasion is movingly recorded in the *Anglo-Saxon Chronicle*; Wulfstan's *Sermo Lupi* considers the "Danes" (a generic name for all the northern tribes) a manifestation of the wrath of God (Appendix D1). Dorothy Whitelock's 1951 *The Audience of Beowulf* argued that the poem's praise of the Danes could *not* have been written after the beginning of these Viking raids; no English audience, she believed, would have willingly listened to a poem celebrating the glory of its enemies. R.I. Page, however, notes that it would be wrong to assume "an unsophisticated audience for a sophisticated poem" (113)—and in any case it must be said that the poem's praise of the Danes is, at best, qualified, and their glory placed firmly in the past. More recently, scholars such as Nicholas Howe have argued that the Anglo-Saxons throughout their history maintained a lively interest in their pre-migration past and kept a clear sense of the difference between the "Danes" of legend and the Danes who were their foes, neighbors, and compatriots. The West-Saxon royal house traced its ancestry back through historical rulers to Woden, then to Scyld and Heremod, legendary Danish kings mentioned in *Beowulf* (Appendix A4); apparently the Christian West-Saxon kings thought it worthwhile to note their descent from the same legendary heroes as the pagan Danes. When the English were converted to Christianity they sent missionaries to save the souls of their continental cousins (Appendix C3a), and virtuous pagans were sometimes held up as a rebuke to evil English kings (Appendix C3b).

From Alfred's time onward, the English lived and worked alongside Danish settlers in the eastern and northern regions of the country, known as the *Danelaw*, and such mixed Anglo-Danish milieus, where integration and assimilation coexisted with difference, division, and no doubt some lingering hostility, may have fostered an interest in the legendary history of the northern tribes. On strictly historical grounds, then, there is no period in Anglo-Saxon history in which a poem like *Beowulf* might not have been written or appreciated.

There is a great deal at stake in these arguments over the poem's origins. *Beowulf* will be read differently if it is imagined to have been produced in the time of Bede (c. 725) or Alfred (c. 880) or Ælfric (c. 1000). The earlier we think the poem to be, the more potentially authentic its historical material; a later *Beowulf*, more openly fictional, is a more complex and "literary" work. Moreover, the more closely we try to assign a date and place of origin to the poem, the more closely we must read it as a text, the intention of a single author or a reflection of a particular ideology, rather than a product of an oral poetic art whose composition may have been collective and whose traditional roots are beyond discovery. Unfortunately there is no consensus, and little hope for one, on the question of the poem's origins. In the final analysis it may be useful, as John Niles has suggested, to divide the question into two parts: "first, what is the probable origin of the discourse, the collective heroic verse-making tradition, that finds textual expression in *Beowulf*? And second, what is the probable origin of this individual poem, in the shape that we now have it?" ("Locating *Beowulf*" 91-92). In its most elementary structures the story of Beowulf may be as old as the migration to Britain itself. Both James Earl and Craig Davis have noted how the poem asserts the dominance of the warrior band or *comitatus*, organized around the great hall, over the tribe, organized around agriculture and family groups; it celebrates the warrior in heroic isolation—fighting for honor and fame rather than hearth and home, rewarded with riches by his kings and patrons but rootless, unmarried, without progeny. The shift in cultural balance from the family tribe to the men's hall probably began before the migration period, but the migration to Britain reinforced a social order founded on military kingship and must have contributed to the force and popularity of stories like *Beowulf* that endorsed and celebrated this new social order.

In the course of its telling and retelling, the poem may have taken on something like its present shape, but constant refinement and adjustment could have been made throughout its growth: its story reimagined in light of later spiritual and historical concerns, allusive tributes to English kings like Offa woven into its narrative fabric, its adventures placed in the framework of Christian history and set against the background of the Scylding dynasty from which the West-Saxons claimed their descent. Finally, as the tradition of aristocratic oral storytelling was declining, replaced even in the vernacular by books of history and chronicle, the poem was set down in writing (Niles, "Oral Poetry Acts"). *Beowulf* may thus reflect the interests of several different eras, its traditional materials coalescing into a rough form before being shaped by the hand of its final author; it may respond to diverse moments of cultural crisis and triumph in early and later Anglo-Saxon society, whether the secularized aristocratic monasteries of Bede's day (as Patrick Wormald suggests) or the nation-building of Athelstan or the reign of Æthelred "the Unready," where stories of generous and noble heroes like Beowulf may have served as a kind of "invention of tradition" (in Eric Hobsbawm's phrase) for the demoralized English nation in the face of Danish attack. In each case the poem's force derives from its projection onto the past of values and attitudes sought in the present, but the values sought in the poem may have been different from one age to the next, or from one reader to another.

Obscure in its origins, inarticulate in its purposes, enigmatic in its history: given these ambiguities, and the poem's allusive complexity, is it possible to read *Beowulf* with modern expectations of unity and coherence? Can the various threads of the poem be gathered into a single pattern? When the poem was first read, some scholars contended that it was a collection of "lays" or *Lieder*; scholars such as Ludwig Ettmüller and Karl Müllenhoff were eager to separate *Beowulf* into different layers from different sources. Woven into the main narrative are numerous "digressions" that most early scholars regarded as structural flaws.[1] The stories of Finn and Sigemund, the long "sermon" of Hrothgar to the triumphant Beowulf (1700-84), the hero's verbal sparring with Unferth, the somewhat murky story of Thryth, even the prologue concerning Scyld Scefing—these have all been regarded at one time or another as detachable parts of a composite structure, in need of explanation and apology. Others, such as Tolkien and Adrien Bonjour, resisted this diachronic view of the poem's structure and argued for the unity of the poem as it now stands. Most modern critics assume that the poem should be read as a unified work, however elusive its principles of unity may sometimes be.[2] The poem's shaping

---

1   See the survey of earlier scholarship by Shippey, and Bjork, "Digressions and Episodes."

2   But the desire to dissect the poem into its component parts did not vanish; F.P. Magoun wrote two articles ("*Beowulf A*" and "*Beowulf B*") arguing for the disunity of the poem, and Kenneth Sisam's *Structure of Beowulf* dismisses the idea that the poem is unified in any modern sense.

aesthetic principles, as Jonathan Evans argues, do not derive from an Aristotelian emphasis on structure and closure; rather, they give rise to a work that is episodic, digressive, and recursive. Edward B. Irving has described this as an "emotional" rather than a structural unity, "a unity based on the very fact of diversity" (193). Even the term "digression" may be misleading if it implies that the reader ought to expect a single narrative strand, with some dangling irrelevancies that are merely decorative or detachable from the main plot. It may be better to follow the lead of John Leyerle, who examined the complex "interlace" structure of the poem's interlocking motifs and stories and concluded that "there are no digressions in *Beowulf*" (13). Every piece of the poem can be read alongside every other piece as an adumbration or refraction of some larger theme: the story of Sigemund reflects on the relation of the heroic individual to his society; the story of Finn foregrounds the tragic insufficiency of marriages and truces to effect lasting peace; the prologue concerning Scyld Scefing (see Bruce) sounds the first note of a repeated motif, the mystery of divine providence, and provides a long foreshadowing of the poem's melancholy conclusion. To say that the various parts of *Beowulf* work together toward an overarching effect, however, is not to say that it is entirely the product of one poet's mind or pen. Like an Anglo-Saxon church made from the salvaged stones of a Roman temple, the structure of *Beowulf* may reveal complex layers of source and context; built perhaps by many hands over many years but according to an ancient plan and with a single purpose, it is unified by use and time rather than by pre-formed design.

Beowulf between Court and Cloister

> ... *both a new world*
> *and the old made explicit, understood*
> *in the completion of its partial ecstasy,*
> *the resolution of its partial horror.*

Critics of *Beowulf* are divided on many issues; perhaps none is more important than the significance of the poem's religious elements. Though it is still sometimes argued that the poem's origin and ethos are essentially pagan, with only a veneer of Christianity or an imperfect grasp of the principal tenets of the Christian faith,[1] Christine Fell pointedly observes that "Rome had been officially Christian only a couple of centuries before Pope Gregory sent his missionaries to the Anglo-Saxons yet we accept that these missionaries came with a full

---

1   See, for example, Moorman, Cherniss.

understanding of Christian teaching. We are curiously reluctant however to accept that within another couple of hundred years the Anglo-Saxon educated mind was equal in understanding and commitment" (14). Most critics agree that the heroic action of the poem is thoroughly accommodated to a Christian paradigm; they disagree, however, on the meaning and purpose of that accommodation. Scholars such as Alan Cabaniss and M.B. McNamee have argued that Beowulf, who gives his life for his people, should be seen as a type of Christ, while others, most notably Margaret Goldsmith, have read *Beowulf* as a condemnation of pagan pride, greed, and violence. These two extreme positions capture quite dramatically the dilemma caused by what can be regarded as the poem's deliberate ambivalence: *Beowulf* is a secular Christian poem about pagans that avoids the easy alternatives of automatic condemnation or enthusiastic anachronism. While early scholars tried to find a single source for the poem's complex and peculiar texture—whether in pure Germanic paganism or orthodox Augustinian Christianity—more recent work recognizes that *Beowulf*, like the culture of the Anglo-Saxons themselves, reflects a variety of interdependent and competing influences and attitudes, even a certain tension inherent in the combination of biblical, patristic, secular Latin, and popular Germanic material. The search for a single "audience" of *Beowulf*, and with it a sense of a single meaning, has given way to a recognition of a plurality of readers and interests in Anglo-Saxon England.

The author of the poem (for the sake of argument, let us say the person who was responsible for its commitment to parchment) was certainly a Christian: the technology of writing in the Anglo-Saxon period was almost entirely confined to monastic scriptoria. The manuscript in which *Beowulf* is preserved contains a saint's legend and a versified Bible story. Moreover the poet indicates a clear familiarity with the Bible and expects the same from his audience—Grendel and his mother are said to be descended from Cain (104-08; 1258-65; cf. Genesis 4:8-16), and apocryphal Old Testament legend is alluded to in the story of the giants who perished in the flood (1688-91).[1] Some of the details of Grendel's lair seem to derive from descriptions of Hell in the Old English homiletic tradition (see Appendix B5). Words borrowed from Latin such as *candel* (1572), *gigant* "giant" (113, 1562), and *non* "the ninth hour" (1600) suggest an easy cohabitation between the heroic story and the vocabulary of the Church. The poem depicts a God who watches over history and secures even the safety of the

---

1 These legends, and the possibility of their being known among the Anglo-Saxons, are discussed by Mellinkoff.

Danes who do not know Him (14-18, 700-02, 1553), and the narrator laments the religious ignorance of his characters (183-88). Equally clearly, however, these characters are pagan—they practice cremation and burial with lavish treasure, foretell the future with auguries (204), make occasional and desperate sacrifice to their deities (recognized by the narrator as devils, 175-88), repeatedly stress their belief in fate, and cling to fame as the only afterlife. The narrator acknowledges that "they did not know the Lord God" (*ne wiston hie Drihten God*, 181).

This explicit admission appears only once, however; the paganism of the characters is otherwise presented in a curiously muted way. None of the more offensive pagan practices is mentioned explicitly. Characters speak of "the Lord" or "the Almighty," using terms that overlap with Christian epithets for God, but they never name any particular pagan deity; their natural piety is evident in the way they thank God for their victories and worry about having offended the Creator. The poet's Christianity neither sets itself against the paganism of his characters in a posture of condemnation (except in the one passage noted above) nor obscures his sense of their difference from his audience. There is no intrusive or anachronistic reference to Christian doctrine, nothing about Christ's mercy, the veneration of Mary, the loving self-sacrifice of the martyrs, the ascetic devotion of the desert fathers, or the miracles of the saints. There is, one might say, an Old Testament feeling about the poem's religiosity, appropriate for the kind of story it tells and the kind of world it represents, in which a somber and hidden King of Heaven battles his demonic foes by proxy through the power of such men as Beowulf. Thomas Hill argues that "the religious language of the poem reflects the religious knowledge of those patriarchs who lived before the covenants and the creation of Israel" (67-68); following Robert Kaske, he describes the poem's spiritual atmosphere as "Noachite." Even the "judgment of the righteous" to which Beowulf's soul goes (line 2820) can be found in the Old Testament book of Ecclesiastes 3:17: "I said in my heart, God will judge the righteous and the wicked, for he has appointed a time for every matter and for every work" (NRSV translation). The poem's religious tone is tailored to its heroic action and scene.

Though the paganism of Beowulf's world is downplayed, however, it is not denied; his world is connected to that of the audience but separated by the gulf of conversion as much as by the seas of migration. The carefully ambiguous religious atmosphere in *Beowulf* is an aspect of the author's sense of history, his appreciation that the past is different from yet prologue to the present, his exploration of the meaning of individual action in the framework of possibilities and limitations imposed by time and place. For some Anglo-

Saxons no connection could be tolerated between the Christian present and the pagan past; the heroes of legend and history were unbaptized, unsaved, and unworthy of remembrance. Alcuin's caustic rebuke (Appendix A3) indicates that, for at least one prominent churchman, tales of the pagan past were of no value whatsoever: we may lament the ignorance and sinfulness of our pagan forebears, but hardly celebrate or emulate their heroic deeds. Other Anglo-Saxons, such as the archbishop Wulfstan at the turn of the millennium, railed against paganism as a religious system (Appendix C4) and sought to suppress its traces in folk customs or "superstitions" (Appendix C5). As Larry Benson argues, however, there is evidence that not all Anglo-Saxons felt such automatic condemnation for the people who were, after all, their ancestors ("Pagan Coloring"). Theological speculation on the salvation of the "naturally good" pagans may have reached England from Ireland, as Charles Donahue has argued; this opens the possibility of imagining a kind of spiritual solidarity between the pagan past and the Christian present. Pope Gregory advised the missionaries to the English to make churches out of the shrines and temples of the heathens, and preserve their celebrations while changing their meaning (Appendix C1); it is easy to imagine a poem like *Beowulf* arising from the same impulse to preserve a story of the past while re-interpreting it in the light of a fuller revelation. The Anglo-Saxons managed to use their inherited traditional poetic modes to write verse saints' lives and biblical history; there must have been some impulse among them to salvage their old stories of kings and heroes as well. *Beowulf* seeks to explore both the bridges and the chasms between the pagan past and the Christian present; it teaches secular readers how to be pious, moral, and thoughtful about their own history, mindful of fame and courage while aware of its limitations and dangers. The poem is a Christian author's imaginative recreation of a pagan mentality, similar in some respects to Bede's eloquent simile of the sparrow, which he places in the mouth of one of King Edwin's retainers in the *Ecclesiastical History* I.30 (Appendix C2)—the warm but fleeting pleasures of life are placed against the somber background of its ultimate meaninglessness, and without the hope of conversion or salvation all that is available to make sense of the world are courage, honor, and a stoical acceptance of one's fate, whether good or bad.

The question of the spiritual status of pagans is not avoided in *Beowulf*, but the possibility of any easy answer to the question is foreclosed in the poem's prologue. The fate of Scyld after his death, the narrator states, is unknown; the shift into the present tense insists on our own suspension of judgment:

                          Men ne cunnon
secgan tō sōðe,   selerædende,
hæleð under heofenum,   hwā þæm hlæste onfēng.

                  Men do not know
how to say truly — not trusted counselors,
nor heroes under the heavens — who received that cargo. (50-52)

It could be said that the poem teaches us how to answer this question;
the answer comes, mournfully triumphant and shadowed with a certain
ambiguity, in lines 2817-20, at the death of Beowulf himself:

þæt wæs þām gomelan   gingæste word
brēostgehygdum,   ær hē bæl cure,
hāte heaðowylmas;   him of hræðre gewāt
sāwol sēcean   sōðfæstra dōm.

That was the last word of the old warrior,
his final thought before he chose the fire,
the hot surging flames — from his breast flew
his soul to seek the judgment of the righteous.

Later (line 3155) we are told of his funeral pyre, "Heaven swallowed
the smoke" (*heofon rece swealg*). Is this a sign of divine favor? If so,
it is a strikingly pagan one (see Appendix B3).

Framed by these moments of metaphysical speculation, the action
of *Beowulf* unfolds, and for most of the poem pains are taken to assert
the distant yet connected relationship between the worlds of the pagan
past and the Christian present, a connection heard most clearly in the
repeated phrase "in that day of this life" (*on þæm dæge þysses lifes*,
197, 790, 806). Clearly we are meant to admire the hero's actions and
accept that his world and ours share certain norms for judging these
actions. Susan Deskis has discussed the poem's numerous generalizing
gnomic passages—the first begins at line 20—which link the world of
the characters to that of the audience; we are explicitly told to admire
and imitate their heroic courage and restraint, and at the end of the
poem we are told again that "it is proper" to praise the dead and cele-
brate their memory (3174). Hospitality, readiness for defense, gen-
erosity, vengeance, courage, and loyalty are all presented in the mirror
of the poem as virtues that we, too, ought to practice, the common
ground of pagan and Christian secular life. The rewards of heroic
success—rings, cups, swords, horses, feasts, and above all fame—are
held up, lovingly, for our admiration; they are the good things of this

world, the just and desirable accoutrements of a warrior's achievements. Moreover, Beowulf fights with God's help against God's enemies; he does God's work and enjoys God's favor. Grendel is a "fiend from hell" (*feond on helle*, 101) descended from the archcriminal Cain; he is "God's adversary" (*Godes andsacan*, 786), he bears "God's anger" (*Godes yrre bær*, 711), and lives among "a host of devils" (*deofla gedræg*, 756). It could hardly be more plain: Beowulf, whether he knows it or not, is on God's side.

For all that, however, Beowulf dies, and his death has none of the triumphant sanctification of the death of a martyr like King Edmund, or a Christian hero like Charlemagne's champion in the French *Chanson de Roland*. In the last third of the poem the dazzling picture of the hero's exploits grows darker and sadder; the glittering of treasure and the sweet songs of fame, all the values celebrated in the earlier episodes, are restated as questions and finally abandoned. The good things of the world and the virtues of heroic nobility they represent are, finally, not enough to save Beowulf's people from destruction. Linda Georgianna has eloquently described how in the poem's long conclusion the possibility of action gives way to the limitations of action; we may feel that even the possibility of telling a true tale is called into question as the narrative weaves in and out of the complex history of Swedish/Geatish relations, the story coils around on itself like a serpent, and the reader is lost in the narrative maze of a history that finally seems to consume even the Geats themselves. It might be that killing monstrous opponents is easier than building a stable society on the volatile values of gold, pride, and violent self-assertion; the world of Beowulf, however noble and attractive, is consumed by its own force, reduced to ashes by the long-smoldering history of raids, feuds, failed truces, and unpaid debts of honor. The so-called "Lay of the Last Survivor" marks the tone of the poem's long twilight as surely as Beowulf's stirring call to action, "Sorrow not, wise one!" (1384-96), marks the tone of its earlier clear day:

> 'Heald þū nū, hrūse,   nū hæleð ne mōstan,
> eorla æhte!   Hwæt, hyt ær on ðē
> gōde begēaton;   gūðdēað fornam,
> feorhbealo frēcne   fȳra gehwylcne
> lēoda mīnra   þāra ðe þis līf ofgeaf,
> gesāwon seledrēam.   Nāh, hwā sweord wege
> oððe forð bere   fæted wæge,
> dryncfæt dēore;   duguð ellor sceōc.
> Sceal se hearda helm   hyrstedgolde,
> fætum befeallen;   feormynd swefað,

þā ðe beadogrīman   bȳwan sceoldon;
gē swylce sēo herepād,   sīo æt hilde gebād
ofer borda gebræc   bite īrena,
brosnað æfter beorne.   Ne mæg byrnan hring
æfter wīgfruman   wīde fēran,
hæleðum be healfe.   Næs hearpan wyn,
gomen glēobēames,   nē gōd hafoc
geond sæl swingeð,   nē se swifta mearh
burhstede bēateð.   Bealocwealm hafað
fela feorhcynna   forð onsended!'

"Hold now, o thou earth, for heroes cannot,
the wealth of men — Lo, from you long ago
those good ones first obtained it! Death in war,
and awful deadly harm have swept away
all of my people who have passed from life,
and left the joyful hall. Now have I none
to bear the sword or burnish the bright cup,
the precious vessel — all that host has fled.
Now must the hardened helm of hammered gold
be stripped of all its trim; the stewards sleep
who should have tended to this battle-mask.
So too this warrior's coat, which waited once
the bite of iron over the crack of boards,
molders like its owner. The coat of mail
cannot travel widely with the war-chief,
beside the heroes. Harp-joy have I none,
no happy song; nor does the well-schooled hawk
soar high throughout the hall, nor the swift horse
stamp in the courtyards. Savage butchery
has sent forth many of the race of men!" (2247-66)

The speech, pronounced over a hoard of treasure that has outlasted its
owners and is being consigned to a burial mound, is an elegy for all the
bright world of the poem's early sections, all the feasts, all the rewards,
all the honor and fame, all now lost to the inevitability of decline and
death. The lines recall the biblical injunction against "storing up treas-
ures on earth" (Matthew 6:19) as well as the classical and Germanic
tradition of lament for lost times; it is perhaps the poem's most char-
acteristic moment, and it would surely have been accepted even by a
monastic audience as an expression of worldly wisdom. But the
wisdom of *Beowulf* is only that—worldly—and that is its tragedy. At
the end of the poem, after the hero has bravely met his fate, we are left

with only the possibility of mourning and the commemoration of values we have been forced to recognize as inadequate. Beowulf, however brave, is unable to secure lasting peace and safety for his people even at the cost of his own life; his fame may endure but things look grim indeed for the rest of the Geats. *Beowulf* is a Christian poet's bittersweet elegy for the doomed heroic life, the futility of forging peace by the works of war, the instability of the bonds formed by gifts and exchange and inter-tribal marriage, and the impossibility of permanence in a world whose knowledge is tragically limited.

It would be wrong to imply, however, that the elegiac turn at the end of *Beowulf* is an unexpected one; even the brightest moments in the poem are set against a darkening awareness of the inevitable end of things. The poem's characteristic word is "until"; the poem continually looks forward from present happiness to future catastrophe. As soon as the great hall Heorot is raised, the narrator says "it awaited hostile fires, / the surges of war" (*heaðowylma bad, / laðan liges*; 82-83); when Hrothgar and his nephew Hrothulf are seated together we are told that "Heorot within was / filled with friends — no false treacheries / did the people of the Scyldings plot *at that time*" (*Heorot innan wæs / freondum afylled; nalles facenstafas / þeod-Scyldingas þenden fremedon*, 1017-19, emphasis added). No happiness is permanent; uncertain and dangerous sleep must follow every feast. This theme of mutability is sounded throughout the poem, and so the ending of *Beowulf* seems inevitable rather than surprising. The career of the hero is depicted against a recognition that his triumph is limited and his defeat unavoidable; all the great works of the poem—the hall, the peace of Hrothgar's kingdom, the gifts of Wealhtheow, perhaps the fame of Beowulf himself—are doomed to fall. Because this realization never quite reaches the hero himself, the poem is suffused with intense and poignant dramatic irony. Characters in *Beowulf* clearly believe in the values of feuding, boasting, gift-giving, thaneship, and peace-weaving, but they do so because their world, at least as the poem constructs it, offers no other choice.[1] As Eric Stanley has observed in *"Beowulf": Continuations and Beginnings*, the pagan heroic ideal is noble, but in comparison to the higher ideal of the Christian world, it is insufficient. At the moment of his death a martyr like Edmund of East Anglia renounces the heroic ideal in favor of a higher ideal whose exemplar is Christ; his reward is not only long-lasting fame, but eternal life.

And yet the poem's encroaching sense of the tragic limitations of the heroic life does not negate its recognition and celebration of its

---

1 A well-argued dissent from this critical consensus may be found in J. Hill.

beauty and value. Whatever attitude the reader may take toward the poem must somehow respect both the overwhelming honor paid to Beowulf and his deeds and the overwhelming sadness with which the poem ends—the hero and his world are precious but precarious, noble but impossible. Our sympathetic suspension of judgment on the doomed world of Beowulf is never quite allowed to resolve itself; the poem's last word praises the hero for being *lofgeornost*, "most eager for fame," and even after nearly 3,200 lines we cannot tell whether this is admiration or condemnation. Perhaps it is both. What else do the pagans have but fame? Richard Schrader (492) has pointed out the relevance to *Beowulf* of a haunting passage from Augustine's *City of God* (V: xiv): "since the Romans were in an earthly city ... and a kingdom, not in heaven but in earth—not in the sphere of eternal life, but in the sphere of demise and succession, where the dead are succeeded by the dying—what else but glory should they love, by which they wished even after death to live in the mouths of their admirers?" But it is the poem *Beowulf* itself that creates and sustains the fame of the hero Beowulf. The Christian poet peers into the pagan past, remembers, seeks connection, celebrates, questions, forswears, recollects, mourns, and finally, by his very participation in the continuum of poetic fame and praise, endorses the values of a lost heroic world.

Nor, in some ways, are the values of a work like Ælfric's *Life of St Edmund* (Appendix D2)—a text nearly contemporary with the manuscript of *Beowulf*—entirely antithetical to those of the poem. The Christian idea of heroic martyrdom is obviously quite different from the heroism of Beowulf's death—his last thoughts are of treasure and his people, not Christ and His angels—and the demonizing of the Danes in Ælfric's work stands in sharp contrast to the historical sympathy of the *Beowulf*-poet. Yet despite these obvious differences many similarities of form and content between the two works can be noted: the rhetoric of challenging speeches and formal promises, a concern with the afterlife (whether of reputation or of Christian salvation), a belief that fidelity to one's ideals is more important than victory or long life, a memorializing of the body, a pattern of reference to other stories of similar people who form a kind of constellation of figures of exemplary value. One work encourages praise of God and His saints, the other praise of secular deeds, heroic integrity, and a hero's sad but noble courage in the face of inevitable defeat, but both present noble figures from the past; both celebrate ideals that are worthy of emulation. Both draw on a similar stock of narrative themes and patterns to present a hero who is at the same time exemplary—available for emulation and contemporary appropriation—and historically rooted. In the end it is not impossible to imagine an Anglo-Saxon reader of a historical turn of mind, interested in stories worthy of remembrance and tales of kings and heroes of whatever nation and lineage, enjoying both works with attention and profit.

Beowulf between Old and Modern English

> Words strain,
> Crack and sometimes break, under the burden,
> Under the tension, slip, slide, perish,
> Decay with imprecision, will not stay in place,
> Will not stay still.

Early in the poem the technique of Hrothgar's court poet is described:

Hwīlum cyninges þegn,
guma gilphlæden,   gidda gemyndig,
sē ðe ealfela   ealdgesegena
worn gemunde   — word ōþer fand
sōðe gebunden —   secg eft ongan
sīð Bēowulfes   snyttrum styrian,
ond on spēd wrecan   spel gerāde,
wordum wrixlan;

At times the king's thane,
full of grand stories, mindful of songs,
who remembered much, a great many
of the old tales, found other words
truly bound together; he began again
to recite with skill the adventure of Beowulf,
adeptly tell an apt tale,
and weave his words. (867-74)

To many readers the descriptive terms "weaving" (*wrixlan*) and "binding" (*gebindan*) are suggestive of the structural principles of Old English verse. Each line of *Beowulf* consists of two half-lines containing (usually) two stressed syllables each and a varying number of unstressed syllables. The half-lines are linked by alliteration between one or both stressed syllables in the first half-line and the first stressed syllable of the second half-line; the most common alliterative pattern is aa:ax. Alliteration and stress held the lines of an Old English poem together, just as meter and rhyme hold together the lines of a Shakespearean sonnet; they were not decorative, as they are in modern poetry, but necessary structural elements.

The opening lines of the poem in Old English illustrate this alliterative structure (the letters þ and ð represent the *th* sounds in *thin* and *then*; *sc* in Old English is pronounced like *sh* in *ship* or *shield*; most words are accented on the first syllable; compound words, indicated here by hyphens, usually have a secondary stress on the second element of the compound; finally, any vowel alliterates with any other):

> Hwæt! Wē Gar-dena   in gēar-dagum,
> þēod-cyninga   þrym gefrūnon,
> hū ðā æþelingas   ellen fremedon.
> Oft Scyld Scēfing   sceaþena þrēatum,
> monegum mǣgþum,   meodo-setla oftēah,
> egsode eorlas.   Syððan ǣrest wearð
> fēasceaft funden,   hē þæs frōfre gebād,
> wēox under wolcnum,   weorð-myndum þāh,
> oðþæt him æghwylc   þara ymbsittendra
> ofer hron-rāde   hȳran scolde,
> gomban gyldan.   þæt wæs gōd cyning. (1-11)

Though the passage of time has placed a thorough disguise upon it, Old English can still be recognized as the ancestor of Modern English. The most stable words through the intervening millennium have been the grammatical function-words: pronouns such as "we," "he," "him," and (despite orthographical differences) "that," prepositions such as "in," "under," and "ofer" (pronounced just like Modern English "over," though the spelling has changed), adverbs such as "hu" (how) and "oft." Other words are related to modern English words: *geardagum* is almost recognizable as "yore-days," i.e., "days of yore," and *wolcnum* survives as the archaic "welkin," i.e., "the heavens"; *funden* is not too far from the participial adjective "found," *hyran* is related to modern "hear" (though it means "obey" as well as "hear" in Old English), and *god* (with a long *o*) is only an older spelling of "good." The word *cyning* (originally meaning "leader of the kin") was sometimes spelled *cyng* or even *kyng* in later Old English manuscripts, which suggests that even then it was pronounced much like its Modern English descendant "king." Still other words, especially those in an aristocratic or poetic register, vanished from the language soon after the arrival of the Normans—*æþelingas* "noblemen," *ellen* "(deeds of) valor," *þrym* "glory," *frofre* "consolation."

Other important differences between Old and Modern English are found in word-order and inflection. A literal translation into Modern English (words in italics are grammatical particles required in Modern

English but expressed by inflectional endings in Old English) clearly reveals this:

What! We *of the* Spear-Danes   in yore-days
of the people-kings   glory heard,
how the noblemen   valor did.
Often Scyld, son-of-Sceaf   *from* enemies' troops
from many tribes   mead-benches took away
terrified nobles.   After first *he* was
destitute found,   he for-that comfort awaited,
grew under *the* skies,   *in* honors prospered
until to him each   of the surrounding ones
over *the* whale-riding   obey had to,
tribute yield.   That was *a* good king.

Old English generally placed verbs after direct objects (as in lines 2, 3, 5, 7, 8, and 11), while Modern English syntax requires a fairly strict Subject-Verb-Object order. Old English could express grammatical relationships by inflection (i.e., endings on nouns, pronouns, and adjectives), but Modern English requires grammatical particles such as prepositions and definite articles.

Other differences, however, reflect features peculiar to the Old English poetic style.[1] One feature that is difficult to reproduce in translation is the profusion of synonyms. Alliterative poetry worked by having a number of different ways of saying the same thing in different lines: depending on the meter, context, and the necessity of making an alliterative link, a king might be called a *cyning, dryhten, hyrde, ræswa, sigedryhten, þeodcyning, weard,* or *wine.* Of course, these words are not quite synonyms, any more than are their nearest equivalents in Modern English ("king," "lord," "shepherd," "prince," "victorious lord," "king of the people," "guardian," "friend"), but it is hard to avoid the suspicion that their use in Old English is only partly determined by the nuances of their connotations. At times metrical necessity must have played a decisive role. The aged and ineffectual king Hrothgar, for example, is called *helm Scyldinga* "protector of the Scyldings" in lines 371, 456, and 1321, presumably not because he is such a great protector of his people—under the circumstances, the title could at best be regarded as a courtesy—but because *helm* alliterates

---

1   Good introductions to Old English poetic style are found in O'Brien O'Keeffe, "Diction," and Schaefer.

with *Hrothgar*. But the elaboration of synonyms is part of what gives the poem its notable formality, another instance of the recurrence-with-variation that is the essence of its art.

Another striking feature of Old English poetry is the restatement and repetition of subjects, predicates, and objects—the use of several different words, grammatically parallel, for the same referent. This "appositive style" (as Fred C. Robinson calls it), also known as "variation" (Brodeur), involves a kind of multiplication of reference: a simple example is the line "Beowulf spoke, son of Ecgtheow" (*Beowulf maþelode, bearn Ecgþeowes*, 631 and elsewhere; see the earlier discussion, p. 20). Elsewhere the use of appositive style or variation is more complex; a closer analysis of the sentence beginning in line 4, for example, reveals a series of restatements with carefully nuanced connotations:

Often Scyld Scefing (1a) took away meadbenches (1b) from
troops of enemies, (2a) terrified nobles (2b) from many tribes.
After he first was found destitute, he (1) awaited comfort for that,
(2) grew under the skies, (3) prospered in honors,
until each of the surrounding tribes over the whale's-riding had to
(1) obey him, (2) pay him tribute.

As the numbering indicates, variants can move from greater to lesser specificity (Scyld "took away meadbenches," that is, deprived his enemies of their halls, and by so doing he "terrified nobles"), or from lesser to greater (surrounding tribes had to "obey" him, which means they had to "pay him tribute"), or express a temporal progression (Scyld "awaits," "grows" and then "prospers") with a measure of compact efficiency. By presenting and re-presenting an action, or naming and re-naming a character, an object is set before the hearer and examined, as it were, from several different angles. Like the elaboration of synonyms, variation contributes to the poem's austere but voluptuous *gravitas*, its stately and deliberate tone that is always full without being florid; it is also responsible for some lively effects of style and scene, and meaningful juxtapositions of thought and theme. When Beowulf and his troop arrive at Heorot, the clangor and gleam of their armor fairly leap off the page:

Strǣt wæs stānfāh,	stīg wīsode
gumum ætgædere.	Gūðbyrne scān
heard hondlocen,	hringīren scīr
song in searwum,	þā hīe tō sele furðum
in hyra gryregeatwum	gangan cwōmon.

Setton sǣmēþe   sīde scyldas,
rondas regnbearde   wið þæs recedes weal;
bugon þā tō bence — byrnan hringdon,
gūðsearo gumena;   gāras stōdon,
sǣmanna searo   samod ætgædere,
æscholt ufan grǣg;   wæs se īrenþrēat
wǣpnum gewurþad.

The road was stone-paved, the path led
the men together. Their mail coats shone
hard, hand-linked, bright rings of iron
rang out on their gear, when right to the hall
they went trooping in their terrible armor.
Sea-weary, they set their broad shields,
wondrously-hard boards, against the building's wall;
they sat on a bench — their byrnies rang out,
their soldiers' war-gear; their spears stood,
the gear of the seamen all together,
a gray forest of ash. That iron troop
was worthy of its weapons. (320-31)

Though their arrival raises the hope of rescue from Grendel's terror,
the Geatish warriors are potentially a threat to the demoralized Danes,
and so the poet dwells on the fact that they are armed, an emphasis
achieved through both repetition—the word *searo* (here translated
"gear") appears three times—and variation: the men are described in
"mail coats" and "rings of iron," "in their gear" and "in their ... armor,"
with "broad shields" and "wondrously-hard boards," in "byrnies"
(shirts of linked mail) and "war-gear," with "spears" and "gear" and "a
forest of ash." Variation often works in a subtle way to expand the
meaning of a given passage or even, at times, the whole poem: when
Beowulf is set upon by Grendel, the poet says that

    hwæþre hē gemunde   mægenes strenge,
    gimfæste gife   ðē him God sealde,
    ond him tō Anwaldan āre gelȳfde,
    frōfre ond fultum;

    he remembered his mighty strength,
    the ample gifts which God had given him,
    and trusted the Almighty for mercy,
    favor and support; (1270-73)

The hero's strength and God's grace are brought together; the variation tells us that they are essentially two aspects of the same thing.

The formality of the poem's compositional principles, including the formulaic expressions and scenes mentioned above, dictates a different approach to reading the poem—a reader must not expect headlong forward movement, bold new language, breathless narrative advance, idiosyncratic turns of phrase, and all the effects one might enjoy in a modern novel or (particularly) a modern poem. Most handbooks of rhetoric and composition define "style" as the characteristics of individual expression, but this is not at all what the term implies in Old English poetry. Rather, like a kind of traditional jazz in which musicians express their individuality within the relatively narrow confines of a standard repertoire and technique, the aim of the Anglo-Saxon poet's art was apparently the capable crafting of a complex and solid story out of traditional materials, the re-making of an old tale in a new register. Recognizing this principle leads to a different kind of reading for a work like *Beowulf*; since a translation is nothing but a long and very explicit reading of a text, embracing it has entailed an adjustment of my own language as well.

The brute fact of translation is that it is a reading that sets out, after all its slow and passionate attention to the text, to replace its original inspiration. Perhaps all readings secretly do this. Like a commentary that obliterates what it explicates, a translation is, in the end, a gesture toward an empty space where a text used to be. In addition, any translation is a gesture *from* one place *to* another. The history of *Beowulf* translation (see Appendix E) shows how literary taste and linguistic knowledge have often shaped the translator's style far more powerfully than any primary responsibility to the poem itself; or rather, our primary responses to the poem occur only within a framework of expectation given to us by the literary world in which we live and move. The distance from Conybeare's Miltonic translation of 1826 to Raffel's vivid and free rendering in 1963 is not measured solely by the increase in knowledge of Old English language and literary form; each translator tries to satisfy the literary expectations of his own time. Each reads, in that sense, a different *Beowulf*. Any translator, then, hoping to rescue the poem from the obscurity of the past, risks plunging it into the obscurity of his own present, and in the act of recovering the past we often lose what we set out to save. Yet one of the meanings of the Latin word *translatio* is "metaphor," a way of suggesting similarity through connections between dissimilar objects, a leap of imagination across a chasm of difference. This is how I have tried to imagine this translation: not as a substitute or simulacrum, nor a re-creation or a replacement, but a suggestion. Without trying to make Old English out of Modern English, I have tried to re-imagine some of what I have felt to be the effects of the language of the poem. But I know too well that my translation is only a sketch.

As with any translation, certain effects are lost in the pursuit of others; placing fluency and precision at the top of my list of goals I have had to abandon any hope of a wholesale sound-for-sound equivalence. In the course of working on the translation I came to believe that this was not altogether a bad thing. Certain features that are structurally important in Old English verse—regular alliteration and a strongly felt caesura—are only decorative in most English poetry since the Renaissance, and are so alien to the sound of Modern English verse that they tend to strike the ear too heavily, overwhelming all other sound-effects and distracting the listener from the larger patterns of the poetry such as sentences and verse-paragraphs. I have tried to write in a poetic idiom that is analogous to, not imitative of, the character of the original; the end result has been a translation that is somewhat quieter than most others. Each verse has four stresses, a medial pause, and alliteration, but these are by no means as marked as they are in the original, and on rare occasion they are foregone altogether. I have allowed myself considerable license in the matter of stress; I have necessarily used far more unstressed syllables than an Anglo-Saxon poet could have tolerated, but each line, when read at a normal tempo, has four beats (occasionally rising to 4 1/2 or even 5, just as certain types of OE lines had a secondary stress within the four-beat structure). At moments of great formality in the poem the lines resolve into decasyllables; this has no parallel in the original—apart from a few hypermetrical lines the poem is written in a single meter throughout—but seemed appropriate for certain passages of quotation or verse-within-the-verse. I have also taken liberties with alliteration, using it suggestively rather than structurally, and allowing alliteration on an unstressed syllable, on the last stress of a line, and in various other ways not found in Old English. I have tried to retain various effects of poetic diction—the metaphorical compounds (the sea is the "whale's riding," a sword a "battle-flame," and so on), the strongly nominal quality of the variations and repetitions, the proliferation of synonyms and compounds, the slightly contorted syntax, and the use of formulaic descriptions and narrative markers—but I have not tried to reproduce OE word order faithfully, and within sentences I have often rearranged a half-line or two to make a smoother sentence.

I have assumed a level of complexity in the sentence structure of the poem that is not always found in other readings and translations. Old English used the same word, *þonne* or *þa*, as both conjunction "then" and adverb "when," and often used a pair of them to introduce consecutive clauses; it is not always easy to tell whether a pair of clauses containing these words ought to be translated paratactically (as a sequence of independent clauses) or hypotactically (as a complex sentence with a subordinate clause). An example is found in lines 126-29, with emphasis added:

Ðā wæs on ūhtan   mid ǣrdæge
Grendles gūðcræft   gumum undyrne;
þā wæs æfter wiste   wōp ūp āhafen,
micel morgenswēg.

When in the dim twilight just before dawn
Grendel's warfare was made known to men,
then lamentation was lifted up after the feasting,
a great morning-sound.

In Old English, the correlative *þa* is used twice; most editors of the Old English text put a semicolon between the two clauses, so that each is read as an independent clause—"Then ... Grendel's warfare was made known to men; then lamentation was lifted up...." This is an entirely plausible reading, and when consistently followed (as it generally is in editions of *Beowulf*) it gives the poem a solid, somewhat squat style, sturdy and stationary like a handmade stone wall. Instead I have translated the first "when" and the second "then," an equally plausible reading that emphasizes the poem's moments of movement and forward momentum, its qualities of logical sequence, subordination, and syntactical complexity.

I have also tried to avoid archaic language, except in a few inevitable cases such as *byrnie* "mail coat" and *liege* (a French loanword that postdates the poem by a century or more) and on some occasions the practically untranslatable OE word for "fate": *wyrd*. Some words in Old English were confined to poetry; these must have struck the listener as "poetic" or "archaic," and some gesture toward this effect seemed reasonable. To simulate the formal diction of the poem I have used a slightly more multisyllabic vocabulary and Latinate syntax at certain points. Still, despite my goal of making a relatively smooth but precise translation, I have tried to leave a bit of the difficulty and sharpness of the syntax and style of the original poem, however alien it may seem at times to a modern reader, in the conviction that such difficulty and sharpness was part of the effect of *Beowulf* even on its Old English audience.

A Note on the Text

In addition to the damage caused by the fire of 1731, the text of *Beowulf* presents many readings that are difficult for an editor; the poem's long history of emendation and supplementation is ably detailed by Birte Kelly. A number of lines are illegible, especially on folios 182 (lines 2207-50) and 201 (lines 3121-82); in many other places the scribes have apparently miscopied a word or more, and modern editors have to guess at what they meant to write. Elsewhere words and even lines are apparently omitted; in other places there are words that seem to have been copied correctly but whose meanings are unknown. For the most part the translation is based on the text of Klaeber's third edition of 1950, though I have ignored some of Klaeber's emendations when I thought the manuscript reading or the suggestions of other scholars made better sense. I have adopted many (though by no means all) of the emendations and explanations for retained manuscript readings found in Bruce Mitchell and Fred C. Robinson's 1998 edition, which first appeared as this translation was being readied for the press, and have used their excellent notes and explanatory glosses in many cases. The paragraphing and to some extent the punctuation of the translation, however, tend to follow the lead of older editors. The frequent paragraph breaks and full punctuation are meant as a convenience to the reader and part of the translator's license, and should not be taken too seriously; they are editorial, not authorial or even scribal. In the translation I have made rather more use of the dash than is commonly allowed in polite society; this is meant to accommodate the numerous parenthetical clauses found in the Old English. In the manuscript, punctuation is by a single dot, usually at the end of a verse, and has little relationship to the syntax and rhetorical structure of the poem's sentences; small capital letters mark the beginnings of paragraphs, nearly all of which are at major turning points in the narrative. This sparse punctuation is not at all unusual in Old English poetry; it forces the audience to work out syntactical relationships for itself. In the translation I have done much of this work for the reader, but it ought to be remembered that it is the translator's opinion, not the author's.

A Note to the Second Edition

The preparation of a second edition has given me the welcome but dreadful opportunity to revisit my work and try to emend or improve it. I have resisted the temptation to rewrite every line of the translation, but I have made some small changes that seemed important to make. Similarly I have tried to clarify some of the muddy prose in the introduction and appendices, and add a few references to more recent scholarship. The most important change is that the publisher has generously allowed me to add a facing-page Old English text, printed with textual variants at the bottom of each page. This is by no means a new critical edition of *Beowulf*, and it makes no claims to originality or authority—the text is a slightly modified reprint of the text found in Friedrich Klaeber's edition, checked against other editions and a facsimile of the manuscript; it follows most of Klaeber's choices in emendation, punctuation, and paragraphing. Readers wishing to understand the complex editorial history of the Old English text or to parse obscure readings should consult Klaeber's edition, not mine. The translated text does not usually correspond word-for-word with the Old English, but in most cases a reader can look across the page to see what the translation is supposed to be a translation of. My hope is that, confronted by this facing-page layout, readers will remember that *Beowulf* is an Old English poem, and some of them may be intrigued, inspired, or exasperated enough by my own work to puzzle out the original for themselves.

The Old English Text

Brackets enclose words altered by emendation, where the manuscript reading is clear but makes no sense. Parentheses indicate letters or words added by conjecture where the original reading is illegible in the manuscript. Often parts of missing letters have been recovered using ultraviolet light or other enhancements, and in most cases all modern editors agree on these conjectural reconstructions. Where they do not, the textual apparatus indicates the manuscript reading and the editors' conjectures.

Reading Old English

What follows is a very rough guide to the pronunciation of Old English (OE); more detailed instructions can be found in standard teaching grammars such as Mitchell and Robinson's *Guide to Old English* and Peter Baker's *Introduction to Old English*.

Old English had seven vowels, *a*, *æ*, *e*, *i*, *o*, *u*, and *y*, as well as two diphthongs, *ea* and *eo*. These were pronounced like the vowels in most non-English languages, i.e.:

a	like	f<u>a</u>ther
e	like	f<u>a</u>te
i	like	f<u>ee</u>t
o	like	b<u>oa</u>t
u	like	t<u>oo</u>l
æ	like	c<u>a</u>t

In Modern English some "long" vowels are, in fact, diphthongs (there is a sharp difference between the *a* sound in *pat* and *pate*, for example); Old English long vowels are just longer versions of the short vowel sounds—they differ in *quantity* but not in quality. The vowel *y*, originally a rounded vowel, is pronounced by rounding the lips as if you were saying "fool," but then trying to say "feel" instead. The sound should be like the umlauted *u* in German *über* or the vowel in French *tu*. The diphthongs *ea* and *eo* are pronounced like *æə*—the second vowel is a schwa, an unstressed vowel in the center of the mouth more or less like the *a* in "sofa"—and *eo*, respectively.

Most Old English consonants are pronounced as in Modern English, with a few complications:

All letters are pronounced; there are no silent letters, not even in words like *hring* "ring," *cniht* "boy" (the origin of Modern English "knight"), or *hlaf* "loaf." Try to pronounce double consonants as double: *sittan* has the consonant sound of "cat-tail," not "mittens." Unstressed vowels at the ends of words should also be pronounced— the word *sealde* "gave" has two syllables, *seal-de*.

The letters *þ* (thorn) and *ð* (eth) are pronounced like *th* in *thin* or *then*. The consonants *f*, *s*, and *þ/ð* are pronounced as voiced *v*, *z*, *ð* when they occur between vowels or other voiced sounds. OE *ofer* and *feðer* are pronounced like Modern English (MnE) "over" and "feather"; *ceosan* has the /z/ sound of MnE "chosen."

Back-of-the-throat consonants, called *velar*, are the most trouble-some in Old English. *c* is pronounced like /k/ in the neighborhood of back vowels like *a*, *o*, *u*; elsewhere it is *palatalized* to the sound spelled *ch* in Modern English. So OE *col* is pronounced more or less like MnE "coal," and *cirice* is roughly like MnE "church." OE *c* is never pronounced like /s/.

In a similar way *g* is pronounced like MnE /g/ (as in "gate") at the beginning of a word and in the neighborhood of back vowels, and like the MnE consonant sound *y* (as in "young") elsewhere; thus OE *god* is like MnE "God," while *gieldan* is the ancestor of MnE "yield." Beowulf's people are the *Geats*, pronounced more like "yats" than "geets." The name of his uncle *Hygelac* is pronounced something like "HEE-ya-lack." Before consonants, *g* and *h* are pronounced with a slight throat-clearing, something like the consonant in Scottish *loch* or German *ach*.

The combination *cg* (as in OE *ecg* "blade, edge") is pronounced like the consonant sound in MnE "edge"; the *sc* in *scip* (OE "ship") is pronounced like *sh* in "ship." The one common exception is the word *ascian*, ancestor of MnE "ask."

Stress is on the first syllable of a word unless it is a verb with a prefix such as *ge-* (pronounced "ye"); in the second line of the poem *gefrunon* is pronounced roughly like "ye-FRU-non." Compound words can have a second stress on the root syllable of the compound; *þeod-cyninga* in the same line can be pronounced like "THAYUD-KIN-ing-ga."

When reading Old English aloud, remember that nobody speaks Old English anymore, and all reconstructions are only approximations, so just let it rip. Stress and style generally matter more than precision, though there's no reason you can't try to have both; try to respect the meaning of the lines as you read, and accent words and phrases as if you knew exactly what they meant, and your reading will be better than most scholars. Excerpts from *Beowulf* read aloud can be found online in various places, including Peter Baker's excellent Old English site at the University of Virginia and the *Norton Anthology of English Literature* website.

BEOWULF

HPÆT PE GARDE
na ingeaji dagum· þeod cyniga
þrym ge frunon huða æþelingaf elle
fremedon· ofz scyld sceping scæþe
þreatum monegū mægþum meodo set
of teah egsode eopl syððan ærest p
fea sceapt funden he þæf frofre geb
peox undeji polcnum peojið myndum þah
oð þ him æghpyle þaja ymb sittendjia
ofeji hjion jiade hyjian scolde gomban
gyldan þþæf god cyning· ðæm eafeja paf
æfteji cenned geong ingeajidum þone god
sende folce toffrofje fyjen ðajife on
geat þ hie ædjuizon aldo ase· lange
hpile him þæf lif fjiea puldjief peal dend
pojold aje foj geaf· beopulf paf bjien
blæd pide sjijian scyl da eafeja scede
landum in Spaces
ge pyji cean gromum peax

Prologue

Hwæt, wē Gār-Dena   in gēardagum,
þēodcyninga   þrym gefrūnon,
hū ðā æþelingas   ellen fremedon!
    Oft Scyld Scēfing   sceaþena þrēatum,
monegum mǣgþum   meodosetla oftēah,   5
egsode eorl[as].   Syððan ǣrest wearð
fēasceaft funden,   hē þæs frōfre gebād —
wēox under wolcnum   weorðmyndum þāh,
oð þæt him æghwylc   þara ymbsittendra
ofer hronrāde   hȳran scolde,   10
gomban gyldan;   þæt wæs gōd cyning!
Ðǣm eafera wæs   æfter cenned
geong in geardum,   þone God sende
folce tō frōfre;   fyrenðearfe ongeat,
þæt hīe ǣr drugon   aldor(l)ēase   15
lange hwīle;   him þæs Liffrea,
wuldres Wealdend   woroldāre forgeaf;
Bēowulf wæs brēme   — blǣd wīde sprang —
Scyldes eafera   Scedelandum in.
Swā sceal ge(ong) guma   gōde gewyrcean,   20
fromum feohgiftum   on fæder (bea)rme,
þæt hine on ylde   eft gewunigen
wilgesīþas,   þonne wīg cume,
lēode gelǣsten;   lofdǣdum sceal
in mǣgþa gehwǣre   man geþeon.   25
    Him ðā Scyld gewāt   tō gescæphwīle
felahrōr fēran   on Frēan wǣre;
hī hyne þā ætbǣron   tō brimes faroðe,

---

6 eorlas] eorl MS

Prologue

Listen!
    We have heard of the glory in bygone days
of the folk-kings of the spear-Danes,[1]
how those noble lords did lofty deeds.
    Often Scyld Scefing[2] seized the mead-benches
from many tribes, troops of enemies,   5
struck fear into earls. Though he first was
found a waif, he awaited solace for that —
he grew under heaven and prospered in honor
until every one of the encircling nations
over the whale's-riding[3] had to obey him,   10
grant him tribute. That was a good king!
A boy was later born to him,
young in the courts, whom God sent
as a solace to the people — he saw their need,
the dire distress they had endured, lordless,   15
for such a long time. The Lord of Life,
Wielder of Glory, gave him worldly honor;
Beowulf,[4] the son of Scyld, was renowned,
his fame spread wide in Scandinavian lands.
Thus should a young man bring about good   20
with pious gifts from his father's possessions,
so that later in life loyal comrades
will stand beside him when war comes,
the people will support him — with praiseworthy deeds
a man will prosper among any people.   25
    Scyld passed away at his appointed hour,
the mighty lord went into the Lord's keeping;
they bore him down to the brimming sea,

---

1 The Danes are described by many different epithets in the poem; see the Glossary of
    Proper Names (p. 247) for further instances.
2 The name means "Shield, Son of Sheaf (i.e., of grain)." The mysterious origins of
    Scyld, who seems to arrive providentially from nowhere and is returned to the sea
    after his death, have occasioned much critical speculation.
3 A condensed descriptive image of the sea—the riding-place of whales. Elsewhere the
    sea is the "gannet's bath" and the "swan's riding."
4 Not the monster-slaying hero of the title, but an early Danish king. Many scholars
    argue that the original name was Beow.

swǣse gesīþas,   swā hē selfa bæd,
þenden wordum wēold   wine Scyldinga —   30
lēof landfruma   lange āhte.
Þǣr æt hȳðe stōd   hringedstefna
īsig ond ūtfūs,   æþelinges fær;
ālēdon þā   lēofne þēoden,
bēaga bryttan   on bearm scipes,   35
mǣrne be mæste.   Þǣr wæs mādma fela
of feorwegum   frætwa gelǣded;
ne hȳrde ic cȳmlīcor   cēol gegyrwan
hildewǣpnum   ond heaðowǣdum,
billum ond byrnum.   Him on bearme læg   40
mādma mænigo,   þā him mid scoldon
on flōdes ǣht   feor gewītan.
Nalæs hī hine lǣssan   lācum tēodan,
þēodgestrēonum,   þon þā dydon,
þē hine æt frumsceafte   forð onsendon   45
ǣnne ofer ȳðe   umborwesende.
Þā gȳt hīe him āsetton   segen gy(l)denne
hēah ofer hēafod,   lēton holm beran,
gēafon on gārsecg;   him wæs geōmor sefa,
murnende mōd.   Men ne cunnon   50
secgan tō sōðe,   selerǣden[d]e,
hǣleð under heofenum,   hwā þǣm hlæste onfēng.

I

Ðā wæs on burgum   Bēowulf Scyldinga,
lēof lēodcyning   longe þrāge
folcum gefrǣge   — fæder ellor hwearf,   55
aldor of earde —   oþ þæt him eft onwōc
hēah Healfdene;   hēold þenden lifde
gamol ond gūðrēouw   glæde Scyldingas.
Ðǣm fēower bearn   forðgerīmed

---

51 selerædende] sele rædenne MS

his dear comrades, as he himself had commanded
while the friend of the Scyldings[1] wielded speech —   30
that dear land-ruler had long held power.
In the harbor stood a ring-prowed ship,
icy, outbound, a nobleman's vessel;
there they laid down their dear lord,
dispenser of rings, in the bosom of the ship,   35
glorious, by the mast. There were many treasures
loaded there, adornments from distant lands;
I have never heard of a more lovely ship
bedecked with battle-weapons and war-gear,
blades and byrnies.[2] In its bosom lay   40
many treasures, which were to travel
far with him into the keeping of the flood.
With no fewer gifts did they furnish him there,
the wealth of nations, than those did who
at his beginning first sent him forth   45
alone over the waves while still a small child.[3]
Then they set a golden ensign
high over his head, and let the waves have him,
gave him to the sea with grieving spirits,
mournful in mind. Men do not know   50
how to say truly — not trusted counselors,
nor heroes under the heavens — who received that cargo.

I

Then Beowulf Scylding, beloved king,
was famous in the strongholds of his folk
for a long while — his father having passed away,   55
a lord from earth — until after him arose
the great Healfdene, who held the glorious Scyldings
all his life, ancient and fierce in battle.
Four children, all counted up,

---

1 The Scyldings are the Danes, "sons of Scyld."
2 A *byrnie* is a coat of ring-mail.
3 Scyld was found destitute—this statement is an example of litotes, or ironic under-
   statement, not uncommon in Anglo-Saxon poetry.

in worold wōcun,   weoroda rǣswa[n],   60
Heorogār ond Hrōðgār   ond Hālga til,
hȳrde ic þæt [......   wæs On]elan cwēn,
Heaðo-Scilfingas   healsgebedda.
    Þā wæs Hrōðgāre   herespēd gyfen,
wīges weorðmynd,   þæt him his winemāgas   65
georne hȳrdon,   oðð þæt sēo geogoð gewēox,
magodriht micel.   Him on mōd bearn
þæt healreced   hātan wolde,
medoærn micel   men gewyrcean
þone yldo bearn   ǣfre gefrūnon,   70
ond þǣr on innan   eall gedǣlan
geongum ond ealdum,   swylc him God sealde,
būton folcscare   ond feorum gumena.
Ðā ic wīde gefrægn   weorc gebannan
manigre mǣgþe   geond þisne middangeard,   75
folcstede frætwan.   Him on fyrste gelomp
ǣdre mid yldum,   þæt hit wearð ealgearo,
healærna mǣst;   scōp him Heort naman
sē þe his wordes geweald   wīde hæfde.
Hē bēot ne ālēh,   bēagas dǣlde,   80
sinc æt symle.   Sele hlīfade
hēah ond horngēap;   heaðowylma bād,
lāðan līges;   ne wæs hit lenge þā gēn,
þæt se [e]cghete   āþumsw[ēor]an
æfter wælnīðe   wæcnan scolde.   85
    Ðā se ellengǣst   earfoðlīce
þrāge geþolode,   sē þe in þȳstrum bād,
þæt hē dōgora gehwām   drēam gehȳrde
hlūdne in healle;   þǣr wæs hearpan swēg,

---

60 rǣswan] rǣswa MS   62 *no gap in* MS   70 þone] *many editors emend to* þonne
84 ecghete] secg hete MS   aþumsweoran] aþum swerian MS

were born to that bold leader of hosts: 60
Heorogar, Hrothgar, and Halga the Good,
I heard that ... was Onela's queen,[1]
dear bedfellow of the Battle-Scylfing.
        Then success in war was given to Hrothgar,
honor in battle, so that his beloved kinsmen 65
eagerly served him, until the young soldiers grew
into a mighty troop of men. It came to his mind
that he should order a hall-building,
have men make a great mead-house
which the sons of men should remember forever,[2] 70
and there within he would share everything
with young and old that God had given him,
except for the common land and the lives of men.
Then the work, as I've heard, was widely proclaimed
to many nations throughout this middle-earth, 75
to come adorn the folk-stead. It came to pass
swiftly among men, and it was soon ready,
the greatest of halls; he gave it the name "Heorot,"[3]
he whose words were heeded far and wide.
He remembered his boast; he gave out rings, 80
treasure at table. The hall towered
high and horn-gabled — it awaited hostile fires,
the surges of war; the time was not yet at hand
when the sword-hate of sworn in-laws
should arise after ruthless violence.[4] 85
        A bold demon who waited in darkness
wretchedly suffered all the while,
for every day he heard the joyful din
loud in the hall, with the harp's sound,

---

1   A name is missing from the manuscript here; it has been conjectured from parallel
    sources that it should be Yrse, or Ursula. The Swedish ("Scylfing") king Onela
    appears later in the story, causing much distress to Beowulf's nation.
2   Or "a greater mead-hall / than the sons of men had ever heard of." The reading
    adopted here is that of Mitchell and Robinson.
3   "Hart." An object recovered from the burial-mound at Sutton Hoo, perhaps a royal
    insignia, is surmounted by the image of a hart.
4   The hall Heorot is apparently fated to be destroyed in a battle between Hrothgar and
    his son-in-law Ingeld the Heathobard, a conflict predicted by Beowulf in 2024-69.
    The battle itself happens outside the action of the poem.

swutol sang scopes.   Sægde sē þe cūþe   90
frumsceaft fīra   feorran reccan,
cwæð þæt se Ælmihtiga   eorðan worh(te),
wlitebeorhtne wang,   swā wæter bebūgeð,
gesette sigehrēþig   sunnan ond mōnan
lēoman tō lēohte   landbūendum,   95
ond gefrætwade   foldan scēatas
leomum ond lēafum,   līf ēac gesceōp
cynna gehwylcum   þāra ðe cwice hwyrfaþ.
Swā ðā drihtguman   drēamum lifdon,
ēadiglīce,   oð ðæt ān ongan   100
fyrene fre(m)man   fēond on helle;
wæs se grimma gæst   Grendel hāten,
mære mearcstapa,   sē þe mōras hēold,
fen ond fæsten;   fīfelcynnes eard
wonsælī wer   weardode hwīle,   105
siþðan him Scyppend   forscrifen hæfde
in Cāines cynne —   þone cwealm gewræc
ēce Drihten,   þæs þe hē Ābel slōg;
ne gefeah hē þære fæhðe,   ac hē hine feor forwræc,
Metod for þȳ māne   mancynne fram.   110
Þanon untȳdras   ealle onwōcon,
eotenas ond ylfe   ond orcneas,
swylce gīgantas,   þā wið Gode wunnon
lange þrāge;   hē him ðæs lēan forgeald.

II

Gewāt ðā nēosian,   syþðan niht becōm,   115
hean hūses,   hū hit Hring-Dene
æfter bēorþege   gebūn hæfdon.
Fand þā ðær inne   æþelinga gedriht

---

106 Scyppend] *alt. from* scyppen   107 Caines] *alt. from* cames

the clear song of the scop.[1] He who knew   90
how to tell the ancient tale of the origin of men
said that the Almighty created the earth,
a bright and shining plain, by seas embraced,
and set, triumphantly, the sun and moon
to light their beams for those who dwell on land,   95
adorned the distant corners of the world
with leaves and branches, and made life also,
all manner of creatures that live and move.
— Thus this lordly people lived in joy,
blessedly, until one began   100
to work his foul crimes — a fiend from hell.
This grim spirit was called Grendel,
mighty stalker of the marches, who held
the moors and fens; this miserable man
lived for a time in the land of giants,   105
after the Creator had condemned him
among Cain's race — when he killed Abel
the eternal Lord avenged that death.[2]
No joy in that feud — the Maker forced him
far from mankind for his foul crime.   110
From thence arose all misbegotten things,
trolls and elves and the living dead,
and also the giants who strove against God
for a long while[3] — He gave them their reward for that.

II

When night descended he went to seek out   115
the high house, to see how the Ring-Danes
had bedded down after their beer-drinking.
He found therein a troop of nobles

---

1   A *scop* is a poet-singer. This is the first of several self-reflexive scenes of poetic
    entertainment in the poem.
2   The story of Cain and Abel is told in Genesis 4:1-16.
3   The poet lists a collection of Germanic, classical, and biblical horrors; all are ulti-
    mately traced to their biblical roots, though the characters in the poem are not aware
    of this.

swefan æfter symble;   sorge ne cūðon,
wonsceaft wera.   Wiht unhǣlo,   120
grim ond grǣdig,   gearo sōna wæs,
rēoc ond rēþe,   ond on ræste genam
þrītig þegna;   þanon eft gewāt
hūðe hrēmig   tō hām faran,
mid þære wælfylle   wīca nēosan.   125
Đā wæs on ūhtan   mid ǣrdæge
Grendles gūðcræft   gumum undyrne;
þā wæs æfter wiste   wōp ūp āhafen,
micel morgenswēg.   Mǣre þēoden,
æþeling ǣrgōd,   unblīðe sæt,   130
þolode ðrȳðswȳð   þegnsorge drēah,
syðþan hīe þæs lāðan   lāst scēawedon,
wergan gāstes;   wæs þæt gewin tō strang,
lāð ond longsum!
    Næs hit lengra fyrst,
ac ymb āne niht   eft gefremede   135
morðbeala māre,   ond nō mearn fore,
fǣhðe ond fyrene;   wæs tō fæst on þām.
Þā wæs ēaðfynde   þē him elles hwǣr
gerūmlīcor   ræste [sōhte],
bed æfter būrum,   ðā him gebēacnod wæs,   140
gesægd sōðlīce   sweotolan tācne
healðegnes hete;   hēold hyne syðþan
fyr ond fæstor   sē þǣm fēonde ætwand.
Swā rīxode   ond wið rihte wan,
āna wið eallum,   oð þæt īdel stōd   145
hūsa sēlest.   Wæs sēo hwīl micel;
twelf wintra tīd   torn geþolode
wine Scyld[ing]a,   wēana gehwelcne,
sīdra sorga;   forðām [secgum] wearð,
ylda bearnum   undyrne cūð   150
gyddum geōmore,   þætte Grendel wan

---

139 sohte] *not in* MS   148 Scyldinga] scyldenda MS   149 secgum] *not in* MS

asleep after the feast; they knew no sorrow
or human misery. The unholy creature,   120
grim and ravenous, was ready at once,
ruthless and cruel, and took from their rest
thirty thanes;[1] thence he went
rejoicing in his booty, back to his home,
to seek out his abode with his fill of slaughter.   125
When in the dim twilight just before dawn
Grendel's warfare was made known to men,
then lamentation was lifted up after the feasting,
a great morning-sound. Unhappy sat
the mighty lord, long-good nobleman;   130
he suffered greatly, grieved for his thanes,
once they beheld that hostile one's tracks,
the accursed spirit; that strife was too strong,
loathsome and long.
            It was no long wait,
but the very next night he committed   135
a greater murder, mourned not at all
for his feuds and sins — he was too fixed in them.
Then it was easy to find a thane
who sought his rest elsewhere, farther away,
a bed in the outbuildings,[2] when they pointed out —   140
truly announced with clear tokens —
that hall-thane's hate; he who escaped the fiend
held himself afterwards farther away and safer.
So he ruled, and strove against right,
one against all, until empty stood   145
the best of houses. And so it was for a great while —
for twelve long winters the lord of the Scyldings
suffered his grief, every sort of woe,
great sorrow, when to the sons of men
it became known, and carried abroad   150
in sad tales, that Grendel strove

---

1   A "thane" is a retainer, one of the troop of companions surrounding a heroic king in
    Germanic literature.
2   Hrothgar's hall is apparently surrounded by smaller buildings, including the women's
    quarters (see lines 662-65, 920-24). Under normal circumstances the men sleep
    together in the hall, ready for battle (1239-50).

hwīle wið Hrōþgār,   hetenīðas wæg,
fyrene ond fæhðe   fela missēra,
singāle sæce;   sibbe ne wolde
wið manna hwone   mægenes Deniga,   155
feorhbealo feorran,   fēa þingian,
nē þǣr nǣnig witena   wēnan þorfte
beorhtre bōte   tō ban[an] folmum;
(ac se) ǣglǣca   ēhtende wæs,
deorc dēaþscua,   duguþe ond geogoþe,   160
seomade ond syrede;   sinnihte hēold
mistige mōras;   men ne cunnon,
hwyder helrūnan   hwyrftum scrīþað.
   Swā fela fyrena   fēond mancynnes,
atol āngengea   oft gefremede,   165
heardra hȳnða;   Heorot eardode,
sincfāge sel   sweartum nihtum;
nō hē þone gifstōl   grētan mōste,
māþðum for Metode,   nē his myne wisse.
Þæt wæs wrǣc micel   wine Scyldinga,   170
mōdes brecða.   Monig oft gesæt
rīce tō rūne;   rǣd eahtedon,
hwæt swīðferhðum   sēlest wǣre
wið fǣrgryrum   tō gefremmanne.
Hwīlum hīe gehēton   æt [h]ærgtrafum   175
wīgweorþunga,   wordum bǣdon,
þæt him gāstbona   gēoce gefremede
wið þēodþrēaum.   Swylc wæs þēaw hyra,
hǣþenra hyht;   helle gemundon
in mōdsefan,   Metod hīe ne cūþon,   180
dǣda Dēmend,   ne wiston hīe Drihten God,
nē hīe hūru heofena Helm   herian ne cūþon,
wuldres Waldend.   Wā bið þǣm ðe sceal

---

158 banan] banū MS   175 hærgtrafum] hrærg trafum MS

long with Hrothgar, bore his hatred,
sins and feuds, for many seasons,
perpetual conflict; he wanted no peace
with any man of the Danish army,   155
nor ceased his deadly hatred, nor settled with money,
nor did any of the counselors need to expect
bright compensation from the killer's hands,[1]
for the great ravager relentlessly stalked,
a dark death-shadow, lurked and struck   160
old and young alike, in perpetual night
held the misty moors. Men do not know
whither such whispering demons wander about.
      Thus the foe of mankind, fearsome and solitary,
often committed his many crimes,   165
cruel humiliations; he occupied Heorot,
the jewel-adorned hall, in the dark nights —
he saw no need to salute the throne,
he scorned the treasures; he did not know their love.[2]
That was deep misery to the lord of the Danes,   170
crushing his spirit. Many a strong man sat
in secret counsel, considered advice,
what would be best for the brave at heart
to save themselves from the sudden attacks.
At times they offered honor to idols   175
at pagan temples, prayed aloud
that the soul-slayer[3] might offer assistance
in the country's distress. Such was their custom,
the hope of heathens — they remembered hell
in their minds, they did not know the Maker,   180
the Judge of deeds, they did not know the Lord God,
or even how to praise the heavenly Protector,
Wielder of glory. Woe unto him

---

1   Germanic and Anglo-Saxon law allowed that a murderer could make peace with the
    family of his victim by paying compensation, or *wergild*. The amount of compensa-
    tion varied with the rank of the victim.
2   This is a much-disputed passage; my reading follows a suggestion made by Fred C.
    Robinson in "Why is Grendel's Not Greeting the *gifstol* a *wræc micel*?" and repeated
    in Mitchell and Robinson's *Beowulf*.
3   I.e., the Devil. In the Middle Ages the gods of the pagans were often regarded as
    demons in disguise.

þurh slīðne nīð   sāwle bescūfan
in fȳres fæþm,   frōfre ne wēnan,   185
wihte gewendan!   Wēl bið þǣm þe mōt
æfter dēaðdæge   Drihten sēcean
ond tō Fæder fæþmum   freoðo wilnian!

III

Swā ðā mǣlceare   maga Healfdenes
singāla sēað;   ne mihte snotor hæleð   190
wēan onwendan;   wæs þæt gewin tō swȳð,
lāþ ond longsum,   þē on ðā lēode becōm,
nȳdwracu nīþgrim,   nihtbealwa mǣst.
     Þæt fram hām gefrægn   Higelāces þegn
gōd mid Gēatum,   Grendles dǣda;   195
sē wæs moncynnes   mægenes strengest
on þǣm dæge   þysses līfes,
æþele ond ēacen.   Hēt him ȳðlidan
gōdne gegyrwan;   cwæð, hē gūðcyning
ofer swanrāde   sēcean wolde,   200
mǣrne þēoden,   þā him wæs manna þearf.
Ðone sīðfæt him   snotere ceorlas
lȳthwōn lōgon,   þēah hē him lēof wǣre;
hwetton hige(r)ōfne,   hǣl scēawedon.
Hæfde se gōda   Gēata lēoda   205
cempan gecorone   þāra þe hē cēnoste
findan mihte;   fīftȳna sum
sundwudu sōhte,   secg wīsade,
lagucræftig mon   landgemyrcu.
Fyrst forð gewāt;   flota wæs on ȳðum,   210
bāt under beorge.   Beornas gearwe
on stefn stigon —   strēamas wundon,
sund wið sande;   secgas bǣron
on bearm nacan   beorhte frætwe,
gūðsearo geatolīc;   guman ūt scufon,   215
weras on wilsīð   wudu bundenne.

who must thrust his soul through wicked force
in the fire's embrace, expect no comfort,   185
no way to change at all! It shall be well for him
who can seek the Lord after his deathday
and find security in the Father's embrace.

III

With the sorrows of that time the son of Healfdene
seethed constantly; nor could the wise hero   190
turn aside his woe — too great was the strife,
long and loathsome, which befell that nation,
violent, grim, cruel, greatest of night-evils.
        Then from his home the thane of Hygelac,[1]
a good man among the Geats, heard of Grendel's deeds —   195
he was of mankind the strongest of might
in those days of this life,
noble and mighty. He commanded to be made
a good wave-crosser, said that he would seek out
that war-king over the swan's-riding,   200
the renowned prince who was in need of men.
Wise men did not dissuade him at all
from that journey, though he was dear to them;
they encouraged his bold spirit, inspected the omens.
From the Geatish nation that good man   205
had chosen the boldest champions, the best
he could find; as one of fifteen
he sought the sea-wood. A wise sailor
showed the way to the edge of the shore.
The time came — the craft was on the waves,   210
moored under the cliffs. Eager men
climbed on the prow — the currents eddied,
sea against sand — the soldiers bore
into the bosom of the ship their bright gear,
fine polished armor; the men pushed off   215
on their wished-for journey in that wooden vessel.

---

1   The hero is not named until more than a hundred lines later. Hygelac is his uncle and
    king. On Hygelac as Chlochilaicus, see Appendix A1; see also Appendix A2.

Gewāt þā ofer wǣgholm winde gefȳsed
flota fāmīheals fugle gelīcost,
oð þæt ymb āntīd ōþres dōgores
wundenstefna gewaden hæfde, 220
þæt ðā līðende land gesāwon,
brimclifu blīcan, beorgas stēape,
sīde sǣnæssas; þā wæs sund liden,
eoletes æt ende. Þanon ūp hraðe
Wedera lēode on wang stigon, 225
sǣwudu sǣldon, syrcan hrysedon,
gūðgewǣdo; Gode þancedon
þæs þe him ȳþlāde ēaðe wurdon.
Þā of wealle geseah weard Scildinga,
sē þe holmclifu healdan scolde, 230
beran ofer bolcan beorhte randas,
fyrdsearu fūslicu; hine fyrwyt brǣc
mōdgehygdum, hwæt þā men wǣron.
Gewāt him þā tō waroðe wicge rīdan
þegn Hrōðgāres, þrymmum cwehte 235
mǣgenwudu mundum, meþelwordum frægn:
"Hwæt syndon gē searohæbbendra,
byrnum werede, þē þus brontne cēol
ofer lagustrǣte lǣdan cwōmon,
hider ofer holmas? [Hwæt, ic hwī]le wæs 240
endesǣta, ǣgwearde hēold,
þē on land Dena lāðra nǣnig
mid scipherge sceðþan ne meahte.
Nō hēr cūðlīcor cuman ongunnon
lindhæbbende, nē gē lēafnesword 245
gūðfremmendra gearwe ne wisson,
māga gemēdu. Nǣfre ic māran geseah
eorla ofer eorþan, ðonne is ēower sum,
secg on searwum; nis þæt seldguma,
wǣpnum geweorðad, næf[n]e him his wlite lēoge, 250
ǣnlīc ansȳn. Nū ic ēower sceal
frumcyn witan, ǣr gē fyr heonan
lēasscēaweras on land Dena

---

240 Hwæt, ic hwile wæs] le wæs MS   250 næfne] næfre MS

Over the billowing waves, urged by the wind,
the foamy-necked floater flew like a bird,
until in due time on the second day
the curved-prowed vessel had come so far   220
that the seafarers sighted land,
shining shore-cliffs, steep mountains,
wide headlands — then the waves were crossed,
the journey at an end. Thence up quickly
the people of the Weders[1] climbed onto the plain,   225
moored their ship, shook out their mail-shirts,
their battle-garments; they thanked God
that the sea-paths had been smooth for them.
       When from the wall the Scyldings' watchman,
whose duty it was to watch the sea-cliffs,   230
saw them bear down the gangplank bright shields,
ready battle-gear, he was bursting with curiosity
in his mind to know who these men were.
This thane of Hrothgar rode his horse
down to the shore, and shook mightily   235
his strong spear, and spoke a challenge:
"What are you, warriors in armor, wearing
coats of mail, who have come thus sailing
over the sea-road in a tall ship,
hither over the waves? Long have I been   240
the coast-warden, and kept sea-watch
so that no enemies with fleets and armies
should ever attack the land of the Danes.
Never more openly have there ever come
shield-bearers here, nor have you heard   245
any word of leave from our warriors
or consent of kinsmen. I have never seen
a greater earl on earth than that one among you,
a man in war-gear; that is no mere courtier,
honored only in weapons — unless his looks belie him,   250
his noble appearance! Now I must know
your lineage, lest you go hence
as false spies, travel further

---

1 The Weders are the Geats.

furþur fēran.   Nū gē feorbūend
merelīðende,   mīn[n]e gehȳrað   255
ānfealdne geþōht: ofost is sēlest
tō gecȳðanne,   hwanan ēowre cyme syndon."

IV

   Him se yldesta   andswarode,
werodes wīsa,   wordhord onlēac:
"Wē synt gumcynnes   Gēata lēode   260
ond Higelāces   heorðgenēatas.
Wæs mīn fæder   folcum gecȳþed,
æþele ordfruma,   Ecgþēow hāten;
gebād wintra worn,   ǣr hē on weg hwurfe,
gamol of geardum;   hine gearwe geman   265
witena wēlhwylc   wīde geond eorþan.
Wē þurh holdne hige   hlāford þīnne,
sunu Healfdenes   sēcean cwōmon,
lēodgebyrgean;   wes þū ūs lārena gōd!
Habbað wē tō þǣm mǣran   micel ǣrende   270
Deniga frean;   ne sceal þǣr dyrne sum
wesan, þæs ic wēne.   Þū wāst, gif hit is
swā wē sōþlīce   secgan hȳrdon,
þæt mid Scyldingum   sceaðona ic nāt hwylc,
dēogol dǣdhata   deorcum nihtum   275
ēaweð þurh egsan   uncūðne nīð,
hȳnðu ond hrāfyl.   Ic þæs Hrōðgār mæg
þurh rūmne sefan   rǣd gelǣran,
hū hē frōd ond gōd   fēond oferswȳðeþ —
gyf him edwend[e]n   ǣfre scolde   280
bealuwa bisigu   bōt eft cuman,
ond þā cearwylmas   cōlran wurðaþ;
oððe ā syþðan   earfoðþrāge,
þrēanȳd þolað,   þenden þǣr wunað
on hēahstede   hūsa sēlest."   285

---

255 minne] mine MS   280 edwenden] edwendan MS

into Danish territory. Now, you sea-travelers
from a far-off land, listen to my   255
simple thought — the sooner the better,
you must make clear from whence you have come."[1]

IV

    The eldest one answered him,
leader of the troop, unlocked his word-hoard:
"We are men of the Geatish nation   260
and Hygelac's hearth-companions.
My father was well-known among men,
a noble commander named Ecgtheow;
he saw many winters before he passed away,
ancient, from the court; nearly everyone   265
throughout the world remembers him well.
With a friendly heart have we come
seeking your lord, the son of Healfdene,
guardian of his people; be of good counsel to us!
We have a great mission to that famous man,   270
ruler of the Danes; nor should any of it be
hidden, I think. You know, if things are
as we have truly heard tell,
that among the Scyldings some sort of enemy,
a hidden evildoer, in the dark nights   275
makes known his terrible mysterious violence,
shame and slaughter. With a generous spirit
I can counsel Hrothgar, advise him how,
wise old king, he may overcome this fiend —
if a change should ever come for him,   280
a remedy for the evil of his afflictions,
and his seething cares turn cooler;
or else forever afterwards a time of anguish
he shall suffer, his sad necessity, while there stands
in its high place the best of houses."   285

---

1   See Appendix E for a selection of other translations of this section of the poem, lines
   229-57.

Weard maþelode,   ðǣr on wicge sæt,
ombeht unforht: "Ǣghwæþres sceal
scearp scyldwiga   gescād witan,
worda ond worca,   sē þe wēl þenceð.
Ic þæt gehȳre,   þæt þis is hold weorod   290
frēan Scyldinga.   Gewītaþ forð beran
wǣpen ond gewǣdu,   ic ēow wīsige;
swylce ic maguþegnas   mīne hāte
wið fēonda gehwone   flotan ēowerne,
nīwtyrwydne   nacan on sande   295
ārum healdan,   oþ ðæt eft byreð
ofer lagustrēamas   lēofne mannan
wudu wundenhals   tō Wedermearce,
gōdfremmendra   swylcum gifeþe bið,
þæt þone hilderǣs   hāl gedīgeð."   300
    Gewiton him þā fēran;   flota stille bād,
seomode on s[ā]le   sīdfæþmed scip,
on ancre fæst.   Eoforlīc scionon
ofer hlēorber[g]an   gehroden golde,
fāh ond fȳrheard,   ferhwearde hēold.   305
gūþmōd gr[i]mmon.   Guman ōnetton,
sigon ætsomne,   oþ þæt hȳ [s]æl timbred
geatolīc ond goldfāh   ongyton mihton;
þæt wæs foremǣrost   foldbūendum
receda under roderum,   on þǣm se rīca bād;   310
līxta se lēoma   ofer landa fela.
Him þā hildedēor   [h]of mōdigra
torht getǣhte,   þæt hīe him tō mihton
gegnum gangan;   gūðbeorna sum
wicg gewende,   word æfter cwæð: 315
"Mǣl is mē tō fēran;   Fæder alwalda
mid ārstafum   ēowic gehealde
sīða gesunde!   Ic tō sǣ wille,
wið wrāð werod   wearde healdan."

---

302 on sale] on sole MS   304 hleorbergan] hleor beran MS   306 grimmon] grummon
MS   307 sæl timbred] æltimbred MS   312 hof] of MS

The watchman spoke, as he sat on his horse,
a fearless officer: "A sharp shield-warrior
must be a judge of both things,
words and deeds, if he would think well.
I understand that to the Scylding lord   290
you are a friendly force. Go forth, and bear
weapons and armor — I shall guide your way;
and I will command my young companions
to guard honorably against all enemies
your ship, newly-tarred, upon the sand,   295
to watch it until the curved-necked wood
bears hence across the ocean-streams
a beloved man to the borders of the Weders —
and such of these good men as will be granted
that they survive the storm of battle."   300
They set off — their vessel stood still,
the roomy ship rested in its riggings,
fast at anchor. Boar-figures shone
over gold-plated cheek-guards,[1]
gleaming, fire-hardened; they guarded the lives   305
of the grim battle-minded. The men hastened,
marched together, until they could make out
the timbered hall, splendid and gold-adorned —
the most famous building among men
under the heavens — where the high king waited;   310
its light shone over many lands.
Their brave guide showed them the bright court
of the mighty ones, so that they might go
straight to it; that fine soldier
wheeled his horse and spoke these words: 315
"Time for me to go. The almighty Father
guard you in his grace,
safe in your journeys! I must to the sea,
and hold my watch against hostile hordes."

---

1   The boar was a sacred animal in Germanic mythology; in his *Germania* the Roman
    historian Tacitus mentions warriors wearing boar-images into battle (ch. 45). Images
    of boars were placed on helmets to protect the wearer from the "bite" of a sword,
    which was often quasi-personified as a serpent. Archaeologists have unearthed
    several Anglo-Saxon helmets with various kinds of boar-images on them.

Strǣt wæs stānfāh,   stīg wīsode   320
gumum ætgædere.   Gūðbyrne scān
heard hondlocen,   hringīren scīr
song in searwum,   þā hīe tō sele furðum
in hyra gryregeatwum   gangan cwōmon.
Setton sǣmēþe   sīde scyldas,   325
rondas regnbearde   wið þæs recedes weal;
bugon þā tō bence —   byrnan hringdon,
gūðsearo gumena;   gāras stōdon,
sǣmanna searo   samod ætgædere,
æscholt ufan grǣg;   wæs se īrenþrēat   330
wǣpnum gewurþad.
                  Þā ðǣr wlonc hæleð
ōretmecgas   æfter [æþel]um frægn:
"Hwanon ferigeað gē   fǣtte scyldas,
grǣge syrcan,   ond grīmhelmas,
heresceafta hēap?   Ic eom Hrōðgāres   335
ār ond ombiht.   Ne seah ic elþēodige
þus manige men   mōdiglīcran.
Wēn' ic þæt gē for wlenco,   nalles for wræcsīðum,
ac for higeþrymmum   Hrōðgār sōhton."
Him þā ellenrōf   andswarode,   340
wlanc Wedera lēod,   word æfter spræc
heard under helme: "Wē synt Higelāces
bēodgenēatas;   Bēowulf is mīn nama.
Wille ic āsecgan   sunu Healfdenes,
mǣrum þēodne   mīn ǣrende,   345
aldre þīnum,   gif hē ūs geunnan wile,
þæt wē hine swā gōdne   grētan mōton."
Wulfgār maþelode   — þæt wæs Wendla lēod,
wæs his mōdsefa   manegum gecȳðed,
wīg ond wīsdōm: "Ic þæs wine Deniga,   350
frēan Scildinga   frīnan wille,
bēaga bryttan,   swā þū bēna eart,
þēoden mǣrne   ymb þīnne sīð,
ond þē þā andsware   ǣdre gecȳðan,

---

332 æþelum] hæleþum MS

V

The road was stone-paved, the path led   320
the men together. Their mail-coats shone
hard, hand-linked, bright rings of iron
rang out on their gear, when right to the hall
they went trooping in their terrible armor.
Sea-weary, they set their broad shields,   325
wondrously-hard boards, against the building's wall;
they sat on a bench — their byrnies rang out,
their soldiers' war-gear; their spears stood,
the gear of the seamen all together,
a gray forest of ash. That iron troop   330
was worthy of its weapons.
                    Then a proud warrior[1]
asked those soldiers about their ancestry:
"From whence do you carry those covered shields,
gray coats of mail and grim helmets,
this troop of spears? I am herald and servant   335
to Hrothgar; never have I seen
so many foreign men so fearless and bold.
For pride, I expect, and not for exile,
and for greatness of heart you have sought out Hrothgar."
The courageous one answered him,   340
proud prince of the Weders, spoke words
hardy in his helmet: "We are Hygelac's
board-companions — Beowulf is my name.
I wish to explain my errand
to the son of Healfdene, famous prince,   345
your lord, if he will allow us,
in his goodness, to greet him."
Wulfgar spoke — a prince of the Wendels,
his noble character was known to many,
his valor and wisdom: "I will convey   350
to the friend of the Danes, lord of the Scyldings,
giver of rings, what you have requested,
tell the famous prince of your travels,
and then quickly announce to you the answer

---

1   Later identified as Wulfgar.

ðē mē se gōda   āgifan þenceð."   355
　Hwearf þā hrædlīce   þǣr Hrōðgār sæt
eald ond [a]nhār   mid his eorla gedriht;
ēode ellenrōf,   þæt hē for eaxlum gestōd
Deniga frean;   cūþe hē duguðe þēaw.
Wulfgār maðelode   tō his winedrihtne: 360
"Hēr syndon geferede,   feorran cumene
ofer geofenes begang   Gēata lēode;
þone yldestan   ōretmecgas
Bēowulf nemnað.   Hȳ bēnan synt,
þæt hīe, þēoden mīn,   wið þē mōton   365
wordum wrixlan;   nō ðū him wearne getēoh
ðīnra gegncwida,   glædman Hrōðgār!
Hȳ on wīggetāwum   wyrðe þinceað
eorla geæhtlan;   hūru se aldor dēah,
sē þǣm heaðorincum   hider wīsade."   370

VI

　Hrōðgār maþelode,   helm Scyldinga:
"Ic hine cūðe   cnihtwesende;
wæs his ealdfæder   Ecgþēo hāten,
ðǣm tō hām forgeaf   Hrēþel Gēata
āngan dohtor;   is his eafor[a] nū   375
heard hēr cumen,   sōhte holdne wine.
Ðonne sægdon þæt   sǣlīþende,
þā ðe gifsceattas   Gēata fyredon
þyder tō þance,   þæt hē þritiges
manna mægencræft   on his mundgripe   380
heaþorōf hæbbe.   Hine hālig God
for ārstafum   ūs onsende,
tō West-Denum,   þæs ic wēn hæbbe,
wið Grendles gryre.   Ic þǣm gōdan sceal
for his mōdþræce   māðmas bēodan.   385
Bēo ðū on ofeste,   hāt in gan
sēon sibbegedriht   samod ætgædere;

---

357 anhar] un har MS   375 eafora] eaforan MS

which that good man sees fit to give me."   355
      He hastily returned to where Hrothgar sat
old and gray-haired, with his band of earls;
he went boldly, stood by the shoulder
of the Danish king — he knew the noble custom.
Wulfgar spoke to his friend and lord: 360
"There have arrived here over the sea's expanse,
come from afar, men of the Geats;
the chief among them the warriors call
Beowulf. They bring a request,
my lord, that they might be allowed   365
to exchange words with you — do not refuse them
your reply, gracious Hrothgar!
In their war-trappings they seem worthy
of noble esteem; notable indeed is that chief
who has shown these soldiers the way hither."   370

                                    VI

      Hrothgar spoke, protector of the Scyldings:
"I knew him when he was nothing but a boy —
his old father was called Ecgtheow,
to whom Hrethel the Geat[1] gave in marriage
his only daughter; now his daring son   375
has come here, sought a loyal friend.
Seafarers, in truth, have said to me,
those who brought to the Geats gifts and money
as thanks, that he has thirty
men's strength, strong in battle,   380
in his handgrip. Holy God
in His grace has guided him to us,
to the West-Danes, as I would hope,
against Grendel's terror. To this good man
I shall offer treasures for his true daring.   385
Be hasty now, bid them enter
to see this troop of kinsmen all assembled;

---

1   Hrethel was the father of Hygelac and grandfather of Beowulf.

gesaga him ēac wordum,   þæt hīe sint wilcuman

Deniga lēodum."   [þā wið duru healle

Wulfgār ēode,]   word inne ābēad: 390

"Ēow hēt secgan   sigedrihten mīn,

aldor Ēast-Dena,   þæt hē ēower æþelu can,

ond gē him syndon   ofer sǣwylmas

heardhicgende   hider wilcuman.

Nū gē mōton gangan   in ēowrum gūðg[e]tawum,   395

under heregrīman   Hrōðgār gesēon;

lǣtað hildebord   hēr onbīdan,

wudu wælsceaftas,   worda geþinges."

    Ārās þā se rīca,   ymb hine rinc manig,

þrȳðlīc þegna hēap;   sume þǣr bidon,   400

heaðorēaf hēoldon,   swā him se hearda bebēad.

Snyredon ætsomne   — secg wīsode —

under Heorotes hrōf;   [ēode hildedēor,]

hear(d) under helme,   þæt hē on heo[r]ðe gestōd.

Bēowulf maðelode   — on him byrne scān,   405

searonet seowed   smiþes orþancum:

"Wæs þū, Hrōðgār, hāl!   Ic eom Higelāces

mǣg ond magoðegn;   hæbbe ic mǣrða fela

ongunnen on geogoþe.   Mē wearð Grendles þing

on mīnre eþeltyrf   undyrne cūð;   410

secgað sǣlīðend,   þæt þæs sele stande,

reced sēlesta   rinca gehwylcum

īdel ond unnyt,   siððan ǣfenlēoht

under heofenes ha[ð]or   beholen weorþeð.

Þā mē þæt gelǣrdon   lēode mīne,   415

þā sēlestan,   snotere ceorlas,

þēoden Hrōðgār,   þæt ic þē sōhte,

forþan hīe mægenes cræft   mīn[n]e cūþon;

selfe ofersāwon,   ðā ic of searwum cwōm,

fāh from fēondum,   þǣr ic fīfe geband,   420

ȳðde eotena cyn,   ond on ȳðum slōg

niceras nihtes,   nearoþearfe drēah,

389-90 þa wið … Wulfgar eode] *no gap in* MS   395 guðgetawum] guð geata wum MS
403 eode hildedeor] *no gap in* MS   404 heorðe] heoðe MS   414 haðor] hador MS
418 minne] mine MS

and tell them in your words that they are welcome
to the Danish people."

He announced from within:[1]   390
"My conquering lord commands me to tell you,
ruler of the East-Danes, that he knows your ancestry,
and you are to him, hardy spirits,
welcome hither from across the rolling waves.
Now you may go in your war-gear   395
under your helmets to see Hrothgar,
but let your battle-shields and deadly spears
await here the result of your words."

The mighty one arose, and many a man with him,
powerful thanes; a few waited there,   400
guarded their battle-dress as the bold man bid them.
They hastened together as the man led them,
under Heorot's roof; [the warrior went][2]
hardy in his helmet, until he stood on the hearth.
Beowulf spoke — his byrnie gleamed on him,   405
war-net sewn by the skill of a smith:
"Be well, Hrothgar! I am Hygelac's kinsman
and young retainer; in my youth I have done
many glorious deeds. This business with Grendel
was made known to me on my native soil;   410
seafarers say that this building stands,
most excellent of halls, idle and useless
to every man, after evening's light
is hidden under heaven's gleaming dome.
Then my own people advised me,   415
the best warriors and the wisest men,
that I should, lord Hrothgar, seek you out,
because they knew the might of my strength;
they themselves had seen me, bloodstained from battle,
come from the fight, when I captured five,   420
slew a tribe of giants, and on the salt waves
fought sea-monsters by night, survived that tight spot,

---

1   There is no gap in the manuscript, but the two halves of the line do not alliterate, and
    something is probably missing from the text at this point. Most editors add two half-
    lines with the sense "Then Wulfgar went to the door."
2   A half-line is missing; the translation follows the most innocuous conjecture.

wræc Wedera nīð   — wēan āhsodon —
forgrand gramum;   ond nū wið Grendel sceal,
wið þām āglǣcan   āna gehēgan   425
ðing wið þyrse.   Ic þē nū ðā,
brego Beorht-Dena,   biddan wille,
eodor Scyldinga,   ānre bēne,
þæt ðū mē ne forwyrne,   wīgendra hlēo,
frēowine folca,   nū ic þus feorran cōm,   430
þæt ic mōte āna   mīnra eorla gedryht,
þes hearda hēap,   Heorot fǣlsian.
Hǣbbe ic ēac geāhsod,   þæt se ǣglǣca
for his wonhȳdum   wǣpna ne recceð;
ic þæt þonne forhicge,   swā mē Higelāc sīe,   435
mīn mondrihten   mōdes blīðe,
þæt ic sweord bere   oþðe sīdne scyld,
geolorand tō gūþe,   ac ic mid grāpe sceal
fōn wið fēonde   ond ymb feorh sacan,
lāð wið lāþum;   ðǣr gelȳfan sceal   440
Dryhtnes dōme   sē þe hine dēað nimeð.
Wēn' ic þæt hē wille,   gif hē wealdan mōt,
in þǣm gūðsele   Gēotena lēode
etan unforhte,   swā hē oft dyde,
mægenhrēð manna.   Nā þū mīnne þearft   445
hafalan hȳdan,   ac hē mē habban wile
d[r]ēore fāhne,   gif mec dēað nimeð;
byreð blōdig wæl,   byrgean þenceð,
eteð āngenga   unmurnlīce,
mearcað mōrhopu;   nō ðū ymb mīnes ne þearft   450
līces feorme   leng sorgian.
Onsend Higelāce,   gif mec hild nime,
beaduscrūda betst,   þæt mīne brēost wereð,
hrægla sēlest;   þæt is Hrǣdlan lāf,
Wēlandes geweorc.   Gǣð ā wyrd swā hīo scel!"   455

---

447 dreore] deore MS

avenged the Weders' affliction — they asked for trouble! —
and crushed those grim foes; and now with Grendel,
that monstrous beast, I shall by myself have   425
a word or two with that giant. From you now I wish,
ruler of the Bright-Danes, to request
a single favor, protector of the Scyldings,
that you should not refuse, having come this far,
protector of warriors, noble friend to his people, —   430
that I might alone, o my own band of earls
and this hardy troop, cleanse Heorot.
I have also heard that this evil beast
in his wildness does not care for weapons,
so too will I scorn — so that Hygelac,   435
my liege-lord, may be glad of me —
to bear a sword or a broad shield,
a yellow battle-board, but with my grip
I shall grapple with the fiend and fight for life,
foe against foe. Let him put his faith   440
in the Lord's judgment, whom death takes!
I expect that if he is allowed to win, he will
eat unafraid the folk of the Geats
in that war-hall, as he has often done,
the host of the Hrethmen. You'll have no need   445
to cover my head[1] — he will have it,
gory, bloodstained, if death bears me away;
he will take his kill, think to taste me,
will dine alone without remorse,
stain his lair in the moor; no need to linger   450
in sorrow over disposing of my body!
Send on to Hygelac, if battle should take me,
the best battledress, which my breast wears,
finest of garments; it is Hrethel's heirloom,
the work of Weland.[2] Wyrd always goes as it must!"[3]   455

---

1 A burial custom. Beowulf grimly jokes that there will be no need to trouble with
  funeral expenses if Grendel wins this fight; he will have no head to bury.
2 Weland is the legendary blacksmith of the Norse gods. The antiquity of weapons and
  armor added to their value.
3 *Wyrd* is the Old English word for "fate"; it is sometimes quasi-personified, though
  apparently not to the extent that the goddess Fortuna was in Roman   (*continued*)

Hrōðgār maþelode,   helm Scyldinga:
"F[or gewyr]htum þū,   wine mīn Bēowulf,
ond for ārstafum   ūsic sōhtest.
Geslōh þīn fæder   fæhðe mæste;
wearþ hē Heaþolāfe   tō handbonan   460
mid Wilfingum;   ðā hine [Wede]ra cyn
for herebrōgan   habban ne mihte.
Þanon hē gesōhte   Sūð-Dena folc
ofer ȳða gewealc,   Ār-Scyldinga;
ðā ic furþum wēold   folce Deni[g]a   465
ond on geogoðe hēold   gi[nn]e rīce,
hordburh hæleþa;   ðā wæs Heregār dēad,
mīn yldra mæg   unlifigende,
bearn Healfdenes;   sē wæs betera ðonne ic!
Siððan þā fæhðe   fēo þingode;   470
sende ic Wylfingum   ofer wæteres hrycg
ealde mādmas;   hē mē āþas swōr.
Sorh is mē tō secganne   on sefan mīnum
gumena ængum,   hwæt mē Grendel hafað
hȳnðo on Heorote   mid his heteþancum,   475
færnīða gefremed;   is mīn fletwerod,
wīghēap gewanod;   hīe wyrd forswēop
on Grendles gryre.   God ēaþe mæg
þone dolsceaðan   dæda getwæfan!
Ful oft gebēotedon   bēore druncne   480
ofer ealowæge   ōretmecgas,
þæt hīe in bēorsele   bīdan woldon
Grendles gūþe   mid gryrum ecga.
Ðonne wæs þeos medoheal   on morgentīd,
drihtsele drēorfāh,   þonne dæg līxte,   485
eal bencþelu   blōde bestȳmed,

---

457 For gewyrhtum] fere fyhtum MS   461 Wedera] gara MS   465 Deniga] deninga
MS   466 ginne] gimme MS

Hrothgar spoke, protector of the Scyldings:
"For past favors, my friend Beowulf,
and for old deeds, you have sought us out.
Your father struck up the greatest of feuds,
when he killed Heatholaf by his own hand   460
among the Wylfings. When the Weder tribe
would not harbor him for fear of war,
thence he sought the South-Dane people
over the billowing seas, the Honor-Scyldings;
then I first ruled the Danish folk   465
and held in my youth this grand kingdom,
city of treasure and heroes — then Heorogar
was dead, my older brother unliving,
Healfdene's firstborn — he was better than I!
Later I settled that feud with fee-money;   470
I sent to the Wylfings over the crest of the waves
ancient treasures; he swore oaths to me.[1]
It is a sorrow to my very soul to say
to any man what Grendel has done to me —
humiliated Heorot with his hateful thoughts,   475
his sudden attacks. My hall-troop,
my warriors, are decimated; wyrd has swept them away
into Grendel's terror. God might easily
put an end to the deeds of this mad enemy!
Often men have boasted, drunk with beer,   480
officers over their cups of ale,
that they would abide in the beer-hall
Grendel's attack with a rush of sword-terror.
Then in the morning this mead-hall,
lordly dwelling, was drenched with blood,   485
when daylight gleamed, the benches gory,

---

poetic mythology. The word survives, via Shakespeare's *Macbeth*, as the Modern
English word "weird."

1   Hrothgar pays the *wergild* for the man Ecgtheow killed, and Ecgtheow swears an
    oath of loyalty and support. It is this oath, passed on to the next generation, that
    Beowulf is fulfilling (at least this is Hrothgar's public sentiment; his thoughts in the
    privacy of his council are somewhat different).

heall heorudrēore;   āhte ic holdra þȳ lǣs,
dēorre duguðe,   þē þā dēað fornam.
Site nū tō symle   ond on sǣl meoto,
sigehrēð secgum,   swā þīn sefa hwette."   490
    Þā wæs Gēatmæcgum   geador ætsomne
on bēorsele   benc gerȳmed;
þǣr swiðferhþe   sittan ēodon,
þrȳðum dealle.   Þegn nytte behēold,
sē þe on handa bær   hroden ealowǣge,   495
scencte scīr wered.   Scop hwīlum sang
hādor on Heorote.   Þǣr wæs hæleða drēam,
duguð unlȳtel   Dena ond Wedera.

VIII

[U]nferð maþelode,   Ecglāfes bearn,
þē æt fōtum sæt   frēan Scyldinga,   500
onband beadurūne —   wæs him Bēowulfes sīð,
mōdges merefaran,   micel æfþunca,
forþon þe hē ne ūþe   þæt ænig ōðer man
ǣfre mǣrða þon mā   middangeardes
gehēdde under heofenum   þonne hē sylfa: 505
"Eart þū sē Bēowulf,   sē þe wið Brecan wunne,
on sīdne sǣ   ymb sund flite,
ðǣr git for wlence   wada cunnedon
ond for dolgilpe   on dēop wæter
aldrum nēþdon?   Nē inc ænig mon,   510
nē lēof nē lāð,   belēan mihte
sorhfullne sīð,   þā git on sund reon;
þǣr git ēagorstrēam   earmum þehton,
mǣton merestrǣta,   mundum brugdon,
glidon ofer gārsecg;   geofon ȳþum wēol,   515
wintrys wylm[e].   Git on wæteres ǣht

---

499 Unferð] HVN ferð MS   516 wylme] wylm MS

the hall spattered and befouled; I had fewer
dear warriors when death took them away.
Now sit down at my feast, drink mead in my hall,[1]
the reward of victory, as your mood urges." 490
    Then a bench was cleared in the beer-hall
for the men of the Geats all together;
the strong-minded men went to sit down,
proud in their strength. A thane did his service,
bore in his hands the gold-bright ale-cup, 495
poured the clear sweet drink. The scop sang
brightly in Heorot — there was the joy of heroes,
no small gathering of Danes and Geats.

VIII

    Unferth[2] spoke, son of Ecglaf,
who sat at the feet of the Scylding lord, 500
unbound his battle-runes[3] — Beowulf's journey,
that brave seafarer, sorely vexed him,
for he did not wish that any other man
on this middle-earth should care for glory
under the heavens, more than he himself: 505
"Are you the Beowulf who strove with Breca
in a swimming contest on the open sea,
where in your pride you tried the waves
and for a foolish boast risked your life
in the deep water? No man, whether 510
friend or foe, could dissuade you two
from that sad venture, when you swam in the sea;
there you seized in your arms the ocean-streams,
measured the sea-ways, flailed your hands
and glided over the waves — the water roiled, 515
wintry surges. In the keeping of the water

---

1   The meaning of this line in Old English is disputed.

2   Unferth's name, which may be significant, means either "un-peace" or "un-reason."
In the manuscript it is always spelled "Hunferth," though it alliterates with a vowel.
His position at Hrothgar's feet appears to be one of honor.

3   Or "unleashed his hostile secret thoughts." *Run* in Old English often means "secret."

seofon niht swuncon;   hē þē æt sunde oferflāt,
hæfde māre mægen.   Þā hine on morgentīd
on Heaþo-Rǣmes   holm ūp ætbær;
ðonon hē gesōhte   swǣsne ēþel,   520
lēof his lēodum,   lond Brondinga,
freoðoburh fægere,   þǣr hē folc āhte,
burh ond bēagas.   Bēot eal wið þē
sunu Bēanstānes   sōðe gelæste.
Ðonne wēne ic tō þē   wyrsan geþingea,   525
ðēah þū heaðorǣsa   gehwǣr dohte,
grimre gūðe,   gif þū Grendles dearst
nihtlongne fyrst   nean bīdan."
Bēowulf maþelode,   bearn Ecgþēowes:
"Hwæt, þū worn fela,   wine mīn [U]nferð,   530
bēore druncen   ymb Brecan sprǣce,
sægdest from his sīðe!   Sōð ic talige,
þæt ic merestrengo   māran āhte,
earfeþo on ȳþum,   ðonne ǣnig ōþer man.
Wit þæt gecwǣdon   cnihtwesende   535
ond gebēotedon   — wǣron bēgen þā gīt
on geogoðfēore —   þæt wit on gārsecg ūt
aldrum nēðdon,   ond þæt geæfndon swā.
Hæfdon swurd nacod,   þā wit on sund reon,
heard on handa;   wit unc wið hronfixas   540
werian þōhton.   Nō hē wiht fram mē
flōdȳþum feor   flēotan meahte,
hraþor on holme,   nō ic fram him wolde.
Ðā wit ætsomne   on sǣ wǣron
fīf nihta fyrst,   oþ þæt unc flōd tōdrāf,   545
wado weallende,   wedera cealdost,
nīpende niht,   ond norþanwind
heaðogrim ondhwearf.   Hrēo wǣron ȳþa;
wæs merefixa   mōd onhrēred.
Þǣr mē wið lāðum   licsyrce mīn   550
heard hondlocen   helpe gefremede,
beadohrægl brōden,   on brēostum læg
golde gegyrwed.   Mē tō grunde tēah
fāh fēondscaða,   fæste hæfde

---

530 Unferð] Hunferð MS

you toiled for seven nights, and he outswam you,
and had more strength. Then in the morning
the swells bore him to the Heathoream shore;
from thence he sought his own sweet land,   520
beloved by his people, the land of the Brondings,
the fair fortress, where he had his folk,
his castle and treasure. He truly fulfilled,
the son of Beanstan, his boast against you.
So I expect a worse outcome from you —   525
though you may have survived the storm of battle,
some grim combats — if for Grendel you dare
to lie in wait the whole night long."
      Beowulf spoke, son of Ecgtheow:
"What a great deal, Unferth my friend,   530
drunk with beer, you have said about Breca,
told his adventures! I will tell the truth —
I had greater strength on the sea,
more ordeals on the waves than any other man.
When we were just boys we two agreed   535
and boasted — we were both still
in our youth — that out on the great ocean
we would risk our lives, and we did just that.
We had bare swords, when we swam in the sea,
hard in our hands; we thought to protect   540
ourselves from whales. Not for anything
could he swim far from me on the sea-waves,
more swiftly on the water, nor would I go from him.
We two were together on the sea
for five nights, until the flood drove us apart,   545
surging waves, coldest of weathers,
darkening night, and a northern wind,
knife-sharp, pushed against us. The seas were choppy;
the fishes of the sea were stirred up by it.
There my coat of armor offered help,   550
hard, hand-locked, against those hostile ones,
my woven battle-dress lay on my breast
adorned with gold. Down to the ocean floor
a grisly foe dragged me, gripped me fast

grim on grāpe;   hwæþre mē gyfeþe wearð,   555
þæt ic āglǣcan   orde gerǣhte,
hildebille;   heaþorǣs fornam
mihtig merēdeor   þurh mīne hand.

IX

Swā mec gelōme   lāðgetēonan
þrēatedon þearle.   Ic him þēnode   560
dēoran sweorde,   swā hit gedēfe wæs.
Næs hīe ðǣre fylle   gefēan hæfdon,
mānfordǣdlan,   þæt hīe mē þēgon,
symbel ymbsǣton   sǣgrunde nēah;
ac on mergenne   mēcum wunde   565
be ȳðlāfe   uppe lǣgon,
sweo[r]dum āswefede,   þæt syðþan nā
ymb brontne ford   brimlīðende
lāde ne letton.   Lēoht ēastan cōm,
beorht bēacen Godes,   brimu swaþredon,   570
þæt ic sǣnæssas   gesēon mihte,
windige weallas.   Wyrd oft nereð
unfǣgne eorl,   þonne his ellen dēah!
Hwæþere mē gesǣlde,   þæt ic mid sweorde ofslōh
niceras nigene.   Nō ic on niht gefrægn   575
under heofones hwealf   heardran feohtan,
nē on ēgstrēamum   earmran mannon;
hw[æ]þere ic fāra feng   fēore gedīgde
sīþes wērig.   Ðā mec sǣ oþbær,
flōd æfter faroðe   on Finna land,   580
w[a]du weallendu.   Nō ic wiht fram þē
swylcra searonīða   secgan hȳrde,
billa brōgan.   Breca nǣfre gīt
æt heaðolāce,   nē gehwæþer incer,
swā dēorlīce   dǣd gefremede   585
fāgum sweordum   — nō ic þæs [fela] gylpe —
þēah ðū þīnum brōðrum   tō banan wurde,

---

567 sweordum] speodū *Thorkelin* A, sweo.. *Thorkelin* B   578 hwæþere] hwaþere MS
581 wadu] wudu MS   586 fela] *not in* MS

in his grim grasp, yet it was given to me   555
to stab that monster with the point of my sword,
my war-blade; the storm of battle took away
that mighty sea-beast, through my own hand.

IX

Time and again those terrible enemies
sorely threatened me. I served them well   560
with my dear sword, as they deserved.
They got no joy from their gluttony,
those wicked maneaters, when they tasted me,
sat down to their feast on the ocean floor —
but in the morning, wounded by my blade,   565
they were washed ashore by the ocean waves,
dazed by sword-blows, and since that day
they never hindered the passage of any
sea-voyager. Light shone from the east,
God's bright beacon; the waves grew calm,   570
so that I could see the sea-cliffs,
the windswept capes. *Wyrd* often spares
an undoomed man, when his courage endures!
And so it was that with my sword I slew
nine of these sea-monsters. I have never heard   575
of a harder night-battle under heaven's vault,
nor a more wretched man on the water's stream;
yet I escaped alive from the clutches of my enemies,
weary from my journey. Then the sea washed me up,
the currents of the flood, in the land of the Finns,   580
the welling waters. I have never heard a word
about any such contest concerning you,
such sword-panic. In the play of battle
Breca has never — nor you either —
done a deed so bold and daring   585
with his decorated blade — I would never boast of it! —
though you became your brothers' killer,

hēafodmǣgum;   þæs þū in helle scealt
werhðo drēogan,   þēah þīn wit duge.
Secge ic þē tō sōðe,   sunu Ecglāfes,   590
þæt nǣfre Gre[n]del swā fela   gryra gefremede,
atol ǣglǣca   ealdre þīnum,
hȳnðo on Heorote,   gif þīn hige wǣre,
sefa swā searogrim,   swā þū self talast;
ac hē hafað onfunden,   þæt hē þā fǣhðe ne þearf,   595
atole ecgþrǣce   ēower lēode
swīðe onsittan,   Sige-Scyldinga;
nymeð nȳdbāde,   nǣnegum ārað
lēode Deniga,   ac hē lust wigeð,
swefeð ond sendeþ,   secce ne wēneþ   600
tō Gār-Denum.   Ac ic him Gēata sceal
eafoð ond ellen   ungeāra nū,
gūþe gebēodan.   Gǣþ eft sē þe mot
tō medo mōdig,   siþþan morgenlēoht
ofer ylda bearn   ōþres dōgores,   605
sunne sweglwered   sūþan scīneð!"
    Þā wæs on sālum   sinces brytta
gamolfeax ond gūðrōf;   gēoce gelȳfde
brego Beorht-Dena;   gehȳrde on Bēowulfe
folces hyrde   fæstrǣdne geþōht.   610
Ðǣr wæs hæleþa hleahtor,   hlyn swynsode,
word wǣron wynsume.   Eode Wealhþēow forð,
cwēn Hrōðgāres   cynna gemyndig,
grētte goldhroden   guman on healle,
ond þā frēolīc wīf   ful gesealde   615
ǣrest Ēast-Dena   eþelwearde,
bæd hine blīðne   æt þǣre bēorþege,
lēodum lēofne;   hē on lust geþeah

---

591 Grendel] gre del MS

your next of kin; for that you needs must suffer
punishment in hell, no matter how clever you are.[1]
I will say it truly, son of Ecglaf,   590
that never would Grendel have worked such terror,
that gruesome beast, against your lord,
or shames in Heorot, if your courage and spirit
were as fierce as you yourself fancy they are;
but he has found that he need fear no feud,   595
no storm of swords from the Victory-Scyldings,[2]
no resistance at all from your nation;
he takes his toll, spares no one
in the Danish nation, but indulges himself,
hacks and butchers and expects no battle   600
from the Spear-Danes. But I will show him
soon enough the strength and courage
of the Geats in war. Afterwards, let him who will
go bravely to mead, when the morning light
of a new day, the sun clothed in glory,   605
shines from the south on the sons of men!"
　　　Then the giver of treasure was greatly pleased,
gray-haired and battle-bold; the Bright-Danes' chief
had faith in his helper; that shepherd of his folk
recognized Beowulf's firm resolution.   610
There was the laughter of warriors, lovely sounds
and winsome words. Wealhtheow went forth,
Hrothgar's queen, mindful of customs;
adorned with gold, she greeted the men in the hall,
then that courteous wife offered the full cup   615
first to the guardian of the East-Danes' kingdom,
bid him be merry at his beer-drinking,
beloved by his people; with pleasure he received

1　Unferth's fratricide brings the general theme of kin-slaying, represented by Grendel's
　　descent from Cain, inside Hrothgar's hall. In reality—at least in the reality of the
　　heroic world depicted in poetry—it may not have been unthinkable for kinsmen to
　　find themselves on opposite sides of a battle; loyalty to one's lord was supposed to
　　outweigh the claims of blood-relation. The word "hell" is not in the manuscript, but it
　　is attested by one of the early transcriptions. Mitchell and Robinson read *healle*, i.e.,
　　"hall."

2　Is this a nasty irony on Beowulf's part, or a conventional epithet used thoughtlessly
　　by the poet?

symbel ond seleful,   sigerōf kyning.
Ymbēode þā   ides Helminga   620
duguþe ond geogoþe   dæl æghwylcne,
sincfato sealde,   oþ þæt sæl ālamp,
þæt hīo Bēowulfe,   bēaghroden cwēn
mōde geþungen   medoful ætbær;
grētte Gēata lēod,   Gode þancode   625
wīsfæst wordum   þæs ðe hire se willa gelamp,
þæt hēo on ænigne   eorl gelȳfde
fyrena frōfre.   Hē þæt ful geþeah,
wælrēow wiga   æt Wealhþeon,
ond þā gyddode   gūþe gefȳsed;   630
Bēowulf maþelode,   bearn Ecgþēowes:
"Ic þæt hogode,   þā ic on holm gestāh,
sæbāt gesæt   mid mīnra secga gedriht,
þæt ic ānunga   ēowra lēoda
willan geworhte,   oþðe on wæl crunge   635
fēondgrāpum fæst.   Ic gefremman sceal
eorlīc ellen,   oþðe endedæg
on þisse meoduhealle   mīnne gebīdan!"
Ðām wīfe þā word   wēl līcodon,
gilpcwide Gēates;   ēode goldhroden   640
frēolicu folccwēn   tō hire frēan sittan.
    Þā wæs eft swā ær   inne on healle
þrȳðword sprecen,   ðēod on sælum,
sigefolca swēg,   oþ þæt semninga
sunu Healfdenes   sēcean wolde   645
æfenræste;   wiste þæm āhlæcan
tō þæm hēahsele   hilde geþinged,
siððan hīe sunnan lēoht   gesēon meahton,
oþðe nīpende   niht ofer ealle,
scaduhelma gesceapu   scrīðan cwōman   650
wan under wolcnum.   Werod eall ārās.
[Ge]grētte þā   guma ōþerne,
Hrōðgār Bēowulf,   ond him hæl ābēad,
wīnærnes geweald,   ond þæt word ācwæð:
"Næfre ic ænegum men   ær ālȳfde,   655
siþðan ic hond ond rond   hebban mihte,

---

652 Gegrette] grette MS

the feast and cup, victorious king.
The lady of the Helmings then went about 620
to young and old, gave each his portion
of the precious cup, until the moment came
when the ring-adorned queen, of excellent heart,
bore the mead-cup to Beowulf;
she greeted the Geatish prince, thanked God 625
with wise words that her wish had come to pass,
that she could rely on any earl for relief
from those crimes. He took the cup,
the fierce warrior, from Wealhtheow,
and then eager for battle he made his announcement. 630
Beowulf spoke, son of Ecgtheow:
"I resolved when I set out over the waves,
sat down in my ship with my troop of soldiers,
that I would entirely fulfill the wishes
of your people, or fall slain, 635
fast in the grip of my foe. I shall perform
a deed of manly courage, or in this mead-hall
I will await the end of my days!"
These words well pleased that woman,
the boasting of the Geat; she went, the gold-adorned 640
and courteous folk-queen, to sit beside her lord.

     Then, as before, there in that hall were
strong words spoken, the people happy,
the sounds of a victorious nation, until shortly
the son of Healfdene wished to seek 645
his evening rest; he knew that the wretched beast
had been planning to do battle in the high building
from the time they could first see the sunrise
until night fell darkening over all,
and creatures of shadow came creeping about 650
pale under the clouds. The company arose.
One warrior greeted another there,
Hrothgar to Beowulf, and wished him luck,
gave him control of the wine-hall in these words:
"I have never entrusted to any man, 655
ever since I could hold and hoist a shield,

ðrýþærn Dena   būton þē nū ðā.
Hafa nū ond geheald   hūsa sēlest,
gemyne mærþo,   mægenellen cýð,
waca wið wrāþum!   Ne bið þē wilna gād,   660
gif þū þæt ellenweorc   aldre gedīgest."

X

    Ðā him Hrōþgār gewāt   mid his hæleþa gedryht,
eodur Scyldinga   ūt of healle;
wolde wīgfruma   Wealhþēo sēcan,
cwēn tō gebeddan.   Hæfde Kyningwuldor   665
Grendle tōgēanes,   swā guman gefrugnon,
seleweard āseted;   sundornytte behēold
ymb aldor Dena,   eotonweard ābēad.
Hūru Gēata lēod   georne trūwode
mōdgan mægnes,   Metodes hyldo,   670
ðā hē him of dyde   īsernbyrnan,
helm of hafelan,   sealde his hyrsted sweord,
īrena cyst   ombihtþegne,
ond gehealdan hēt   hildegeatwe.
Gespræc þā se gōda   gylpworda sum,   675
Bēowulf Gēata,   ær hē on bed stige:
"Nō ic mē an herewæsmun   hnāgran talige
gūþgeweorca,   þonne Grendel hine;
forþan ic hine sweorde   swebban nelle,
aldre benēotan,   þēah ic eal mæge;   680
nāt hē þāra gōda,   þæt hē mē ongēan slea,
rand gehēawe,   þēah ðe hē rōf sīe
nīþgeweorca;   ac wit on niht sculon
secge ofersittan,   gif h[ē] gesēcean dear
wīg ofer wǣpen,   ond siþðan wītig God   685
on swā hwæþere hond   hālig Dryhten
mǣrðo dēme,   swā him gemet þince."
Hylde hine þā heaþodēor,   hlēorbolster onfēng
eorles andwlitan,   ond hine ymb monig
snellīc sǣrinc   selereste gebēah.   690

---

684 he] het MS

the great hall of the Danes — except to you now.
Have it and hold it, protect this best of houses,
be mindful of glory, show your mighty valor,
watch for your enemies! You will have all you desire,   660
if you emerge from this brave undertaking alive."

X

    Then Hrothgar and his troop of heroes,
protector of the Scyldings, departed the hall;
the war-chief wished to seek Wealhtheow,
his queen's bedchamber. The glorious king[1]   665
had set against Grendel a hall-guardian
— as men had heard said — who did special service
for the king of the Danes, kept guard against a giant.
Surely the Geatish prince greatly trusted
his mighty strength, the Maker's favor,   670
when he took off his iron byrnie,
undid his helmet, and gave his decorated sword,
most excellent iron, to his servant
and bid him hold his battle-gear.
The good man, Beowulf the Geat,   675
spoke a few boasting words before he lay down:
"I consider myself no poorer in strength
and battle-deeds than Grendel does himself;
and so I will not kill him with a sword,
put an end to his life, though I easily might;   680
he knows no arts of war, no way to strike back,
hack at my shield-boss, though he be brave
in his wicked deeds; but tonight we two will
forego our swords, if he dare to seek out
a war without weapons — and then let the wise Lord,   685
the holy God, grant the judgment of glory
to whichever hand seems proper to Him."
    Battle-brave, he lay down; the bolster took
the earl's cheek, and around him many
a bold seafarer sank to his hall-rest.   690

---

1   Or "King of Glory," i.e., God?

Nǣnig heora þōhte   þæt hē þanon scolde
eft eardlufan   ǣfre gesēcean,
folc oþðe frēoburh,   þǣr hē āfēded wæs,
ac hīe hæfdon gefrūnen,   þæt hīe ǣr tō fela micles
in þǣm wīnsele   wældēað fornam,   695
Denigea lēode.   Ac him Dryhten forgeaf
wīgspēda gewiofu,   Wedera leōdum,
frōfor ond fultum,   þæt hīe fēond heora
ðurh ānes cræft   ealle ofercōmon,
selfes mihtum.   Sōð is gecȳþed,   700
þæt mihtig God   manna cynnes
wēold [w]īdeferhð.
                    Cōm on wanre niht
scrīðan sceadugenga.   Scēotend swǣfon,
þā þæt hornreced   healdan scoldon,
ealle būton ānum.   Þæt wæs yldum cūþ,   705
þæt hīe ne mōste,   þā Metod nolde,
se s[c]ynscaþa   under sceadu bregdan; —
ac hē wæccende   wrāþum on andan
bād bolgenmōd   beadwa geþinges.

                    XI

    Ðā cōm of mōre   under misthleoþum   710
Grendel gongan,   Godes yrre bær;
mynte se mānscaða   manna cynnes
sumne besyrwan   in sele þām hēan.
Wōd under wolcnum   tō þæs þe hē wīnreced,
goldsele gumena   gearwost wisse   715
fǣttum fāhne.   Ne wæs þæt forma sīð,
þæt hē Hrōþgāres   hām gesōhte;
nǣfre hē on aldordagum   ǣr nē siþðan
heardran hǣle,   healðegnas fand.
Cōm þā tō recede   rinc sīðian   720
drēamum bedǣled.   Duru sōna onarn
fȳrbendum fæst,   syþðan hē hire folmum (æt)hrān;
onbrǣd þā bealohȳdig,   ðā (hē ge)bolgen wæs,

---

702 wideferhð] ride ferhð MS   707 scynscaþa] synscaþa MS

None of them thought that he should thence
ever again seek his own dear homeland,
his tribe or the town in which he was raised,
for they had heard it said that savage death
had swept away far too many of the Danish folk   695
in that wine-hall. But the Lord gave
a web of victory to the people of the Weders,
comfort and support, so that they completely,
overcame their enemy through one man's craft,
by his own might. It is a well-known truth   700
that mighty God has ruled mankind
always and forever.
                        In the dark night he came
creeping, the shadow-goer. The bowmen slept
who were to hold that horned hall —
all but one. It was well-known to men   705
that the demon foe could not drag them
under the dark shadows if the Maker did not wish it;
but he, wakeful, keeping watch for his enemy,
awaited, enraged, the outcome of battle.

                                XI

Then from the moor, in a blanket of mist,   710
Grendel came stalking — he bore God's anger;
the evil marauder meant to ensnare
some of human-kind in that high hall.
Under the clouds he came until he clearly knew
he was near the wine-hall, men's golden house,   715
finely adorned. It was not the first time
he had sought out the home of Hrothgar,
but never in his life, early or late,
did he find harder luck or a hardier hall-thane.
To the hall came that warrior on his journey,   720
bereft of joys. The door burst open,
fast in its forged bands, when his fingers touched it;
bloody-minded, swollen with rage, he swung open

recedes mūþan.   Raþe æfter þon
on fāgne flōr   fēond treddode,   725
ēode yrremōd;   him of ēagum stōd
ligge gelīcost   lēoht unfǣger.
Geseah hē in recede   rinca manige,
swefan sibbegedriht   samod ætgædere,
magorinca hēap —   þā his mōd āhlōg;   730
mynte þæt hē gedælde,   ǣr þon dæg cwōme,
atol āglǣca   ānra gehwylces
līf wið līce,   þā him ālumpen wæs
wistfylle wēn.   Ne wæs þæt wyrd þā gēn,
þæt hē mā mōste   manna cynnes   735
ðicgean ofer þā niht.   Þrӯðswӯð behēold
mǣg Higelāces,   hū se mānscaða
under fǣrgripum   gefaran wolde.
Nē þæt se āglǣca   yldan þōhte,
ac hē gefēng hraðe   forman sīðe   740
slǣpendne rinc,   slāt unwearnum,
bāt bānlocan,   blōd ēdrum dranc,
synsnǣdum swealh;   sōna hæfde.
unlyfigendes   eal gefeormod,
fēt ond folma.   Forð nēar ætstōp,   745
nam þā mid handa   higeþīhtigne
rinc on ræste,   him ræhte ongēan
fēond mid folme;   hē onfēng hraþe
inwitþancum   ond wið earm gesæt.
Sōna þæt onfunde   fyrena hyrde,   750
þæt hē ne mētte   middangeardes,
eorþan scēa[t]a   on elran men
mundgripe māran;   hē on mōde wearð
forht on ferhðe;   nō þӯ ǣr fram meahte.
Hyge wæs him hinfūs,   wolde on heolster flēon,   755
sēcan dēofla gedræg;   ne wæs his drohtoð þǣr

---

752 sceata] sceatta MS

the hall's mouth, and immediately afterwards
the fiend strode across the paved floor,   725
went angrily; in his eyes stood
a light not fair, glowing like fire.
He saw in the hall many a soldier,
a peaceful troop sleeping all together,
a large company of thanes — and he laughed inside;   730
he meant to divide, before day came,
this loathsome creature, the life of each man
from his body, when there befell him
the hope of a feast. But it was not his fate
to taste any more of the race of mankind   735
after that night. The kinsman of Hygelac,
mighty one, beheld how that maneater
planned to proceed with his sudden assault.
Not that the monster[1] meant to delay —
he seized at once at his first pass   740
a sleeping man, slit him open suddenly,
bit into his joints, drank the blood from his veins,
gobbled his flesh in gobbets, and soon
had completely devoured that dead man,
feet and fingertips. He stepped further,   745
and took in his hands the strong-hearted
man in his bed; the monster reached out
towards him with his hands — he quickly grabbed him
with evil intent, and sat up against his arm.[2]
As soon as that shepherd of sins discovered   750
that he had never met on middle-earth,
in any region of the world, another man
with a greater handgrip, in his heart he was
afraid for his life, but none the sooner could he flee.
His mind was eager to escape to the darkness,   755
seek out a host of devils — his habit there

---

1   The OE word *æglæca*, which literally means "awesome one" or "terror," is elsewhere
    applied to the dragon-slaying Sigemund (line 893, where it is translated "fierce crea-
    ture") and to Beowulf himself. Its translation here is admittedly tendentious. The
    word appears elsewhere, variously translated, in lines 159, 433, 556, 732, etc.
2   It is not entirely clear who grabs whom—apparently Grendel reaches out to Beowulf,
    who is lying down; the hero then grabs Grendel's arm and sits up against it.

swylce hē on ealderdagum ǣr gemētte.
Gemunde þā se gōda, mǣg Higelāces,
ǣfensprǣce, ūplang āstōd
ond him fæste wiðfēng; fingras burston; 760
eoten wæs ūtweard, eorl furþur stōp.
Mynte se mǣra, (hw)ær hē meahte swā,
wīdre gewindan ond on weg þanon
flēon on fenhopu; wiste his fingra geweald
on grames grāpum. Þæt wæs gēocor sīð, 765
þæt se hearmscaþa tō Heorute ātēah!
Dryhtsele dynede; Denum eallum wearð,
ceasterbūendum, cēnra gehwylcum,
eorlum ealuscerwen. Yrre wǣron bēgen,
rēþe renweardas. Reced hlynsode. 770
þā wæs wundor micel, þæt se wīnsele
wiðhaefde heaþodēorum, þæt hē on hrūsan ne fēol,
fǣger foldbold; ac hē þæs fæste wæs
innan ond ūtan īrenbendum
searoþoncum besmiþod. Þǣr fram sylle ābēag 775
medubenc monig mīne gefrǣge
golde geregnad, þǣr þā graman wunnon.
Þæs ne wēndon ǣr witan Scyldinga,
þæt hit ā mid gemete manna ǣnig
[b]etlic ond bānfāg tōbrecan meahte, 780
listum tōlūcan, nymþe līges fæþm
swulge on swaþule. Swēg ūp āstāg
nīwe geneahhe: Norð-Denum stōd
atelic egesa, ānra gehwylcum
þāra þe of wealle wōp gehȳrdon, 785
gryrelēoð galan Godes andsacan,
sigelēasne sang, sār wānigean
helle hæfton. Hēold hine fæste
sē þe manna wæs mægene strengest
on þǣm dæge þysses līfes. 790

---

780 betlic] hetlic MS

was nothing like he had ever met before.
The good kinsman of Hygelac remembered then
his evening speech, and stood upright
and seized him fast. His fingers burst;   760
the giant turned outward, the earl stepped inward.
The notorious one meant — if he might —
to turn away further and flee, away
to his lair in the fen; he knew his fingers
were held in a hostile grip. That was an unhappy journey 765
that the harm-doer took to Heorot!
The great hall resounded; to the Danes it seemed,
the city's inhabitants and every brave earl,
like a wild ale-sharing.[1] Both were angry,
fierce house-wardens — the hall echoed.   770
It was a great wonder that the wine-hall
withstood their fighting and did not fall to the ground,
that fair building — but it was fastened
inside and out with iron bands,
forged with skill. From the floor there flew   775
many a mead-bench, as men have told me,
gold-adorned, where those grim foes fought.
The Scylding elders had never expected
that any man, by any ordinary means,
could break it apart, beautiful, bone-adorned,   780
or destroy it with guile, unless the embrace of fire
might swallow it in flames. The noise swelled
new and stark — among the North-Danes was
horrible terror, in each of them
who heard through the wall the wailing cry —   785
God's adversary shrieked a grisly song
of horror, defeated, the captive of Hell
bewailed his pain. He pinned him fast,
he who was the strongest of might among men
in those days of this life.   790

---

1 The general sense of the OE word *ealuscerwen* is "panic" or "terror," but its precise
 meaning (probably "a dispensing of ale") is unclear: did the Danes think a wild party
 was going on? or were they dismayed by the loss of their mead-hall? or does OE *ealu*
 mean "luck"?

Nolde eorla hlēo   ǣnige þinga
þone cwealmcuman   cwicne forlǣtan,
nē his līfdagas   lēoda ǣnigum
nytte tealde.   Þǣr genehost brǣgd
eorl Bēowulfes   ealde lāfe,   795
wolde frēadrihtnes   feorh ealgian,
mǣres þēodnes,   ðǣr hīe meahton swā.
Hīe þæt ne wiston,   þā hīe gewin drugon,
heardhicgende   hildemecgas,
ond on healfa gehwone   hēawan þōhton,   800
sāwle sēcan: þone synscaðan
ǣnig ofer eorþan   īrenna cyst,
gūðbilla nān   grētan nolde;
ac hē sigewǣpnum   forsworen hæfde,
ecga gehwylcre.   Scolde his aldorgedāl   805
on ðǣm dæge   þysses līfes
earmlīc wurðan,   ond se ellorgāst
on fēonda geweald   feor siðian.
Ðā þæt onfunde   sē þē fela ǣror
mōdes myrðe   manna cynne,   810
fyrene gefremede   — hē [wæs] fāg wið God —
þæt him se līchoma   lǣstan nolde,
ac hine se mōdega   mǣg Hygelāces
hæfde be honda;   wæs gehwæþer ōðrum
lifigende lāð.   Līcsār gebād   815
atol ǣglǣca;   him on eaxle wearð
syndolh sweotol,   seonowe onsprungon,
burston bānlocan.   Bēowulfe wearð
gūðhrēð gyfeþe;   scolde Grendel þonan
feorhsēoc fleon   under fenhleoðu,   820
sēcean wynlēas wīc;   wiste þē geornor,
þæt his aldres wæs   ende gegongen,
dōgera dægrīm.   Denum eallum wearð
æfter þām wælrǣse   willa gelumpen.
Hæfde þā gefǣlsod   sē þe ǣr feorran cōm   825
snotor ond swȳðferhð   sele Hrōðgāres,

---

811 wæs] *not in* MS

XII

Not for anything would that protector of earls
let that murderous visitor escape alive —
he did not consider his days on earth
of any use at all. Many an earl
in Beowulf's troop drew his old blade,   795
longed to protect the life of his liege-lord,
the famous captain, however they could.
But they did not know as they entered the fight,
those stern-minded men of battle,
and thought to strike from all sides   800
and seek his soul, that no sword,
not the best iron anywhere in the world,
could even touch that evil sinner,
for he had worked a curse on weapons,
every sort of blade. His separation from the world   805
in those days of this life
would be a wretched work, and that alien spirit
would travel far into the keeping of fiends.
Then he discovered, who had done before
so much harm to the race of mankind,   810
so many crimes — he was marked by God —
that his body could bear it no longer,
but the courageous kinsman of Hygelac
had him in hand — hateful to each
was the life of the other. The loathsome creature felt   815
a great pain in his body; a gaping wound opened
in his shoulder-joint, his sinews sprang apart,
his joints burst asunder. Beowulf was given
glory in battle — Grendel was forced
to flee, fatally wounded, into the fen,   820
seek a sorry abode; he knew quite surely
that the end of his life had arrived,
the sum of his days. The wishes of the Danes
were entirely fulfilled in that bloody onslaught!
He who had come from afar had cleansed,   825
wise and stout-hearted, the hall of Hrothgar,

genered wið nīðe.   Nihtweorce gefeh,
ellenmǣrþum.   Hæfde Ēast-Denum
Gēatmecga lēod   gilp gelǣsted,
swylce oncȳþðe   ealle gebētte,   830
inwidsorge   þē hīe ǣr drugon
ond for þrēanȳdum   þolian scoldon,
torn unlȳtel.   Þæt wæs tācen sweotol,
syþðan hildedēor   hond ālegde,
earm ond eaxle   — þǣr wæs eal geador   835
Grendles grāpe —   under gēapne hr(ōf).

XIII

   Ðā wæs on morgen   mīne gefrǣge
ymb þā gifhealle   gūðrinc monig
fērdon folctogan   feorran ond nean
geond wīdwegas   wundor scēawian,   840
lāþes lāstas.   Nō his līfgedāl
sārlīc þūhte   secga ǣnegum
þāra þe tīrlēases   trode scēawode,
hū hē wērigmōd   on weg þanon,
nīða ofercumen,   on nicera mere   845
fǣge ond geflȳmed   feorhlāstas bǣr.
Ðǣr wæs on blōde   brim weallende,
atol ȳða geswing   eal gemenged,
hāton heolfre,   heorodrēore wēol;
dēaðfǣge dēog;   siððan drēama lēas   850
in fenfreoðo   feorh ālegde,
hǣþene sāwle;   þǣr him hel onfēng.
   Þanon eft gewiton   ealdgesīðas
swylce geong manig   of gomenwāþe,
fram mere mōdge   mēarum rīdan,   855
beornas on blancum.   Ðǣr wæs Bēowulfes
mǣrðo mǣned;   monig oft gecwæð,
þætte sūð nē norð   be sǣm twēonum
ofer eormengrund   ōþer nǣnig

---

836 hrof] hr .. *end of line in* MS

warded off attack. He rejoiced in his night-work,
his great deed of courage. That man of the Geats
had fulfilled his boast to the East-Danes,
and entirely remedied all their distress,   830
the insidious sorrows they had suffered
and had to endure from sad necessity,
no small affliction. That was a clear sign
when the battle-brave one laid down the hand,
arm and shoulder — there all together   835
was Grendel's claw — under the curved roof.

XIII

Then in the morning was many a warrior,
as I have heard, around that gift-hall,
leaders of the folk came from far and near
throughout the wide land to see that wonder,   840
the loathsome one's tracks. His parting from life
hardly seemed sad to any man
who examined the trail of that inglorious one,
how he went on his weary way,
defeated by force, to a pool of sea-monsters,   845
doomed, put to flight, and left a fatal trail.
The water was welling with blood there —
the terrible swirling waves, all mingled together
with hot gore, heaved with the blood of battle,
concealed that doomed one when, deprived of joys,   850
he lay down his life in his lair in the fen,
his heathen soul — and hell took him.
Then the old retainers returned from there,
and many a youth on the joyful journey,
bravely rode their horses back from the mere,   855
men on their steeds. There they celebrated
Beowulf's glory: it was often said
that south or north, between the two seas,[1]
across the wide world, there was none

---

1   A conventional expression like Modern English "coast to coast"; apparently it origi-
    nally referred to the North and Baltic seas.

under swegles begong   sēlra nǣre   860
rondhæbbendra,   rīces wyrðra —
nē hīe hūru winedrihten   wiht ne lōgon,
glǣdne Hrōðgār,   ac þæt wæs gōd cyning.
Hwīlum heaþorōfe   hlēapan lēton,
on geflit faran   fealwe mēaras,   865
ðǣer him foldwegas   fægere þūhton,
cystum cūðe.   Hwīlum cyninges þegn,
guma gilphlǣden,   gidda gemyndig,
sē ðe ealfela   ealdgesegena
worn gemunde   — word ōþer fand   870
sōðe gebunden —   secg eft ongan
sīð Bēowulfes   snyttrum styrian,
ond on spēd wrecan   spel gerāde,
wordum wrixlan;   wēlhwylc gecwæð,
þæt hē fram Sigemunde[s]   secgan hȳrde   875
ellendǣdum,   uncūþes fela,
Wælsinges gewin,   wīde sīðas,
þāra þe gumena bearn   gearwe ne wiston,
fǣhðe ond fyrena,   būton Fitela mid hine,
þonne hē swulces hwæt   secgan wolde,   880
eam his nefan,   swā hīe ā wǣron
æt nīða gehwām   nȳdgesteallan;
hæfdon ealfela   eotena cynnes
sweordum gesǣged.   Sigemunde gesprong
æfter dēaðdæge   dōm unlȳtel,   885
syþðan wīges heard   wyrm ācwealde,
hordes hyrde;   hē under hārne stān,

---

875 Sigemundes] sige munde MS

better under the broad billowing sky 860
among shield-warriors, nor more worthy to rule —
though they found no fault with their own friendly lord,
gracious Hrothgar, but said he was a good king.
At times the proud warriors let their horses prance,
their fallow mares fare in a contest, 865
wherever the footpaths seemed fair to them,
the way tried and true. At times the king's thane,
full of grand stories, mindful of songs,
who remembered much, a great many
of the old tales, found other words 870
truly bound together; he began again
to recite with skill the adventure of Beowulf,
adeptly tell an apt tale,
and weave his words. He told nearly all
that he had heard said of Sigemund's 875
stirring deeds,[1] many strange things,
the Volsung's strife, his distant voyages
obscure, unknown to all the sons of men,
his feuds and crimes — except for Fitela,
when of such things he wished to speak to him, 880
uncle to nephew[2] — for always they were,
in every combat, companions at need;
a great many of the race of giants
they slaughtered with their swords. For Sigemund
no small fame grew after his final day, 885
after that hardened soldier, prince's son,
had killed a dragon, keeper of a hoard;

---

1   Beowulf is praised indirectly, by being compared first to Sigemund, another famous
    monster-slayer (a different version of whose story is told in the Old Norse *Volsun-
    gasaga* and the Middle High German *Nibelungenlied*; there the dragon-slaying is
    attributed to Sigemund's son Siegfried), and then contrasted to Heremod, an earlier
    king of the Danes who descended into tyranny (it is sometimes assumed that the dis-
    astrous ending of Heremod's reign is the cause of the Danes' lordlessness and distress
    mentioned at the beginning of the poem). The implication is that Beowulf's deeds
    place him in the ranks of other exemplary figures. The method of narration is allusive
    and indirect, as though the audience were expected to know the details of the story
    and appreciate an elliptical reference to them.
2   Fitela is actually Sigemund's son by his own sister—either the poet is being discreet,
    or his version of the story differs from that of the Norse.

æþelinges bearn   āna genēðde
frēcne dǣde,   ne wæs him Fitela mid;
hwæþre him gesǣlde,   ðæt þæt swurd þurhwōd   890
wrǣtlīcne wyrm,   þæt hit on wealle ætstōd,
dryhtlīc īren;   draca morðre swealt.
Hæfde āglǣca   elne gegongen,
þæt hē bēahhordes   brūcan mōste
selfes dōme;   sǣbāt gehleōd,   895
bær on bearm scipes   beorhte frætwa,
Wælses eafera;   wyrm hāt gemealt.
Sē wæs wreccena   wīde mǣrost
ofer werþēode,   wīgendra hlēo
ellendǣdum   — hē þæs ǣr onðāh —   900
siððan Heremōdes   hild sweðrode,
[ea]foð ond ellen.   Hē mid Ēotenum wearð
on fēonda geweald   forð forlācen,
snūde forsended.   Hine sorhwylmas
lemede tō lange;   hē his lēodum wearð,   905
eallum æþellingum   tō aldorceare;
swylce oft bemearn   ǣrran mǣlum
swīðferhþes sīð   snotor ceorl monig,
sē þe him bealwa tō   bōte gelȳfde,
þæt þæt ðeōdnes bearn   geþēon scolde,   910
fæderæþelum onfōn,   folc gehealdan,
hord ond hlēoburh,   hæleþa rīce,
ēþel Scyldinga.   Hē þǣr eallum wearð
mǣg Higelāces   manna cynne,
frēondum gefægra;   hine fyren onwōd.   915
    Hwīlum flītende   fealwe strǣte
mēarum mǣton.   Ðā wæs morgenlēoht
scofen ond scynded.   Ēode scealc monig
swīðhicgende   tō sele þām hēan
searowundor sēon;   swylce self cyning   920
of brȳdbūre,   bēahhorda weard,
tryddode tīrfæst   getrume micle,

---

902 eafoð] earfoð MS

alone, he dared to go under gray stones,
a bold deed — nor was Fitela by his side;
yet so it befell him that his sword pierced   890
the wondrous serpent, stood fixed in the wall,
the manly iron; the dragon met his death.
That fierce creature had gone forth in courage
so that he could possess that store of rings
and use them at his will; the son of Wæls   895
loaded his sea-boat, bore the bright treasure
to the ship's hold. The serpent melted in its own heat.
    He was the most famous of exiles, far and wide,
among all people, protector of warriors,
for his noble deeds — he had prospered for them —   900
since the struggles of Heremod had ceased,
his might and valor. Among the Jutes[1]
he was betrayed into his enemies' hands,
quickly dispatched. The surging of cares
had crippled him too long; he became a deadly burden   905
to his own people, to all noblemen;
for many a wise man had mourned
in earlier times over his headstrong ways
who had looked to him for relief from affliction,
hoped that that prince's son would prosper,   910
receive his father's rank, rule his people,
hoard and fortress, a kingdom of heroes,
the Scylding homeland. The kinsman of Hygelac
became to all the race of mankind
a more pleasant friend; sin possessed him.[2]   915
    Sometimes, competing, the fallow paths
they measured on horseback. When morning's light
raced on and hastened away, many a retainer,
stout-hearted, went to see the high hall
to see the strange wonder; the king himself,   920
guard of the treasure-hoard, strode glorious
from the woman's chambers with a great entourage,

---

1 Perhaps "Eoten." The word literally means "giants" and may be a tribal name, or an
   epithet, or may in fact refer to an actual race of giants.
2 I.e., Heremod.

cystum gecȳþed,   ond his cwēn mid him
medostigge mæt   mægþa hōse.

XIV

Hrōðgār maþelode   — hē tō healle gēong,   925
stōd on stapole,   geseah stēapne hrōf
golde fāhne   ond Grendles hond:
"Ðisse ansȳne   Alwealdan þanc
lungre gelimpe!   Fela ic lāþes gebād,
grynna æt Grendle;   ā mæg God wyrcan   930
wunder æfter wundre,   wuldres Hyrde.
Ðæt wæs ungeāra,   þæt ic ænigra mē
wēana ne wēnde   tō wīdan feore
bōte gebīdan,   þonne blōde fāh
hūsa sēlest   heorodrēorig stōd,   935
wēa wīdscofen   witena gehwylc[um]
ðāra þe ne wēndon,   þæt hīe wīdeferhð
lēoda landgeweorc   lāþum beweredon
scuccum ond scinnum.   Nū scealc hafað
þurh Drihtnes miht   dǣd gefremede,   940
ðē wē ealle   ǣr ne meahton
snyttrum besyrwan.   Hwæt, þæt secgan mæg
efne swā hwylc mægþa,   swā ðone magan cende
æfter gumcynnum,   gyf hēo gȳt lyfað,
þæt hyre ealdmetod   ēste wǣre   945
bearngebyrdo.   Nū ic, Bēowulf, þec,
secg[a] betsta,   mē for sunu wylle
frēogan on ferhþe;   heald forð tela
nīwe sibbe.   Ne bið þē [n]ænigre gād
worolde wilna,   þe ic geweald hæbbe.   950
Ful oft ic for lǣssan   lēan teohhode,
hordweorþunge   hnāhran rince,
sǣmran æt sæcce.   Þū þē self hafast
dǣdum gefremed,   þæt þīn [dōm] lyfað
āwa tō aldre.   Alwalda þec   955

---

936 gehwylcum] gehwylcne MS   947 secga] secg MS   949 nænigre] ænigre MS
954 dom] *not in* MS

a chosen retinue, and his royal queen with him
measured the mead-hall path with a troop of maidens.

XIV

Hrothgar spoke — he went to the hall,   925
stood on the steps, beheld the steep roof
plated with gold, and Grendel's hand:
"For this sight let us swiftly offer thanks
to the Almighty! Much have I endured
of dire grief from Grendel, but God may always   930
work, Shepherd of glory, wonder upon wonder.
It was not long ago that I did not expect
ever in my life to experience relief
from any of my woes, when, stained with blood,
this best of houses stood dripping, gory,   935
a widespread woe to all wise men
who did not expect that they might ever
defend the people's fortress from its foes,
devils and demons. Now a retainer has done
the very deed, through the might of God,   940
which we all could not contrive to do
with all our cleverness. Lo, that woman could say,
whosoever has borne such a son
into the race of men, if she still lives,
that the God of Old was good to her   945
in childbearing. Now I will cherish you,
Beowulf, best of men, like a son
in my heart; hold well henceforth
your new kinship. You shall have no lack
of any worldly goods which I can bestow.   950
Often have I offered rewards for less,
honored with gifts a humbler man,
weaker in battle. Now by yourself
you have done such deeds that your fame will endure
always and forever — may the Almighty   955

gōde forgylde,   swā hē nū gȳt dyde!"

Bēowulf maþelode,   bearn Ec[g]þēowes:
"Wē þæt ellenweorc   ēstum miclum,
feohtan fremedon,   frēcne genēðdon
eafoð uncūþes.   Ūþe ic swīþor,   960
þæt ðū hine selfne   gesēon mōste,
fēond on frætewum   fylwerigne!
Ic hi[ne] hrædlīce   heardan clammum
on wælbedde   wrīþan þōhte,
þæt hē for [mu]ndgripe   mīnum scolde   965
licgean līfbysig,   būtan his līc swice;
ic hine ne mihte,   þā Metod nolde,
ganges getwǣman,   nō ic him þǣs georne ætfealh,
feorhgenīðlan;   wæs tō foremihtig
fēond on fēþe.   Hwæþere hē his folme forlēt   970
tō līfwraþe   lāst weardian,
earm ond eaxle;   nō þǣr ǣnige swā þēah
fēasceaft guma   frōfre gebohte;
nō þȳ leng leofað   lāðgetēona
synnum geswenced,   ac hyne sār hafað   975
in [n]īdgripe   nearwe befongen,
balwon bendum;   ðǣr ābīdan sceal
maga māne fāh   miclan dōmes,
hū him scīr Metod   scrīfan wille."
Ðā wæs swīgra secg,   sunu Ec[g]lāfes,   980
on gylpsprǣce   gūðgeweorca,
siþðan æþelingas   eorles cræfte
ofer hēanne hrōf   hand scēawedon,
fēondes fingras;   foran ǣghwylc wæs,
steda nægla gehwylc   stȳle gelīcost,   985
hǣþenes handsporu   hilderinces
egl[u] unhēoru;   ǣghwylc gecwæð,
þæt him heardra nān   hrīnan wolde
īren ǣrgōd,   þæt ðæs āhlǣcan
blōdge beadufolme   onberan wolde.   990

---

957 Ecgþeowes] ec þeo wes MS   963 hine] him MS   965 mundgripe] hand gripe MS
976 nidgripe] mid gripe MS   980 Ecglafes] eclafes MS   987 eglu] egl MS

reward you with good, as He has already done!"
   Beowulf spoke, son of Ecgtheow:
"Freely and gladly have we fought this fight,
done this deed of courage, daringly faced
this unknown power. I would much prefer   960
that you could have seen the foe himself
decked in his finery,[1] fallen and exhausted!
With a hard grip I hoped to bind him
quickly and keenly on the killing floor,
so that in my handgrasp he would have to   965
lie squirming for life, unless he might slip away;
I could not — the Creator did not wish it —
hinder his going, no matter how hard I held
that deadly enemy; too overwhelming was
that fiend's flight. Yet he forfeited his hand,   970
his arm and shoulder, to save his life,
to guard his tracks — though he got little
comfort thereby, pathetic creature;
the loathsome destroyer will live no longer,
rotten with sin, but pain has seized him,   975
grabbed him tightly in its fierce grip,
its baleful bonds — and there he shall abide,
guilty of his crimes, the greater judgment,
how the shining Maker wishes to sentence him."
   Then the son of Ecglaf[2] was more silent   980
in boasting words about his battle-works
after the noblemen, through the earl's skill,
looked on the hand over the high roof,
the enemy's fingers; at the end of each nail
was a sharp tip, most like steel,   985
heathen talons, the terrible spikes
of that awful warrior; each of them agreed
that not even the hardest of ancient and honorable
irons could touch him, or injure at all
the bloody battle-paw of that baleful creature.   990

---

1   Literally "in his adornments," a peculiar phrase since Grendel is notoriously *not*
    armed and unadorned. Perhaps Beowulf means "covered in a garment of blood"?
2   I.e., Unferth.

Đā wæs hāten hreþe   Heort innanweard
folmum gefrætwod;   fela þǣra wæs,
wera ond wīfa,   þē þæt wīnreced,
gestsele gyredon.   Goldfāg scinon
web æfter wāgum,   wundorsīona fela   995
secga gehwylcum   þāra þe on swylc staraδ.
Wæs þæt beorhte bold   tōbrocen swiδe
eal inneweard   īrenbendum fæst,
heorras tōhlidene;   hrōf āna genæs
ealles ansund,   þē se āglǣca   1000
fyrendǣdum fāg   on flēam gewand
aldres orwēna.   Nō þæt ȳδe byδ
tō befleonne   — fremme sē þe wille —
ac ges[ē]can sceal   sāwlberendra
nȳde genȳdde,   niþδa bearna,   1005
grundbūendra   gearwe stōwe,
þǣr his līchoma   legerbedde fæst
swefeþ æfter symle.
              Þā wæs sǣl ond mǣl,
þæt tō healle gang   Healfdenes sunu;
wolde self cyning   symbel þicgan.   1010
Ne gefrægen ic þā mǣgþe   māran weorode
ymb hyra sincgyfan   sēl gebǣran.
Bugon þā tō bence   blǣdāgande,
fylle gefǣgon,   fægere geþǣgon
medoful manig;   māgas þāra   1015
swīδhicgende   on sele þām hēan,
Hrōδgār ond Hrōþulf.   Heorot innan wæs
frēondum āfylled;   nalles fācenstafas
þēod-Scyldingas   þenden fremedon.

1004 gesecan] ge sacan MS

Then it was quickly commanded that Heorot
be adorned by hands. There were many
men and women who prepared that wine-hall,
the guest-house; gold-dyed tapestries
shone on the walls, many a wonderful sight   995
to any man who might look on them.
That shining building was nearly shattered
inside, entirely, fast in its iron bands,
its hinges sprung; the roof alone survived
unharmed, when that horrible creature,   1000
stained with foul deeds, turned in his flight,
despairing of life. Death is not an easy
thing to escape — try it who will —
but compelled by necessity all must come
to that place set aside for soul-bearers,   1005
children of men, dwellers on earth,
where the body, fast on its bed of death,
sleeps after the feast.
     Then was the set time
that the son of Healfdene went to the hall;
the king himself wished to share in the feast.   1010
I have never heard of a greater host
who bore themselves better before their treasure-giver.
Those men in their glory moved to their benches,
rejoiced in the feast; fairly those kinsmen
took many a full mead-cup,   1015
stouthearted in the high hall,
Hrothgar and Hrothulf. Heorot within was
filled with friends — no false treacheries
did the people of the Scyldings plot at that time.[1]

---

1 Implicit in this statement is the idea that, at some later time, the people of the Scyld-
  ings *did* plot false treacheries; from other sources it is possible to infer that after the
  death of Hrothgar, his nephew Hrothulf ruled rather than Hrethric, Hrothgar's son.
  Many scholars assume that the story of some sort of treacherous usurpation was
  known to the audience; this gives a special urgency to much of what happens in these
  scenes of feasting, especially the speeches of Wealhtheow.

Forgeaf þā Bēowulfe   brand Healfdenes   1020
segen gyldenne   sigores tō lēane,
hroden hil[d]ecumbor,   helm ond byrnan;
mǣre māðþumsweord   manige gesāwon
beforan beorn beran.   Bēowulf geþah
ful on flette;   nō hē þǣre feohgyfte   1025
for sc[ē]oten[d]um   scamigan ðorfte —
ne gefrægn ic frēondlīcor   fēower mādmas
golde gegyrede   gummanna fela
in ealobence   ōðrum gesellan.
Ymb þæs helmes hrōf   hēafodbeorge   1030
wīrum bewunden   wal[u] ūtan hēold,
þæt him fēla lāf   frēcne ne meaht[e]
scūrheard sceþðan,   þonne scyldfreca
ongēan gramum   gangan scolde.
Heht ðā eorla hlēo   eahta mēaras   1035
fǣtedhlēore   on flet teon,
in under eoderas;   þāra ānum stōd
sadol searwum fāh,   since gewurþad;
þæt wæs hildesetl   hēahcyninges,
ðonne sweorda gelāc   sunu Healfdenes   1040
efnan wolde;   nǣfre on ōre læg
wīdcūþes wīg,   ðonne walu fēollon.
Ond ðā Bēowulfe   bēga gehwæþres
eodor Ingwina   onweald gēteah,
wicga ond wǣpna;   hēt hine wēl brūcan.   1045
Swā manlīce   mǣre þēoden,
hordweard hæleþa   heaþorǣsas geald
mēarum ond mādmum,   swā hȳ nǣfre man lyhð,
sē þe secgan wile   sōð æfter rihte.

XVI

Ðā gȳt ǣghwylcum   eorla drihten   1050
þāra þe mid Bēowulfe   briml[ā]de tēah,

1022 hildecumbor] hilte cumbor MS   1026 sceotendum] scotenum MS
1031 walu] walan MS   1032 meahte] meahton MS   1051 brimlade] brim leade MS

He gave to Beowulf the blade of Healfdene,[1] 1020
a golden war-standard as a reward for victory,
the bright banner, a helmet and byrnie,
a great treasure-sword — many saw them
borne before that man. Beowulf received
the full cup in the hall, he felt no shame 1025
at that gift-giving before his bowmen;
never have I heard tell of four treasures
given more graciously, gold-adorned,
from one man to another on the ale-benches.
On the crown of the helmet as a head-protector 1030
a ridge, wound with wire, stood without,
so that the file-sharp swords might not terribly
harm him, storm-hardened, when shield-fighters
had to go against hostile forces.
The protector of earls ordered eight horses 1035
with ornamented bridles led into the building,
in under the eaves; on one sat
a saddle, skillfully tooled, set with gemstones;
that was the warseat of the high-king
when the son of Healfdene sought to perform 1040
his swordplay — the widely-known warrior
never failed at the front, when the slain fell about him.
And the lord of the Ingwines[2] gave ownership
of both of them to Beowulf,
the horses and weapons, bid him use them well. 1045
So manfully did the mighty prince,
hoard-guard of warriors, reward the storm of battle
with steeds and treasures that none who will speak
the truth rightfully could ever reproach them.

XVI

Then the lord of earls, to each of those 1050
on the mead-benches who had made with Beowulf

---

1 The translation follows the reading of Mitchell and Robinson, and see also Mitchell.
   The manuscript is usually emended to mean "the son of Healfdene gave to Beowulf."
2 The "Ingwines" or "friends of Ing" are the Danes.

on þære medubence   māþðum gesealde,
yrfeláfe,   ond þone ænne heht
golde forgyldan,   þone ðe Grendel ær
māne ācwealde —   swā hē hyra mā wolde,   1055
nefne him wītig God   wyrd forstōde
ond ðæs mannes mōd.   Metod eallum wēold
gumena cynnes,   swā hē nū gīt dēð.
Forþan biō andgit   æghwær sēlest,
ferhðes foreþanc.   Fela sceal gebīdan   1060
lēofes ond lāþes   sē þe longe hēr
on ðyssum windagum   worolde brūceð.
      Þær wæs sang ond swēg   samod ætgædere
fore Healfdenes   hildewīsan,
gomenwudu grēted,   gid oft wrecen,   1065
ðonne healgamen   Hrōþgāres scop
æfter medobence   mænan scolde,
[be] Finnes eaferum,   ðā hīe se fær begeat,
hæleð Healf-Dena,   Hnæf Scyldinga,
in Frēswæle   feallan scolde.   1070
Nē hūru Hildeburh   herian þorfte
Ēotena trēowe;   unsynnum wearð
beloren lēofum   æt þām [lind]plegan
bearnum ond brōðrum;   hīe on gebyrd hruron
gāre wunde;   þæt wæs geōmuru ides!   1075
Nalles hōlinga   Hōces dohtor
meotodsceaft bemearn,   syþðan morgen cōm,
ðā hēo under swegle   gesēon meahte
morþorbealo māga,   þær hē[o] ær mæste hēold
worolde wynne.   Wīg ealle fornam   1080
Finnes þegnas   nemne fēaum ānum,
þæt hē ne mehte   on þæm meðelstede
wīg Hengeste   wiht gefeohtan,
nē þā wēaláfe   wīge forþringan

1068 be Finnes eaferum] finnes eaferum MS   1073 lindplegan] hildplegan MS
1079 heo] he MS

a sea-journey, gave jeweled treasures,
antique heirlooms, and then ordered
that gold be paid for the man whom Grendel
had wickedly slain — he would have done more, 1055
if wise God and one man's courage
had not prevented that fate. The Maker ruled all
of the race of mankind, as He still does.
Therefore understanding is always best,
spiritual foresight — he must face much, 1060
both love and hate, who long here
endures this world in these days of strife.

    Noise and music mingled together
before the leader of Healfdene's forces,
the harp was touched, tales often told, 1065
when Hrothgar's scop was set to recite
among the mead-tables his hall-entertainment
about the sons of Finn, surprised in ambush,
when the hero of the Half-Danes, Hnæf the Scylding
had to fall in a Frisian slaughter.[1] 1070

    Hildeburh, indeed, had no need to praise
the good faith of the Jutes. Guiltless, she was
deprived of her dear ones in that shieldplay,
her sons and brothers — sent forth to their fate,
dispatched by spears; she was a sad lady! 1075
Not without cause did she mourn fate's decrees,
the daughter of Hoc, after daybreak came
and she could see the slaughter of her kin
under the very skies where once she held
the greatest worldly joys. War took away 1080
all of the thanes of Finn, except a few,
so that he could not continue at all
a fight with Hengest on the battlefield,
nor could that woeful remnant drive away

---

1   The story is obscure; the survival of a fragment of another poem telling the same
story (see Appendix A5) helps clarify the action somewhat. Hnæf, prince of the
Danes, is visiting his sister Hildeburh at the home of her husband Finn, king of the
Frisians. While there, the Danish party is treacherously attacked (perhaps by a Jutish
contingent among Finn's troops, unless the "Jutes" and Frisians are one and the same
people); after five days of fighting Hnæf lies dead, along with many casualties on
either side. Hnæf's retainer Hengest is left to lead the remnant of Danish survivors.

þēodnes ðegne;   ac hig him geðingo budon,   1085
þæt hīe him ōðer flet   eal gerȳmdon,
healle ond hēahsetl,   þæt hīe healfre geweald
wið Ēotena bearn   āgan mōston,
ond æt feohgyftum   Folcwaldan sunu
dōgra gehwylce   Dene weorþode,   1090
Hengestes hēap   hringum wenede
efne swā swīðe   sincgestrēonum
fǣttan goldes,   swā hē Frēsena cyn
on bēorsele   byldan wolde.
Ðā hīe getrūwedon   on twā healfa   1095
fæste frioðuwǣre.   Fin Hengeste
elne unflitme   āðum benemde,
þæt hē þā wēalāfe   weotena dōme
ārum hēolde,   þæt ðǣr ǣnig mon
wordum nē worcum   wǣre ne brǣce,   1100
nē þurh inwitsearo   ǣfre gemǣnden,
ðēah hīe hira bēaggyfan   banan folgedon
ðēodenlēase,   þā him swā geþearfod wæs;
gyf þonne Frȳsna hwylc   frēcn[a]n sprǣce
ðæs morðorhetes   myndgiend wǣre,   1105
þonne hit sweordes ecg   syððan sc[ē]de.
Āð wæs geæfned,   ond icge gold
āhæfen of horde.   Here-Scyldinga
betst beadorinca   wæs on bǣl gearu.
Æt þǣm āde wæs   ēþgesȳne   1110
swātfāh syrce,   swȳn ealgylden,
eofer īrenheard,   æþeling manig
wundum āwyrded;   sume on wæle crungon!
Hēt ðā Hildeburh   æt Hnæfes āde
hire selfre sunu   sweoloðe befæstan,   1115
bānfatu bærnan,   ond on bǣl dōn
[ēa]me on eaxle.   Ides gnornode,
geōmrode giddum.   Gūðrinc āstāh.
Wand tō wolcnum   wælfyra mǣst,

1104 frecnan] frecnen MS   1106 scede] scolde MS   1107 Að] *this is the* MS *reading;*
many editors emend to ad   1117 eame] earme MS

the prince's thane — so they offered them terms:[1]   1085
they would clear out another hall for them,
a house and high-seat, of which they should have
half the control with the sons of the Jutes,
and Folcwalda's son, with feasting and gifts,
should honor the Danes each and every day,   1090
gladden the troops of Hengest with gold rings
and ancient treasures, ornamented gold,
just as often as he would encourage
the hosts of the Frisians in the beer-hall.
They swore their pledges then on either side,   1095
a firm compact of peace. With unfeigned zeal
Finn swore his oaths to Hengest, pledged that he,
with the consent of his counselors, would
support with honor those sad survivors,
and that none should break their pact in word or deed,   1100
nor through malice should ever make mention,
though they should serve their ring-giver's slayer,
without a lord, as they were led by need —
and if, provoking, any Frisian spoke
reminding them of all their murderous hate,   1105
then with the sword's edge they should settle it.
     The oath[2] was made ready, and ancient gold
was brought from the hoard; the Battle-Scyldings'
best fighting-man was ready for the fire.
It was easy to see upon that pyre   1110
the bloodstained battle-shirt, the gilded swine,
iron-hard boar-images, the noblemen
with fatal wounds — so many felled by war!
Then Hildeburh commanded at Hnæf's pyre
that her own son be consigned to the flames   1115
to be burnt, flesh and bone, placed on the pyre
at his uncle's shoulder; the lady sang
a sad lament. The warrior ascended;
to the clouds coiled the mighty funeral fire,

---

1   The referent of this pronoun is not entirely clear—who offers what to whom? The
    terms of the truce are unthinkable—no hero could honorably follow the killer of his
    lord. In the following line "they" refers to the Frisians, "them" to the Danes.
2   Some editors emend *að* "oath" to *ad* "pyre."

hlynode for hlāwe;   hafelan multon,   1120
bengeato burston,   ðonne blōd ætspranc,
lāðbite līces.   Līg ealle forswealg,
gæsta gīfrost,   þāra ðē þǣr gūð fornam
bēga folces;   wæs hira blǣd scacen.

XVII

Gewiton him ðā wīgend   wīca nēosian   1125
frēondum befeallen,   Frȳsland gesēon,
hāmas ond hēaburh.   Hengest ðā gȳt
wælfāgne winter   wunode mid Finne
[ea]l unhlitme;   eard gemunde,
þēah þe hē [ne] meahte   on mere drīfan   1130
hringedstefnan —   holm storme wēol,
won wið winde,   winter ȳþe belēac
īsgebinde —   oþ ðæt ōþer cōm
gēar in geardas,   swā nū gȳt deð,
þā ðe syngāles   sēle bewitiað,   1135
wuldortorhtan weder.   Ðā wæs winter scacen,
fæger foldan bearm;   fundode wrecca,
gist of geardum;   hē tō gyrnwræce
swīðor þōhte   þonne tō sǣlāde,
gif hē torngemōt   þurhtēon mihte,   1140
þæt hē Ēotena bearn   inne gemunde.
Swā hē ne forwyrnde   woroldrǣdenne,
þonne him Hūnlāfing   hildelēoman,
billa sēlest   on bearm dyde;
þæs wǣron mid Ēotenum   ecge cūðe.   1145
Swylce ferhðfrecan   Fin eft begeat
sweordbealo slīðen   æt his selfes hām,
siþðan grimne gripe   Gūðlāf ond Ōslāf
æfter sǣsīðe   sorge mǣndon,

1128-29 Finne / eal unhlitme] finnel unhlitme MS   1130 ne] *not in* MS

and roared before their mound; their heads melted,   1120
their gashes burst open and spurted blood,
the deadly body-bites. The flame devoured,
most greedy spirit, those whom war destroyed
of both peoples — their glory departed.

XVII

          The warriors left to seek their native lands,   1125
bereft of friends, to behold Frisia,
their homes and high fortresses. Hengest still
stayed there with Finn that slaughter-stained winter,
unwilling, desolate. He dreamt of home,
though on the frozen sea he could not[1] steer   1130
his ring-prowed ship — the ocean raged with storms,
strove with the wind, and winter locked the waves
in icy bonds, until there came another
year to the courtyard — as it yet does,
always observing its seasons and times,   1135
bright glorious weather. Gone was the winter,
and fair the bosom of earth; the exile burned
to take leave of that court, yet more he thought
of stern vengeance than of sea-voyages,
how he might arrange a hostile meeting,   1140
remind the Jutish sons of his iron sword.
So he did not refuse the world's custom
when the son of Hunlaf[2] placed a glinting sword,
the best of battle-flames, upon his lap;
its edge was not unknown among the Jutes.   1145
And so, in turn, to the bold-minded Finn
befell cruel sword-evil in his own home,
when Guthlaf and Oslaf spoke of their grief,
the fierce attack after their sea voyage,

---

1   OE *ne* "not" is not in the manuscript; most editors and translators add it to make
    better sense of the passage and of Hengest's character.
2   It is not clear who this is: perhaps Guthlaf or Oslaf (mentioned a few lines later),
    perhaps not; apparently some retainers remained with Hengest in Finn's hall, nursing
    their resentment throughout the winter. Some scholars take the OE word *hunlafing* as
    the name of a sword.

ætwiton wēana dǣl;   ne meahte wǣfre mōd   1150
forhabban in hreþre.   Ðā wæs heal [r]oden
fēonda fēorum,   swilce Fin slægen,
cyning on corþre,   ond sēo cwēn numen.
Scēotend Scyldinga   tō scypon feredon
eal ingesteald   eorðcyninges,   1155
swylce hīe æt Finnes hām   findan meahton
sigla searogimma.   Hīe on sǣlāde
drihtlīce wīf   tō Denum feredon,
lǣddon tō lēodum.
    Lēoð wæs āsungen,
glēomannes gyd.   Gamen eft āstāh,   1160
beorhtode bencswēg,   byrelas sealdon
wīn of wunderfatum.   Þā cwōm Wealhþēo forð
gān under gyldnum bēage   þǣr þā godan twēgen
sǣton suhtergefæderan;   þā gȳt wæs hiera sib ætgædere,
ǣghwylc ōðrum trȳwe.   Swylce þǣr [Un]ferþ þyle   1165
æt fōtum sæt frēan Scyldinga;   gehwylc hiora his ferhðe trēowde,
þæt hē hæfde mōd micel,   þēah þe hē his māgum nǣre
ārfæst æt ecga gelācum.   Spræc ðā ides Scyldinga:
"Onfōh þissum fulle,   frēodrihten mīn,
sinces brytta!   Þū on sǣlum wes,   1170
goldwine gumena,   ond tō Gēatum spræc
mildum wordum,   swā sceal man dōn!
Bēo wið Gēatas glæd,   geofena gemyndig,
nēan ond feorran   [þa] þū nū hafast.
Mē man sægde,   þæt þū ðē for sunu wolde   1175
hereri[n]c habban.   Heorot is gefǣlsod,
bēahsele beorhta;   brūc þenden þū mōte
manigra mēdo,   ond þīnum māgum lǣf
folc ond rīce,   þonne ðū forð scyle,
metodsceaft seon.   Ic mīnne can   1180
glædne Hrōþulf,   þæt hē þā geogoðe wile
ārum healdan,   gyf þū ǣr þonne hē,
wine Scildinga,   worold oflǣtest;
wēne ic þæt hē mid gōde   gyldan wille

1151 roden] hroden MS   1165 Unferþ] hun ferþ MS   1174 þa] *not in* MS
1176 hererinc] here ric MS

and cursed their wretched lot — the restless heart 1150
could not restrain itself. The hall was stained
with the lifeblood of foes, and Finn was slain,
the king among his host; the queen was seized.
The Scylding bowmen carried to their ships
all the house property of that earth-king, 1155
whatever they could find in Finn's homestead,
brooches and bright gems. On their sea journey
they bore that noble queen back to the Danes
and led her to her people.
                                    The lay was sung,
the entertainer's song. Glad sounds rose again, 1160
the bench-noise glittered, cupbearers gave
wine from wondrous vessels. Wealhtheow came forth
in her golden crown to where the good two
sat, nephew and uncle; their peace was still whole then,
each true to the other. Likewise Unferth, spokesman,[1] 1165
sat at the foot of the Scylding lord; everyone trusted his spirit,
that he had great courage, though to his kinsmen he had not been
merciful in sword-play. Then the lady of the Scyldings spoke:
      "Take this cup, my noble courteous lord,
giver of treasure! Be truly joyful, 1170
gold-friend of men, and speak to the Geats
in mild words, as a man should do!
Be gracious to the Geats, mindful of the gifts
which you now have from near and far.
I have been told that you would take this warrior 1175
for your son. Heorot is cleansed,
the bright ring-hall — use your many rewards
while you can, and leave to your kinsmen
the folk and kingdom, when you must go forth
to face the Maker's decree. I know that my own 1180
dear gracious Hrothulf will hold in honors
these youths, if you should give up the world
before him, friend of the Scyldings;
I expect that he would wish to repay

---

1   The Old English word *thyle* has been variously interpreted, from "court jester" to
    "official speechmaker." The present translation grants Unferth a measure of dignity
    and position to which, perhaps, he is not entitled.

uncran eaferan,　　　gif hē þæt eal gemon,　　　　　　　1185
hwæt wit tō willan　　ond tō worðmyndum
umborwesendum ǣr　　ārna gefremedon."
Hwearf þā bī bence,　　þǣr hyre byre wǣron,
Hrēðrīc ond Hrōðmund,　　ond hæleþa bearn,
giogoð ætgædere;　　þǣr se gōda sæt,　　　　　　　　1190
Bēowulf Gēata　　be þǣm gebrōðrum twǣm.

XVIII

Him wæs ful boren,　　ond frēondlaþu
wordum bewægned,　　ond wunden gold
ēstum geēawed,　　earm[h]rēade twā,
hrægl ond hringas,　　healsbēaga mǣst　　　　　　　1195
þāra þe ic on foldan　　gefrægen hæbbe.
Nǣnigne ic under swegle　　sēlran hȳrde
hordmā[ðð]um hæleþa,　　syþðan Hāma ætwæg
tō [þǣ]re byrhtan byrig　　Brōsinga mene,
sigle ond sincfæt —　　searonīðas f[lēa]h　　　　　1200
Eormenrīces,　　gecēas ēcne rǣd.
Þone hring hæfde　　Higelāc Gēata,
nefa Swertinges　　nȳhstan sīðe,
siðþan hē under segne　　sinc ealgode,
wælrēaf werede;　　hyne wyrd fornam,　　　　　　1205
syþðan hē for wlenco　　wēan āhsode,
fǣhðe tō Frȳsum.　　Hē þā frætwe wæg,
eorclanstānas　　ofer ȳða ful,
rīce þēoden;　　hē under rande gecranc.
Gehwearf þā in Francna fæþm　　feorh cyninges,　　1210
brēostgewǣdu,　　ond se bēah somod;
wyrsan wīgfrecan　　wæl rēafeden

1194 earmhreade] earm reade MS　　1198 hordmaððum] hord mad mum
1199 þære] here MS　　1200 fleah] fealh MS

both our sons kindly, if he recalls all 1185
the pleasures and honors that we have shown him,
in our kindness, since he was a child."
She turned to the bench where her boys sat,
Hrethric and Hrothmund, and the son of heroes,
all the youths together; the good man, 1190
Beowulf the Geat, sat between the two brothers.

XVIII

The flagon was brought forth, a friendly greeting
conveyed with words, and wound gold
offered with good will, two armlets,
garments and rings, and the greatest neck-collar 1195
ever heard of anywhere on earth.
Under heaven I have not heard tell of a better
hoard-treasure of heroes, since Hama carried off
to the bright city the Brosinga necklace,
the gem and its treasures; he fled the treachery 1200
of Eormanric,[1] chose eternal counsel.
    Hygelac the Geat on his last journey
had that neck-ring,[2] nephew of Swerting,
when under the banner he defended his booty,
the spoils of slaughter. Fate struck him down 1205
when in his pride he went looking for woe,
a feud with the Frisians. He wore that finery,
those precious stones, over the cup of the sea,
that powerful lord, and collapsed under his shield.
Into Frankish hands came the life of that king, 1210
his breast-garments, and the great collar too;
a lesser warrior looted the corpses

---

1 The Brosinga necklace had apparently been worn by the Norse goddess Freya.
  Nothing much is known of Hama, who apparently stole the necklace from Eormanric,
  famous king of the Goths. The "bright city" and "eternal counsel" may refer to his
  retreat into a monastery and conversion to Christianity (a story told in the Old Norse
  Thidrekssaga), though this is not entirely certain.
2 The first of several mentions of Hygelac's ill-fated raid against the Frisians. Later we
  are told that Beowulf gives the necklace to Hygd, Hygelac's wife; she apparently let
  him borrow it when he went on his piratical raid.

æfter gūðsceare,   Gēata lēode
hrēawīc hēoldon.
               Heal swēge onfēng.
Wealhðēo maþelode,   hēo fore þǣm werede spræc: 1215
"Brūc ðisses bēages,   Bēowulf lēofa,
hyse, mid hǣle,   ond þisses hrægles nēot,
þēo[d]gestrēona,   ond geþēoh tela,
cen þec mid cræfte,   ond þyssum cnyhtum wes
lāra līðe!   Ic þē þæs lēan geman.   1220
Hafast þū gefēred,   þæt ðe feor ond nēah
ealne wīdeferhþ   weras ehtigað,
efne swā sīde   swā sǣ bebūgeð
windgeard weallas.   Wes þenden þū lifige,
æþeling, ēadig!   Ic þē an tela   1225
sincgestrēona.   Bēo þū suna mīnum
dǣdum gedēfe,   drēamhealdende!
Hēr is ǣghwylc eorl   ōþrum getrȳwe,
mōdes milde,   mandrihtne hol[d],
þegnas syndon geþwǣre,   þēod ealgearo,   1230
druncne dryhtguman   dōð swā ic bidde!"
    Ēode þā tō setle.   þǣr wæs symbla cyst,
druncon wīn weras.   Wyrd ne cūþon,
geōsceaft grim[m]e,   swā hit āgangen wearð
eorla manegum,   syþðan ǣfen cwōm,   1235
ond him Hrōþgār gewāt   tō hofe sīnum,
rīce tō ræste.   Reced weardode
unrīm eorla,   swā hīe oft ǣr dydon.
Bencþelu beredon;   hit geondbrǣded wearð
beddum ond bolstrum.   Bēorscealca sum   1240
fūs ond fǣge   fletræste gebēag.
Setton him tō hēafdon   hilderandas,
bordwudu beorhtan;   þǣr on bence wæs
ofer æþelinge   ȳþgesēne
heaþostēapa helm,   hringed byrne,   1245
þrecwudu þrymlīc.   Wæs þēaw hyra,
þæt hīe oft wǣron   an wīg gearwe,
gē æt hām gē on herge,   gē gehwæþer þāra

1218 þeodgestreona] þeo ge streona MS   1229 hold] hol MS   1234 grimme] grimne
MS

mown down in battle; Geatish men
held that killing field.
                    The hall swallowed the noise.
Wealhtheow stood before the company and spoke: 1215
"Beowulf, beloved warrior, wear this neck-ring
in good health, and enjoy this war-garment,
treasure of a people, and prosper well,
be bold and clever, and to these boys be
mild in counsel — I will remember you for that.   1220
You have made it so that men will praise you
far and near, forever and ever,
as wide as the seas, home of the winds,
surround the shores of earth. Be while you live
blessed, o nobleman! I wish you well   1225
with these bright treasures. Be to my sons
kind in your deeds, keeping them in joys!
Here each earl is true to the other,
mild in his heart, loyal to his liege-lord,
the thanes united, the nation alert,   1230
the troop, having drunk at my table, will do as I bid."
        She went to her seat. The best of feasts it was —
the men drank wine, and did not know *wyrd*,
the cruel fate which would come to pass
for many an earl once evening came,   1235
and Hrothgar departed to his own dwelling,
the mighty one to his rest. Countless men
held that hall, as they often had before.
They cleared away bench-planks, spread cushions
and bedding on the floor. One of those beer-drinkers   1240
lay down to his rest fated, ripe for death.
They set at their heads their round battle-shields,
bright boards; there on the bench,
easily seen over the noblemen,
were the high battle-helmet, the ringed byrnie,   1245
the mighty wooden spear. It was their custom
to be always ready, armed for battle,
at home or in the field, every one of them,

efne swylce mæla,   swylce hira mandryhtne
þearf gesælde;   wæs sēo þēod tilu.   1250

XIX

  Sigon þā tō slæpe.   Sum sāre angeald
æfenræste,   swā him ful oft gelamp,
siþðan goldsele   Grendel warode,
unriht æfnde,   oþ þæt ende becwōm,
swylt æfter synnum.   Þæt gesȳne wearþ,   1255
widcūþ werum,   þætte wrecend þā gȳt
lifde æfter lāþum,   lange þrāge,
æfter gūðceare;   Grendles mōdor,
ides āglæcwīf   yrmþe gemunde,
sē þe wæteregesan   wunian scolde,   1260
cealde strēamas,   siþðan Cā[in] wearð
tō ecgbanan   āngan brēþer,
fæderenmæge;   hē þā fāg gewāt,
morþre gemearcod   mandrēam fleon,
wēsten warode.   Þanon wōc fela   1265
geōsceaftgāsta;   wæs þæra Grendel sum,
heorowearh hetelīc,   sē æt Heorote fand
wæccendne wer   wīges bīdan.
Þær him āglæca   ætgræpe wearð,
hwæþre hē gemunde   mægenes strenge,   1270
gimfæste gife,   ðē him God sealde,
ond him tō Anwaldan   āre gelȳfde,
frōfre ond fultum;   ðȳ hē þone fēond ofercwōm,
gehnægde helle gāst.   Þā hē hēan gewāt,
drēame bedæled   dēaþwīc seon,   1275
mancynnes fēond.   Ond his mōdor þā gȳt
gīfre ond galgmōd   gegān wolde
sorhfulne sīð,   sunu [dēoð] wrecan.
  Cōm þā tō Heorote,   ðær Hring-Dene
geond þæt sæld swæfun.   Þā ðær sōna wearð   1280
edhwyrft eorlum,   siþðan inne fealh
Grendles mōdor.   Wæs se gryre læssa

1261 Cain] camp MS   1278 deoð] ðeod MS

on whatever occasion their overlord
had need of them; that was a good troop.

XIX

They sank into sleep — one paid sorely
for his evening rest, as had often happened
when Grendel guarded that gold-hall,
committed his wrongs until he came to his end,
died for his sins. It was soon all too clear, 1255
obvious to all men, that an avenger still
lived on after that enemy for a long time
after that grim battle — Grendel's mother,
monstrous woman, remembered her misery,
she who dwelt in those dreadful waters, 1260
the cold streams, ever since Cain
killed with his blade his only brother,
his father's kin; he fled bloodstained,
marked for murder, left the joys of men,
dwelled in the wasteland. From him awoke 1265
many a fateful spirit — Grendel among them,
hateful accursed foe, who found at Heorot
a wakeful warrior waiting for battle.
When the great beast began to seize him,
he remembered his mighty strength, 1270
the ample gifts which God had given him,
and trusted the Almighty for mercy,
favor and support; thus he overcame the fiend,
subdued the hellish spirit. He went away wretched,
deprived of joy, to find his place of death, 1275
mankind's foe. But his mother — greedy,
grim-minded — still wanted to go
on her sad journey to avenge her son's death.
 She reached Heorot, where the Ring-Danes
slept throughout the building; a sudden upset 1280
came to men, when Grendel's mother
broke into the hall. The horror was less

efne swā micle,   swā bið mægþa cræft,
wīggryre wīfes   be wǣpnedmen,
þonne heoru bunden,   hamere geþ[rū]en,   1285
sweord swāte fāh   swīn ofer helme
ecgum dyhtig   andweard scireð.
Ðā wæs on healle   heardecg togen
sweord ofer setlum,   sīdrand manig
hafen handa fæst;   helm ne gemunde,   1290
byrnan sīde,   þā hine se brōga angeat.
Hēo wæs on ofste,   wolde ūt þanon,
fēore beorgan,   þā hēo onfunden wæs;
hraðe hēo æþelinga   ānne hæfde
fæste befangen,   þā hēo tō fenne gang.   1295
Sē wæs Hrōþgāre   hæleþa lēofost
on gesīðes hād   be sǣm twēonum,
rīce randwiga,   þone ðe hēo on ræste ābrēat,
blǣdfæstne beorn.   Næs Bēowulf þǣr,
ac wæs ōþer in   ǣr geteohhod   1300
æfter māþðumgife   mǣrum Gēate.
Hrēam wearð in Heorote;   hēo under heolfre genam
cūþe folme;   cearu wæs genīwod,
geworden in wīcun.   Ne wæs þæt gewrixle til,
þæt hīe on bā healfa   bicgan scoldon   1305
frēonda fēorum!
          Þā wæs frōd cyning,
hār hilderinc   on hrēon mōde,
syðþan hē aldorþegn   unlyfigendne,
þone dēorestan   dēadne wisse.
Hraþe wæs tō būre   Bēowulf fetod,   1310
sigorēadig secg.   Samod ǣrdæge
ēode eorla sum,   æþele cempa
self mid gesīðum   þǣr se snotera bād,
hwæþ[er] him A[l]walda   ǣfre wille
æfter wēaspelle   wyrpe gefremman.   1315
Gang ðā æfter flōre   fyrdwyrðe man
mid his handscale   — healwudu dynede —
þæt hē þone wīsan   wordum [n]ǣgde

1285 geþruen] geþuren MS   1314 hwæþer] hwæþre MS   Alwalda] alf walda MS
1318 nægde] hnægde MS

by as much as a maiden's strength,
a woman's warfare, is less than an armed man's
when a bloodstained blade, its edges strong, 1285
hammer-forged sword, slices through
the boar-image on a helmet opposite.[1]
Then in the hall was the hard edge drawn,
swords over seats, many a broad shield
raised in hands — none remembered his helmet 1290
or broad mail-shirt when that terror seized them.
She came in haste and meant to hurry out,
save her life, when she was surprised there,
but she quickly seized, fast in her clutches,
one nobleman when she went to the fens. 1295
He was the dearest of heroes to Hrothgar
among his comrades between the two seas,
mighty shield-warrior, whom she snatched from his rest,
a glorious thane. Beowulf was not there,
but another place had been appointed 1300
for the famous Geat after the treasure-giving.
Heorot was in an uproar — she took the famous hand,
covered in gore; care was renewed,
come again to the dwellings. That was no good exchange,
that those on both sides should have to bargain 1305
with the lives of friends.

                   Then the wise old king,
Grey-bearded warrior, was grieved at heart
when he learned that he no longer lived —
the dearest of men, his chief thane, was dead.
Quickly Beowulf was fetched to the chambers, 1310
victory-blessed man. Just before dawn
that noble champion came with his companions,
went with his men to where the old king waited
wondering whether the Almighty would ever
work a change after his tidings of woe. 1315
Across the floor walked the worthy warrior
with his small troop — the hall-wood resounded —
and with his words he addressed the wise one,

---

1   In fact Grendel's mother is a much more dangerous opponent for Beowulf; the point
    of these lines is not clear.

frēan Ingwina,   frægn gif him wǣre
æfter nēodlaðu[m]   niht getǣse.   1320

XX

Hrōðgār maþelode,   helm Scyldinga:
"Ne frīn þū æfter sǣlum!   Sorh is genīwod
Denigea lēodum.   Dēad is Æschere,
Yrmenlāfes   yldra brōþor,
mīn rūnwita   ond mīn rǣdbora,   1325
eaxlgestealla,   þonne wē on orlege
hafelan weredon,   þonne hniton fēþan,
eoferas cnysedan.   Swy(lc) scolde eorl wesan,
[æþeling] ǣrgōd,   swylc Æschere wæs!
Wearð him on Heorote   tō handbanan   1330
wælgǣst wǣfre;   ic ne wāt hwæþer
atol ǣse wlanc   eftsiðas tēah,
fylle ge[f]ægnod.   Hēo þā fǣhðe wræc,
þē þū gystran niht   Grendel cwealdest
þurh hǣstne hād   heardum clammum,   1335
forþan hē tō lange   lēode mīne
wanode ond wyrde.   Hē æt wīge gecrang
ealdres scyldig,   ond nū ōþer cwōm
mihtig mānscaða,   wolde hyre mǣg wrecan,
gē feor hafað   fǣhðe gestǣled,   1340
þæs þe þincean mæg   þegne monegum,
sē þe æfter sincgyfan   on sefan grēoteþ,
hreþerbealo hearde;   nū sēo hand ligeð,
sē þe ēow wēlhwylcra   wilna dohte.
Ic þæt londbūend,   lēode mine,   1345
selerǣdende   secgan hȳrde,
þæt hīe gesāwon   swylce twēgen
micle mearcstapan   mōras healdan,
ellorgǣstas.   Ðǣra ōðer wæs,
þæs þe hīe gewislīcost   gewitan meahton,   1350
idese onlīcn[e]s;   ōðer earmsceapen

1320 neodlaðum] neodlaðu MS   1329 æþeling] *not in* MS   1333 gefægnod]
gefrægnod MS   1351 onlicnes] onlicnæs MS

lord of the Ingwines, asked him whether
the night had been agreeable, after his urgent summons.　　　1320

XX

Hrothgar spoke, protector of the Scyldings:
"Ask not of joys! Sorrow is renewed
for the Danish people. Æschere is dead,
elder brother of Yrmenlaf,
my confidant, my counselor,　　　　　　　　　　　　　　1325
my shoulder-companion in every conflict
when we defended our heads when the footsoldiers clashed
and struck boar-helmets. As a nobleman should be,
always excellent, so Æschere was!
In Heorot he was slain by the hand　　　　　　　　　　　1330
of a restless death-spirit; I do not know
where that ghoul went, gloating with its carcass,
rejoicing in its feast. She avenged that feud
in which you killed Grendel yesterday evening
in your violent way with a crushing vice-grip,　　　　　　1335
for he had diminished and destroyed my people
for far too long. He fell in battle,
it cost him his life, and now another has come,
a mighty evil marauder who means to avenge
her kin, and too far has carried out her revenge,　　　　1340
as it may seem to many a thane
whose spirit groans for his treasure-giver,
a hard heart's distress — now that hand lies dead
which was wont to give you all good things.
　　I have heard countrymen and hall-counselors　　　1345
among my people report this:
they have seen two such creatures,
great march-stalkers holding the moors,
alien spirits. The second of them,
as far as they could discern most clearly,　　　　　　　1350
had the shape of a woman; the other, misshapen,

on weres wæstmum   wræclāstas træd,
næfne hē wæs māra   þonne ǣnig man ōþer;
þone on gēardagum   Grendel nemdo[n]
foldbūende;   nō hīe fæder cunnon,   1355
hwæþer him ǣnig wæs   ǣr ācenned
dyrnra gāsta.   Hīe dȳgel lond
warigeað wulfhleoþu,   windige næssas,
frēcne fengelād,   ðǣr fyrgenstrēam
under næssa genipu   niþer gewīteð,   1360
flōd under foldan.   Nis þæt feor heonon
mīlgemearces,   þæt se mere stan[d]eð;
ofer þǣm hongiað   hrinde bearwas,
wudu wyrtum fæst   wæter oferhelmað.
Þǣr mæg nihta gehwǣm   nīðwundor sēon,   1365
fȳr on flōde.   Nō þæs frōd leofað
gumena bearna,   þæt þone grund wite.
Ðēah þe hǣðstapa   hundum geswenced,
heorot hornum trum   holtwudu sēce,
feorran geflȳmed,   ǣr hē feorh seleð,   1370
aldor on ōfre,   ǣr hē in wille,
hafelan [beorgan];   nis þæt hēoru stōw!
þonon ȳðgeblond   ūp āstīgeð
won tō wolcnum,   þonne wind styreþ
lāð gewidru,   oð þæt lyft drysmaþ,   1375
roderas rēotað.   Nū is se rǣd gelang
eft æt þē ānum.   Eard gīt ne const,
frēcne stōwe,   ðǣr þū findan miht
sinnigne secg;   sēc gif þū dyrre!
Ic þē þā fæhðe   fēo lēanige,   1380
ealdgestrēonum,   swā ic ǣr dyde,
wund[num] golde,   gyf þū on weg cymest."

XXI

Bēowulf maþelode,   bearn Ecgþēowes:
"Ne sorga, snotor guma!   Sēlre bið ǣghwǣm,

1354 nemdon] nemdod MS   1362 standeð] stanðeð MS   1372 beorgan] *not in* MS
1382 wundnum] wundini *or* wundmi MS

marched the exile's path in the form of a man,
except that he was larger than any other;
in bygone days he was called 'Grendel'
by the local folk. They knew no father, 1355
whether before him had been begotten
any more mysterious spirits. That murky land
they hold, wolf-haunted slopes, windy headlands,
awful fenpaths, where the upland torrents
plunge downward under the dark crags, 1360
the flood underground. It is not far hence
— measured in miles — that the mere stands;
over it hangs a grove hoar-frosted,
a firm-rooted wood looming over the water.
Every night one can see there an awesome wonder, 1365
fire on the water. There lives none so wise
or bold that he can fathom its abyss.
Though the heath-stepper beset by hounds,
the strong-horned hart, might seek the forest,
pursued from afar, he will sooner lose 1370
his life on the shore than save his head
and go in the lake — it is no good place!
The clashing waves climb up from there
dark to the clouds, when the wind drives
the violent storms, until the sky itself droops, 1375
the heavens groan. Now once again all help
depends on you alone. You do not yet know
this fearful place, where you might find
the sinful creature — seek it if you dare!
I will reward you with ancient riches 1380
for that feud, as I did before,
with twisted gold, if you return alive."

XXI

   Beowulf spoke, son of Ecgtheow:
"Sorrow not, wise one! It is always better

þæt hē his frēond wrece,   þonne hē fela murne.   1385
Ūre ǣghwylc sceal   ende gebīdan
worolde līfes;   wyrce sē þe mōte
dōmes ǣr dēaþe;   þæt bið drihtguman
unlifgendum   æfter sēlest.
Ārīs, rīces weard,   uton hraþe fēran,   1390
Grendles māgan   gang scēawigan.
Ic hit þē gehāte: nō hē on helm losaþ,
nē on foldan fæþm,   nē on fyrgenholt,
nē on gyfenes grund,   gā þǣr hē wille!
Ðȳs dōgor þū   geþyld hafa   1395
wēana gehwylces,   swā ic þē wēne tō."
Āhlēop ðā se gomela,   Gode þancode,
mihtigan Drihtne,   þæs se man gespræc.
    Þā wæs Hrōðgāre   hors gebǣted,
wicg wundenfeax.   Wīsa fengel   1400
geatolīc gende;   gumfēþa stōp
lindhæbbendra.   Lāstas wǣron
æfter waldswaþum   wīde gesȳne,
gang ofer grundas,   [þǣr] gegnum fōr
ofer myrcan mōr,   magoþegna bǣr   1405
þone sēlestan   sāwollēasne
þāra þe mid Hrōðgāre   hām eahtode.
Oferēode þā   æþelinga bearn
stēap stānhliðo,   stīge nearwe,
enge ānpaðas,   uncūð gelād,   1410
neowle næssas,   nicorhūsa fela;
hē fēara sum   beforan gengde
wīsra monna   wong scēawian,
oþ þæt hē fǣringa   fyrgenbēamas
ofer hārne stān   hleonian funde,   1415
wynlēasne wudu;   wæter under stōd
drēorig ond gedrēfed.   Denum eallum wæs,
winum Scyldinga   weorce on mōde
tō geþolianne,   ðegne monegum,
oncȳð eorla gehwǣm,   syðþan Æscheres   1420
on þām holmclife   hafelan mētton.

1404 þær] *not in* MS

to avenge one's friend than to mourn overmuch.   1385
Each of us must await the end
of this world's life; let him who can
bring about fame before death — that is best
for the unliving man after he is gone.
Arise, kingdom's guard, let us quickly go   1390
and inspect the path of Grendel's kin.
I promise you this: he[1] will find no protection —
not in the belly of the earth nor the bottom of the sea,
nor the mountain groves — let him go where he will!
For today, you must endure patiently   1395
all your woes, as I expect you will."
The old man leapt up, thanked the Lord,
the mighty God, for that man's speech.
            Then for Hrothgar a horse was bridled
with plaited mane. The wise prince   1400
rode in full array; footsoldiers marched
with shields at the ready. The tracks were seen
far and wide on the forest paths,
a trail through the woods, where she went forth
over the murky moor, bore the young man's   1405
lifeless body, the best of all those
who had held watch over Hrothgar's home.
The son of nobles crossed over
the steep stone cliffs, the constricted climb,
a narrow solitary path, a course unknown,   1410
the towering headlands, home of sea-monsters.
He went before with just a few
wise men to see the way,
until suddenly he saw mountain-trees,
stunted and leaning over gray stone,   1415
a joyless wood; the water went under
turbid and dreary. To all the Danes,
the men of the Scyldings, many a thane,
it was a sore pain at heart to suffer,
a grief to every earl, when on the seacliff   1420
they came upon the head of Æschere.

---

1   The hero does not note carefully enough the gender of Grendel's mother, or else the
    pronoun *he* refers to OE *magan* "kinsman," a masculine noun.

Flōd blōde wēol   — folc tō sǣgon —
hātan heolfre.   Horn stundum song
fūslīc f(yrd)lēoð.   Fēþa eal gesæt;
gesāwon ðā æfter wætere   wyrmcynnes fela,   1425
sellice sǣdracan   sund cunnian,
swylce on næshleoðum   nicras licgean,
ðā on undernmǣl   oft bewitigað
sorhfulne sīð   on seglrāde,
wyrmas ond wildēor.   Hīe on weg hruron   1430
bitere ond gebolgne;   bearhtm ongēaton,
gūðhorn galan.   Sumne Gēata lēod
of flānbogan   fēores getwǣfde,
ȳðgewinnes,   þæt him on aldre stōd
herestrǣl hearda;   hē on holme wæs   1435
sundes þē sǣnra,   ðē hyne swylt fornam.
Hræþe wearð on ȳðum   mid eofersprēotum
heorohōcyhtum   hearde genearwod,
nīða genǣged,   ond on næs togen,
wundorlic wǣgbora;   weras scēawedon   1440
gryrelīcne gist.

                Gyrede hine Bēowulf
eorlgewǣdum,   nalles for ealdre mearn;
scolde herebyrne   hondum gebrōden,
sīd ond searofāh   sund cunnian,
sēo ðe bāncofan   beorgan cūþe,   1445
þæt him hildegrāp   hreþre ne mihte,
eorres inwitfeng   aldre gesceþðan;
ac se hwīta helm   hafelan werede,
sē þe meregrundas   mengan scolde,
sēcan sundgebland   since geweorðad,   1450
befongen frēawrāsnum,   swā hine fyrndagum
worhte wǣpna smið,   wundrum tēode,
besette swīnlīcum,   þæt hine syðþan nō
brond nē beadomēcas   bītan ne meahton.
Næs þæt þonne mǣtost   mægenfultuma,   1455
þæt him on ðearfe lāh   ðyle Hrōðgþares;
wæs þǣm hæftmēce   Hrunting nama;
þæt wæs ān foran   ealdgestrēona;

1424 fyrdleoð] f(. . .)leoð MS

The flood boiled with blood — the folk gazed on —
and hot gore. At times a horn sang
its eager war-song. The footsoldiers sat down.
They saw in the water many kinds of serpents,   1425
strange sea-creatures testing the currents,
and on the sloping shores lay such monsters
as often attend in early morning
a sorrowful journey on the sail-road,
dragons and wild beasts. They rushed away   1430
bitter, enraged; they heard the bright noise,
the sound of the battle-horn. A Geatish bowman
cut short the life of one of those swimmers
with a bow and arrow, so that in his body stood
the hard war-shaft; he was a slower swimmer   1435
on the waves, when death took him away.
At once in the water he was assailed
with the barbed hooks of boar-pikes,
violently attacked and dragged ashore,
the strange wave-roamer; the men inspected   1440
this grisly visitor.
                 Beowulf geared up
in his warrior's clothing, cared not for his life.
The broad war-shirt, woven by hand,
cunningly made, had to test the mere —
it knew well how to protect his bone-house   1445
so that a battle-grip might not hurt his breast
nor an angry malicious clutch touch his life.
The shining helmet protected his head,
set to stir up the sea's depths,
seek that troubled water, decorated with treasure,   1450
encircled with a splendid band, as a weapon-smith
in days of old had crafted it with wonders,
set boar-images, so that afterwards
no blade or battle-sword might ever bite it.
Not the smallest of powerful supports was that   1455
which Hrothgar's spokesman lent him at need;
that hilted sword was named Hrunting,
unique among ancient treasures —

ecg wæs īren,   ātertānum fāh,
āhyrded heaþoswāte;   nǣfre hit æt hilde ne swāc   1460
manna ǣngum   þāra þe hit mid mundum bewand,
sē ðe gryresīðas   gegān dorste,
folcstede fāra;   næs þæt forma sīð
þæt hit ellenweorc   æfnan scolde.
Hūru ne gemunde   mago Ecglāfes   1465
eafoþes cræftig,   þæt hē ǣr gespræc
wīne druncen,   þā hē þæs wǣpnes onlāh
sēlran sweordfrecan;   selfa ne dorste
under ȳða gewin   aldre genēþan,
drihtscype drēogan;   þǣr hē dōme forlēas,   1470
ellenmǣrðum.   Ne wæs þǣm ōðrum swā,
syðþan hē hine tō gūðe   gegyred hæfde.

XXII

Bēowulf maþelode,   bearn Ecgþēowes:
"Geþenc nū, se mǣra   maga Healfdenes,
snottra fengel,   nū ic eom sīðes fūs,   1475
goldwine gumena,   hwæt wit geō sprǣcon,
gif ic æt þearfe   þīnre scolde
aldre linnan,   þæt ðū mē ā wǣre
forðgewitenum   on fæder stǣle.
Wes þū mundbora   mīnum magoþegnum,   1480
hondgesellum,   gif mec hild nime;
swylce þū ðā mādmas,   þē þū mē sealdest,
Hrōðgār lēofa,   Higelāce onsend.
Mæg þonne on þǣm golde ongitan   Gēata dryhten,
gesēon sunu Hrǣdles,   þonne hē on þæt sinc starað,   1485
þæt ic gumcystum   gōdne funde
bēaga bryttan,   brēac þonne mōste.
Ond þū [Un]ferð lǣt   ealde lāfe,
wrǣtlīc wǣgsweord   wīdcūðne man
heardecg habban;   ic mē mid Hruntinge   1490
dōm gewyrce,   oþðe mec dēað nimeð."

1488 Unferð] hunferð MS

its edge was iron, etched with poison stripes,
hardened with the blood of war; it had never failed 1460
any man who grasped it in his hands in battle,
who dared to undertake a dreadful journey
into the very home of the foe — it was not the first time
that it had to perform a work of high courage.
Truly, the son of Ecglaf, crafty in strength, 1465
did not remember what he had said before,
drunk with wine, when he lent that weapon
to a better swordsman; he himself did not dare
to risk his life under the rushing waves,
perform a lordly act; for that he lost honor, 1470
his fame for courage. Not so with the other,
when he had geared himself up for battle.

XXII

Beowulf spoke, son of Ecgtheow:
"Consider now, famous kinsman of Healfdene,
wise prince, now that I am eager to depart, 1475
gold-friend to men, what we spoke of before:
if ever in your service I should
lose my life, that you would always be
like a father to me when I have gone forth.
Be a protector to my band of men, 1480
my boon-companions, if battle should take me,
beloved Hrothgar, and send on to Hygelac
the gifts of treasure which you have given me.
The lord of the Geats will understand by that gold,
the son of Hrethel will see by that treasure, 1485
that I found a ring-giver who was good
in ancient customs, and while I could, enjoyed it.
And let Unferth have that ancient heirloom,
that well-known man have my wave-patterned sword,
hard-edged, splendid; with Hrunting I shall 1490
win honor and fame, or death will take me!"

Æfter þæm wordum   Weder-Gēata lēod
efste mid elne,   nalas andsware
bīdan wolde;   brimwylm onfēng
hilderince.   Ðā wæs hwīl dæges,   1495
ær hē þone grundwong   ongytan mehte.
Sōna þæt onfunde   sē ðe flōda begong
heorogīfre behēold   hund missēra,
grim ond grǣdig,   þæt þǣr gumena sum
ælwihta eard   ufan cunnode.   1500
Grāp þā tōgēanes,   gūðrinc gefēng
atolan clommum;   nō þȳ ær in gescōd
hālan līce;   hring ūtan ymbbearh,
þæt hēo þone fyrdhom   ðurhfōn ne mihte,
locene leoðosyrcan   lāþan fingrum.   1505
Bær þā sēo brimwyl[f],   þā hēo tō botme cōm,
hringa þengel   tō hofe sīnum,
swā hē ne mihte   — nō hē þǣ[s] mōdig wæs —
wǣpna gewealdan,   ac hine wundra þæs fela
swe[n]cte on sunde,   sǣdēor monig   1510
hildetūxum   heresyrcan bræc,
ēhton āglǣcan.
          Ðā se eorl ongeat,
þæt hē [in] nīðsele   nāthwylcum wæs,
ðǣr him nǣnig wæter   wihte ne sceþede,
nē him for hrōfsele   hrīnan ne mehte   1515
fǣrgripe flōdes;   fȳrlēoht geseah,
blācne lēoman   beorhte scīnan.
Ongeat þā se gōda   grundwyrgenne,
merewīf mihtig;   mægenrǣs forgeaf
hildebille,   ho[n]d swen[g] ne oftēah,   1520
þæt hire on hafelan   hringmæl āgōl
grǣdig gūðlēoð.   Ðā se gist onfand,
þæt se beadolēoma   bītan nolde,
aldre sceþðan,   ac sēo ecg geswāc
ðēodne æt þearfe;   ðolode ær fela   1525
hondgemōta,   helm oft gescær,

1506 brimwylf] brym wyl MS   1508 þæs] þæm MS   1510 swencte] swecte MS
1513 in] *not in* MS   1520 hond sweng] hord swenge MS

After these words the Wether-Geat man
hastened boldly, by no means wished to
stay for an answer; the surging sea received
the brave soldier. It was the space of a day[1]   1495
before he could perceive the bottom.
Right away she who held that expanse of water,
bloodthirsty and fierce, for a hundred half-years,
grim and greedy, perceived that some man
was exploring from above that alien land.   1500
She snatched at him, seized the warrior
in her savage clutches, but none the sooner
injured his sound body — the ring-mail encircled him,
so that she could not pierce that war-dress,
the locked coat of mail, with her hostile claws.   1505
Then that she-wolf of the sea swam to the bottom,
and bore the prince of rings into her abode,
so that he might not — no matter how strong —
wield his weapons, but so many wonders
set upon him in the water, many a sea-beast   1510
with battle-tusks tearing at his war-shirt,
monsters pursuing him.[2]
            Then the earl perceived
that he was in some sort of battle-hall
where no water could harm him in any way,
and, for the hall's roof, he could not be reached   1515
by the flood's sudden rush — he saw a fire-light,
a glowing blaze shining brightly.
Then the worthy man saw that water-witch,
a great mere-wife; he gave a mighty blow
with his battle-sword — he did not temper that stroke —   1520
so that the ring-etched blade rang out on her head
a greedy battle-song. The guest discovered then
that the battle-flame would not bite,
or wound her fatally — but the edge failed
the man in his need; it had endured many   1525
hand-to-hand meetings, often sheared through helmets,

---

1   Or "it was daylight."
2   Or "attacked their adversary." The Old English word *æglæcan* may refer here to
   Beowulf or the sea-monsters.

fǣges fyrdhrægl;   ðā wæs forma sīð
dēorum mādme,   þæt his dōm ālæg.
  Eft wæs anrǣd,   nalas elnes læt,
mǣrða gemyndig   mǣg Hȳlāces: 1530
wearp ðā wunde[n]mǣl   wrǣttum gebunden
yrre ōretta,   þæt hit on eorðan læg,
stīð ond stȳlecg;   strenge getruwode,
mundgripe mægenes.   Swā sceal man dōn,
þonne hē æt gūðe   gegān þenceð   1535
longsumne lof;   nā ymb his līf cearað.
Gefēng þā be eaxle   — nalas for fǣhðe mearn —
Gūð-Gēata lēod   Grendles mōdor;
brægd þā beadwe heard,   þā hē gebolgen wæs,
feorhgenīðlan,   þæt hēo on flet gebēah.   1540
Hēo him eft hraþe   handlēan forgeald
grimman grāpum   ond him tōgēanes fēng;
oferwearp þā wērigmōd   wigena strengest,
fēþecempa,   þæt hē on fylle wearð.
Ofsæt þā þone selegyst,   ond hyre seaxe getēah   1545
brād [ond] brūnecg;   wolde hire bearn wrecan,
āngan eaferan.   Him on eaxle læg
brēostnet brōden;   þæt gebearh fēore,
wið ord ond wið ecge   ingang forstōd.
Hæfde ðā forsīðod   sunu Ecgþēowes   1550
under gynne grund,   Gēata cempa,
nemne him heaðobyrne   helpe gefremede,
herenet hearde,   ond hālig God
gewēold wīgsigor;   wītig Drihten,
rodera Rǣdend   hit on ryht gescēd   1555
ȳðelīce,   syþðan hē eft āstōd.

XXIII

  Geseah ðā on searwum   sigeēadig bil,
ealdsweord eotenisc   ecgum þȳhtig,
wigena weorðmynd;   þæt [wæs] wǣpna cyst,
būton hit wæs māre   ðonne ǣnig mon ōðer   1560

1531 wundenmæl] wundel mæl MS   1546 ond] *not in* MS   1559 wæs] *not in* MS

fated war-garments. It was the first time
that the fame of that precious treasure had failed.
     Again he was stalwart, not slow of zeal,
mindful of glory, that kinsman of Hygelac —   1530
the angry challenger threw away that etched blade,
wrapped and ornamented, so that it lay on the earth,
strong, steel-edged. He trusted his strength,
the might of his handgrip — as a man should do
if by his warfare he thinks to win   1535
long-lasting praise: he cares nothing for his life.
The man of the War-Geats grabbed by the shoulder
Grendel's mother — he had no regret for that feud;
battle-hardened, enraged, he swung her around,
his deadly foe, so she fell to the ground.   1540
Quickly she gave him requital for that
with a grim grasp, and grappled him to her —
weary, he stumbled, strongest of warriors,
of foot-soldiers, and took a fall.
She set upon her hall-guest[1] and drew her knife,   1545
broad, bright-edged; she would avenge her boy,
her only offspring. On his shoulders lay
the linked corselet; it defended his life,
prevented the entrance of point and blade.
There the son of Ecgtheow would have ended his life   1550
under the wide ground, the Geatish champion,
had not his armored shirt offered him help,
the hard battle-net, and holy God
brought about war-victory — the wise Lord,
Ruler of the heavens, decided it rightly,   1555
easily, once he stood up again.

XXIII

     He saw among the armor a victorious blade,
ancient giant-sword strong in its edges,
worthy in battles; it was the best of weapons,
except that it was greater than any other man   1560

---

1   Some translations read "sat down upon"; the meaning of OE *ofsæt* is disputed.

tō beadulāce   ætberan meahte,
gōd ond geatolīc,   gīganta geweorc.
Hē gefēng þā fetelhilt,   freca Scyldinga
hrēoh ond heorogrim,   hringmǣl gebrægd
aldres orwēna,   yrringa slōh,   1565
þæt hire wið halse   heard grāpode,
bānhringas bræc;   bil eal ðurhwōd
fǣgne flǣschoman;   hēo on flet gecrong,
sweord wæs swātig,   secg weorce gefeh.
    Līxte se lēoma,   lēoht inne stōd,   1570
efne swā of hefene   hādre scīneð
rodores candel.   Hē æfter recede wlāt;
hwearf þā be wealle,   wǣpen hafenade
heard be hiltum   Higelāces ðegn
yrre ond anrǣd —   næs sēo ecg fracod   1575
hilderince,   ac hē hraþe wolde
Grendle forgyldan   gūðrǣsa fela
ðāra þe hē geworhte   tō West-Denum
oftor micle   ðonne on ǣnne sīð,
þonne hē Hrōðgāres   heorðgenēatas   1580
slōh on sweofote,   slǣpende frǣt
folces Denigea   fȳftȳne men,
ond ōðer swylc   ūt offerede,
lāðlicu lāc.   Hē him þæs lēan forgeald,
rēþe cempa,   tō ðæs þe hē on ræste geseah   1585
gūðwērigne   Grendel licgan,
aldorlēasne,   swā him ǣr gescōd
hild æt Heorote.   Hrā wīde sprong,
syþðan hē æfter dēaðe   drepe þrōwade,
heorosweng heardne,   ond hine þā hēafde becearf.   1590
    Sōna þæt gesāwon   snottre ceorlas,
þā ðe mid Hrōðgāre   on holm wliton,
þæt wæs ȳðgeblond   eal gemenged,
brim blōde fāh.   Blondenfeaxe,
gomele ymb gōdne   ongeador sprǣcon,   1595
þæt hig þæs æðelinges   eft ne wēndon,
þæt hē sigehrēðig   sēcean cōme

might even bear into the play of battle,
good, adorned, the work of giants.[1]
The Scyldings' champion seized its linked hilt,
fierce and ferocious, drew the ring-marked sword
despairing of his life, struck in fury   1565
so that it caught her hard in the neck,
broke her bone-rings; the blade cut through
the doomed flesh — she fell to the floor,
the sword was bloody, the soldier rejoiced.

      The flames gleamed, a light glowed within   1570
even as from heaven the firmament's candle
shines clearly. He looked around the chamber,
passed by the wall, hefted the weapon
hard by its hilt, that thane of Hygelac,
angry and resolute — nor was the edge useless   1575
to that warrior, but he quickly wished
to pay back Grendel for the many battle-storms
which he had wrought on the West-Danes
much more often than on one occasion,
when Hrothgar's hall-companions   1580
he slew in their beds, devoured sleeping
fifteen men of the Danish folk,
and made off with as many more,
a loathsome booty. He paid him back for that,
the fierce champion, for on a couch he saw   1585
Grendel lying lifeless,
battle-weary from the wound he received
in the combat at Heorot. His corpse burst open
when he was dealt a blow after death,
a hard sword-stroke, and his head chopped off.   1590
      Soon the wise troops saw it,
those who kept watch on the water with Hrothgar —
all turbid were the waves, and troubled,
the sea stained with blood. The graybearded
elders spoke together about the good one,   1595
said they did not expect that nobleman
would return, triumphant, to seek

---

1   Old, highly praised weapons are often called "the work of giants"—whether this is
    meant to connect the sword to the giants "who fought against God" is not clear.

mǣrne þēoden;   þā ðæs monige gewearþ,
þæt hine sēo brimwylf   ābr[o]ten hæfde.
Ðā cōm nōn dæges.   Næs ofgēafon   1600
hwate Scyldingas;   gewāt him hām þonon
goldwine gumena.   Gistas s[æt]an
mōdes sēoce   ond on mere staredon;
wīston ond ne wēndon,   þæt hīe heora winedrihten
selfne gesāwon.

           Þā þæt sweord ongan   1605
æfter heaþoswāte   hildegicelum,
wīgbil wanian;   þæt wæs wundra sum,
þæt hit eal gemealt   īse gelīcost,
ðonne forstes bend   Fæder onlǣteð,
onwindeð wælrāpas,   sē geweald hafað   1610
sǣla ond mǣla;   þæt is sōð Metod.
Ne nōm hē in þǣm wīcum,   Weder-Gēata lēod,
māðmǣhta mā,   þēh hē þǣr monige geseah,
būton þone hafelan   ond þā hilt somod
since fāge;   sweord ǣr gemealt,   1615
forbarn brōdenmǣl;   wæs þæt blōd tō þæs hāt,
ættren ellorgǣst,   sē þǣr inne swealt.
Sōna wæs on sunde   sē þe ǣr æt sæcce gebād
wīghryre wrāðra,   wæter ūp þurhdēaf;
wǣron ȳðgebland   eal gefǣlsod,   1620
ēacne eardas,   þā se ellorgāst
oflēt līfdagas   ond þās lǣnan gesceaft.

    Cōm þā tō lande   lidmanna helm
swīðmōd swymman;   sǣlāce gefeah,
mægenbyrþenne   þāra þe hē him mid hæfde.   1625
Ēodon him þā tōgēanes,   Gode þancodon,
ðrȳðlīc þegna hēap,   þēodnes gefēgon,
þæs þe hī hyne gesundne   gesēon mōston.
Ðā wæs of þǣm hrōran   helm ond byrne
lungre ālȳsed.   Lagu drūsade,   1630
wæter under wolcnum,   wældrēore fāg.
Fērdon forð þonon   fēþelāstum
ferhþum fægne,   foldweg mǣton,
cūþe strǣte;   cyningbalde men

1599 abroten] abreoten MS   1602 sætan] secan MS

the mighty prince; to many it seemed
that the sea-wolf had destroyed him.
The ninth hour came; the noble Scyldings 1600
abandoned the headland, and home went
the gold-friend of men. The guests[1] sat
sick at heart, and stared into the mere;
they wished, but did not hope, that they would
see their lord himself.
            Then the sword began, 1605
that blade, to dissolve away in battle-icicles
from the war-blood; it was a great wonder
that it melted entirely, just like ice
when the Father loosens the frost's fetters,
unwraps the water's bonds — He wields power 1610
over times and seasons; that is the true Maker.
The man of the Geats took no more precious treasures
from that place — though he saw many there —
than the head, and the hilt as well,
bright with gems; the blade had melted, 1615
the ornamented sword burned up; so hot was the blood
of the poisonous alien spirit who died in there.
Soon he was swimming who had survived in battle
the downfall of his enemies, dove up through the water;
the sea-currents were entirely cleansed, 1620
the spacious regions, when that alien spirit
gave up life-days and this loaned world.
        The defender of seafarers came to land,
swam stout-hearted; he rejoiced in his sea-booty,
the great burden which he brought with him. 1625
That splendid troop of thanes went towards him,
thanked God, rejoiced in their prince,
that they might see him safe and sound.
Then from that bold man helmet and byrnie
were quickly unstrapped. Under the clouds 1630
the mere stewed, stained with gore.
They went forth, followed the trail,
rejoicing in their hearts; they marched along the road,
the familiar path; proud as kings

---

1   I.e., the Geats who had come to Heorot with Beowulf.

from þæm holmclife   hafelan bǣron   1635
earfoðlīce   heora ǣghwæþrum
felamōdigra;   fēower scoldon
on þæm wælstenge   weorcum geferian
tō þǣm goldsele   Grendles hēafod,
oþ ðæt semninga   tō sele cōmon   1640
frome fyrdhwate   fēowertȳne
Gēata gongan;   gumdryhten mid
mōdig on gemonge   meodowongas træd.
Ðā cōm in gan   ealdor ðegna,
dǣdcēne mon   dōme gewurþad,   1645
hæle hildedēor,   Hrōðgār grētan.
Þā wæs be feaxe   on flet boren
Grendles hēafod,   þǣr guman druncon,
egeslīc for eorlum   ond þǣre idese mid,
wlitesēon wrǣtlīc;   weras on sāwon.   1650

XXIV

Bēowulf maþelode,   bearn Ecgþēowes:
"Hwæt, wē þē þās sǣlāc,   sunu Healfdenes,
lēod Scyldinga,   lustum brōhton
tīres tō tācne,   þē þū hēr tō lōcast.
Ic þæt unsōfte   ealdre gedīgde,   1655
wigge under wætere,   weorc genēþde
earfoðlīce;   ætrihte wæs
gūð getwǣfed,   nymðe mec God scylde.
Ne meahte ic æt hilde   mid Hruntinge
wiht gewyrcan,   þēah þæt wǣpen duge;   1660
ac mē geūðe   ylda Waldend,
þæt ic on wāge geseah   wlitig hangian
ealdsweord ēacen   — oftost wīsode
winigea lēasum —   þæt ic ðȳ wǣpne gebrǣd.
Ofslōh ðā æt þǣre sæcce,   þā mē sǣl āgeald,   1665
hūses hyrdas.   Þā þæt hildebil
forbarn brogdenmǣl,   swā þæt blōd gesprang,
hātost heaþoswāta.   Ic þæt hilt þanan
fēondum ætferede;   fyrendǣda wræc,
dēaðcwealm Denigea,   swā hit gedēfe wæs.   1670

they carried the head from the sea-cliff   1635
with great trouble, even for two pairs
of stout-hearted men; four of them had to
bear, with some strain, on a battle-pole
Grendel's head to the gold-hall,
until presently fourteen proud   1640
and battle-hardy Geats came to the hall,
warriors marching; the lord of those men,
mighty in the throng, trod the meadhall-plain.
Then the ruler of thanes entered there,
daring in actions, honored in fame,   1645
battle-brave hero, to greet Hrothgar.
Then, where men were drinking, they dragged by its hair
Grendel's head across the hall-floor,
a grisly spectacle for the men and the queen.
Everyone stared at that amazing sight.   1650

XXIV

Beowulf spoke, son of Ecgtheow:
"Look! son of Healfdene, prince of the Scyldings,
we have brought you gladly these gifts from the sea
which you gaze on here, a token of glory.
Not easily did I escape with my life   1655
that undersea battle, did my brave deed
with difficulty — indeed, the battle would have been
over at once, if God had not guarded me.
Nor could I achieve anything at that battle
with Hrunting, though that weapon is good;   1660
but the Ruler of Men granted to me
that I might see on the wall a gigantic old sword,
hanging glittering — He has always guided
the friendless one — so I drew that weapon.
In that conflict, when I had the chance, I slew   1665
the shepherds of that house. Then that battle-sword
burned up with its ornaments, as the blood shot out,
hot sweat of battle. I have brought the hilt
back from the enemy; I avenged the old deeds,
the slaughter of Danes, as seemed only right.   1670

Ic hit þē þonne gehāte,   þæt þū on Heorote mōst
sorhlēas swefan   mid þīnra secga gedryht,
ond þegna gehwylc   þīnra lēoda,
duguðe ond iogoþe,   þæt þū him ondrǣdan ne þearft,
þēoden Scyldinga,   on þā healfe,   1675
aldorbealu eorlum,   swā þū ǣr dydest."
Ðā wæs gylden hilt   gamelum rince,
hārum hildfruman   on hand gyfen,
enta ǣrgeweorc;   hit on ǣht gehwearf
æfter dēofla hryre   Denigea frean,   1680
wundorsmiþa geweorc;   ond þā þās worold ofgeaf
gromheort guma,   Godes andsaca,
morðres scyldig,   ond his mōdor ēac;
on geweald gehwearf   woroldcyninga
ðǣm sēlestan   be sǣm twēonum   1685
ðāra þe on Scedenigge   sceattas dǣlde.
    Hrōðgār maðelode —   hylt scēawode,
ealde lāfe,   on ðǣm wæs ōr writen
fyrngewinnes,   syðþan flōd ofslōh,
gifen gēotende   gīganta cyn,   1690
frēcne gefērdon;   þæt wæs fremde þēod
ēcean Dryhtne;   him þæs endelēan
þurh wæteres wylm   Waldend sealde.
Swā wæs on ðǣm scennum   scīran goldes
þurh rūnstafas   rihte gemearcod,   1695
geseted ond gesǣd,   hwām þæt sweord geworht,
īrena cyst   ǣrest wǣre,
wreoþenhilt ond wyrmfāh.   Ðā se wīsa spræc
sunu Healfdenes;   swīgedon ealle:
"Þæt, lā, mæg secgan   sē þe sōð ond riht   1700
fremeð on folce,   feor eal gemon,
eald eþelweard,   þæt ðes eorl wǣre
geboren betera!   Blǣd is ārǣred
geond wīdwegas,   wine mīn Bēowulf,
ðīn ofer þēoda gehwylce.   Eal þū hit geþyldum healdest,   1705
mægen mid mōdes snyttrum.   Ic þē sceal mīne gelǣstan
frēode, swā wit furðum sprǣcon.   Ðū scealt tō frōfre weorþan

Now you have my word that you may in Heorot
sleep without care with your company of men,
and every thane, young and old,
in your nation; you need fear nothing,
prince of the Scyldings, from that side,   1675
no deadly manslaughters, as you did before."
        Then the golden hilt was placed in the hand
of the gray-haired war-chief, wise old leader,
that old work of giants; it came to the keeping
of the Danish lord after the fall of demons,   1680
a work of wonder-smiths; and when that evil-hearted man,
God's adversary, gave up the world,
guilty of murders — and his mother too —
it passed to the possession of the best
of world-kings between the two seas,   1685
of all those that dealt out treasures in Danish lands.
        Hrothgar spoke — he studied the hilt
of the old heirloom, where was written[1] the origin
of ancient strife, when the flood slew,
rushing seas, the race of giants —   1690
they suffered awfully. That was a people alien
to the eternal Lord; a last reward
the Ruler gave them through the raging waters.
Also, on the sword-guard of bright gold
was rightly marked in rune-letters,   1695
set down and said for whom that sword,
best of irons, had first been made,
with scrollery and serpentine patterns. Then spoke
the wise son of Healfdene — all fell silent:
        "One may, indeed, say, if he acts in truth   1700
and right for the people, remembers all,
old guardian of his homeland, that this earl was
born a better man! Beowulf my friend,
your glory is exalted throughout the world,
over every people; you hold it all with patient care,   1705
and temper strength with wisdom. To you I shall fulfill
our friendship, as we have said. You shall become a comfort

---

1   Or "carved." It is not clear whether the scene is visual or textual, depicted or written
    in (presumably runic) characters.

eal langtwidig   lēodum þīnum,
hæleðum tō helpe.

                 Ne wearð Heremōd swā
eaforum Ecgwelan,   Ār-Scyldingum;   1710
ne gewēox hē him tō willan,   ac tō wælfealle
ond tō dēaðcwalum   Deniga lēodum;
brēat bolgenmōd   bēodgenēatas,
eaxlgesteallan,   oþ þæt hē āna hwearf,
mǣre þēoden   mondrēamum from.   1715
Ðēah þe hine mihtig God   mægenes wynnum,
eafeþum stēpte,   ofer ealle men
forð gefremede,   hwæþere him on ferhþe grēow
brēosthord blōdrēow;   nallas bēagas geaf
Denum æfter dōme;   drēamlēas gebād,   1720
þæt hē þæs gewinnes   weorc þrōwade,
lēodbealo longsum.   Ðū þē lǣr be þon,
gumcyste ongit!   Ic þis gid be þē
āwræc wintrum frōd.

                 Wundor is tō secganne,
hū mihtig God   manna cynne   1725
þurh sīdne sefan   snyttru bryttaþ,
eard ond eorlscipe;   hē āh ealra geweald.
Hwīlum hē on lufan   lǣteð hworfan
monnes mōdgeþonc   mǣran cynnes,
seleð him on ēþle   eorþan wynne   1730
tō healdanne   hlēoburh wera,
gedēð him swā gewealdene   worolde dǣlas,
sīde rīce,   þæt hē his selfa ne mæg
his unsnyttrum   ende geþencean.
Wunað hē on wiste;   nō hine wiht dweleð   1735
ādl nē yldo,   nē him inwitsorh
on sefa[n] sweorceð,   nē gesacu ōhwǣr
ecghete ēoweð,   ac him eal worold
wendeð on willan;   hē þæt wyrse ne con,

1737 sefan] sefað MS

everlasting to your own people,
and a help to heroes.

                    Not so was Heremod
to the sons of Ecgwala, the Honor-Scyldings;   1710
he grew not for their delight, but for their destruction
and the murder of Danish men.
Enraged, he cut down his table-companions,
comrades-in-arms, until he turned away alone
from the pleasures of men, that famous prince;   1715
though mighty God exalted him in the joys
of strength and force, advanced him far
over all men, yet in his heart he nursed
a blood-ravenous breast-hoard. No rings did he give
to the Danes for their honor; he endured, joyless,   1720
to suffer the pains of that strife,
a long-lasting harm to his people. Learn from him,
understand virtue! For your sake I am telling this,
in the wisdom of my winters.

                     It is a wonder to say
how mighty God in His great spirit   1725
allots wisdom, land and lordship
to mankind; He has control of everything.
At times He permits the thoughts of a man
in a mighty race to move in delights,
gives him to hold in his homeland   1730
the sweet joys of earth, a stronghold of men,
grants him such power over his portion of the world,
a great kingdom, that he himself cannot
imagine an end to it, in his folly.
He dwells in plenty; in no way plague him   1735
illness or old age, nor do evil thoughts
darken his spirit, nor any strife
or sword-hate shows itself, but all the world
turns to his will; he knows nothing worse.

oð þæt him on innan   oferhygda dæl   1740
weaxeð ond wrīdað;   þonne se weard swefeð,
sāwele hyrde;   bið se slǣp tō fæst,
bisgum gebunden,   bona swīðe nēah,
sē þe of flānbogan   fyrenum scēoteð.
   Þonne bið on hreþre   under helm drepen   1745
biteran strǣle   — him bebeorgan ne con —
wōm wundorbebodum   wergan gāstes;
þinceð him tō lȳtel,   þæt hē lange hēold,
gȳtsað gromhȳdig,   nallas on gylp seleð
fǣ[tt]e bēagas,   ond hē þā forðgesceaft   1750
forgyteð ond forgȳmeð,   þæs þe him ǣr God sealde,
wuldres Waldend,   weorðmynda dæl.
Hit on endestæf   eft gelimpeð,
þæt se līchoma   lǣne gedrēoseð,
fǣge gefealleð;   fēhð ōþer tō,   1755
sē þe unmurnlīce   mādmas dǣleþ,
eorles ǣrgestrēon,   egesan ne gȳmeð.
Bebeorh þē ðone bealonīð,   Bēowulf lēofa,
secg betsta,   ond þē þæt sēlre gecēos,
ēce rǣdas;   oferhȳda ne gȳm,   1760
mǣre cempa!   Nū is þīnes mægnes blǣd
āne hwīle;   eft sōna bið,
þæt þec ādl oððe ecg   eafoþes getwǣfeð,
oððe fȳres feng,   oððe flōdes wylm,
oððe gripe mēces,   oððe gāres fliht,   1765
oððe atol yldo;   oððe ēagena bearhtm
forsiteð ond forsworceð;   semninga bið,
þæt ðec, dryhtguma,   dēað oferswȳðeð.
   Swā ic Hring-Dena   hund missēra
wēold under wolcnum   ond hig wigge belēac   1770
manigum mǣgþa   geond þysne middangeard,
æscum ond ecgum,   þæt ic mē ǣnigne
under swegles begong   gesacan ne tealde.
Hwæt, mē þæs on ēþle   edwend[e]n cwōm,

1750 fætte] fædde MS   1774 edwenden] ed wendan MS

XXV

At last his portion of pride within him   1740
grows and flourishes, while the guardian sleeps,
the soul's shepherd — that sleep is too sound,
bound with cares, the slayer too close
who, sinful and wicked, shoots from his bow.[1]
Then he is struck in his heart, under his helmet   1745
with a bitter dart — he knows no defense —
the strange, dark demands of evil spirits;
what he has long held seems too little,
angry and greedy, he gives no golden rings
for vaunting boasts, and his final destiny   1750
he neglects and forgets, since God, Ruler of glories,
has given him a portion of honors.
In the end it finally comes about
that the loaned life-dwelling starts to decay
and falls, fated to die; another follows him   1755
who doles out his riches without regret,
the earl's ancient treasure; he heeds no terror.
Defend yourself from wickedness, dear Beowulf,
best of men, and choose better,
eternal counsel; care not for pride,   1760
great champion! The glory of your might
is but a little while; too soon it will be
that sickness or the sword will shatter your strength,
of the grip of fire, or the surging flood,
or the cut of a sword, or the flight of a spear,   1765
or terrible old age — or the light of your eyes
will fail and flicker out; in one fell swoop
death, o warrior, will overwhelm you.
            Thus, a hundred half-years I held the Ring-Danes
under the skies, and kept them safe from war   1770
from many tribes throughout this middle-earth,
from spears and swords, so that I considered none
under the expanse of heaven my enemy.
Look! Turnabout came in my own homeland,

---

1 The slayer is sin or vice; the soul's guardian is reason, conscience or prudence.

gyrn æfter gomene,   seoþðan Grendel wearð,   1775
ealdgewinna,   ingenga mīn;
ic þǣre sōcne   singāles wæg
mōdceare micle,   þæs sig Metode þanc,
ēcean Dryhtne,   þæs ðe ic on aldre gebād,
þæt ic on þone hafelan   heorodrēorigne   1780
ofer eald gewin   ēagum starige!
Gā nū tō setle,   symbelwynne drēoh
wīggeweorþad;   unc sceal worn fela
māþma gemǣnra,   siþðan morgen bið."
    Gēat wæs glædmōd,   gēong sōna tō,   1785
setles nēosan,   swā se snottra heht.
Þā wæs eft swā ǣr   ellenrōfum,
fletsittendum   fægere gereorded
nīowan stefne.   Nihthelm geswearc
deorc ofer dryhtgumum.   Duguð eal ārās;   1790
wolde blondenfeax   beddes nēosan,
gamela Scylding.   Gēat unigmetes wēl,
rōfne randwigan   restan lyste;
sōna him seleþegn   sīðes wērgum,
feorrancundum   forð wīsade,   1795
sē for andrysnum   ealle beweote[d]e
þegnes þearfe,   swylce þȳ dōgore
heaþolīðende   habban scoldon.
Reste hine þā rūmheort;   reced hlīuade
gēap ond goldfāh;   gæst inne swæf,   1800
oþ þæt hrefn blaca   heofones wynne
blīðheort bodode.   Ðā cōm beorht [lēoma]
[ofer sceadwa] scacan;   scaþan ōnetton,
wǣron æþelingas   eft tō lēodum
fūse tō faren[n]e;   wolde feor þanon   1805
cuma collenferhð   cēoles nēosan.
Heht þā se hearda   Hrunting beran
sunu Ecglāfes,   heht his sweord niman,
lēoflīc īren;   sægde him þæs lēanes þanc,

1796 beweotede] be weotene MS   1802-03 leoma / ofer sceadwa] *no gap in* MS
1805 farenne] farene ne MS

grief after gladness, when Grendel became   1775
my invader, ancient adversary;
for that persecution I bore perpetually
the greatest heart-cares. Thanks be to the Creator,
eternal Lord, that I have lived long enough
to see that head, stained with blood,   1780
with my own eyes, after all this strife!
Go to your seat, enjoy the feast,
honored in battle; between us shall be shared
a great many treasures, when morning comes."
    Glad-hearted, the Geat went at once   1785
to take his seat, as the wise one told him.
Then again as before, a feast was prepared
for the brave ones who occupied the hall
on this new occasion. The dark helm of night
overshadowed the troop. The soldiers arose;   1790
the gray-haired ruler was ready for bed,
the aged Scylding. Immeasurably well
did rest please the Geat, proud shield-warrior;
at once a chamberlain led him forth,
weary from his adventure, come from afar,   1795
he who attended to all the needs
of that thane, for courtesy, as in those days
all heroes and warriors used to have.
    The great-hearted one rested; the hall towered
vaulted and gold-adorned; the guest slept within   1800
until the black[1] raven, blithe-hearted, announced
the joy of heaven. Then light came hurrying
bright over shadows; the soldiers hastened,
the noblemen were eager to travel
back to their people; the bold-spirited visitor   1805
wished to seek his far-off ship.
    The hardy one ordered Hrunting to be borne
to the son of Ecglaf,[2] bid him take his sword,
lordly iron; he thanked him for the loan,

---

1 Either OE *blac* "shining" or *blæc* "black"; the translation prefers the irony of the
    image of the black raven, not otherwise known as a harbinger of joy, announcing the
    surprising good news of a dawn without slaughter.

2 I.e., Unferth.

cwæð hē þone gūðwine   gōdne tealde,   1810
wīgcræftigne,   nales wordum lōg
mēces ecge;   þæt wæs mōdig secg.
Ond þā siðfrome,   searwum gearwe
wīgend wǣron,   ēode weorð Denum
æþeling tō yppan,   þǣr se ōþer wæs,   1815
h[æ]le hildedēor   Hrōðgār grētte.

XXVI

Bēowulf maþelode,   bearn Ecgþēowes:
"Nū wē sǣlīðend   secgan wyllað
feorran cumene,   þæt wē fundiaþ
Higelāc sēcan.   Wǣron hēr tela,   1820
willum bewenede;   þū ūs wēl dohtest.
Gif ic þonne on eorþan   ōwihte mæg
þīnre mōdlufan   māran tilian,
gumena dryhten,   ðonne ic gȳt dyde,
gūðgeweorca,   ic bēo gearo sōna.   1825
Gif ic þæt gefricge   ofer flōda begang,
þæt þec ymbsittend   egesan þȳwað,
swā þec hetende   hwīlum dydon,
ic ðē þūsenda   þegna bringe,
hæleþa tō helpe.   Ic on Higelāce wāt,   1830
Gēata dryhten,   þēah ðe hē geong sȳ,
folces hyrde,   þæt hē mec fremman wile
w[o]rdum ond w[eo]rcum,   þæt ic þē wēl herige
ond þē tō gēoce   gārholt bere,
mægenes fultum,   þǣr ðē bið manna þearf.   1835
Gif him þonne Hrēþrī[c]   tō hofum Gēata
geþingeð þēodnes bearn,   hē mæg þǣr fela
frēonda findan;   feorcȳþðe bēoð
sēlran gesōhte   þǣm þe him selfa dēah."
Hrōðgār maþelode   him on andsware: 1840
"Þē þā wordcwydas   wigtig drihten
on sefan sende;   ne hȳrde ic snotorlīcor

1816 hæle] helle MS   1833 wordum ond weorcum] weordum ond worcum MS
1836 Hreþric] hreþrinc MS   1837 geþingeð] geþinged MS

and said that he regarded it as a good war-friend, 1810
skillful in battle, and the sword's edges
he did not disparage; he was a noble man.
And when the warriors were eager for their journey,
equipped in their war-gear, the nobleman went,
honoring the Danes, to the high seat where the other was: 1815
the hero, brave in battle, saluted Hrothgar.

XXVI

Beowulf spoke, son of Ecgtheow:
"Now we seafarers, come from afar,
wish to say that we desire
to seek Hygelac. Here we were honorably 1820
entertained with delights; you have treated us well.
If ever on earth I can do any thing
to earn more of your affection,
than the battle-deeds I have done already,
ruler of men, I will be ready at once. 1825
If ever I hear over the sea's expanse
that your neighbors threaten you with terror
as your enemies used to do,
I will bring you a thousand thanes,
heroes to help you. I have faith in Hygelac — 1830
the lord of the Geats, though he be young,
shepherd of his people, will support me
with words and deeds, that I might honor you well
and bring to your side a forest of spears,
the support of my might, whenever you need men. 1835
If ever Hrethric, son of a prince, decides
to come to the Geatish court, he will find
many friends there; far-off lands
are better sought by one who is himself good."
Hrothgar spoke in answer to him: 1840
"The wise Lord has sent those words
into your heart; I have never heard

on swā geongum feore   guman þingian.
Þū eart mægenes strang,   ond on mōde frōd,
wīs wordcwida!   Wēn ic talige,   1845
gif þæt gegangeð,   þæt ðe gār nymeð,
hild heorugrimme   Hrēþles eaferan,
ādl oþðe īren   ealdor ðīnne,
folces hyrde,   ond þū þīn feorh hafast,
þæt þe Sǣ-Gēatas   sēlran næbben   1850
tō gecēosenne   cyning ǣnigne,
hordweard hæleþa,   gyf þū healdan wylt
māga rīce.   Mē þīn mōdsefa
līcað leng swā wēl,   lēofa Bēowulf.
Hafast þū gefēred,   þæt þām folcum sceal,   1855
Gēata lēodum   ond Gār-Denum
sib gemǣn[e],   ond sacu restan,
inwitnīþas,   þē hīe ǣr drugon,
wesan, þenden ic wealde   wīdan rīces,
māþmas gemǣne,   manig ōþerne   1860
gōdum gegrēttan   ofer ganotes bæð
sceal hringnaca   ofer hea[f]u bringan
lāc ond luftācen.   Ic þā lēode wāt
gē wið fēond gē wið frēond   fæste geworhte,
ǣghwæs untǣle   ealde wīsan."   1865
    Ðā gīt him eorla hlēo   inne gesealde,
mago Healfdenes   māþmas twelfe;
hēt [h]ine mid þǣm lācum   lēode swǣse
sēcean on gesyntum,   snūde eft cuman.
Gecyste þā   cyning æþelum gōd,   1870
þēoden Scyldinga   ðegn betstan
ond be healse genam;   hruron him tēaras
blondenfeaxum.   Him wæs bēga wēn
ealdum infrōdum,   ōþres swīðor,
þæt h[ī]e seoðða(n) [nō]   gesēon mōston,   1875
mōdige on meþle.   Wæs him se man tō þon lēof,
þæt hē þone brēostwylm   forberan ne mehte;
ac him on hreþre   hygebendum fæst
æfter dēorum men   dyrne langað

1857 gemæne] gemænum MS   1862 heafu] hea þu MS   1868 hine] inne MS
1875 hie seoððan no] he seoðða . . . MS

a shrewder speech from such a young man.
You are strong in might, and sound in mind,
prudent in speech! I expect it is likely   1845
that if it should ever happen that the spear
or the horrors of war take Hrethel's son,[1]
or sickness or sword strike the shepherd of his people,
your lord, and you still live,
that the sea-Geats could not select   1850
a better choice anywhere for king,
hoard-guard of heroes, if you will hold
the realm of your kinsmen. Your character pleases me
better and better, beloved Beowulf.
You have brought it about that between our peoples,   1855
the Geatish nation and the spear-Danes,
there shall be peace, and strife shall rest,
the malicious deeds they endured before,
as long as I shall rule this wide realm,
and treasures together. Many shall greet   1860
another with gifts across the gannet's bath;
the ring-necked ship shall bring over the sea
tribute and tokens of love. I know these nations
will be made fast against friend and foe,
blameless in everything, in the old way."   1865
        The protector of heroes, kinsman of Healfdene,
gave him twelve great treasures in the hall;
bid him seek his own dear people in safety
with those gifts, and quickly come again.
Then the good king, of noble kin, kissed   1870
that best of thanes and embraced his neck,
the Scylding prince; tears were shed
by that gray-haired man. He was of two minds —
but in his old wisdom knew it was more likely
that never again would they see one another,   1875
brave in their meeting-place. The man was so dear to him
that he could not hold back the flood in his breast,
but in his heart, fast in the bonds of his thought,
a deep-felt longing for the dear man

---

1   I.e., Hygelac.

b[o]rn wið blōde.   Him Bēowulf þanan,   1880
gūðrinc goldwlanc   græsmoldan træd
since hrēmig;   sægenga bād
āge[n]dfrean,   sē þe on ancre rād.
Þā wæs on gange   gifu Hrōðgāres
oft geæhted;   þæt wæs ān cyning   1885
æghwæs orleahtre,   oþ þæt hine yldo benam
mægenes wynnum,   sē þe oft manegum scōd.

XXVII

Cwōm þā tō flōde   felamōdigra,
hægstealdra [hēap];   hringnet bæron,
locene leoðosyrcan.   Landweard onfand   1890
eftsīð eorla,   swā hē ǣr dyde;
nō hē mid hearme   of hliðes nōsan
gæs(tas) grētte,   ac him tōgēanes rād,
cwæð þæt wilcuman   Wedera lēodum
scaþan scīrhame   tō scipe fōron.   1895
Þā wæs on sande   sægēap naca
hladen herewǣdum   hringedstefna,
mēarum ond māðmum;   mǣst hlīfade
ofer Hrōðgāres   hordgestrēonum.
Hē þǣm bātweard   bunden golde   1900
swurd gesealde,   þæt hē syðþan wæs
on meodubence   māþm[e] þȳ weorþr[a],
yrfelāfe.   Gewāt him on nac[a]
drēfan dēop wæter,   Dena land ofgeaf.
Þā wæs be mæste   merehrægla sum,   1905
segl sāle fæst;   sundwudu þunede;
nō þǣr wēgflotan   wind ofer ȳðum
sīðes getwǣfde;   sægenga fōr,
flēat fāmigheals   forð ofer ȳðe,
bundenstefna   ofer brimstrēamas,   1910
þæt hīe Gēata clifu   ongitan meahton,

1880 born] beorn MS   1883 agendfrean] aged frean MS   1889 heap] *not in* MS
1893 gæstas] gæs. . . MS   1902 maþme þy weorþra] maþma þy weorþre MS
1903 naca] nacan MS

burned in his blood. Beowulf from thence,   1880
gold-proud warrior, trod the grassy lawn,
exulting in treasure; the sea-goer awaited
its lord and owner, where it rode at anchor.
As they were going, the gift of Hrothgar
was often praised; that king was peerless,   1885
blameless in everything, until old age took from him
— it has injured so many — the joy of his strength.

XXVII

Those men of high courage then came to the sea,
that troop of young retainers, bore their ring-mail,
locked shirts of armor. The coast-guard observed   1890
the return of those earls, as he had once before;
he did not greet those guests with insults
on the clifftop, but rode towards them,
said that the warriors in their shining armor
would be welcome in their ships to the people of the Weders. 1895
The sea-curved prow, the ring-necked ship,
as it lay on the sand was laden with war-gear,
with horses and treasures; the mast towered high
over Hrothgar's hoard-gifts.
To the ship's guardian he[1] gave a sword,   1900
bound with gold, so that on the mead-benches
he was afterwards more honored by that heirloom,
that old treasure. Onward they went, the ship
sliced through deep water, gave up the Danish coast.
The sail by the mast was rigged fast with ropes,   1905
a great sea-cloth; the timbers creaked,
the wind over the sea did not hinder at all
the wave-floater on its way; the sea-goer sped on,
floated foamy-necked, forth upon the waves,
the bound prow over the briny streams,   1910
until they could make out the cliffs of Geatland,

---

1   I.e., Beowulf.

cūþe næssas;   cēol ūp geþrang
lyftgeswenced,   on lande stōd.
Hraþe wæs æt holme   hȳðweard geara,
sē þe ǣr lange tīd   lēofra manna   1915
fūs æt faroðe   feor wlātode;
sǣlde tō sande   sīdfæþme scip
onc[e]rbendum fæst,   þȳ lǣs hym ȳþa ðrym
wudu wynsuman   forwrecan meahte.
Hēt þā ūp beran   æþelinga gestrēon,   1920
frætwe ond fǣtgold;   næs him feor þanon
tō gesēcanne   sinces bryttan,
Higelāc Hrēþling,   þǣr æt hām wunað
selfa mid gesīðum   sǣwealle nēah.
    Bold wæs betlīc,   bregorōf cyning,   1925
hea[h on] healle,   Hygd swīðe geong,
wīs wēlþungen,   þēah ðe wintra lȳt
under burhlocan   gebiden hæbbe,
Hæreþes dohtor;   næs hīo hnāh swā þēah,
nē tō gnēað gifa   Gēata lēodum,   1930
māþmgestrēona.   Mōd þrȳðo wæg,
fremu folces cwēn   firen' ondrysne;
nænig þæt dorste   dēor genēþan
swǣsra gesīða,   nefne sinfrea,
þæt hire an dæges   ēagum starede;   1935
ac him wælbende   weotode tealde
handgewriþene;   hraþe seoþðan wæs
æfter mundgripe   mēce geþinged,
þæt hit sceādenmǣl   scȳran mōste,
cwealmbealu cȳðan.   Ne bið swylc cwēnlīc þēaw   1940
idese tō efnanne,   þēah ðe hīo ǣnlicu sȳ,
þætte freoðuwebbe   fēores onsǣce

1918 oncer] oncear MS   1926 heah on healle] hea healle MS

familiar capes; the keel drove forward
thrust by the wind, and came to rest on land.
Right away the harbor-guard was ready at the shore,
who for a long time had gazed far   1915
over the currents, eager for the beloved men;
he moored the broad-beamed ship on the beach
fast with anchor-ropes, lest the force of the waves
should drive away the handsome wooden vessel.
He bade that the nobleman's wealth be borne ashore,   1920
armor and plated gold; they had not far to go
to seek their dispenser of treasure,
Hygelac son of Hrethel, where he dwelt at home
with his companions, near the sea-wall.

      The building was splendid, the king quite bold,   1925
high in his hall, Hygd[1] very young,
wise, well-mannered, though few winters
had the daughter of Hæreth passed within
the palace walls — yet not poor for that,
nor stingy of gifts to the Geatish people,   1930
of great treasures. She considered Thryth's pride,[2]
famous folk-queen, and her terrible crimes:
no man, however bold, among her own retainers
dared to approach her, except as her prince,[3]
or dared to look into her eyes by day;   1935
for he knew that deadly bonds, braided by hand,
were waiting for him — first the hand-grip,
and quickly after a blade appointed,
so that a patterned sword had to settle things,
proclaim the execution. That is no queenly custom   1940
for a lady to perform — no matter how lovely —
that a peace-weaver[4] should deprive of life

---

1 Hygelac's queen.

2 These lines are difficult. Some editions and translations read the name as
    "Modthryth"; the reading adopted here smoothes out a transition that is otherwise
    abrupt even by the standards of this poem. This "digression" on the character of a
    queen, with some elements of a folktale, is the counterpart to the story of Heremod in
    earlier sections.

3 I.e., as a husband; or else the line means "except the prince himself," i.e., her father.

4 This epithet reflects the common practice, whose sometimes tragic consequences are
    explored at length elsewhere in the poem, of settling intertribal feuds with a marriage
    between the daughter of one lord and the son of another.

æfter ligetorne   lēofne mannan.
Hūru þæt onhōhsnod[e]   Hem[m]inges mǣg:
ealodrincende   ōðer sǣdan,   1945
þæt hīo lēodbealewa   lǣs gefremede,
inwitnīða,   syððan ǣrest wearð
gyfen goldhroden   geongum cempan,
æðelum dīore,   syððan hīo Offan flet
ofer fealone flōd   be fæder lāre   1950
sīðe gesōhte;   ðǣr hīo syððan well
in gumstōle,   gōde mǣre,
līfgesceafta   lifigende brēac,
hīold hēahlufan   wið hæleþa brego,
ealles moncynnes   mīne gefrǣge   1955
þ[one] sēlestan   bī sǣm twēonum,
eormencynnes;   forðām Offa wæs
geofum ond gūðum,   gārcēne man,
wīde geweorðod,   wīsdōme hēold
ēðel sīnne;   þonon [Ē]om[ē]r wōc   1960
hæleðum tō helpe,   Hem[m]inges mǣg,
nefa Gārmundes,   nīða cræftig.

XXVIII

Gewāt him ðā se hearda   mid his hondscole
sylf æfter sande   sǣwong tredan,
wīde waroðas.   Woruldcandel scān,   1965
sigel sūðan fūs.   Hī sīð drugon,
elne geēodon,   tō ðæs ðe eorla hlēo,
bonan Ongenþēoes   burgum in innan,
geongne gūðcyning   gōdne gefrūnon
hringas dǣlan.   Higelāce wæs   1970
sīð Bēowulfes   snūde gecȳðed,

1944 onhohsnode] on hohsnod MS   Hemminges] hem ninges MS
1956 þone] þæs MS   1960 Eomer] geomor MS   1961 Hemminges] hem inges MS

a friendly man after a pretended affront.
The kinsman of Hemming[1] put a halt to that:
then ale-drinkers told another tale,   1945
said she caused less calamity to the people,
less malicious evil, after she was
given gold-adorned to the young champion,
fair to that nobleman, when to Offa's floor
she sought a journey over the fallow sea   1950
at her father's wish, where she afterwards
on the throne, famous for good things,
used well her life while she had it,
held high love with that chief of heroes,
of all mankind, as men have told me,   1955
the best between the two seas,
of all the races of men; therefore Offa,
in gifts and battle, spear-bold man,
was widely honored, and held in wisdom
his own homeland. From him arose Eomer   1960
as a help to heroes, kinsman of Hemming,
grandson of Garmund, skilled in violence.

XXVIII

The hardy man[2] with his hand-picked troop
went across the sand, trod the sea-plain,
the wide shore. The world's candle shone,   1965
hastening from the south. They had survived their journey,
went boldly to where they knew
the protector of earls, slayer of Ongentheow,[3]
good young battle-king, gave out rings
in his fortress. To Hygelac   1970
the arrival of Beowulf was quickly reported,

---

1   Offa I, fourth-century king of the continental Angles, not Offa II, the eighth-century
    king of Mercia. The elaborate praise offered to Offa I has been taken to suggest that
    the poem may have been written or circulated in the court of Offa II, but there is oth-
    erwise no evidence for this.
2   I.e., Beowulf.
3   I.e., Hygelac. The death of the Swedish king Ongentheow (at the hands of Wulf and
    Eofor, retainers of Hygelac) is told below, section XL-XLI.

þæt ðǣr on worðig   wīgendra hlēo,
lindgestealla   lifigende cwōm,
heaðolāces hāl   tō hofe gongan.
Hraðe wæs gerȳmed,   swā se rīca bebēad,   1975
fēðegestum   flet innanweard.
    Gesæt þā wið sylfne   sē ðā sæcce genæs,
mǣg wið mǣge,   syððan mandryhten
þurh hlēoðorcwyde   holdne gegrētte,
mēaglum wordum.   Meoduscencum hwearf   1980
geond þæt [heal]reced   Hǣreðes dohtor,
lufode ðā lēode,   līðwǣge bær
hæ[leð]um tō handa.   Higelāc ongan
sīnne geseldan   in sele þām hēan
fægre fricgcean,   hyne fyrwet bræc,   1985
hwylce Sǣ-Gēata   sīðas wǣron:
"Hū lomp ēow on lāde,   lēofa Bīowulf,
þā ðū fǣringa   feorr gehogodest
sæcce sēcean   ofer sealt wæter,
hilde tō Hiorote?   Ac ðū Hrōðgāre   1990
wī[d]cūðne wēan   wihte gebēttest,
mǣrum ðēodne?   Ic ðæs mōdceare
sorhwylmum sēað,   sīðe ne trūwode
lēofes mannes;   ic ðē lange bæd,
þæt ðū þone wælgǣst   wihte ne grētte,   1995
lēte Sūð-Dene   sylfe geweorðan
gūðe wið Grendel.   Gode ic þanc secge,
þæs ðe ic ðē gesundne   gesēon mōste."
    Bīowulf maðelode,   bearn Ecgðīoes:
"þæt is undyrne,   dryhten Hige(lāc),   2000
(mǣru) gemēting,   monegum fīra,
hwyl(c) or(leg)hwīl   uncer Grendles
wearð on ðām wange,   þǣr hē worna fela
Sige-Scyldingum   sorge gefremede,
yrmðe tō aldre;   ic ðæt eall gewræc,   2005
swā begylpan [ne] þearf   Grendeles māga

1981 healreced] side reced MS   1983 hæleðum] hæ . nū *with* ð *partly erased* MS
1991 widcuðne] wið cuðne MS   2000 Higelac] Hige . . . *at edge of* MS
2001 mǣru] *word lost at edge of* MS   2002 orleghwil] . . . hwil MS   2006 swa begyl-
pan ne þearf] swa . . gylpan þearf MS

that to the enclosures his battle-companion,
protector of warriors, came walking alive
back to his court, safe from his battle-play.
Quickly, as the powerful one commanded,   1975
the hall was cleared out inside for the foot-guests.
 He sat down with him, he who had survived the fight,
kinsmen together, after he greeted
his friend and liege-lord with a formal speech,
with courteous words and cups of mead.   1980
The daughter of Hæreth passed through the hall,
cared for the people, bore the cup
to the hand of the hero.[1] Hygelac began
to question his companion courteously
in the high hall — curiosity pressed him   1985
to know how the sea-Geats' adventures had gone:
 "How did you fare, beloved Beowulf,
in your journey, when you suddenly resolved
to seek a far-off strife over the salt sea,
a battle in Heorot? Did you better at all   1990
the well-known woe of Hrothgar,
the famous prince? For that I seethed
with heart-care and distress, mistrusted the adventure
of my beloved man; long I implored
that you not seek that slaughter-spirit at all,   1995
let the south-Danes themselves make
war against Grendel. I say thanks to God
that I might see you again safe and sound."
 Beowulf spoke, son of Ecgtheow:
"It is no mystery to many men,   2000
my lord Hygelac — the great meeting,
what a time of great struggle Grendel and I
had in that place where he made so many
sorrows for the victory-Scyldings,
life-long misery — I avenged them all,   2005
so that none of Grendel's tribe needs to boast

---

1 The manuscript reads "to the hands of heathens," which makes sense, but is usually
   emended. The "daughter of Hæreth" is Hygd.

(ǣnig) ofer eorðan   ūhthlem þone,
sē ðe lengest leofað   lāðan cynnes,
f(ācne) bifongen.   Ic ðǣr furðum cwōm
tō ðām hringsele   Hrōðgār grētan;   2010
sōna mē se mǣra   mago Healfdenes,
syððan hē mōdsefan   mīnne cūðe,
wið his sylfes sunu   setl getǣhte.
Weorod wæs on wynne;   ne seah ic wīdan feorh
under heofones hwealf   healsittendra   2015
medudrēam māran.   Hwīlum mǣru cwēn,
friðusibb folca   flet eall geondhwearf,
bǣdde byre geonge;   oft hīo bēahwriðan
secge (sealde),   ǣr hīe tō setle gēong.
Hwīlum for (dugu)ðe   dohtor Hrōðgāres   2020
eorlum on ende   ealuwǣge bær,
þā ic Frēaware   fletsittende
nemnan hȳrde,   þǣr hīo (næ)gled sinc
hæleðum sealde.   Sīo gehāten (is),
geong goldhroden,   gladum suna Frōdan;   2025
(h)afað þæs geworden   wine Scyldinga,
rīces hyrde,   ond þæt rǣd talað,
þæt hē mid ðȳ wīfe   wælfǣhða dǣl,
sæcca gesette.   Oft seldan hwǣr
æfter lēodhryre   lȳtle hwīle   2030
bongār būgeð,   þēah sēo brȳd duge!
Mæg þæs þonne ofþyncan   ðēod[ne] Heaðo-Beardna
ond þegna gehwām   þāra leoda,
þonne hē mid fǣmnan   on flett gǣð,
dryhtbearn Dena   duguða biwenede;   2035
on him gladiað   gomelra lāfe,
heard ond hringmǣl   Heaða-Bear[d]na gestrēon,
þenden hīe ðām   wǣpnum wealdan mōston —

2007 ænig] *word lost at edge of* MS   2009 facne] f. . . . MS   2019 sealde] *word lost at edge of* MS   2020 duguðe] . . . . ðe MS   2023 nægled] . . . gled MS   2024 is] *word lost at edge of* MS   2026 hafað] . . afað MS   2032 ðeodne] ðeoden MS 2037 Heaða-Beardna] heaðabearna MS

anywhere on earth of that uproar at dawn,
whoever lives longest of that loathsome kind,
enveloped in foul evil. First I came there
to the ring-hall to greet Hrothgar;   2010
quickly the famous kinsman of Healfdene,
once he knew of my intentions,
assigned me a seat with his own sons.
That troop was in delight; never in my life
have I seen among hall-sitters, under heaven's vault, 2015
a more joyous feast. At times the famous queen,
bond of peace to nations, passed through the hall,
urged on her young sons; often she gave
twisted rings before she took her seat.
At times before the hall-thanes the daughter of Hrothgar 2020
bore the ale-cup to the earls in the back —
Freawaru, I heard the men in the hall
call her, when the studded treasure-cup
was passed among them. She is promised,
young, gold-adorned, to the gracious son of Froda;[1]   2025
the ruler of the Scyldings has arranged this,
the kingdom's shepherd, and approves the counsel
that he might settle his share of feud and slaughter
with this young woman. But seldom anywhere
after the death of a prince does the deadly spear rest   2030
for even a brief while, though the bride be good!
    It may, perhaps, displease the Heathobards' prince,
and every retainer among his tribe,
when across the floor, following that woman, goes
a noble son of the Danes, received with honors;   2035
on him glitters an ancestral heirloom,
hard, ring-adorned, once a Heathobard treasure
as long as they were able to wield their weapons —

---

1   Ingeld, prince of the Heathobards. His attack on the Danes, alluded to earlier in the
    poem (80-85), was apparently unsuccessful; another Old English poem, *Widsith* (see
    Appendix A6) reports that "Hrothulf and Hrothgar ... humbled Ingeld's battle-array."

oð ðæt hīe forlǣddan tō ðām lindplegan
swǣse gesīðas ond hyra sylfra feorh.   2040
Þonne cwið æt bēore sē ðe bēah gesyhð,
eald æscwiga, sē ðe eall ge(man),
gārcwealm gumena — him bið grim (se)fa —
onginneð geōmormōd geong(um) cempan
þurh hreðra gehygd higes cunnian,   2045
wīgbealu weccean, ond þæt word ācwyð:
'Meaht ðū, mīn wine, mēce gecnāwan,
þone þīn fæder tō gefeohte bær
under heregrīman hindeman sīðe,
dȳre īren, þǣr hyne Dene slōgon,   2050
wēoldon wælstōwe, syððan Wiðergyld læg,
æfter hæleþa hryre, hwate Scyldungas?
Nū hēr þāra banena byre nāthwylces
frætwum hrēmig on flet geað,
morðres gylpe[ð], ond þone māðþum byreð, 2055
þone þe ðū mid rihte rǣdan sceoldest.'
Manað swā ond myndgað mǣla gehwylce
sārum wordum, oð ðæt sǣl cymeð,
þæt se fǣmnan þegn fore fæder dǣdum
æfter billes bite blōdfāg swefeð,   2060
ealdres scyldig; him se ōðer þonan
losað (li)figende, con him land geare.
Þonne bīoð (āb)rocene on bā healfe
āðsweor[d] eorla; (syð)ðan Ingelde
weallað wælnīðas, ond him wīflufan   2065
æfter cearwælmum cōlran weorðað.
Þȳ ic Heaðo-Bear[d]na hyldo ne telge,
dryhtsibbe dǣl Denum unfǣcne,
frēondscipe fæstne.
    Ic sceal forð sprecan

2042 geman] ge . . . MS 2043 sefa] fa MS 2044 geongum] geong . . MS
2055 gylpeð] gylped MS 2062 lifigende] . . figende MS 2063 abrocene] . . rocene
MS 2064 aðsweord] að sweorð (*last letter obscure*) MS syððan] . . . ðan MS
2067 Heaðo-Beardna] heaðobearna MS

until in that deadly shield-play they undid
their beloved comrades and their own lives.   2040
Then an old spear-bearer[1] speaks over his beer,
who sees that ring-hilt and remembers all
the spear-deaths of men — his spirit is grim —
begins, sad-minded, to test the mettle
of a young thane with his innermost thoughts,   2045
to awaken war, and says these words:
　　　'Can you, my friend, recognize that sword,
which your father bore into battle
in his final adventure beneath the helmet,
that dear iron, when the Danes struck him,   2050
ruled the field of slaughter after the rout of heroes,
when Withergyld[2] fell — those valiant Scyldings?
Now here some son or other of his slayer
walks across this floor, struts in his finery,
brags of the murder and bears that treasure   2055
which ought, by right, to belong to you.'
　　　He urges and reminds him on every occasion
with cruel words, until the time comes
that Freawaru's thane, for his father's deeds,
sleeps, bloodstained from the bite of a sword,   2060
forfeits his life; from there the other
escapes alive, for he knows the land well.
Then on both sides the sworn oaths of earls
will be broken, once bitter violent hate
wells up in Ingeld, and his wife-love   2065
grows cooler after his surging cares.
Thus I expect that the Heathobards' part
in the Danish alliance is not without deceit,
nor their friendship fast.
　　　　　　I will speak further

1　I.e., of the Heathobards, outraged by the presence of his former enemies, the Danes.
　　In heroic poetry when a warrior falls, his killer is often awarded his armor; the sword
　　is a vivid reminder of the fate of its former owner and the duty of revenge that is
　　passed on to the next generation.
2　Apparently a famous Heathobard warrior.

gēn ymbe Grendel,   þæt ðū geare cunne,   2070
sinces brytta,   tō hwan syððan wearð
hondrǣs hæleða.   Syððan heofones gim
glād ofer grundas,   gǣst yrre cwōm,
eatol ǣfengrom   ūser nēosan,
ðǣr wē gesunde   sæl weardodon.   2075
þǣr wæs Hondsciō   hil[d] onsǣge,
feorhbealu fǣgum;   hē fyrmest læg,
gyrded cempa;   him Grendel wearð,
mǣrum mag[u]þegne   tō mūðbonan,
lēofes mannes   līc eall forswealg.   2080
Nō ðȳ ǣr ūt ðā gēn   īdelhende
bona blōdigtōð,   bealewa gemyndig,
of ðām goldsele   gongan wolde;
ac hē mægnes rōf   mīn costode,
grāpode gear[o]folm.   Glōf hangode   2085
sīd ond syllīc,   searobendum fæst;
sīo wæs orðoncum   eall gegyrwed
dēofles cræftum   ond dracan fellum.
Hē mec þǣr on innan   unsynnigne,
dīor dǣdfruma   gedōn wolde   2090
manigra sumne;   hyt ne mihte swā,
syððan ic on yrre   uppriht āstōd.

[XXX]

Tō lang ys tō reccenne,   hū i[c ð]ām lēodsceaðan
yfla gehwylces   [o]ndlēan forgeald;
þǣr ic, þēoden mīn,   þīne lēode   2095

2076 hild] hilde MS   2079 magu] magū MS   2085 gearofolm] gearefolm MS
2092 *not in* MS   2093 hu ic ðam] huiedā MS   2094 ondlean] hondlean MS

concerning Grendel, so that you might certainly know,   2070
giver of treasure, how it turned out,
the heroic wrestling-match. When heaven's gem
slipped under the ground, the angry spirit came,
horrible, evening-grim, sought us out
where, unharmed, we guarded the hall.   2075
The attack came first against Hondscio[1] there,
deadly to that doomed man — he fell first,
a girded champion; Grendel was
that famous young retainer's devourer,
gobbled up the body of that beloved man.   2080
None the sooner did that slayer, blood in his teeth,
mindful of misery, mean to leave
that gold-hall empty-handed,
but in his mighty strength he tested me,
grabbed with a ready hand. A glove[2] hung   2085
huge, grotesque, fast with cunning clasps;
it was all embroidered with evil skill,
with the devil's craft and dragons' skins.
Inside there, though I was innocent,
that proud evil-doer wanted to put me,   2090
one of many; but it was not to be,
once I angrily stood upright.

XXX[3]

It is too long to tell how I handed back payment
to the people's enemy for all his evils —
there, my prince, I did honor to your people   2095

---

1 We finally learn the name of the retainer killed in section XI. The name, as in modern
German, means "glove."

2 It is not clear what this is, but apparently it is a pouch of some kind. It is characteris-
tic of a troll in Norse legend. In any case it does not figure in the narrator's own
description of Grendel's attack, and is but one of the discrepancies between the two
tellings of the story. Is Beowulf embellishing his tale? or do such inconsistencies
matter in a story like this?

3 The placement of this section is conjectural; the MS sectional divisions are confused
at this point.

weorðode weorcum.   Hē on weg losade,
lȳtle hwīle   līfwynna br[ēa]c;
hwæþre him sīo swīðre   swaðe weardade
hand on Hiorte,   ond hē hēan ðonan,
mōdes geōmor   meregrund gefēoll.   2100
Mē þone wælrǣs   wine Scildunga
fǣttan golde   fela lēanode,
manegum māðmum,   syððan mergen cōm,
ond wē tō symble   geseten hæfdon.
Þǣr wæs gidd ond glēo;   gomela Scilding,   2105
felafricgende   feorran rehte
hwīlum hildedēor   hearpan wynne,
gome[n]wudu grētte,   hwīlum gyd āwræc
sōð ond sārlīc,   hwīlum syllīc spell
rehte æfter rihte   rūmheort cyning;   2110
hwīlum eft ongan   eldo gebunden,
gomel gūðwiga   gioguðe cwīðan,
hildestrengo;   hreðer inne wēoll,
þonne hē wintrum frōd   worn gemunde.
Swā wē þǣr inne   andlangne dæg   2115
nīode nāman,   oð ðæt niht becwōm
ōðer tō yldum.   Þā wæs eft hraðe
gearo gyrnwræce   Grendeles mōdor,
sīðode sorhfull;   sunu dēað fornam,
wīghete Wedra.   Wīf unhȳre   2120
hyre bearn gewræc,   beorn ācwealde
ellenlīce;   þǣr wæs Æschere,
frōdan fyrnwitan   feorh ūðgenge.
Nōðer hȳ hine ne mōston,   syððan mergen cwōm,
dēaðwērigne   Denia lēode   2125
bronde forbærnan,   nē on bēl hladan,
lēofne mannan;   hīo þæt līc ætbær
fēondes fæð(mum   un)der firgenstrēam.
Þæt wæs Hrōðgāre   hrēowa tornost
þāra þe lēodfruman   lange begēate.   2130
Þā se ðēoden mec   ðine līfe

2097 breac] br . c MS   2108 gomenwudu] gomel wudu MS   2128 fæðmum under]
fæð . . . . der MS

with my actions. He escaped away,
enjoyed his life a little while longer;
yet behind him, guarding his path, was his right
hand in Heorot, and wretched, he went hence,
sad at heart, and sank to the sea-floor. 2100
       For that bloody onslaught the friend of the Scyldings
repaid me greatly with plated gold,
many treasures, when morning came,
and we had gathered together to the feast again.
There was song and joy; the aged Scylding,[1] 2105
widely learned, told of far-off times;
at times the brave warrior touched the song-wood,
delight of the harp, at times made lays
both true and sad, at times strange stories
he recounted rightly. That great-hearted king, 2110
gray-bearded old warrior wrapped in his years,
at times began to speak of his youth again,
his battle-strength; his heart surged within him
when, old in winters, he remembered so much.
And so there inside we took our ease 2115
all day long, until night descended
again upon men. There, quickly ready
with revenge for her griefs, Grendel's mother
journeyed sorrowful; death took her son,
the war-hate of the Weders. That monstrous woman 2120
avenged her son, killed a soldier
boldly at once — there the life of Æschere,
wise old counselor, came to its end.
And when morning came the men of the Danes
were not able to burn his death-weary body 2125
with flames, nor place him on a funeral pyre,
beloved man; she bore away his corpse
in her evil embrace under the upland streams.
That, to Hrothgar, was the most wrenching distress
of all those that had befallen that folk-leader. 2130
Then the prince — by your life — implored me,

---

1   It is not clear whether this is Hrothgar or not, or how many storytellers and singers
    are at this banquet.

healsode hrēohmōd,   þæt ic on holma geþring
eorlscipe efnde,   ealdre genēðde,
mǣrðo fremede;   hē mē mēde gehēt.
Ic ðā ðæs wælmes,   þe is wīde cūð,   2135
grim[n]e gryrelīcne   grundhyrde fond.
Þǣr unc hwīle wæs   hand gemǣne;
holm heolfre wēoll,   ond ic hēafde becearf
in ðām [gūð]sele   Grendeles mōdor
ēacnum ecgum;   unsōfte þonan   2140
feorh oðferede;   næs ic fǣge þā gȳt;
ac mē eorla hlēo   eft gesealde
māðma menigeo,   maga Healfdenes.

XXXI

Swā se ðēodkyning   þēawum lyfde;
nealles ic ðām lēanum   forloren hæfde,   2145
mægnes mēde,   ac hē mē (māðma)s geaf,
sunu Healfdenes   on (mīn)ne sylfes dōm;
ðā ic ðē, beorncyning,   bringan wylle,
ēstum geȳwan.   Gēn is eall æt ðē
lissa gelong;   ic lȳt hafo   2150
hēafodmāga   nefne, Hygelāc, ðec."
Hēt ðā in beran   eaforhēafodsegn,
heaðostēapne helm,   hāre byrnan,
gūðsweord geatolīc,   gyd æfter wræc:
"Mē ðis hildesceorp   Hrōðgār sealde,   2155
snotra fengel;   sume worde hēt,
þæt ic his ǣrest ðē   ēst gesægde;
cwæð þæt hyt hæfde   Hiorogār cyning,
lēod Scyldunga   lange hwīle;
nō ðȳ ǣr suna sīnum   syllan wolde,   2160
hwatum Heorowearde,   ðēah hē him hold wǣre,
brēostgewǣdu.   Brūc ealles well!"
Hȳrde ic ðæt ðām frætwum   fēower mēaras

2136 grimne] grimme MS   2139 guð] *not in* MS   2146 maðmas] *word lost at edge of* MS   2147 minne] . . ne MS

his mind wracked, that in the roaring waves
I should do a noble deed, put my life in danger,
perform glorious things — he promised me reward.
In the waves I found, as is widely known,   2135
a grim, horrible guardian of the abyss.
There for a while, we fought hand-to-hand;
the sea foamed with blood, and I severed the head
of Grendel's mother with a mighty sword
in that [battle-]hall;[1] I barely managed   2140
to get away with my life — I wasn't doomed yet —
and the protector of earls once again gave me
many treasures, that kinsman of Healfdene.

XXXI

So that nation's king followed good customs;
in no wise have I lost those rewards,   2145
the prize for my strength, but the son of Healfdene
offered me treasures at my own choice,
which I wish to bring to you, o war-king,
to show good will. Still all my joys
are fixed on you alone; I have few   2150
close kinsmen, my Hygelac, except for you."
He ordered to be borne in the boar standard,
the helmet towering in battle, the gray byrnie,
the decorated sword, and told this story:
"Hrothgar gave me this battle-gear,   2155
wise prince, and commanded particularly
that first I should tell you the story of his gift —
he said that Heorogar[2] the king first had it,
lord of the Scyldings, for a long while;
none the sooner would he give to his own son,   2160
the valiant Heoroweard — loyal though he was —
that breast-armor. Use all well!"
Then, as I've heard, four swift horses,

---

1   A word is missing; other editors and translators supply different words, such as *grund*
    or "earth."

2   I.e., the eldest brother of Hrothgar.

lungre, gelīce,   lāst weardode,
æppelfealuwe;   hē him ēst getēah   2165
mēara ond māðma.   Swā sceal mǣg dōn,
nealles inwitnet   ōðrum bregdon
dyrnum cræfte,   dēað rēn(ian)
hondgesteallan.   Hygelāce wæs
nīða heardum   nefa swȳðe hold,   2170
ond gehwæðer ōðrum   hrōþra gemyndig.
Hȳrde ic þæt hē þone healsbēah   Hygde gesealde,
wrǣtlicne wundurmāððum,   ðone þe him Wealhðēo
    geaf,
ðēod(nes) dohtor,   þrīo wicg somod
swancor ond sadolbeorht;   hyre syððan wæs   2175
æfter bēahðege   br[ē]ost geweorðod.
    Swā bealdode   bearn Ecgðēowes,
guma gūðum cūð,   gōdum dǣdum,
drēah æfter dōme;   nealles druncne slōg
heorðgenēatas;   næs him hrēoh sefa,   2180
ac hē mancynnes   mǣste cræfte
ginfæstan gife,   þē him God sealde,
hēold hildedēor.   Hēan wæs lange,
swā hyne Gēata bearn   gōdne ne tealdon,
nē hyne on medobence   micles wyrðne   2185
drihten wereda   gedōn wolde;
swȳðe (wēn)don,   þæt hē slēac wǣre,
æðeling unfrom.   Edwenden cwōm
tīrēadigum menn   torna gehwylces.
    Hēt ðā eorla hlēo   in gefetian,   2190
heaðorōf cyning   Hrēðles lāfe
golde gegyrede;   næs mid Gēatum ðā
sincmāðþum sēlra   on sweordes hād;
þæt hē on Bīowulfes   bearm ālegde,
ond him gesealde   seofan þūsendo,   2195

2168 renian] ren . . . MS   2174 ðeodnes] ðeod . . . MS   2176 breost] brost MS
2186 wereda] *most editors emend to* Wedera   2187 wendon] . . . don MS

fallow as apples, well-matched, followed
that war-gear; he gave him as a gift   2165
the horses and harness — as kinsman should behave,
never knitting a net of malice for another
with secret plots, preparing death
for his hand-picked comrades. Hygelac's nephew
was loyal to him, hardy in the fight,   2170
and each man to the other mindful of benefits. —
I heard that he gave the necklace to Hygd,
the wondrous ornamented treasure which Wealhtheow had
    given him,
to that lord's daughter, along with three horses
graceful and saddle-bright; her breast was adorned   2175
the more graciously after that ring-giving.
        So the son of Ecgtheow showed himself brave,
renowned for battles and noble deeds,
pursued honor, by no means slew, drunken,
his hearth-companions; he had no savage heart,   2180
but the great gift which God had given him,
the greatest might of all mankind, he held,
brave in battle. He had been long despised,[1]
as the sons of the Geats considered him no good,
nor did the lord of the Weders wish to bestow   2185
many good things upon him on the mead-benches,
for they assumed that he was slothful,
a cowardly nobleman. Reversal came
to the glorious man for all his griefs.
        The protector of earls, battle-proud king,   2190
ordered the heirloom of Hrethel[2] brought in,
adorned with gold; among the Geats there was
no finer treasure in the form of a sword.
He laid the sword in Beowulf's lap,
and gave him seven thousand hides of land,[3]   2195

---

1   The reasons for ascribing to the hero an unpromising youth, elsewhere not men-
    tioned, are not clear.
2   I.e., the father of Hygelac.
3   The "hide" is a unit of land, originally the amount of land that could support a
    peasant and his family; its actual size varied from one region to another. Seven
    thousand hides is by any measure a very generous gift.

bold ond bregostōl.   Him wæs bām samod
on ðām lēodscipe   lond gecynde,
eard ēðelriht,   ōðrum swīðor
sīde rīce   þǣr ðǣr sēlra wæs.

Eft þæt geīode   ufaran dōgrum   2200
hildehlæmmum,   syððan Hygelāc læg,
ond Hear[dr]ēde   hildemēceas
under bordhrēoðan   tō bonan wurdon,
ðā hyne gesōhtan   on sigeþēode
hearde hil[d]frecan,   Heaðo-Scilfingas,   2205
nīða genǣgdan   nefan Hererīces:
syððan Bēowulfe   br[ā]de rīce
on hand gehwearf;   hē gehēold tela
fiftig wintra   — wæs ðā frōd cyning,
eald ēþelweard —   oð ðæt [ā]n ongan   2210
deorcum nihtum   draca rīcs(i)an,
sē ðe on hēa(um) h(of)e   hord beweotode,
stānbeorh stēar[c]ne;   stīg under læg
eldum uncūð.   Þær on innan gīong
nið[ð]a nāthwylc,   (se þe nē)h gefe(al)g   2215
hǣðnum horde,   hond (wǣge nam),
(searo) since fāh;   nē hē þæt syððan (bemāð),
þ(ēah) ð(e hē) slǣpende   besyre(d wur)de
þēofes cræfte;   þæt sīe ðīod (onfand),
būfolc beorna,   þæt hē gebolge(n) wæs.   2220

XXXII

Nealles mid gewealdum   wyrmhord ā[bræc],
sylfes willum,   sē ðe him sāre gesceōd,
ac for þrēanēdlan   þ(ēow) nāthwylces

2202 Heardrede] hearede MS   2205 hildfrecan] hildefrecan MS   2207 brade] bræde
MS   2210 an] on MS   2211 ricsian] *lost at edge of* MS   2212 heaum hofe] hea . . .
ho . . MS   2213 stearcne] stearne MS   2215 niðða] nið. MS   se þe neh gefealg]
. . . g . f . . g (*mostly illegible*) MS   2216 wæge nam] *illegible* MS   2217 searo] *illegi-*
ble MS   bemað] *illegible* MS   2218 þeah ðe he] þ . . . ð . . . . MS   besyred wurde]
besyre. . . . . de MS   2219 onfand] *illegible* MS   2220 gebolgen] gebolge . MS
2221 wyrmhord abræc] wyrm horda cræft MS   2223 þeow] þ MS

a hall and a princely throne. Both of them held
inherited land in that nation, a home
and native rights, but the wider rule
was reserved to the one who was higher in rank.

      Then it came to pass[1] amid the crash of battle   2200
in later days, after Hygelac lay dead,
and for Heardred[2] the swords of battle held
deadly slaughter under the shield-wall,
when the Battle-Scylfings sought him out,
those hardy soldiers, and savagely struck down   2205
the nephew of Hereric in his victorious nation —
then came the broad kingdom
into Beowulf's hands; he held it well
for fifty winters — he was then a wise king,
old guardian of his homeland — until   2210
in the dark nights a dragon began his reign,
who guarded his hoard in the high heaths
and the steep stone barrows; the path below
lay unknown to men. Some sort of man
went inside there, found his way to   2215
the heathen hoard — his hand ...
inlaid with jewels.[3] He[4] got no profit there,
though he had been trapped in his sleep
by a thief's trickery: the whole nation knew,
and all the people around them, that he was enraged.   2220

XXXII

Not for his own sake did he who sorely harmed him
break into that worm-hoard, or by his own will,
but in sad desperation some sort of slave[5]

---

1 This section is easier to follow if the reader refers to the Genealogies (p. 251). The stories are told in greater detail later in the poem.

2 I.e., son of Hygelac.

3 The manuscript is damaged here and some text is unreadable. Among many conjectural restorations one thing is clear—a cup is taken from the dragon's hoard.

4 I.e., the thief; "he" in the following line refers to the dragon. These lines are nearly illegible, and other readings have been proposed.

5 The word is illegible in the manuscript; the translation follows most editions.

hæleða bearna   heteswengeas flē[a]h,
ærnes þearfa,   ond ðær inne [fealh],   2225
secg synbysig.   Sōna [in þ]a tide
þæt (þær) ðām gyst(e   gryre)brōga stōd;
hwæðre (earm)sceapen   . . . .

. . . .
. . . .   (þā hyne) se fæ[r] begeat,   2230
sincfæt (sohte).
                  Þǣr wæs swylcra fela
in ðām eorðse(le)   ǣrgestrēona,
swā hȳ on gēardagum   gumena nāthwylc,
eormenlāfe   æðelan cynnes,
þanchycgende   þǣr gehȳdde,   2235
dēore māðmas.   Ealle hīe dēað fornam
ǣrran mǣlum,   ond s[ē] ān ðā gēn
lēoda duguðe,   sē ðǣr lengest hwearf,
weard winegeōmor   wēnde þæs ylcan,
þæt hē lȳtel fæc   longgestrēona   2240
brūcan mōste.   Beorh eallgearo
wunode on wonge   wæterȳðum nēah,
nīwe be næsse,   nearocræftum fæst;
þǣr on inn(a)n bær   eorlgestrēona
hrīnga hyrde   h[o]rdwyrðne dæl,   2245
fættan goldes,   fēa worda cwæð:
"Heald þū nū, hrūse,   nū hæleð ne m[ō]stan,
eorla ǣhte!   Hwæt, hyt ǣr on ðē
gōde begēaton;   gūðdēað fornam,
feorhbealo frēcne   fȳr[a] gehwylcne   2250
lēoda mīnra   þā[r]a ðe þis [līf] ofgeaf,
gesāwon seledrēam.   Nāh hwā sweord wege
oððe f(orð bere)   fǣted wǣge,
dryncfæt dēore;   dug(uð) ellor s[c]eōc.

2224 fleah] fleoh (*with* o *written over* a?) MS   2225 fealh] weall MS
2226 in þa tide] mwatide MS   2227 þær] *illegible* MS   gyste] gyst . MS   gryrebroga]
br . . . . g . . MS   2228 earmsceapen] . . . .sceapen MS   *the rest of* 2228b-2230a *is
barely legible*   2230 fær] fæs MS   2231 sohte] *lost at edge of* MS   2232 eorðsele]
eorðse . . MS   2237 se] si MS   2244 innan] innon (*with* o *alt. from* a?) MS
2245 hordwyrðne] hard wyrðne MS   2247 mostan] mæstan MS   2250 fyra] fyrena
MS   2251 þara] þana MS   lif] *not in* MS   2253 forð bere] f . . . . . . MS
2254 duguð] dug . . . MS   sceoc] seoc MS

of a warrior's son fled the savage lash,
the servitude of a house, and slipped in there, 2225
a man beset by sins. Soon he gazed around
and felt the terror of that evil spirit;
yet ...[1]

    ... made ...

        ... when the terror seized him 2230
he snatched a jeweled cup.

                There were many such
antique riches in that earth-hall,
for in ancient days an unknown man
had thought to hide them carefully there,
the rich legacy of a noble race, 2235
precious treasures. In earlier times
death had seized them all, and he who still survived
alone from that nation's army lingered there,
a mournful sentry, expected the same,
that he might enjoy those ancient treasures 2240
for just a little while. A waiting barrow
stood in an open field near the ocean waves,
new on the cape, safe with crafty narrow entrances;
he bore within the noble wealth,
the plated gold, that guardian of rings, 2245
a share worthy of a hoard, and spoke few words:
    "Hold now, o thou earth, for heroes cannot,
the wealth of men — Lo, from you long ago
those good ones first obtained it! Death in war,
and awful deadly harm have swept away 2250
all of my people who have passed from life,
and left the joyful hall. Now have I none
to bear the sword or burnish the bright cup,
the precious vessel — all that host has fled.

---

1   The manuscript is unreadable at this point.

Sceal se hearda helm   (hyr)stedgolde,   2255
fǣtum befeallen;   feormynd swefað,
þā ðe beadogrīman   bȳwan sceoldon;
gē swylce sēo herepād,   sīo æt hilde gebād
ofer borda gebræc   bite īrena,
brosnað æfter beorne.   Ne mæg byrnan hring   2260
æfter wīgfruman   wīde fēran,
hæleðum be healfe.   Næs hearpan wyn,
gomen glēobēames,   nē gōd hafoc
geond sæl swingeð,   nē se swifta mearh
burhstede bēateð.   Bealocwealm hafað   2265
fela feorhcynna   forð onsended!"
Swā giōmormōd   giohðo mænde
ān æfter eallum,   unblīðe hwe(arf)
dæges ond nihtes,   oð ðæt dēaðes wylm
hrān æt heortan.   Hordwynne fond   2270
eald ūhtsceaða   opene standan,
sē ðe byrnende   biorgas sēceð,
nacod nīðdraca,   nihtes flēogeð
fȳre befangen;   hyne foldbūend
(swīðe ondrǣ)da(ð).   Hē gesēcean sceall   2275
(ho)r(d on) hrūsan,   þǣr hē hǣðen gold
warað wintrum frōd;   ne byð him wihte ðȳ sēl.
    Swā se ðēodsceaða   þrēo hund wintra
hēold on hrūsa[n]   hordærna sum
ēacencræftig,   oð ðæt hyne ān ābealch   2280
mon on mōde;   mandryhtne bær
fǣted wǣge,   frioðowǣre bæd
hlāford sīnne.   Ðā wæs hord rāsod,
onboren bēaga hord,   bēne getīðad
fēasceaftum men;   frēa scēawode   2285
fīra fyrngeweorc   forman sīðe.
Þā se wyrm onwōc,   wrōht wæs genīwad;
stonc ðā æfter stāne,   stearcheort onfand
fēondes fōtlāst;   hē tō forð gestōp
dyrnan cræfte   dracan hēafde nēah.   2290

2255 hyrsted] . . . .sted MS   2268 hwearf] hwe. . . MS   2275 swiðe ondrædað] . . . . . .
da . . MS   2276 hord on hrusan] . . r . . . . rusan MS   2279 hrusan] hrusam MS

Now must the hardened helm of hammered gold   2255
be stripped of all its trim; the stewards sleep
who should have tended to this battle-mask.
So too this warrior's coat, which waited once
the bite of iron over the crack of boards,
molders like its owner. The coat of mail   2260
cannot travel widely with the war-chief,
beside the heroes. Harp-joy have I none,
no happy song; nor does the well-schooled hawk
soar high throughout the hall, nor the swift horse
stamp in the courtyards. Savage butchery   2265
has sent forth many of the race of men!"
    So, grieving, he mourned his sorrow,
alone after all. Unhappy sped
both days and nights, until the flood of death
broke upon his heart. An old beast of the dawn   2270
found that shining hoard standing open —
he who, burning, seeks the barrows,
a fierce and naked dragon, who flies by night
in a pillar of fire; people on earth
fear him greatly. It is his nature to find   2275
a hoard in the earth, where, ancient and proud,
he guards heathen gold, though it does him no good.[1]
    Three hundred winters that threat to the people
held in the ground his great treasury,
wondrously powerful, until one man   2280
made him boil with fury; he[2] bore to his liege-lord
the plated cup, begged for peace
from his lord. Then the hoard was looted,
the hoard of rings fewer, a favor was granted
the forlorn man; for the first time   2285
his lord looked on that ancient work of men.
    When the dragon stirred, strife was renewed;
he slithered along the stones, stark-hearted he found
his enemy's footprint — he had stepped too far
in his stealthy skill, too close to the serpent's head.   2290

---

1   The association of dragons and hoarded treasure is ancient and proverbial.
2   I.e., the thief.

Swā mæg unfǣge　　ēaðe gedīgan
wēan ond wrǣcsið　　sē ðe waldendes
hyldo gehealdeþ!　　Hordweard sōhte
georne æfter grunde,　　wolde guman findan
þone þe him on sweofote　　sāre gerēode;　　　　2295
hāt ond hrēohmōd　　hlǣ[w] oft ymbehwearf
ealne ūtanweard;　　nē ðǣr ǣnig mon
on þ(am) wēstenne —　　hwæðre [wīges] gefeh,
bea(du)[we] weorces;　　hwīlum on beorh æthwearf,
sincfæt sōhte;　　hē þæt sōna onfand,　　　　2300
ðæt hæfde gumena sum　　goldes gefandod,
hēahgestrēona.　　Hordweard onbād
earfoðlīce,　　oð ðæt ǣfen cwōm;
wæs ðā gebolgen　　beorges hyrde,
wolde [s]e lāða　　līge forgyldan　　　　2305
drincfæt dȳre.　　Þā wæs dæg sceacen
wyrme on willan;　　nō on wealle læ[n]g
bīdan wolde,　　ac mid bǣle fōr,
fȳre gefȳsed.　　Wæs se fruma egeslīc
lēodum on lande,　　swā hyt lungre wearð　　　　2310
on hyra sincgifan　　sāre geendod.

XXXIII

　Ðā se gǣst ongan　　glēdum spīwan,
beorht hofu bærnan,　　brynelēoma stōd
eldum on andan;　　nō ðǣr āht cwices
lāð lyftfloga　　lǣfan wolde.　　　　2315
Wæs þæs wyrmes wīg　　wīde gesȳne,
nearofāges nīð　　nēan ond feorran,
hū se gūðsceaða　　Gēata lēode
hatode ond hȳnde;　　hord eft gescēat,
dryhtsele dyrnne　　ǣr dæges hwīle.　　　　2320
Hæfde landwara　　līge befangen,
bǣle ond bronde;　　beorges getrūwode,
wīges ond wealles;　　him sēo wēn gelēah.

2296 hlæw] hlǣwū MS　　2298 þam] þ . . MS　　wiges] hilde MS　　2299 beaduwe]
bea MS　　2305 se lāða] fela ða MS　　2307 læng] læg MS

Thus can an undoomed man easily survive
wrack and ruin, if he holds to the Ruler's
grace and protection![1] The hoard-guardian
searched along the ground, greedy to find
the man who had sorely harmed him while he slept;   2295
hot, half-mad, he kept circling his cave
all around the outside, but no one was there
in that wilderness to welcome his warfare
and the business of battle. Soon he returned to his barrow,
sought his treasure; he soon discovered   2300
that some man had disturbed his gold,
his great wealth. The hoard-guardian waited
impatiently until evening came;
the barrow's shepherd was swollen with rage,
the loathsome foe would repay with fire   2305
his precious drinking-cup. Then day was departed
to the delight of that worm; he did not linger
on the barrow wall, but took off burning
in a burst of flames. The beginning was terror
to the people on land, and to their ring-giving lord   2310
the ending soon would be sore indeed.

XXXIII

Then that strange visitor began to spew flames
and burn the bright courts; his burning gleams
struck horror in men. That hostile flier
would leave nothing alive.   2315
The worm's warfare was widely seen,
his ferocious hostility, near and far,
how the destroyer hated and harmed
the Geatish people, then hastened to his hoard,
his dark and hidden hall, before the break of day.   2320
He had surrounded the people of that region with fire,
flames and cinders; he took shelter in his barrow,
his walls and warfare — but that trust failed him.

---

1   This is the narrator's version of Beowulf's comment at lines 572-73.

Þā wæs Bīowulfe   brōga gecȳðed
snūde tō sōðe,   þæt his sylfes h[ā]m,   2325
bolda sēlest   brynewylmum mealt,
gifstōl Gēata.   Þæt ðām gōdan wæs
hrēow on hreðre,   hygesorga mǣst;
wēnde se wīsa,   þæt hē wealdende
ofer ealde riht   ēcean dryhtne   2330
bitre gebulge;   brēost innan wēoll
þēostrum geþoncum,   swā him geþȳwe ne wæs.
Hæfde līgdraca   lēoda fæsten,
ēal ond ūtan,   eorðweard ðone
glēdum forgrunden;   him ðæs gūðkyning,   2335
Wedera þīoden   wræce leornode.
Heht him þā gewyrcean   wīgendra hlēo
eallīrenne,   eorla dryhten,
wīgbord wrǣtlīc;   wisse hē gearwe,
þæt him holtwudu   he(lpan) ne meahte,   2340
lind wið līge.   Sceolde (lī)þend daga
æþeling ǣrgōd   ende gebīdan,
worulde līfes,   ond se wyrm somod,
þēah ðe hordwelan   hēolde lange.
Oferhogode ðā   hringa fengel,   2345
þæt hē þone wīdflogan   weorode gesōhte,
sīdan herge;   nō hē him þ[a] sæcce ondrēd,
nē him þæs wyrmes wīg   for wiht dyde,
eafoð ond ellen,   forðon hē ǣr fela
nearo nēðende   nīða gedīgde,   2350
hildehlemma,   syððan hē Hrōðgāres,
sigorēadig secg,   sele fǣlsode,
ond æt gūðe forgrāp   Grendeles mǣgum
lāðan cynnes.

        Nō þæt lǣsest wæs
hondgemōt[a],   þǣr mon Hygelāc slōh,   2355
syððan Gēata cyning   gūðe rǣsum,
frēawine folca   Frēslondum on,
Hrēðles eafora   hiorodryncum swealt,
bille gebēaten.   Þonan Bīowulf cōm

2325 ham] him MS   2340 helpan] he . . . . MS   2341 liþend daga] . . . þend daga MS
2347 þa] þā MS   2355 gemota] gemot MS

To Beowulf the news was quickly brought
of that horror — that his own home,   2325
best of buildings, had burned in waves of fire,
the gift-throne of the Geats. To the good man that was
painful in spirit, greatest of sorrows;
the wise one believed he had bitterly offended
the Ruler of all, the eternal Lord,   2330
against the old law; his breast within groaned
with dark thoughts — that was not his custom.
The fire-dragon had razed that fortress,
the folk-stronghold, with searing flames
within and without; for that the war-king,   2335
prince of the Weders, devised revenge.
Then the lord of men bade them make,
protector of warriors, a wondrous war-shield,
all covered with iron; he understood well
that wood from the forest would not help him,   2340
linden against flames. The long-good nobleman
had to endure the end of his loaned days,
this world's life — and so did the worm,
though he had held for so long his hoarded wealth.

      Then that prince of rings scorned to seek out   2345
the far-flung flier with his full force of men,
a large army; he did not dread that attack,
nor did he worry much about the dragon's warfare,
his strength or valor, because he had survived
many battles, barely escaping alive   2350
in the crash of war, after he had cleansed,
triumphant hero, the hall of Hrothgar,
and crushed Grendel and his kin in combat,
that loathsome race.
        It was not the least
of hand-to-hand combats when Hygelac was slain;   2355
in the chaos of battle, the king of the Geats,
the lord of his people, in the land of the Frisians,
the son of Hrethel, died sword-drunk,
beaten by blades. Beowulf escaped from there

sylfes cræfte,   sundnytte drēah;   2360
hæfde him on earme   (eorla) þrītig
hildegeatwa,   þā hē tō holme (stā)g.
Nealles Hetware   hrēmge þorf(t)on
fēðewīges,   þē him foran ongēan
linde bǣron;   lȳt eft becwōm   2365
fram þām hildfrecan   hāmes nīosan!
Oferswam ðā sioleða bigong   sunu Ecgðēowes,
earm ānhaga   eft tō lēodum;
þǣr him Hygd gebēad   hord ond rīce,
bēagas ond bregostōl;   bearne ne trūwode,   2370
þæt hē wið ælfylcum   ēþelstōlas
healdan cūðe,   ðā wæs Hygelāc dēad.
Nō ðȳ ǣr fēasceafte   findan meahton
æt ðām æðelinge   ǣnige ðinga,
þæt hē Heardrēde   hlāford wǣre,   2375
oððe þone cynedōm   cīosan wolde
hwæðre hē him on folce   frēondlārum hēold,
ēstum mid āre,   oð ðæt hē yldra wearð,
Weder-Gēatum wēold.

                Hyne wræcmæcgas
ofer sǣ sōhtan,   suna Ōhteres;   2380
hæfdon hȳ forhealden   helm Scylfinga,
þone sēlestan   sǣcyninga
þāra ðe in Swīorīce   sinc brytnade,
mǣrne þēoden.   Him þæt tō mearce wearð;
hē þǣr [f]or feorme   feorhwunde hlēat,   2385
sweordes swengum,   sunu Hygelāces;
ond him eft gewāt   Ongenðīoes bearn
hāmes nīosan,   syððan Heardrēd læg,

2361 eorla] *lost at corner of page* MS   2362 stag] . . . g MS   2363 þorfton] þorf *at*
end of line MS   2385 for] or MS

through his own strength, took a long swim;   2360
he had in his arms the battle-armor
of thirty men, when he climbed to the cliffs.
By no means did the Hetware[1] need to exult
in that fight, when they marched on foot to him,
bore their linden shields; few came back   2365
from that brave soldier to seek their homes.
The son of Ecgtheow crossed the vast sea,
wretched, solitary, returned to his people,
where Hygd offered him the hoard and kingdom,
rings and royal throne; she did not trust   2370
that her son could hold the ancestral seat
against foreign hosts, now that Hygelac was dead.
But despite their misery, by no means
could they prevail upon that prince at all
that he should become lord over Heardred,   2375
or choose to rule the kingdom.
Yet he upheld him[2] in the folk with friendly counsel,
good will and honors, until he was older,
and ruled the Weder-Geats.
                      Wretched exiles,
the sons of Ohthere,[3] sought him out across the seas;   2380
they had rebelled against the Scylfings' ruler,[4]
the best of all the sea-kings
who dispensed treasure in the Swedish lands,
a famous king. That cost him[5] his life:
for his hospitality he took a mortal hurt   2385
with the stroke of a sword, that son of Hygelac;
and the son of Ongentheow afterwards went
to seek out his home, once Heardred lay dead,

---

1   I.e., a Frankish tribe apparently on the side of the Frisians.

2   Beowulf upheld Heardred, as champion and in effect a kind of regent.

3   I.e., Eanmund and Eadgils.

4   Onela, son of Ongentheow. Ohthere had succeeded his father Ongentheow, but after his death his brother Onela apparently seized the throne and drove the two young men Eanmund and Eadgils into exile. They take refuge at the Geatish court, for which Heardred is attacked and killed by Onela. Later Eanmund is killed by Weohstan (see section XXXVI below) but Eadgils, with the help of Beowulf, becomes king (section XXXIV).

5   I.e., Heardred.

lēt ðone bregostōl   Bīowulf healdan,
Gēatum wealdan;   þæt wæs gōd cyning.   2390

XXXIV

Sē ðæs lēodhryres   lēan gemunde
uferan dōgrum,   Ēadgilse wearð
fēasceaftum frēond;   folce gestēpte
ofer sǣ sīde   sunu Ōhteres,
wigum ond wǣpnum;   hē gewræc syððan   2395
cealdum cearsīðum,   cyning ealdre binēat.
Swā hē nīða gehwane   genesen hæfde,
slīðra geslyhta,   sunu Ecgðīowes,
ellenweorca,   oð ðone ānne dæg,
þē hē wið þām wyrme   gewegan sceolde.   2400
    Gewāt þā twelfa sum   torne gebolgen
dryhten Gēata   dracan scēawian;
hæfde þā gefrūnen,   hwanan sīo fǣhð ārās,
bealonīð biorna;   him tō bearme cwōm
mā[ð]þumfæt mǣre   þurh ðæs meldan hond.   2405
Sē wæs on ðām ðrēate   þreottēoða secg,
sē ðæs orleges   ōr onstealde,
hæft hygegiōmor,   sceolde hēan ðonon
wong wīsian.   Hē ofer willan gīong
tō ðæs ðe hē eorðsele   ānne wisse,   2410
hlǣw under hrūsan   holmwylme nēh,
ȳðgewinne;   sē wæs innan full
wrǣtta ond wīra.   Weard unhīore,
gearo gūðfreca   goldmāðmas hēold
eald under eorðan;   næs þæt ȳðe cēap   2415
tō gegangenne   gumena ǣnigum.
Gesæt ðā on næsse   nīðheard cyning;
þenden hǣlo ābēad   heorðgenēatum,

2405 maðþum] madþum MS

and let Beowulf hold the high throne
and rule the Geats — that was a good king.   2390

XXXIV

In later days he[1] did not forget
that prince's fall, and befriended Eadgils
the wretched exile; across the open sea
he gave support to the son of Ohthere
with warriors and weapons. He[2] wreaked his revenge   2395
with cold sad journeys, and took the king's life.
        And so the son of Ecgtheow had survived
every struggle, every terrible onslaught,
with brave deeds, until that one day
when he had to take his stand against the serpent.   2400
Grim and enraged, the lord of the Geats
took a dozen men[3] to seek out the dragon;
he had found out by then how the feud arose,
the baleful violence; the precious vessel
had come to him through the thief's hands.   2405
He was the thirteenth man among that troop,
who had brought about the beginning of that strife,
a sad-minded captive — wretched and despised
he led the way to that plain. He went against his will
to where he alone knew the earth-hall stood,   2410
an underground cave near the crashing waves,
the surging sea; inside it was full
of gems and metal bands. A monstrous guardian,
eager for combat, kept his gold treasures
ancient under the ground; getting them   2415
was no easy bargain for any man.
        The battle-hardened king sat down on the cape,
then wished good health to his hearth-companions,

---

1 I.e., Beowulf, whose revenge for the death of his lord Heardred takes a curiously
   indirect form—he supports Eadgils' return to Sweden, where Onela is killed.
2 I.e., Eadgils.
3 Literally "one of twelve"—Beowulf, Wiglaf, and ten others. The thief who leads the
   way is the thirteenth man.

goldwine Gēata.   Him wæs geōmor sefa,
wǣfre ond wælfūs,   wyrd ungemete nēah,   2420
sē ðone gomelan   grētan sceolde,
sēcean sāwle hord,   sundur gedǣlan
līf wið līce;   nō þon lange wæs
feorh æþelinges   flǣsce bewunden.

    Bīowulf maþelade,   bearn Ecgðēowes: 2425
"Fela ic on giogoðe   gūðrǣsa genæs,
orleghwīla;   ic þæt eall gemon.
Ic wæs syfanwintre   þā mec sinca baldor,
frēawine folca   æt mīnum fæder genam;
hēold mec ond hæfde   Hrēðel cyning,   2430
geaf mē sinc ond symbel,   sibbe gemunde;
næs ic him tō līfe   lāðra ōwihte
beorn in burgum   þonne his bearna hwylc,
Herebeald ond Hæðcyn   oððe Hygelāc mīn.
Wæs þām yldestan   ungedēfe   2435
mǣges dǣdum   morþorbed stred,
syððan hyne Hæðcyn   of hornbogan,
his frēawine   flāne geswencte,
miste mercelses   ond his mǣg ofscēt,
brōðor ōðerne   blōdigan gāre.   2440
Þæt wæs feohlēas gefeoht,   fyrenum gesyngad,
hreðre hygemēðe;   sceolde hwæðre swā þēah
æðeling unwrecen   ealdres linnan.

    Swā bið geōmorlīc   gomelum ceorle
tō gebīdanne,   þæt his byre rīde   2445
giong on galgan;   þonne hē gyd wrece,
sārigne sang,   þonne his sunu hangað
hrefne tō hrōðre,   ond hē him help[e] ne mæg
eald ond infrōd   ænige gefremman.

2448 helpe] helpan MS

the gold-friend of the Geats. His heart was grieving,
restless, ripe for death — the doom was immeasurably near   2420
that was coming to meet that old man,
seek his soul's treasure, split asunder
his life and his body; not for long was
the spirit of that noble king enclosed in its flesh.

      Beowulf spoke, the son of Ecgtheow: 2425
"In my youth I survived many storms of battle,
times of strife — I still remember them all.
I was seven years old when the prince of treasures,
friend to his people, took me from my father;[1]
Hrethel the king held me and kept me,   2430
gave me gems and feasts, remembered our kinship.
I was no more hated to him while he lived
— a man in his stronghold — than any of his sons,
Herebeald and Hæthcyn and my own Hygelac.
For the eldest,[2] undeservedly,   2435
a death-bed was made by the deeds of a kinsman,
after Hæthcyn with his horn bow
struck down his own dear lord with an arrow —
he missed his mark and killed his kinsman,
one brother to another with a bloody shaft.   2440
That was a fight beyond settling, a sinful crime,
shattering the heart; yet it had to be
that a nobleman lost his life unavenged.

      It was as sad as if an old man
should live to see his young son   2445
ride on the gallows[3] — let him recount a story,
a sorry song, while his son hangs
a comfort only to the ravens, and he cannot,
though old and wise, offer him any help.

---

1 Beowulf was brought up as a noble foster-child in the royal court.

2 I.e., Herebeald.

3 It is usually suggested that this is a kind of epic simile, comparing Hrethel's grief
over his son's death—a death beyond the scope of vengeance—to the grief of a crim-
inal's father, who cannot claim compensation for the execution of his son. Mitchell
and Robinson suggest that this is rather a reference to a pagan practice, part of the
cult of Odin, in which the body of a man who did not die in battle was ritually
hanged on a gallows. If this interpretation is correct, the "old man" is Hrethel
himself.

Symble bið gemyndgad   morna gehwylce   2450
eaforan ellorsīð;   ōðres ne gȳmeð
tō gebīdanne   burgum in innan
yrfeweardas,   þonne se ān hafað
þurh dēaðes nȳd   dǣda gefondad.
Gesyhð sorhcearig   on his suna būre   2455
wīnsele wēstne,   windge reste
rēote berofene —   rīdend swefað,
hæleð in hoðman;   nis þǣr hearpan swēg,
gomen in geardum,   swylce ðǣr iū wǣron.

XXXV

Gewīteð þonne on sealman,   sorhlēoð gæleð   2460
ān æfter ānum;   þūhte him eall tō rūm,
wongas ond wīcstede.
           Swā Wedra helm
æfter Herebealde   heortan sorge
weallende wæg;   wihte ne meahte
on ðām feorhbonan   fǣghðe gebētan;   2465
nō ðȳ ǣr hē þone heaðorinc   hatian ne meahte
lāðum dǣdum,   þēah him lēof ne wæs.
Hē ðā mid þǣre sorhge,   þē him sīo sār belamp,
gumdrēam ofgeaf,   Godes lēoht gecēas;
eaferum lǣfde,   swā dēð ēadig mon,   2470
lond ond lēodbyrig,   þā hē of līfe gewāt.
    Þā wæs synn ond sacu   Swēona ond Gēata
ofer [w]īd wæter   wrōht gemǣne,
herenīð hearda,   syðõan Hrēðel swealt,
oðõe him Ongenðeowes   eaferan wǣran   2475
frome fyrdhwate,   frēode ne woldon
ofer heafo healdan,   ac ymb Hrēosnabeorh

2473 wid] rid MS

Each and every morning calls to mind   2450
his son's passing away; he will not care
to wait for any other heir or offspring
in his fortress, when the first one has
tasted evil deeds and fell death.
He looks sorrowfully on his son's dwelling,   2455
the deserted wine-hall, the windswept home,
bereft of joy — the riders sleep,
heroes in their graves; there is no harp-music,
no laughter in the court, as there had been long before.

XXXV

He takes to his couch and keens a lament   2460
all alone for his lost one; all too vast to him
seem the fields and townships.
                                So the protector of the Weders[1]
bore surging in his breast heartfelt sorrows
for Herebeald. He could not in any way
make amends for the feud with his murderer,   2465
but neither could he hate that warrior
for his hostile deeds, though he was not dear to him.
Then with the sorrow which oppressed him too sorely,
he gave up man's joys, chose God's light;[2]
he left to his children his land and strongholds   2470
— as a blessed man does — when he departed this life.
        Then there was strife between Swedes and Geats,[3]
a quarrel in common across the wide water,
hard hostility after Hrethel died,
until the sons of Ongentheow[4]   2475
were bold and warlike, wanted no peace
over the sea, but around the Hill of Sorrows[5]

---

1 I.e., Hrethel.
2 I.e., he died.
3 This refers to a time a generation before the conflicts of Heardred, Eanmund, and
   Eadgils; the Swedish-Geatish feud is longstanding.
4 I.e., Ohthere and Onela.
5 A hill in Geatland, in OE *Hreosnabeorh*.

eatolne inwitscear   oft gefremedon.
Þæt mægwine   mīne gewrǣcan,
fǣhðe ond fyrene,   swā hyt gefrǣge wæs,   2480
þēah ðe ōðer his   ealdre gebohte,
heardan cēape;   Hæðcynne wearð,
Gēata dryhtne   gūð onsǣge.
Þā ic on morgne gefrægn   mǣg ōðerne
billes ecgum   on bonan stǣlan,   2485
þǣr Ongenþēow   Eofores nīosað;
gūðhelm tōglād,   gomela Scylfing
hrēas [hilde]blāc;   hond gemunde
fǣhðo genōge,   feorhsweng ne oftēah.
    Ic him þā māðmas   þē hē mē sealde   2490
geald æt gūðe,   swā mē gifeðe wæs,
lēohtan sweorde;   hē mē lond forgeaf,
eard ēðelwyn.   Næs him ǣnig þearf,
þæt hē tō Gifðum   oððe tō Gār-Denum
oððe in Swīorīce   sēcean þurfe   2495
wyrsan wīgfrecan,   weorðe gecȳpan;
symle ic him on fēðan   beforan wolde,
āna on orde,   ond swā tō aldre sceall
sæcce fremman,   þenden þis sweord þolað,
þæt mec ǣr ond sīð   oft gelǣste,   2500
syððan ic for dugeðum   Dæghrefne wearð
tō handbonan,   Hūga cempan —
nalles hē ðā frætwe   Frēscyning[e],
brēostweorðunge   bringan mōste,
ac in c[a]mp[e] gecrong   cumbles hyrde,   2505
æþeling on elne;   ne wæs ecg bona,
ac him hildegrāp   heortan wylmas,
bānhūs gebræc.   Nū sceall billes ecg,
hond ond heard sweord   ymb hord wīgan."

2488 hilde] *not in* MS   2503 Frescyninge] fres cyning MS   2505 in campe] incempan
MS

they carried out a terrible and devious campaign.
My friends and kinsmen got revenge for those
feuds and evils[1] — as it is said —   2480
although one of them paid for it with his own life,
a hard bargain; that battle was fatal
for Hæthcyn, king of the Geats.
Then, I've heard, the next morning, one kinsman
avenged the other with the sword's edge,[2]   2485
when Ongentheow attacked Eofor;
his battle-helm slipped, the old Scylfing
staggered, corpse-pale; Eofor's hand recalled
his fill of feuds, and did not withhold the fatal blow.
        I have paid in battle for the precious treasures   2490
he[3] gave me, as was granted to me,
with a gleaming sword; he gave me land,
a joyous home. He had no need
to have to go seeking among the Gifthas
or the Spear-Danes or the Swedes   2495
for a worse warrior, or buy one with his wealth;
always on foot I would go before him,
alone in the front line — and all my life
I will wage war, while this sword endures,
which before and since has served me well,   2500
since I slew Dæghrefn, champion of the Hugas,[4]
with my bare hands in front of the whole army.
He could not carry off to the Frisian king
that battle-armor and that breast-adornment,[5]
but there in the field the standard-bearer fell,   2505
a nobleman in his strength; no blade was his slayer,
but my warlike grip broke his beating heart,
cracked his bone-house. Now the blade's edge,
hand and hard sword, shall fight for the hoard."

---

1 The scene of this revenge is apparently Sweden, in a place called "Ravenswood"; this
   battle is described again in sections XL and XLI.
2 Hygelac avenged the death of Hæthcyn on his slayer Ongentheow—not directly but
   through his man Eofor.
3 I.e., Hygelac.
4 The Hugas, like the Hetware, are Frankish tribes allied to the Frisians; the battle in
   question may be the same as Hygelac's fatal raid.
5 Possibly the same as the necklace described in 1195-1214.

Bēowulf maðelode,   bēotwordum spræc   2510
nīehstan sīðe: "Ic genēðde fela
gūða on geogoðe;   gȳt ic wylle,
frōd folces weard   fæhðe sēcan,
mærð[u] fremman,   gif mec se mānsceaða
of eorðsele   ūt gesēceð."   2515
Gegrētte ðā   gumena gehwylcne,
hwate helmberend   hindeman sīðe,
swǣse gesīðas: "Nolde ic sweord beran,
wǣpen tō wyrme,   gif ic wiste hū
wið ðām āglǣcean   elles meahte   2520
gylpe wiðgrīpan,   swā ic giō wið Grendle dyde;
ac ic ðǣr heaðufȳres   hātes wēne,
[o]reðes ond [a]ttres;   forðon ic mē on hafu
bord ond byrnan.   Nelle ic beorges weard
oferflēon fōtes trem,   ac unc [feohte] sceal   2525
weorðan æt wealle,   swā unc wyrd getēoð,
metod manna gehwæs.   Ic eom on mōde from,
þæt ic wið þone gūðflogan   gylp ofersitte.
Gebīde gē on beorge   byrnum werede,
secgas on searwum,   hwæðer sēl mæge   2530
æfter wælrǣse   wunde gedȳgan
uncer twēga.   Nis þæt ēower sīð,
nē gemet mannes,   nef(ne) mīn ānes,
[þæ]t hē wið āglǣcean   eofoðo dǣle,
eorlscype efne.   Ic mid elne sceall   2535
gold gegangan,   oððe gūð nimeð,
feorhbealu frēcne   frēan ēowerne!"
    Ārās ðā bī ronde   rōf ōretta,
heard under helme,   hiorosercean bær
under stāncleofu,   strengo getrūwode   2540
ānes mannes;   ne bið swylc earges sīð!
Geseah ðā be wealle   sē ðe worna fela
gumcystum gōd   gūða gedīgde,
hildehlemma,   þonne hnitan fēðan,
sto[n]dan stānbogan,   strēam ūt þonan   2545
brecan of beorge;   wæs þǣre burnan wælm

2514 mærðu] mærðū MS   2523 oreðes ond attres] reðes 7 hattres MS   2525 feohte]
not in MS   2533 nefne] nef . . MS   2534 þæt] wat MS   2545 stondan] stodan MS

Beowulf spoke, said boasting words   2510
for the very last time: "I have survived
many battles in my youth; I will yet,
an old folk-guardian, seek out a feud
and do a glorious deed, if only that evildoer
will come out to me from his earth-hall."   2515
Then for the last time he saluted
each of the soldiers, his own dear comrades,
brave in their helmets: "I would not bear a sword
or weapon to this serpent, if I knew any other way
I could grapple with this great beast[1]   2520
after my boast, as I once did with Grendel;
but I expect the heat of battle-flames,
steam and venom; therefore shield and byrnie
will I have on me. From the hoard's warden
I will not flee a single foot, but for us   2525
it shall be at the wall as *wyrd* decrees,
the Ruler of every man. My mind is firm —
I will forego boasting against this flying foe.
Wait on the barrow, protected in your byrnies,
men in war-gear, to see which of the two of us   2530
after the bloody onslaught can better
bear his wounds. This is not your path,
nor proper for any man except me alone
that he should match his strength against this monster,
do heroic deeds. With daring I shall   2535
get that gold — or grim death
and fatal battle will bear away your lord!"
        Then that brave challenger stood up by his shield,
stern under his helmet, bore his battle-shirt
under the stone-cliffs, trusted the strength   2540
of a single man — such is not the coward's way.
He saw then by the wall — he who had survived
a great many conflicts, good in manly virtues,
the crash of battles when footsoldiers clashed —
stone arches standing, and a stream   2545
shooting forth from the barrow; its surge

---

1   The OE word *æglæcan* is here used to refer to the dragon.

heaðofȳrum hāt;   ne meahte horde nēah
unbyrnende   ǣnige hwīle
dēop gedȳgan   for dracan lēge.
Lēt ðā of brēostum,   ðā hē gebolgen wæs,   2550
Weder-Gēata lēod   word ūt faran,
stearcheort styrmde;   stefn in becōm
heaðotorht hlynnan   under hārne stān.
Hete wæs onhrēred,   hordweard oncnīow
mannes reorde;   næs ðǣr māra fyrst   2555
frēode tō friclan.   From ǣrest cwōm
oruð āglǣcean   ūt of stāne,
hāt hildeswāt;   hrūse dynede.
Biorn under beorge   bordrand onswāf
wið ðām gryregieste,   Gēata dryhten;   2560
ðā wæs hringbogan   heorte gefȳsed
sæcce tō sēceanne.   Sweord ǣr gebrǣd
gōd gūðcyning,   gomele lāfe,
ecgum un[s]lāw;   ǣghwæðrum wæs
bealohycgendra   brōga fram ōðrum.   2565
Stīðmōd gestōd   wi[ð] stēapne rond
winia bealdor,   ðā se wyrm gebēah
snūde tōsomne;   hē on searwum bād.
Gewāt ðā byrnende   gebogen scrīðan,
tō gescipe scyndan.   Scyld wēl gebearg   2570
līfe ond līce   lǣssan hwīle
mǣrum þēodne,   þonne his myne sōhte;
ðǣr hē þȳ fyrste   forman dōgore
wealdan mōste,   swā him wyrd ne gescrāf
hrēð æt hilde.   Hond ūp ābrǣd   2575
Gēata dryhten,   gryrefāhne slōh
incge lāfe,   þæt sīo ecg gewāc
brūn on bāne,   bāt unswīðor,
þonne his ðīodcyning   þearfe hæfde
bysigum gebǣded.   Þā wæs beorges weard   2580
æfter heaðuswenge   on hrēoum mōde,
wearp wælfȳre;   wīde sprungon
hildelēoman.   Hrēðsigora ne gealp
goldwine Gēata;   gūðbill geswāc

2564 unslaw] un gl . aw MS   2566 wið] wid MS

was hot with deadly flames, and near the hoard
he could not survive for very long
unburnt, for the dragon's flaming breath.
Enraged, the ruler of the Weder-Geats —   2550
let a word burst forth from his breast,
shouted starkly; the sound echoed,
resounding battle-clear under the gray stone.
Hate was stirred up — the hoard-warden recognized
the voice of a man; there was no more time   2555
to sue for peace. First there issued
the steam of that great creature out of the stone,
hot battle-sweat; the earth bellowed.
The warrior in the barrow turned his shield-board —
against the grisly stranger, lord of the Geats,   2560
when the writhing beast's heart was roused
to seek combat. The good war-king   —
had drawn his sword, its edges undulled,
an ancient heirloom; each of the two
hostile ones stood in horror of the other.   —   2565
He stood stouthearted behind his steep shield,
beloved commander, when the worm coiled itself —
swiftly together — he waited in his war-gear.
Then coiled, burning, slithering he came,
rushing to his fate. The shield defended well   2570
the life and limb of the famous lord
for less time than he might have liked;
there on that day for the first time
he faced the outcome,[1] and Fate did not
grant victory in battle. The lord of the Geats   2575
raised his hand, struck that mottled horror
with his ancient sword, so that that edge failed,
bright against the bony scales, bit less strongly —
than the king of that nation needed it to do,
hard-pressed in battle. Then the barrow-warden   2580
was more savage after that stroke,
and spit out gruesome fire; wide sprang
the battle-flames. The gold-friend of the Geats
did not boast of his glorious victories; his bare sword

---

1   Or "if he could have controlled the outcome for the first time."

nacod æt nīðe,   swā hyt nō sceolde,
īren ǣrgōd.   Ne wæs þæt ēðe sīð,
þæt se mǣra   maga Ecgðēowes
grundwong þone   ofgyfan wolde;
sceolde [ofer] willan   wīc eardian
elles hwergen,   swā sceal ǣghwylc mon   2590
ālǣtan lǣndagas.
    Næs ðā long tō ðon,
þæt ðā āglǣcean   hȳ eft gemētton.
Hyrte hyne hordweard,   hreðer ǣðme wēoll,
nīwan stefne;   nearo ðrōwode
fȳre befongen   sē ðe ǣr folce wēold.   2595
Nealles him on hēape   h[a]ndgesteallan,
æðelinga bearn   ymbe gestōdon
hildecystum,   ac hȳ on holt bugon,
ealdre burgan.   Hiora in ānum wēoll
sefa wið sorgum;   sibb' ǣfre ne mæg   2600
wiht onwendan   þām ðe wēl þenceð.

XXXVI

    Wīglāf wæs hāten,   Wēoxstānes sunu,
lēoflīc lindwiga,   lēod Scylfinga,
mǣg Ælfheres;   geseah his mondryhten
under heregrīman   hāt þrōwian.   2605
Gemunde ðā ðā āre,   þē hē him ǣr forgeaf,
wīcstede weligne   Wǣgmundinga,
folcrihta gehwylc,   swā his fæder āhte;
ne mihte ðā forhabban,   bond rond gefēng,
geolwe linde,   gomel swyrd getēah;   2610
þæt wæs mid eldum   Ēanmundes lāf,
suna Ōhtere[s];   þām æt sæcce wearð,
wræcca(n) winelēasum   Wēohstā[n] bana

2589 ofer] *not in* MS   2596 hand] heand MS   2612 Ohteres] ohtere MS
2613 Weohstan] weohstanes MS

failed at need, as it should never have done,   2585
that ancient good iron. It was no easy journey
when the great offspring of Ecgtheow
had to give up ground in that place;
he was forced, against his will, to find
a place of rest elsewhere — just as every one of us   2590
must give up these loaned days.
                                  It was not long
until those two great creatures[1] came together again.
The hoard-guard took heart, his breast swelled with breath
once again; he[2] suffered anguish,
trapped by flames, he who had once ruled his folk.   2595
His comrades, hand-chosen, sons of noblemen,
did not take their stand in a troop around him
with warlike valor — they fled to the woods
and saved their lives. The spirit rose up in sorrow
in the heart of one of them; nothing can overrule   2600
kinship at all, in one who thinks well.

XXXVI

He was called Wiglaf, Weohstan's son,
a worthy shield-warrior, a prince of the Scylfings,[3]
kinsman of Ælfhere. He saw his liege-lord
suffer heat under his war-helmet;   2605
he recalled the honors he had received from him,
the wealthy homestead of the Waegmundings,
every folk-right that his father had possessed;
he could not hold back — his hand seized
the pale linden shield, and he drew his old sword.   2610
It was known among men as the heirloom of Eanmund,
son of Ohthere; that friendless exile
was slain in battle with the edge of that sword

---

1 OE *æglæcan* again, here referring to Beowulf and the dragon together.
2 I.e., Beowulf.
3 Wiglaf's nationality is in question—he is both a Swede and a Wægmunding (like
   Beowulf; see lines 2813-14). His father fought on the Swedish side in their feuds
   with the Geats. Tribal allegiance is more fluid than modern nationality.

mēces ecgum,   ond his māgum ætbær
brūnfāgne helm,   hringde byrnan,   2615
ealdsweord etonisc;   þæt him Onela forgeaf,
his gædelinges   gūðgewædu,
fyrdsearo fūslīc —   nō ymbe ðā fæhðe spræc,
þēah ðe hē his brōðor bearn   ābredwade.
Hē [ðā] frætwe gehēold   fela missēra,   2620
bill ond byrnan,   oð ðæt his byre mihte
eorlscipe efnan   swā his ærfæder;
geaf him ðā mid Gēatum   gūðgewæda,
æghwæs unrīm,   þā hē of ealdre gewāt
frōd on forðweg.   Þā wæs forma sīð   2625
geongan cempan,   þæt hē gūðe ræs
mid his frēodryhtne   fremman sceolde.
Ne gemealt him se mōdsefa,   nē his mægenes lāf
gewāc æt wīge;   þ[æt] se wyrm onfand,
syððan hīe tōgædre   gegān hæfdon.   2630
    Wīglāf maðelode,   wordriht fela
sægde gesīðum   — him wæs sefa geōmor:
"Ic ðæt mæl geman,   þær wē medu þēgun,
þonne wē gehēton   ūssum hlāforde
in bīorsele,   ðē ūs ðās bēagas geaf,   2635
þæt wē him ðā gūðgetawa   gyldan woldon,
gif him þyslicu   þearf gelumpe,
helmas ond heard sweord.   Ðē hē ūsic on herge gecēas
tō ðyssum sīðfate   sylfes willum,
onmunde ūsic mærða,   ond mē þās māðmas geaf,   2640
þē hē ūsic gārwīgend   gōde tealde,
hwate helmberend —   þēah ðe hlāford ūs
þis ellenweorc   āna āðōhte
tō gefremmanne,   folces hyrde,
forðām hē manna mæst   mærða gefremede,   2645
dæda dollīcra.   Nū is sē dæg cumen,
þæt ūre mandryhten   mægenes behōfað,
gōdra gūðrinca;   wutun gongan tō,
helpan hildfruman,   þenden hyt sȳ,

2620 ðā] *not in* MS   2629 þæt] þa MS

by Weohstan, who brought to his kinsman
the burnished helmet, the ringed byrnie   2615
the old giant-work sword; Onela gave to him
the war-equipment of his young kinsman,
the shining armor — he never spoke of a feud,
though he had slain his brother's son.[1]
He[2] kept that war-gear for a great many years,   2620
the blade and byrnie, until his boy could
perform brave deeds like his father before him;
he gave him among the Geats that battle-gear,
every piece of it, when, old, he departed this life
and went forth. That was the first time   2625
that the young warrior had to weather
the storm of battle beside his noble lord.
His courage did not melt, nor did his kinsman's legacy
weaken in war; the worm discovered that,
when they began to meet together.   2630
          Wiglaf spoke, said to his companions
many true words — he was mournful at heart —
"I remember the time that we took mead together,
when we made promises to our prince
in the beer-hall — he gave us these rings —   2635
that we would pay him back for this battle-gear,
these helmets and hard swords, if such a need
as this ever befell him. For this he chose us from the army
for this adventure by his own will,
thought us worthy of glory, and gave me these treasures — 2640
for this he considered us good spear-warriors,
proud helmet-wearers, even though our prince,
shepherd of his people, intended to perform
this act of courage all alone,
because he has gained the most glory among men,   2645
reckless heroic deeds. Now the day has come
that our noble lord has need of the support
of good warriors; let us go to it,
help our warlord, despite the heat,

---

1   Onela never spoke of a feud, though Weohstan had killed Onela's brother's son, for
    he wished him dead. As elsewhere in the poem, a sword is the reminder of both
    victory and vengeance.
2   I.e., Weohstan.

glēdegesa grim! God wāt on mec, 2650
þæt mē is micle lēofre, þæt mīnne līchaman
mid mīnne goldgyfan glēd fæðmie.
Ne þynceð mē gerysne, þæt wē rondas beren
eft tō earde, nemne we ǣror mægen
fāne gefyllan, feorh ealgian 2655
Wedra ðēodnes. Ic wāt geare,
þæt nǣron ealdgewyrht, þæt hē āna scyle
Gēata duguðe gnorn þrōwian,
gesīgan æt sæcce; ūrum sceal sweord ond helm,
byrne ond b[ea]duscrūd bām gemǣne." 2660
Wōd þā þurh þone wælrēc, wīgheafolan bær
frēan on fultum, fēa worda cwæð:
"Lēofa Bīowulf, lǣst eall tela,
swā ðū on geoguðfēore geāra gecwǣde,
þæt ðū ne ālǣte be ðē lifigendum 2665
dōm gedrēosan; scealt nū dǣdum rōf,
æðeling anhȳdig, ealle mægene
feorh ealgian; ic ðē fullǣstu."
    Æfter ðām wordum wyrm yrre cwōm,
atol inwitgæst ōðre sīðe 2670
fȳrwylmum fāh fīonda nīos[i]an,
lāðra manna. Līg ȳðum for,
born bord wið ronde; byrne ne meahte
geongum gārwigan gēoce gefremman,
ac se maga geonga under his mǣges scyld 2675
elne geēode, þā his āgen (wæs)
glēdum forgrunden. Þā gēn gūðcyning
m(ærða) gemunde, mægenstrengo slōh
hildebille, þæt hyt on heafolan stōd
nīpe genȳded; Nægling forbærst, 2680
geswāc æt sæcce sweord Bīowulfes
gomol ond grǣgmǣl. Him þæt gifeðe ne wæs,
þæt him īrenna ecge mihton
helpan æt hilde; wæs sīo hond tō strong,
sē ðe mēca gehwane mīne gefrǣge 2685
swenge ofersōhte, þonne hē tō sæcce bær

2660 beaduscrud] byrdu scrud MS   2671 niosian] niosnan (with nan marked for dele-
tion) MS   2676 wæs] word lost at edge of MS   2678 mærða] m . . . MS

grim fire-terror. God knows for my part   2650
that I would much prefer that the flames should enfold
my body alongside my gold-giving lord.
It seems wrong to me that we should bear shields
back to our land, unless we first might
finish off this foe, defend the life   2655
of the prince of the Weders. I know full well
that he does not deserve to suffer
this torment all alone among the Geatish troop,
or fall in the struggle; now sword and helmet,
byrnie and battle-dress, shall be ours together!"   2660
He hurried through the deadly fumes, bore his helmet
to the aid of his lord, spoke little:
"Dear Beowulf, do all well,
as in your youth you said you would,
that you would never let in your whole life   2665
your fame decline; now firm in deeds,
single-minded nobleman, with all your strength
you must protect your life — I will support you."
      After these words the worm came angrily,
terrible vicious creature, a second time,   2670
scorched with surging flames, seeking out his enemies,
the hated men. The hot flames rolled in waves,
burned the shield to its rim; the byrnie was not
of any use to the young soldier,
but he showed his courage under his kinsman's shield,   2675
the young warrior, when his own was
charred to cinders. Still the battle-king
remembered his glory, and with his mighty strength
swung his warblade with savage force,
so that it stuck in the skull. Nægling shattered —   2680
the sword of Beowulf weakened at battle,
ancient and gray. It was not granted to him
that iron-edged weapons might ever
help him in battle; his hand was too strong,
he who, I am told, overtaxed every blade   2685
with his mighty blows, when he bore to battle

wǣpen wundum heard;   næs him wihte ðē sēl.
Þā wæs þēodsceaða   þriddan sīðe,
frēcne fȳrdraca   fǣhða gemyndig,
rǣsde on ðone rōfan,   þā him rūm āgeald,   2690
hāt ond heaðogrim,   heals ealne ymbefēng
biteran bānum;   hē geblōdegod wearð
sāwuldrīore,   swāt ȳðum wēoll.

XXXVII

Ðā ic æt þearfe [gefrægn]   þēodcyninges
andlongne eorl   ellen cȳðan,   2695
cræft ond cēnðu,   swā him gecynde wæs.
Ne hēdde hē þæs heafolan,   ac sīo hand gebarn
mōdiges mannes,   þǣr hē his mǣg[es] healp,
þæt hē þone nīðgæst   nioðor hwēne slōh,
secg on searwum,   þæt ðæt sweord gedēaf   2700
fāh ond fǣted,   þæt ðæt fȳr ongon
sweðrian syððan.   Þā gēn sylf cyning
gewēold his gewitte,   wællseaxe gebrǣd
biter ond beaduscearp,   þæt hē on byrnan wæg;
forwrāt Wedra helm   wyrm on middan.   2705
Fēond gefyldan   — ferh ellen wræc —
ond hī hyne þā bēgen   ābroten hæfdon,
sibæðelingas;   swylc sceolde secg wesan,
þegn æt ðearfe!   Þæt ðām þēodne wæs
sīðas[t] sigehwīle   sylfes dǣdum,   2710
worlde geweorces.
                Ðā sīo wund ongon,
þē him se eorðdraca   ǣr geworhte,
swelan ond swellan;   hē þæt sōna onfand,
þæt him on brēostum   bealo[nīðe] wēoll
attor on innan.   Ðā se æðeling gīong,   2715
þæt hē bī wealle   wīshycgende
gesæt on sesse;   seah on enta geweorc,
hū ðā stānbogan   stapulum fæste

2694 gefrægn] *not in* MS   2698 mæges] mægenes MS   2710 siðast] siðas MS
2714 bealoniðe] bealomð MS

a wound-hardened[1] weapon — it was no help to him at all.
    Then that threat to the people for a third time,
fierce fire-dragon, remembering his feud,
rushed on the brave man, hot and bloodthirsty,   2690
when he saw the chance, seized him by the neck
in his bitter jaws; he was bloodied
by his mortal wounds — blood gushed in waves.

XXXVII

Then, I have heard, in his king's hour of need
the earl[2] beside him showed his bravery,   2695
the noble skill which was his nature.
He did not heed that head when he helped his kinsman;
that brave man's hand was burned, so that
he struck that savage foe a little lower down,
the soldier in armor, so that his sword plunged in   2700
bejeweled and bloody, so that the fire began
to subside afterwards. The king himself
still had his wits, drew the war-dagger,
bitter and battle-sharp, that he wore in his byrnie;
the protector of the Weders carved through the worm's midsection. 2705
They felled their foe — their force took his life —
and they both together had brought him down,
the two noble kinsmen; a thane at need,
as a man should be! But that, for the prince, was
his last work of victory, by his own will,   2710
of worldly adventures.
            When the wound
which the earth-dragon had worked on him
began to burn and swell, he soon realized
that in his breast was an evil force,
a poison welling; then the nobleman went,   2715
still wise in thought, so that he sat
on a seat by the wall. On that work of giants he gazed,
saw how stone arches and sturdy pillars

---

1 Or "wondrously hard"; the OE text is unclear.
2 I.e., Wiglaf.

ēce eorðreced   innan healde.

Hyne þā mid handa   heorodrēorigne,   2720
þēoden mǣrne   þegn ungemete till,
winedryhten his   wǣtere gelafede
hilde sǣdne   ond his hel[m] onspēon.

    Bīowulf maþelode —   hē ofer benne sprǣc,
wunde wælblēate;   wisse hē gearwe,   2725
þæt hē dæghwīla   gedrogen hæfde,
eorðan wyn(ne);   ðā wæs eall sceacen
dōgorgerīmes,   dēað ungemete nēah:
"Nū ic suna mīnum   syllan wolde
gūðgewǣdu,   þǣr mē gifeðe swā   2730
ǣnig yrfeweard   æfter wurde
līce gelenge.   Ic ðās lēode hēold
fīftig wintra;   næs sē folccyning,
ymbesittendra   ǣnig ðāra,
þē mec gūðwinum   grētan dorste,   2735
egesan ðēon.   Ic on earde bād
mǣlgesceafta,   hēold mīn tela,
ne sōhte searonīðas,   nē mē swōr fela
āða on unriht.   Ic ðæs ealles mæg
feorhbennum sēoc   gefēan habban;   2740
forðām mē wītan ne ðearf   waldend fīra
morðorbealo māga,   þonne mīn sceaceð
līf of līce.   Nū ðū lungre geong
hord scēawian   under hārne stān,
Wīglāf lēofa,   nū se wyrm ligeð,   2745
swefeð sāre wund,   since berēafod.
Bīo nū on ofoste,   þæt ic ǣrwelan,
goldǣht ongite,   gearo scēawige
swegle searogimmas,   þæt ic ðȳ sēft mæge
æfter māððumwelan   mīn ālǣtan   2750
līf ond lēodscipe,   þone ic longe hēold."

2723 helm] helo MS   2727 wynne] wyn . . MS

held up the inside of that ancient earth-hall.
Then with his hands the thane, immeasurably good,   2720
bathed with water his beloved lord,
the great prince, spattered with gore,
sated with battle, and unstrapped his helmet.
Beowulf spoke — despite his wound,
that deadly cut — he knew clearly   2725
that his allotted life had run out,
and his joys in the earth; all gone
was his portion of days, death immeasurably near:
      "Now I should wish to give my war-gear
to my son, if there had been such,   2730
flesh of my flesh, if fate had granted me
any heir. I held this people
fifty winters; there was no folk-king,
not any of the neighboring tribes,
who dared to face me with hostile forces   2735
or threaten attack. The decrees of fate
I awaited on earth, held well what was mine,
I sought no intrigues, nor swore many
false or wrongful oaths. For all that I may
have joy, though sick with mortal wounds,   2740
because the Ruler of men need not reproach me
with the murder of kinsmen, when my life
quits my body. Now go quickly
to look at the hoard under the hoary stone,
dear Wiglaf, now that the worm lies dead,   2745
sleeps with his wounds, stripped of his treasure.
Hurry, so I might witness that ancient wealth,
those golden goods, might eagerly gaze on
the bright precious gems, and I might more gently,
for that great wealth, give up my   2750
life and lordship, which I have held so long."

Ðā ic snūde gefrægn   sunu Wīhstānes
æfter wordcwydum   wundum dryhtne
hȳran heaðosīocum,   hringnet beran,
brogdne beadusercean   u[n]der beorges hrōf.   2755
Geseah ðā sigehrēðig,   þā hē bī sesse gēong,
magoþegn mōdig   māððumsigla fealo,
gold glitnian   grunde getenge,
wundur on wealle,   ond þæs wyrmes denn,
ealdes ūhtflogan,   orcas stondan,   2760
fyrnmanna fatu,   feormendlēase,
hyrstum behrorene;   þǣr wæs helm monig
eald ond ōmig,   earmbēaga fela
searwum gesǣled.   Sinc ēaðe mæg,
gold on grund(e)   gumcynnes gehwone   2765
oferhīgian,   hȳde sē ðe wylle!
Swylce hē siomian geseah   segn eallgylden
hēah ofer horde,   hondwundra mǣst,
gelocen leoðocræftum;   of ðām lēom[a] stōd,
þæt hē þone grundwong   ongitan meahte,   2770
wrǣ[t]e giondwlītan.   Næs ðæs wyrmes þǣr
onsȳn ǣnig,   ac hyne ecg fornam.
Ðā ic on hlǣwe gefrægn   hord rēafian,
eald enta geweorc   ānne mannan,
him on bearm hl[a]don   bunan ond discas   2775
sylfes dōme;   segn ēac genōm,
bēacna beorhtost.   Bill ǣr gescōd
— ecg wæs īren —   ealdhlāfordes
þām ðāra māðma   mundbora wæs
longe hwīle,   līgegesan wæg   2780
hātne for horde,   hioroweallende
middelnihtum,   oð þæt hē morðre swealt.
Ār wæs on ofoste,   eftsīðes georn,
frætwum gefyrðred;   hyne fyrwet bræc,
hwæðer collenferð   cwicne gemētte   2785
in ðām wongstede   Wedra þēoden

2755 under] urder MS   2765 grund(e)] grunde gru . . . MS   2769 leoma] leoman MS
2771 wræte] wræce MS   2775 hladon] hlodon MS

XXXVIII

Then swiftly, I have heard, the son of Weohstan
after these words obeyed his lord,
sick with wounds, wore his ring-net,
the woven battle-shirt, under the barrow's roof.   2755
As he went by the seat he saw there, triumphant,
the brave young warrior, many bright jewels,
glittering gold scattered on the ground,
wonders on the walls, and the lair of that worm,
the old dawn-flier — flagons standing,   2760
ancient serving-vessels without a steward,
their trappings all moldered; there was many a helmet
old and rusty, a number of arm-bands
with twisted ornaments. — Treasure may easily,
gold in the ground, give the slip   2765
to any one of us: let him hide it who will![1] —
Likewise he saw an ensign, all golden,
hanging high over the hoard, greatest hand-work,
linked together with skill; light gleamed from it
so that he could see the cave's floor,   2770
survey those strange artifacts. There was no sign
of the serpent there — a sword had finished him off.
Then the hoard in that barrow, as I've heard, was looted,
ancient work of giants, by one man alone;
he piled in his arms cups and plates,   2775
whatever he wanted; he took the ensign too,
brightest of beacons. His aged lord's blade
— its edge was iron — had earlier harmed
the one who was protector of those treasures
for such a long time, who bore his fiery terror   2780
flaming before the hoard, seething fiercely
in the darkest night, until he died a bloody death.
        The messenger rushed out, eager to return,
burdened with treasures; he was burning to know
whether, stout-hearted, he would find still alive   2785
the prince of the Weders, weakened by wounds,

---

1   Or "can get the better of any man—heed [these words] who will!" The OE is uncer-
    tain; the translation follows Mitchell and Robinson.

ellensīocne,   þǣr hē hine ǣr forlēt.
Hē ðā mid þām māðmum   mǣrne þīoden,
dryhten sīnne   drīorigne fand
ealdres æt ende;   hē hine eft ongon   2790
wæteres weorpan,   oð þæt wordes ord
brēosthord þurhbræc.   [Biorncyning spræc]
gomel on gio[h]ðe   gold scēawode:
"Ic ðāra frætwa   Frēan ealles ðanc,
wuldurcyninge   wordum secge,   2795
ēcum Dryhtne,   þē ic hēr on starie,
þæs ðe ic mōste   mīnum lēodum
ǣr swyltdæge   swylc gestrȳnan.
Nū ic on māðma hord   mī[n]e bebohte
frōde feorhlege,   fremmað gēna   2800
lēoda þearfe;   ne mæg ic hēr leng wesan.
Hātað heaðomǣre   hlǣw gewyrcean
beorhtne æfter bǣle   æt brimes nōsan;
sē scel tō gemyndum   mīnum lēodum
hēah hlīfian   on Hronesnæsse,   2805
þæt hit sǣlīðend   syððan hātan
Bīowulfes Biorh,   ðā ðe brentingas
ofer flōda genipu   feorran drīfað."
Dyde him of healse   hring gyldenne
þīoden þrīsthȳdig,   þegne gesealde,   2810
geongum gārwigan,   goldfāhne helm,
bēah ond byrnan,   hēt hyne brūcan well:
"Þū eart endelāf   ūsses cynnes,
Wǣgmundinga;   ealle wyrd fors[w]ēo[p]
mīne māgas   tō metodsceafte,   2815
eorlas on elne;   ic him æfter sceal."
Þæt wæs þām gomelan   gingæste word
brēostgehygdum,   ǣr hē bǣl cure,
hāte heaðowylmas;   him of h[r]æðre gewāt
sāwol sēcean   sōðfæstra dōm.   2820

2792 Biorncyning spræc] *no gap in* MS   2793 giohðe] giogoðe MS
2799 mine] minne MS   2814 forsweop] forspeof MS   2819 hræðre] hwæðre MS

in the place where he had left him on that plain.
Then with the treasures he found the famous prince,
his own lord, his life at an end,
all bloody; he began once more 2790
to sprinkle water on him, until the point of a word
escaped from his breast.[1]
Old, full of grief, he looked on the gold:
       "For all these treasures, I offer thanks
with these words to the eternal Lord, 2795
King of Glory, for what I gaze upon here,
that I was able to acquire such wealth
for my people before my death-day.
Now that I have sold my old lifespan
for this hoard of treasures, they will attend[2] 2800
to the needs of the people; I can stay no longer.
The brave in battle will bid a tomb be built
shining over my pyre on the cliffs by the sea;
it will be as a monument to my people
and tower high on Whale's Head, 2805
so that seafarers afterwards shall call it
'Beowulf's Barrow,' when their broad ships
they drive from afar over the darkening flood."
       The boldminded nobleman took from his neck
a golden circlet, and gave it to the thane, 2810
the young spear-carrier, and the gold-covered helmet,
ring and byrnie, bid him use them well:
"You are the last survivor of our lineage,
the Waegmundings; fate has swept away
all of my kinsmen, earls in their courage, 2815
to their final destiny; I must follow them."
That was the last word of the old warrior,
his final thought before he chose the fire,
the hot surging flames — from his breast flew
his soul to seek the judgment of the righteous.[3] 2820

---

1   Half a line (or more?) is missing from the manuscript at this point.

2   Usually translated "you [Wiglaf] will attend ..."; the OE verb may be indicative or imperative, but it is unambiguously plural, and the imperative plural is not used elsewhere in the poem to address a single person.

3   Literally "the *dom* (fame) of the truth-fast," an ambiguous pronouncement. It is not clear whether this means that Beowulf's soul will receive the sort of   (*continued*)

Ðā wæs gegongen   gum[an] unfrōdum
earfoðlīce,   þæt hē on eorðan geseah
þone lēofestan   līfes æt ende
blēate gebǣran.   Bona swylce læg,
egeslīc eorðdraca   ealdre berēafod,   2825
bealwe gebǣded.   Bēahhordum leng
wyrm wōhbogen   wealdan ne mōste,
ac him īrenna   ecga fornāmon,
hearde heaðoscearde   homera lāfe,
þæt se wīdfloga   wundum stille   2830
hrēas on hrūsan   hordærne nēah.
Nalles æfter lyfte   lācende hwearf
middelnihtum,   māðmǣhta wlonc
ansȳn ȳwde,   ac hē eorðan gefēoll
for ðæs hildfruman   hondgeweorce.   2835
Hūru þæt on lande   lȳt manna ðāh
mægenāgendra   mīne gefrǣge,
þēah ðe hē dǣda gehwæs   dyrstig wǣre,
þæt hē wið attorsceaðan   oreðe gerǣsde,
oððe hringsele   hondum styrede,   2840
gif hē wæccende   weard onfunde
būon on beorge.   Bīowulfe wearð
dryhtmāðma dæl   dēaðe forgolden;
hæfde æghwæð[er]   ende gefēred
lænan līfes.   2845
    Næs ðā lang tō ðon,
þæt ðā hildlatan   holt ofgēfan,
tȳdre trēowlogan   tȳne ætsomne,
ðā ne dorston ǣr   dareðum lācan
on hyra mandryhtnes   miclan þearfe;
ac hȳ scamiende   scyldas bǣran,   2850
gūðgewǣdu   þǣr se gomela læg;
wlitan on Wīlāf.   Hē gewērgad sæt,
fēðecempa   frēan eaxlum nēah,
wehte hyne wætre;   him wiht ne spēo[w].

2821 guman] gumū MS   2844 æghwæðer] æghwæðre MS   2854 speow] speop MS

XXXIX

Then it came to pass with piercing sorrow
that the young warrior had to watch
his most precious lord fare so pitifully,
his life at an end. Likewise his slayer lay dead,
the awesome earth-dragon deprived of his life,   2825
overcome by force. The coiled serpent
could no longer rule his hoard of rings —
edges of iron did away with him,
the hard, battle-scarred shards of the smithy,
so that the wide-flier, stilled by his wounds,   2830
toppled to the ground near his treasure-house.
No more soaring about in the skies
at midnight, preening in his precious treasures,
showing his face — he fell to earth
through that war-commander's handiwork.   2835
Indeed, few men on earth, no matter how strong,
could succeed at that, as I have heard tell,
though he were daring in every deed,
could rush against the reek of that venomous foe,
or rifle through that ring-hall with his hands,   2840
if he should find a waking warden
waiting in that barrow. Beowulf's share
of that royal treasure was repaid by his death —
each of them had journeyed to the end
of this loaned life.   It was not long before   2845
the men late for battle left the woods,
those ten weak traitors all together
who had not dared to hoist their spears
when their lord of men needed them most;
now shamefaced, they carried their shields   2850
and battle-dress to where the old man lay dead,
to stare at Wiglaf. He sat exhausted,
a foot-soldier at his lord's shoulder,
tried to rouse him with water — but it was no use.

---

judgment that a righteous soul ought to receive (and so go to Heaven), or that it will be
judged by those "fast in truth" (and so go to Hell as an unbaptized pagan).

Ne meahte hē on eorðan,   ðēah hē ūðe wēl,   2855
on ðām frumgāre   feorh gehealdan,
nē ðæs wealdendes   wiht oncirran;
wolde dōm Godes   dǣdum rǣdan
gumena gehwylcum,   swā hē nū gēn deð.
Þā wæs æt ðām geong[an]   grim andswaru   2860
ēðbegēte   þām ðe ǣr his elne forlēas.
Wīglāf maðelode,   Wēohstānes sunu,
sec[g] sārigferð   seah on unlēofe:
"Þæt, lā, mæg secgan   sē ðe wyle sōð specan,
þæt se mondryhten,   sē ēow þā māðmas geaf,   2865
ēoredgeatwe,   þē gē þǣr on standað,
þonne hē on ealubence   oft gesealde
healsittendum   helm ond byrnan,
þēoden his þegnum,   swylce hē þrȳðlīcost
ōwer feor oððe nēah   findan meahte —   2870
þæt hē gēnunga   gūðgewǣdu
wrāðe forwurpe,   ðā hyne wīg beget.
Nealles folccyning   fyrdgesteallum
gylpan þorfte;   hwæðre him God ūðe,
sigora Waldend,   þæt hē hyne sylfne gewræc   2875
āna mid ecge,   þā him wæs elnes þearf.
Ic him līfwraðe   lȳtle meahte
ætgifan æt gūðe,   ond ongan swā þēah
ofer mīn gemet   mǣges helpan;
symle wæs þȳ sǣmra,   þonne ic sweorde drep   2880
ferhðgenīðlan,   fȳr unswīðor
wēoll of gewitte.   [W]ergendra tō lȳt
þrong ymbe þēoden,   þā hyne sīo þrāg becwōm.
[N]ū sceal sincþego   ond swyrdgifu,
eall ēðelwyn   ēowrum cynne,   2885
lufen ālicgean;   londrihtes mōt
þǣre mǣgburge   monna ǣghwylc
īdel hweorfan,   syððan æðelingas
feorran gefricgean   flēam ēowerne,
dōmlēasan dǣd.   Dēað bið sēlla   2890
eorla gehwylcum   þonne edwītlīf!"

2860 geongan] geongū MS   2863 secg] sec MS   2882 Wergendra] fergendra MS
2884 Nu] Hu MS

He could not, no matter how much he wanted,   2855
keep the life in the body of his captain,
nor change any bit of the Ruler's decree;
the judgment of God would guide the deeds
of every man, as it still does today.
Then that youth was ready with a grim rebuke   2860
for those who had thrown away their courage.
Wiglaf spoke, son of Weohstan,
looked, sick at heart, on those unloved:
        "Lo! the man who would speak the truth must say
that the lord who gave you those gifts of treasures,   2865
the soldier's trappings you stand in there,
when often on the ale-benches he handed out
helmets and byrnies to the hall-sitters,
a lord to his followers, whatever he could find
the finest anywhere, far or near —   2870
that all that battle-dress he absolutely
and entirely threw away, when war beset him.
Our nation's king had no need to boast
of his comrades-in-arms! But the Ruler of victories
allowed that he, alone with his blade,   2875
might avenge himself when he needed your valor.
Only a little life-protection could I offer
him in battle, but began nevertheless
to support my kinsman beyond my own strength;
ever the worse was the deadly enemy   2880
when I struck with my sword, a fire less severe
surging from his head. Too few supporters
thronged around our prince in his great peril.
Now the getting of treasure, the giving of swords,
and all the happy joys of your homeland,   2885
shall end for your race; empty-handed
will you go, every man, among your tribe,
stripped of land-rights, when noblemen learn
far and wide of your flight,
your inglorious deed. Death is better   2890
for any earl than a life of dishonor!"

Heht ðā þæt heaðoweorc   tō hagan bīodan
ūp ofer ecgclif,   þǣr þæt eorlweorod
morgenlongne dæg   mōdgiōmor sæt,
bordhæbbende,   bēga on wēnum,   2895
endedōgores   ond eftcymes
lēofes monnes.   Lȳt swīgode
nīwra spella   sē ðe næs gerād,
ac hē sōðlīce   sægde ofer ealle:
"Nū is wilgeofa   Wedra lēoda,   2900
dryhten Gēata   dēaðbedde fæst,
wunað wælreste   wyrmes dǣdum;
him on efn ligeð   ealdorgewinna
s[e]xbennum sēoc;   sweorde ne meahte
on ðām āglǣcean   ǣnige þinga   2905
wunde gewyrcean.   Wīglāf siteð
ofer Bīowulfe,   byre Wīhstānes,
eorl ofer ōðrum   unlifigendum,
healdeð higemǣðum   hēafodwearde
lēofes ond lāðes.
        Nū ys lēodum wēn   2910
orleghwīle,   syððan under[ne]
Froncum ond Frȳsum   fyll cyninges
wīde weorðeð.   Wæs sīo wrōht scepen
heard wið Hūgas,   syððan Higelāc cwōm
faran flotherge   on Frēsna land,   2915
þǣr hyne Hetware   hilde ge[n]ǣgdon,
elne geēodon   mid ofermægene,
þæt se byrnwiga   būgan sceolde,
fēoll on fēðan;   nalles frætwe geat
ealdor dugoðe.   Ūs wæs ā syððan   2920
Merewīoingas   milts ungyfeðe.
    Nē ic te Swēoðēode   sibbe oððe trēowe
wihte ne wēne,   ac wæs wīde cūð,
þætte Ongenðīo   ealdre besnyðede
Hæðcen Hrēþling   wið Hrefnawudu,   2925

2904 sexbennum] siexbennum MS   2911 underne] under MS   2916 genægdon] ge
hnægdon MS

He ordered the battle-work announced to the camp
up by the cliff's edge, where that troop of earls,
shield-bearers, sat sad-minded
all the long morning, expecting either   2895
the final day of their dear lord
or his homecoming. He who rode up to the cape
was not at all silent with his new tidings,
but he spoke truly in the hearing of all:
    "Now is the joy-giver of the Geatish people,   2900
the lord of the Weders, laid on his deathbed,
holding a place of slaughter by the serpent's deeds;
beside him lies his life-enemy,
sick with knife-slashes; he could not with his sword
make in the monstrous beast   2905
any kind of wound. Wiglaf sits,
Weohstan's offspring, over Beowulf,
one earl over the other, now dead;
he holds with desperate heart the watch
over friend and foe.
        Now this folk may expect   2910
a time of trouble, when this is told
to the Franks and Frisians, and the fall of our king
becomes widespread news. The strife was begun
hard with the Hugas, after Hygelac came
travelling with his ships to the shores of Frisia,   2915
where the Hetware attacked him in war,
advanced with valor and a vaster force,
so that the warrior in his byrnie had to bow down,
and fell amid the infantry; not at all did that lord
give treasure to his troops. Ever after that   2920
the Merovingians have never shown us mercy.
    Nor do I expect any peace or truce
from the Swedish nation, but it has been well-known
that Ongentheow ended the life
of Hæthcyn, son of Hrethel, in Ravenswood,[1]   2925

---

1   See Section XXXV above. The allusive complexity of the narration of human feuds
    and battles is in striking contrast to the straightforward telling of the hero's battles
    against non-human opponents.

þā for onmēdlan   ǣrest gesōhton
Gēata lēode   Gūð-Scilfingas.
Sōna him se frōda   fæder Ōhtheres,
eald ond egesfull   [o]ndslyht āgeaf,
ābrēot brimwīsan,   brȳd āh[red]de,   2930
gomela iōmēowlan   golde berofene,
Onelan mōdor   ond Ōhtheres;
ond ðā folgode   feorhgenīðlan,
oð ðær hī oðēodon   earfoðlīce
in Hrefnesholt   hlāfordlēase.   2935
Besæt ðā sinherge   sweorda lāfe
wundum wērge;   wēan oft gehēt
earmre teohhe   ondlonge niht,
cwæð, hē on mergenne   mēces ecgum
gētan wolde,   sum[e] on galgtrēowu[m]   2940
[fuglum] tō gamene.   Frōfor eft gelamp
sārigmōdum   somod ǣrdæge,
syððan hīe Hygelāces   horn ond bȳman,
gealdor ongēaton,   þā se gōda cōm
lēoda dugoðe   on lāst faran.   2945

XLI

Wæs sīo swātswaðu   Sw[ē]ona ond Gēata,
wælrǣs weora   wīde gesȳne,
hū ðā folc mid him   fǣhðe tōwehton.
Gewāt him ðā se gōda   mid his gædelingum,
frōd felageōmor   fæsten sēcean,   2950
eorl Ongenþīo   ufor oncirde;
hæfde Higelāces   hilde gefrūnen,
wlonces wīgcræft;   wiðres ne trūwode,
þæt hē sǣmannum   onsacan mihte,

2929 ondslyht] hond slyht MS   2930 bryd ahredde] bryda heorde MS   2940 sume on galgtreowum] sum on galg treowu MS   2941 fuglum] *not in* MS   2946 Sweona] swona MS

when in their arrogant pride the Geatish people
first sought out the Battle-Scylfings.
Immediately the ancient father of Ohthere,
old and terrifying, returned the attack —
the old warrior cut down the sea-captain,[1]   2930
rescued his wife, bereft of her gold,
Onela's mother and Ohthere's;
and then hunted down his deadly enemies
until they escaped, with some difficulty,
bereft of their lord, into Ravenswood.   2935
With his standing army he besieged those sword-leavings,
weary, wounded; he kept threatening woe
to that wretched troop the whole night through —
in the morning, he said, with the edge of his sword
he would gut them, and leave some on the gallows-tree   2940
as sport for birds.[2] But for those sad-hearted men
solace came along with the sunrise,
after they heard Hygelac's horn and trumpet
sounding the charge, when the good man came
following the trail of that people's troop.   2945

XLI

The bloody swath of the Swedes and Geats,
the slaughter of men, was easily seen,
how the folk had stirred up feud between them.
That good man[3] then departed, old, desperate,
with a small band of kinsmen, sought his stronghold,   2950
the earl Ongentheow turned farther away;
he had heard of proud Hygelac's prowess in battle,
his war-skill, and did not trust the resistance
he might muster against the seafarers' might

---

1   I.e., Ongentheow killed Hæthcyn. Hygelac is not present at this battle, but arrives
    later.
2   Ongentheow may be threatening to sacrifice the corpses of his defeated enemies to a
    pagan god of war.
3   I.e., Ongentheow, whose vicious hostility toward the Geats does not earn him the nar-
    rator's censure.

heaðolīðendum   hord forstandan,   2955
bearn ond brȳde;   bēah eft þonan
eald under eorðweall.   Þā wæs ǣht boden
Swēona lēodum,   segn Higelāce[s]
freoðowong þone   for[ð] oferēodon,
syððan Hrēðlingas   tō hagan þrungon.   2960
Þǣr wearð Ongenðiow   ecgum sweord[a],
blondenfexa   on bid wrecen,
þæt se þēodcyning   ðafian sceolde
Eafores ānne dōm.   Hyne yrringa
Wulf Wonrēding   wǣpne gerǣhte,   2965
þæt him for swenge   swāt ǣdrum sprong
forð under fexe.   Næs hē forht swā ðēh,
gomela Scilfing,   ac forgeald hraðe
wyrsan wrixle   wælhlem þone,
syððan ðēodcyning   þyder oncirde.   2970
Ne meahte se snella   sunu Wonrēdes
ealdum ceorle   [o]ndslyht giofan,
ac hē him on hēafde   helm ǣr gescer,
þæt hē blōde fāh   būgan sceolde,
fēoll on foldan;   næs hē fǣge þā gīt,   2975
ac hē hyne gewyrpte,   þēah ðe him wund hrine.
Lēt se hearda   Higelāces þegn
brād[n]e mēce,   þā his brōðor læg,
ealdsweord eotonisc   entiscne helm
brecan ofer bordweal;   ðā gebēah cyning,   2980
folces hyrde,   wæs in feorh dropen.
Ðā wǣron monige,   þē his mǣg wriðon,
ricone ārǣrdon,   ðā him gerȳmed wearð,
þæt hīe wælstōwe   wealdan mōston.
Þenden rēafode   rinc ōðerne,   2985
nam on Ongenðīo   īrenbyrnan,
heard swyrd hilted,   ond his helm somod;
hāres hyrste   Higelāce bær.
Hē ð(ām) frætwum fēng   ond him fægre gehēt

2958 Higelaces] hige lace MS   2959 forð] ford MS   2961 sweorda] sweordū MS
2972 ondslyht] hond slyht MS   2978 bradne] brade MS   2989 ðam] *lost at edge of* MS

to defend from the wave-borne warriors his treasure,   2955
his women and children; he ran away from there,
old, into his fortress. Then the pursuit was offered
to the Swedish people, the standard of Hygelac
overran the place of refuge,
after the Hrethlings thronged the enclosure.   2960
There with the edge of a sword, Ongentheow,
old graybeard, was brought to bay,
so that the king of that nation had to yield
to Eofor's will. Angrily he struck;
Wulf the son of Wonred lashed at him with his weapon,   2965
so that with his blow the blood sprang in streams
from under his hair. Yet the ancient Scylfing
was undaunted, and dealt back quickly
a worse exchange for that savage stroke,
once the ruler of that people turned around.   2970
The ready son of Wonred could not
give a stroke in return to the old soldier,
for he had cut through the helmet right on his head
so that he collapsed, covered in blood,
fell to the ground — he was not yet fated to die,   2975
but he recovered, though the cut hurt him.
The hardy thane of Hygelac[1] then let
his broad blade, as his brother lay there,
his ancient giant-made sword, shatter that gigantic helmet
over the shield-wall; then the king stumbled,   2980
shepherd of his people, mortally stricken.
        There were many there who bandaged his[2] kinsman,
quickly raised him up, when a way was clear for them,
so that they had control of that killing field.
Then one warrior plundered another,[3]   2985
took from Ongentheow the iron byrnie,
his hard hilted sword and his helmet too,
and carried the old man's armor to Hygelac.
He[4] took that war-gear and promised him gifts

---

1   I.e., Eofor, Wulf's brother.
2   I.e., Eofor's.
3   I.e., Eofor plundered Ongentheow.
4   I.e., Hygelac.

lēana (mid) lēodum,   ond gelæst[e] swā;   2990
geald þone gūðræs   Gēata dryhten,
Hrēðles eafora,   þā hē tō hām becōm,
Iofore ond Wulfe   mid ofermāðmum,
sealde hiora gehwæðrum   hund þūsenda
landes ond locenra bēaga —   ne ðorfte him ðā lēan oðwītan   2995
mon on middangearde,   syðða[n] hīe ðā mærða geslōgon —
ond ðā Iofore forgeaf   āngan dohtor,
hāmweorðunge,   hyldo tō wedde.

Þæt ys sīo fæhðo   ond se fēondscipe,
wælnīð wera,   ðæs ðe ic [wēn] hafo,   3000
þē ūs sēceað tō   Swēona lēoda,
syððan hīe gefricgeað   frēan ūserne
ealdorlēasne,   þone ðe ǣr gehēold
wið hettendum   hord ond rīce,
æfter hæleða hryre,   hwate Scyldingas,   3005
folcrēd fremede,   oððe furður gēn
eorlscipe efnde.   [Nū] is ofost betost,
þæt wē þēodcyning   þǣr scēawian,
ond þone gebringan,   þē ūs bēagas geaf,
on ādfære.   Ne scel ānes hwæt   3010
meltan mid þām mōdigan,   ac þǣr is māðma hord,
gold unrīme   grimme gecēa(po)d,
ond nū æt sīðestan   sylfes fēore
bēagas (geboh)te;   þā sceall brond fretan,
ǣled þeccean —   nalles eorl wegan   3015
māððum tō gemyndum,   nē mægð scȳne
habban on healse   hringweorðunge,
ac sceal geōmormōd,   golde berēafod
oft nalles ǣne   elland tredan,
nū se herewīsa   hleahtor ālegde,   3020
gamen ond glēodrēam.   Forðon sceall gār wesan
monig morgenceald   mundum bewunden,
hæfen on handa,   nalles hearpan swēg

2990 mid] *lost at edge of* MS   gelæste] gelæsta MS   2996 syððan] syðða MS
3000 wen] *not in* MS   3007 Nu] me MS   3012 geceapod] gecea . . d MS
3014 gebohte] . . . . te MS

among his people — and he kept that promise; 2990
the king of the Geats repaid that carnage,
the offspring of Hrethel, when he made it home,
gave to Eofor and Wulf extravagant treasures,
gave them each lands and locked rings,
worth a hundred thousand.[1] Not a man in this world could 2995
reproach those rewards, since they had won them with their deeds;
and to Eofor he gave his only daughter,
the pride of his home, as a pledge of his friendship.
　　　That is the feud and the fierce enmity,
savage hatred of men, that I expect now, 3000
when the Swedish people seek us out
after they have learned that our lord
has perished, who had once protected
his hoard and kingdom against all hostility,
after the fall of heroes, the valiant Scyldings,[2] 3005
worked for the people's good, and what is more,
performed noble deeds. Now we must hurry
and look upon our people's king,
and go with him who gave us rings
on the way to the pyre. No small part 3010
of the hoard shall burn with that brave man,
but countless gold treasures, grimly purchased,
and rings, here at last with his own life
paid for; then the flames shall devour,
the fire enfold — let no warrior wear 3015
treasures for remembrance, nor no fair maiden
have a ring-ornament around her neck,
but sad in mind, stripped of gold, she must
walk a foreign path, not once but often,
now that leader of our troop has laid aside laughter, 3020
his mirth and joy. Thus many a cold morning
shall the spear be grasped in frozen fingers,
hefted by hands, nor shall the sound of the harp

1　A monetary unit, though it is not clear which one.
2　The manuscript reading ("Scyldings" is a further object of "protected") is often
　emended to *Scylfingas*, i.e., Swedes, or *scildwigan* "shield-warriors"; the present
　reading is that of Mitchell and Robinson. As it stands in the manuscript, the Geatish
　herald is referring to Beowulf's earlier adventures against Grendel and his mother.

wīgend weccean,   ac se wonna hrefn
fūs ofer fǣgum   fela reordian,   3025
earne secgan,   hū him æt ǣte spēow,
þenden hē wið wulf   wæl rēafode."
    Swā se secg hwata   secggende wæs
lāðra spella;   hē ne lēag fela
wyrda nē worda.   Weorod eall ārās;   3030
ēodon unblīðe   under Earna Næs,
wollentēare   wundur scēawian.
Fundon ðā on sande   sāwullēasne
hlimbed healdan   þone þe him hringas geaf
ǣrran mǣlum;   þā wæs endedæg   3035
gōdum gegongen,   þæt se gūðcyning,
Wedra þēoden   wundordēaðe swealt.
Ǣr hī þǣr gesēgan   syllīcran wiht,
wyrm on wonge   wiðerrǣhtes þǣr
lāðne licgean;   wæs se lēgdraca   3040
grimlīc gry(refāh)   glēdum beswǣled;
sē wæs fīftiges   fōtgemearces
lang on legere;   lyftwynne hēold
nihtes hwīlum,   nyðer eft gewāt
dennes nīosian;   wæs ðā dēaðe fæst,   3045
hæfde eorðscrafa   ende genyttod.
Him big stōdan   bunan ond orcas,
discas lāgon   ond dȳre swyrd,
ōmige þurhetone,   swā hīe wið eorðan fæðm
þūsend wintra   þǣr eardodon;   3050
þonne wæs þæt yrfe   ēacencræftig,
iūmonna gold   galdre bewunden,
þæt ðām hringsele   hrīnan ne mōste
gumena ǣnig,   nefne God sylfa,
sigora Sōðcyning   sealde þām ðe hē wolde   3055
— hē is manna gehyld —   hord openian,
efne swā hwylcum manna,   swā him gemet ðūhte.

3041 gryrefah] gry . . . . MS

rouse the warriors, but the dark raven,
greedy for carrion, shall speak a great deal,   3025
ask the eagle how he fared at his feast
when he plundered corpses with the wolf."[1]
     Thus that brave speaker was speaking
a most unlovely truth; he did not lie much
in words or facts. The troop of warriors arose;   3030
they went, unhappy, to the Cape of Eagles,
with welling tears to look at that wonder.
There on the sand they found the soulless body
of the one who gave them rings in earlier times
laid out to rest; the last day   3035
had come for the good man, when the war-king,
prince of the Weders, died a wondrous death.
But first they saw an even stranger creature,
a loathsome serpent lying on the plain
directly across from him; grim with his colors   3040
the fire-dragon was, and scorched with his flames.
He was fifty feet long, lying there
stretched out; once he had joy in the air
in the dark night, and then down he would go
to seek his den, but now he was fast in death;   3045
he had come to the end of his cave-dwelling.
Cups and vessels stood beside him,
plates lay there and precious swords,
eaten through with rust, as if in the bosom of the earth
they had lain for a thousand winters;   3050
all that inheritance was deeply enchanted,
the gold of the ancients was gripped in a spell
so that no man in the world would be able to touch
that ring-hall, unless God himself,
the true King of Victories, Protector of men,   3055
granted to whomever He wished to open the hoard,
to whatever person seemed proper to Him.[2]

---

1   The eagle, wolf, and raven, the "beasts of battle," are a recurring motif in Old
     English poetry.

2   The power of the pagan spell can be overruled by the will of the true God.

Þā wæs gesȳne,   þæt se sīð ne ðāh
þām ðe unrihte   inne gehȳdde
wræ[t]e under wealle.   Weard ǣr ofslōh   3060
fēara sumne;   þā sīo fǣhð gewearð
gewrecen wrāðlīce.   Wundur hwār þonne
eorl ellenrōf   ende gefēre
līfgesceafta,   þonne leng ne mæg
mon mid his (mā)gum   meduseld būan.   3065
Swā wæs Bīowulfe,   þā hē biorges weard
sōhte searonīðas;   seolfa ne cūðe,
þurh hwæt his worulde gedāl   weorðan sceolde.
Swā hit oð dōmes dæg   dīope benemdon
þēodnas mǣre,   þā ðæt þǣr dydon,   3070
þæt se secg wǣre   synnum scildig,
hergum geheaðerod,   hellbendum fæst,
wommum gewītnad,   sē ðone wong str[u]de,
næ[fn]ē goldhwæte   gearwor hæfde
āgendes ēst   ǣr gescēawod.   3075
   Wīglāf maðelode,   Wīhstānes sunu:
"Oft sceall eorl monig   ānes willan
wrǣc ādrēog[an],   swā ūs geworden is.
Ne meahton wē gelǣran   lēofne þēoden,
rices hyrde   rǣd ǣnigne,   3080
þæt hē ne grētte   goldweard þone,
lēte hyne licgean   þǣr hē longe wæs,
wīcum wunian   oð woruldende,
heold on hēahgesceap.   Hord ys gescēawod,
grimme gegongen;   wæs þæt gifeðe tō swīð,   3085
þē ðone [þeodcyning]   þyder ontyhte.
Ic wæs þǣr inne   ond þæt eall geondseh,

3060 wræte] wræce MS   3065 magum] . . gū MS   3073 strude] strade MS   3074
næfne] næs he MS   3078 adreogan] adreogeð MS   3086 þeodcyning] *not in* MS

Then it was plain that the journey did not profit
the one[1] who had wrongfully hidden under a wall
that great treasure. The guardian had slain   3060
that one and few others;[2] then that feud was
swiftly avenged. It is a wonder to say
where a valiant earl should meet the end
of his span of life, when he may no longer
dwell in the mead-hall, a man with his kinsmen.   3065
So it was with Beowulf, when he sought the barrow's guardian
and a hostile fight; even he did not know
how his parting from life should come to pass,
since until doomsday mighty princes had deeply
pronounced, when they placed it there,   3070
that the man who plundered that place would be
harried by hostile demons, fast in hellish bonds,
grievously tortured, guilty of sins,
unless the Owner's grace had earlier
more readily favored the one eager for gold.[3]   3075
  Wiglaf spoke, son of Weohstan:
"Often many earls must suffer misery
through the will of one man, as we have now seen.
We could not persuade our dear prince,
shepherd of a kingdom, with any counsel,   3080
that he should not greet that gold-guardian,
let him lie there where he long had been,
inhabit the dwellings until the end of the world:
he held to his high destiny. The hoard is opened,
grimly gotten; that fate was too great   3085
which impelled the king of our people thither.
I was in there, and looked over it all,

---

1 I.e., the dragon.
2 Or "that one of a few," i.e., "a unique man" or "a man of rare greatness."
3 The OE text is corrupt and the precise meaning of this passage is not certain; the
  present translation tries to incorporate several suggested interpretations. The general
  sense seems to be clear enough—the gold was cursed, and only God's special grace
  would enable anyone to remove it. What this implies about Beowulf's failure, and his
  moral status, is less clear.

recedes geatwa,   þā mē gerȳmed wæs,
nealles swǣslīce   sīð ālȳfed
inn under eorðweall.   Ic on ofoste gefēng   3090
micle mid mundum   mægenbyrðenne
hordgestrēona,   hider ūt ætbær
cyninge mīnum.   Cwico wæs þā gēna,
wīs ond gewittig;   worn eall gespræc
gomol on gehðo,   ond ēowic grētan hēt,   3095
bæd þæt gē geworhton   æfter wines dǣdum
in bǣlstede   beorh þone hean,
micelne ond mǣrne,   swā hē manna wæs
wīgend weorðfullost   wīde geond eorðan,
þenden hē burhwelan   brūcan mōste.   3100
Uton nū efstan   ōðre [sīðe],
sēon ond sēcean   searo[gimma] geþræc,
wundur under wealle;   ic ēow wīsige,
þæt gē genōge   nēon scēawiað
bēagas ond brād gold.   Sīe sīo bǣr gearo,   3105
ǣdre geæfned,   þonne wē ūt cymen,
ond þonne geferian   frēan ūserne,
lēofne mannan   þǣr hē longe sceal
on ðæs waldendes   wǣre geþolian.”
Hēt ðā gebēodan   byre Wīhstānes,   3110
hæle hildedīor   hæleða monegum,
boldāgendra,   þæt hīe bǣlwudu
feorran feredon,   folcāgende,
gōdum tōgēnes: “Nū sceal glēd fretan
— weaxan wonna lēg —   wigena strengel,   3115
þone ðe oft gebād   īsernscūre,
þonne strǣla storm   strengum gebǣded
scōc ofer scildweall,   sceft nytte hēold,
fæ[ð]ergearwum fūs   flāne fullēode.”
Hūru se snotra   sunu Wīhstānes   3120
ācīgde of corðre   cyniges þegnas
syfone (tō)somne,   þā sēlestan,
ēode eahta sum   under inwithrōf
hilderinc[a];   sum on handa bær

3101 sīðe] *not in* MS   3102 searogimma] searo MS   3119 fæðergearwum] fæder-
gearwū MS   3122 syfone tosomne] *only partly legible*   3124 hilderinca] hilde rinc MS

the hall's ornaments, when a way was open to me;
by no means gently was a journey allowed
in under that earth-wall. In eager haste I seized 3090
in my hands a great mighty burden
of hoard-treasure, and bore it out hither
to my king. He was still conscious then,
thoughtful and alert; he spoke of many things,
an old man in his sorrow, and ordered that I greet you; 3095
he asked that you build a great high barrow
for your prince's deeds, in the place of his pyre,
mighty and glorious, since he was of men
the most worthy warrior throughout the wide world,
while he could enjoy the wealth of a hall. 3100
Let us now make haste for one more time
to see and seek out that store of cunning gems,
the wonder under the wall; I will direct you
so that you can inspect them up close,
abundant rings and broad gold. Let the bier be ready, 3105
quickly prepared, when we come out,
then let us bear our beloved lord,
that dear man, to where he must long
rest in the keeping of the Ruler."
        Then the son of Weohstan, brave battle-warrior, 3110
let it be made known to many heroes
and householders, that they should bring from afar
the wood for the pyre to that good one,[1]
the leader of his folk: "Now the flames must devour,
the black blaze rise over the ruler of warriors, 3115
who often awaited the showers of iron
when the storm of arrows hurled from bow-strings
shot over the wall, the shafts did their duty
swift on feather-wings, sent on the arrow-heads."
        Lo, then the wise son of Weohstan 3120
summoned from that host some of the best
of the king's thanes, seven altogether;
he went, one of eight, under that evil roof;
one of the brave warriors bore in his hands

---

1   I.e., the dead Beowulf.

æledlēoman,   sē ðe on orde gēong.   3125
Næs ðā on hlytme   hwā þæt hord strude,
syððan orwearde   ænigne dæl
secgas gesēgon   on sele wunian,
lǣne licgan;   lȳt ænig mearn,
þæt hī ofostlīc(e)   ūt geferedon   3130
dȳre māðmas;   dracan ēc scufun,
wyrm ofer weallclif,   lēton wēg niman,
flōd fæðmian   frætwa hyrde.
Þ[ā] wæs wunden gold   on wǣn hladen,
æghwæs unrīm,   æþelin[g] boren,   3135
hār hilde(rinc)   tō Hronesnæsse.

XLIII

Him ðā gegiredan   Gēata lēode
ād on eorðan   unwāclīcne,
helm[um] behongen,   hildebordum,
beorhtum byrnum,   swā hē bēna wæs;   3140
ālegdon ðā tōmiddes   mǣrne þēoden
hæleð hīofende,   hlāford lēofne.
Ongunnon þā on beorge   bǣlfȳra mǣst
wīgend weccan;   wud(u)rēc āstāh
sweart ofer swi[o]ðole,   swōgende lē[g]   3145
wōpe bewunden   — windblond gelæg —
oð þæt hē ðā bānhūs   gebrocen hæfde
hāt on hreðre.   Higum unrōte
mōdceare mǣndon,   mondryhtnes cw(e)alm;
swylce giōmorgyd   G[ē]at(isc) mēowle   3150
(æfter Bīowulfe   b)undenheorde
(sang) sorgcearig,   sǣ[d]e geneah[he],
þæt hīo hyre (hearmda)gas   hearde ond(r)ēde,

3130 ofostlice] ofostlic . MS   3134 Þa] þæt MS   3135 æþeling] æþelinge MS
3136 hilderinc] hilde . . . . MS   3139 helmum] helm MS   3144 wudurec] wud . . ec MS
3145 swioðole] swicðole MS   leg] let MS   3149 cwealm] cw . . lm MS
3150 Geatisc] . . iat . . MS   3151 æfter Biowulfe bundenheorde] . . . . unden heord . MS
3152 sang] *illegible* MS   sæde] sælðe MS   geneahhe] ge neahl MS
3153 hearmdagas] . . . . . gas MS   ondrede] . . . . . de MS

a flaming torch, and went before them. 3125
It was not chosen by lots who should loot that hoard,[1]
once the men saw it sitting in the hall,
every part of it unprotected,
lying there wasting; there was little lament
that they should have to hurry out with 3130
the precious treasures. They also pushed the dragon,
the worm over the cliff-wall, let the waves take him,
the flood embrace the guard of that finery;
then the twisted gold, an uncountable treasure,
was loaded in a wagon, and the noble one was carried, 3135
the gray-haired warrior, to the Cape of Whales.

XLIII

The people of the Geats then prepared for him
a splendid pyre upon the earth,
hung with battle-shields and helmets
and bright byrnies, as he had bidden; 3140
there in the middle they laid the mighty prince,
the heroes lamenting their dear lord.
Then the warriors kindled there on the cliff
the greatest of funeral pyres; dark over the flames
the woodsmoke rose, the roaring fire 3145
mingled with weeping — the wind lay still —
until it had broken that bone-house
hot at the heart. With heavy spirits
they mourned their despair, the death of their lord;
and a sorrowful song sang the Geatish woman,[2] 3150
with hair bound up, for Beowulf the king,
with sad cares, earnestly said
that she dreaded the hard days ahead,

---

1   I.e., everybody had a share; there was enough for all.
2   The MS is damaged throughout this section, and the readings in this passage are con-
    jectural; it is not clear who the "Geatish woman" is, though her advanced age is indi-
    cated by her bound-up hair. Typically, in Germanic poetry, it is women (and poets)
    who mourn.

wælfylla wo[r]n,   (w)erudes egesan,
hȳ[n]ðo ond hæf(t)nȳd.   Heofon rēce swealg.   3155
    Geworhton ðā   Wedra lēode
hlǣ(w) on h[ō]e,   sē wæs hēah ond brād,
(w)eglīðendum   wīde gesȳne,
ond beti(m)bredon   on tȳn dagum
beadurōfes bēcn,   bronda lāfe   3160
wealle beworhton,   swā hyt weorðlīcost
foresnotre men   findan mihton.
Hī on beorg dydon   bēg ond siglu,
eall swylce hyrsta,   swylce on horde ǣr
nīðhēdige men   genumen hæfdon;   3165
forlēton eorla gestrēon   eorðan healdan,
gold on grēote,   þǣr hit nū gēn lifað
eldum swā unnyt,   swā hit (ǣro)r wæs.
Þā ymbe hlǣw riodan   hildedēore,
æþelinga bearn,   ealra twelf[e],   3170
woldon (care) cwīðan,   [ond] cyning mǣnan,
wordgyd wrecan,   ond ymb w(er) sprecan;
eahtodan eorlscipe   ond his ellenweorc
duguðum dēmdon —   swā hit gedē(fe) bið,
þæt mon his winedryhten   wordum herge,   3175
ferhðum frēoge,   þonne hē forð scile
of l[ī]chaman   (lǣ)ded weorðan.
Swā begnornodon   Gēata lēode
hlāfordes (hry)re,   heorðgenēatas;
cwǣdon þæt hē wǣre   wyruldcyning[a]   3180
manna mildust   ond mon[ðw]ǣrust,
lēodum līðost   ond lofgeornost.

3154 worn] wonn MS   werudes] . erudes MS   3155 hynðo] hyðo MS   ond
hæftnyd] 7 hæf . nyd MS   3157 hlæw on hoe] hlæ . on hde (*nearly illegible*) MS
3158 wegliðendum] . egliðendū MS   3159 betimbredon] beti . bredon MS
3168 hit æror] hyt . . . r MS   3170 twelfe] twelfa MS   3171 care] *lost at beginning
of line* MS   ond cyning] scyning MS   3172 wer] w . . MS   3174 gedefe] ḡde . . MS
3177 lichaman] lachaman MS   læded] *nearly illegible* MS   3179 hryre] . . . re MS
3180 wyruldcyninga] wyruldcyning MS   3181 monðwærust] mondrærust (?) MS

the times of slaughter, the host's terror,
harm and captivity. Heaven swallowed the smoke.   3155
  Then the Weder people wrought for him
a barrow on the headland; it was high and broad,
visible from afar to sea-voyagers,
and in ten days they built the beacon
of that battle-brave one; the ashes of the flames   3160
they enclosed with a wall, as worthily
as the most clever of men could devise it.
In the barrow they placed rings and bright jewels,
all the trappings that those reckless men
had seized from the hoard before,   3165
let the earth hold the treasures of earls,
gold in the ground, where it yet remains,
just as useless to men as it was before.
Then round the mound rode the battle-brave men,
offspring of noblemen, twelve in all,   3170
they wished to voice their cares and mourn their king,
utter sad songs and speak of that man;
they praised his lordship and his proud deeds
judged well his prowess. As it is proper
that one should praise his lord with words,   3175
should love him in his heart when the fatal hour comes,
when he must from his body be led forth,
so the men of the Geats lamented
the fall of their prince, those hearth-companions;
they said that he was of all the kings of the world   3180
the mildest of men and the most gentle,
the kindest to his folk and the most eager for fame.

Glossary of Proper Names

Abel	slain by his brother **Cain**; the story is told in Genesis 4:1-16
Ælfhere	kinsman of **Wiglaf**
Æschere	a prominent Dane, advisor to **Hrothgar**; slain by Grendel's mother
Battle-Scylding	see **Scyldings**
Battle-Scylfing	see **Scylfings**
Beanstan	father of **Breca**
Beowulf	(prologue) Danish king, son of **Scyld**
Breca	engaged in a youthful swimming contest with Beowulf
Bright-Danes	see **Danes**
Brondings	the people of **Breca**
Brosings	(= Old Norse Brísings) makers of the magical necklace of Freya in Norse myth, to which a necklace in the story is compared
Cain	slayer of **Abel** in Genesis 4:1-16; father of the race of monsters
Dæghrefn	a warrior of the **Hugas** slain by Beowulf in hand-to-hand combat during **Hygelac**'s ill-fated raid on the **Frisians**
Danes	**Hrothgar**'s people; the **Scyldings**; also called Bright-, Half-, Ring-, Spear-, East-, West-, North-, and South-Danes
Eadgils	son of **Ohthere**, brother of **Eanmund**
Eanmund	son of **Ohthere**, brother of **Eadgils**; slain by **Weohstan**
East-Danes	see **Danes**
Ecglaf	father of **Unferth**
Ecgtheow	father of Beowulf
Ecgwala	a Danish king; the "sons of Ecgwala" are the **Danes**
Eofor	a warrior of the **Geats**; brother of **Wulf**; slayer of **Ongentheow**; son-in-law of **Hygelac**
Eomer	son of **Offa**
Eormanric	king of the Ostrogoths
Eotens	unclear: perhaps the **Jutes**, perhaps the **Frisians**, perhaps "giants" (the literal meaning of the word) as a nickname for one group or the other
Finn	king of the **Frisians**, husband of **Hildeburh**; killed by **Hengest**

Finns	the people of Finland; the Lapps
Fitela	legendary companion, nephew (and son) of **Sigemund**
Folcwalda	father of **Finn**
Franks	a Germanic tribe; see **Hetware**, **Hugas**, **Merovingians**
Freawaru	daughter of **Hrothgar** betrothed to **Ingeld**
Frisians	a Germanic tribe; **Finn**'s people
Froda	chief of the **Heathobards**, father of **Ingeld**
Garmund	father of **Offa**
Geats	**Hygelac**'s people and Beowulf's; a Germanic tribe; also called War-Geats, Hrethmen, Hrethlings, Weders
Gifthas	an East Germanic tribe
Grendel	descendent of **Cain**; monstrous marauder of the **Danes**
Guthlaf	a Danish warrior, companion of **Hengest**
Hæreth	father of **Hygd**
Hæthcyn	Geatish prince, second son of **Hrethel**
Half-Danes	see **Danes**
Halga	Danish prince, younger brother of **Hrothgar**
Hama	legendary Goth; stole **Brosings'** necklace
Healfdene	king of the **Danes**, father of **Hrothgar**
Heardred	king of the **Geats**, son of **Hygelac**
Heathobards	**Ingeld**'s people; a Germanic tribe
Heatholaf	a **Wylfing** slain by **Ecgtheow**
Heathoream	a Scandinavian tribe: Norwegians, more or less
Helmings	the family of **Wealhtheow**
Hemming	kinsman of **Offa** and **Eomer**
Hengest	leader of the **Danes**; killed **Finn** in **Frisia**
Heorogar	Dane, eldest brother of **Hrothgar**
Heorot	the great hall of **Hrothgar**
Heoroweard	Dane; son of **Heorogar**
Herebeald	Geatish prince, eldest son of **Hrethel**; killed by his brother **Hæthcyn**
Heremod	king of the **Danes** in the poem's distant past, before the Scylding dynasty; he came to a bad end
Hereric	brother of **Hygd**, uncle of **Heardred**
Hetware	a Frankish tribe, allied with the **Frisians**; fought against **Hygelac**
Hildeburh	sister of the Danish **Hnæf**, wife of the Frisian **Finn**
Hnæf	chief of the **Half-Danes**, brother of **Hildeburh**; killed by **Finn**

Hoc	Dane, father of **Hildeburh** and **Hnæf**
Hondscio	Geatish warrior, comrade of Beowulf; slain by **Grendel**
Honor-Scyldings	see **Scyldings**
Hrethel	king of the **Geats**, father of **Hygelac**, grandfather of Beowulf
Hrethlings	sons of **Hrethel**, i.e., the **Geats**
Hrethmen	the **Geats**
Hrethric	Dane, son of **Hrothgar**
Hrothgar	aged king of the **Danes** beset by **Grendel**; helped by Beowulf
Hrothmund	Dane, son of **Hrothgar**
Hrothulf	Dane, son of **Halga**, nephew of **Hrothgar**; not to be trusted
Hrunting	the sword of **Unferth**
Hugas	the **Franks**, allies of the **Frisians**
Hunlaf	father of one of the warriors in **Hengest**'s troop
Hygd	queen of the **Geats**, wife of **Hygelac**, daughter of **Hæreth**
Hygelac	king of the **Geats**, uncle of Beowulf
Ingeld	prince of the **Heathobards**, son of **Froda**, betrothed to **Freawaru**; after the events narrated in the poem he presumably burns down the great hall of **Heorot**
Ingwines	the "friends of Ing": the **Danes**
Jutes	allies of the **Frisians**; see **Eotens**
Merovingians	the **Franks**
Nægling	Beowulf's sword
North-Danes	see **Danes**
Offa	king of the Angles, husband of **Thryth**
Ohthere	Swede, son of **Ongentheow**
Onela	Swede, son of **Ongentheow**; usurped throne
Ongentheow	Swedish king; killed by **Wulf** and **Eofor**
Oslaf	a Danish warrior, companion of **Hengest**
Ring-Danes	see **Danes**
Scyld Scefing	legendary founder of the Danish royal family
Scyldings	the Danes; also called Battle-, Honor-, Victory-Scyldings
Scylfings	the Swedes
Sigemund	legendary Germanic hero, son of **Wæls**
South-Danes	see **Danes**
Spear-Danes	see **Danes**
Swerting	uncle of **Hygelac**

Thryth	(often construed as Modthryth) wife of **Offa**
Unferth	Danish spokesman ("thyle") and courtier of **Hrothgar**
Victory-Scyldings	see **Scyldings**
Volsung	another name for **Sigemund**, son of **Wæls**
Waegmundings	the family of **Weohstan**, **Wiglaf**, and Beowulf
Wæls	father of **Sigemund**
War-Geats	see **Geats**
Wealhtheow	Danish queen, wife of **Hrothgar**
Weders	the **Geats**
Weland	legendary Germanic smith
Wendels	a Germanic tribe; perhaps the Vandals, perhaps not
Weohstan	father of **Wiglaf**; killed **Eanmund**
West-Danes	see **Danes**
Wiglaf	son of **Weohstan**, young retainer of Beowulf
Withergyld	a dead **Heathobard**
Wonred	a Geat, father of **Wulf** and **Eofor**
Wulf	a warrior of the **Geats**, brother of **Eofor**; assisted in killing **Ongentheow**
Wulfgar	a warrior of the **Danes**; herald at the court of **Hrothgar**
Wylfings	a Germanic tribe of which **Heatholaf** was a member, until **Ecgtheow** killed him
Yrmenlaf	a Dane, younger brother of Æschere

Genealogies

1. The Danes (Scyldings)

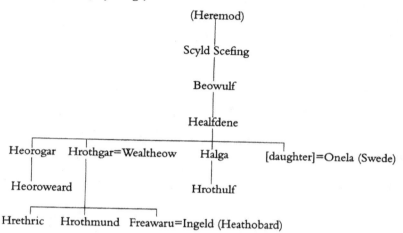

(Heremod)

Scyld Scefing

Beowulf

Healfdene

Heorogar   Hrothgar=Wealtheow   Halga   [daughter]=Onela (Swede)

Heoroweard   Hrothulf

Hrethric   Hrothmund   Freawaru=Ingeld (Heathobard)

2. The Geats

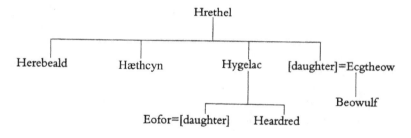

Hrethel

Herebeald   Hæthcyn   Hygelac   [daughter]=Ecgtheow

Beowulf

Eofor=[daughter]   Heardred

3. The Swedes (Scylfings)

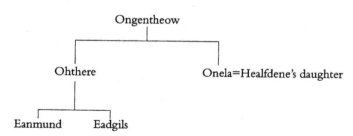

Ongentheow

Ohthere   Onela=Healfdene's daughter

Eanmund   Eadgils

The Geatish-Swedish Wars

When the story of Beowulf's fight with the dragon begins, the narrator leaps over fifty years in one brief passage. It is a tumultuous condensation of a complex chain of events (2200-08):

> Then it came to pass amid the crash of battle
> in later days, after Hygelac lay dead,
> and for Heardred the swords of battle held
> deadly slaughter under the shield-wall,
> when the Battle-Scylfings sought him out,
> those hardy soldiers, and savagely struck down
> the nephew of Hereric in his victorious nation —
> then came the broad kingdom
> into Beowulf's hands;

These events are referred to throughout the last thousand lines of the poem, but they are not told in a straightforward way or in chronological order. The fortunes of the Geatish royal house may be reconstructed as follows:

1. Hæthcyn accidentally kills his brother Herebeald; their father Hrethel dies of grief (2432-71). Hæthcyn becomes king of the Geats.
2. After the death of Hrethel, Ohthere and Onela, the sons of the Swedish king Ongentheow, attack the Geats (2472-78).
3. In retaliation, Hæthcyn attacks Ongentheow in Sweden (2479-84); at first he is successful, but he is later killed at Ravenswood (2922-41). Hygelac's men Wulf and Eofor kill Ongentheow, and Hygelac (Hæthcyn's brother) is victorious (2484-89, 2942-99). Hygelac becomes king of the Geats; Ohthere becomes king of the Swedes.
4. Hygelac is killed in Frisia; his son Heardred becomes king of the Geats (2354-78).
5. Ohthere's brother Onela seizes the Swedish throne and drives out the sons of Ohthere, Eanmund and Eadgils (2379-84). Heardred takes in these exiles, and Onela attacks Heardred for this hospitality and kills him. Onela allows Beowulf to rule the Geats (2385-90).
6. Around this time Weohstan, father of Wiglaf, kills Eanmund on behalf of Onela (2611-19).
7. Eadgils escapes, later to kill Onela in Sweden, with help sent by Beowulf (2391-96); he presumably becomes king of the Swedes.
8. During Beowulf's fifty-year reign, the death of Eanmund is unavenged. After Beowulf's death, Eanmund's brother Eadgils will probably seek vengeance against Wiglaf, son of Weohstan (2999-3005).

Appendix A: Characters Mentioned in Beowulf

1. From Gregory of Tours,[1] *History of the Franks* **III.3**

[Source: Latin text in Klaeber, 3rd ed., 268. Trans. R.M. Liuzza (RML).]

After this, the Danes and their king, whose name was Chlochilaicus, attacked the Franks by ship from the sea. When they came ashore they devastated one district of the kingdom of Theuderic [king of the Franks] and took prisoners; after loading their ships with these prisoners and the rest of their plunder, they sought to return to their own land. But their king stayed on the shore while the ships were taking to the deep sea, for he was going to follow a short time after. When the news had been brought to Theudericus that one of his districts had been plundered by foreigners, he sent his son Theudebertus to those parts with a great army and a large stock of weapons. After killing the king, he set upon the enemy in a battle at sea and conquered them, and restored all the plunder to his own land.

2. From the *Liber Monstrorum*[2] **I.2**

[Source: The Latin text of the *Liber Monstrorum* and an English translation are found in Orchard 258. Trans. RML.]

There are also monsters of amazing size, like King Higlacus, who ruled the Getae and was slain by the Franks. When he was only twelve years old no horse could carry him. His bones are preserved on an island in the Rhine, where it empties into the ocean, and are shown as a wonder to people who come from afar.

---

1   Gregory of Tours (539-594), Frankish historian and Bishop of Tours. In his *History* he mentions that the Danes plundered the coastal regions of the Franks; the event is also mentioned in the anonymous eighth-century *Liber Historiae Francorum*, ch. 19. Gregory's Chlochilaicus is Beowulf's uncle Hygelac.

2   Anonymous eighth-century (?) Anglo-Latin catalogue of monstrosities, surviving in five ninth- and tenth-century manuscripts.

3. From Alcuin,[1] Letter to "Speratus" (797)

[Source: Latin text in Dümmler 183. Trans. RML.]

Let the Word of God be read at the clergy's meals. There it is proper to hear the reader, not the harpist; the sermons of the Fathers, not the songs of the heathens. What has Ingeld to do with Christ? The house is narrow, it cannot hold them both. The King of heaven will have no fellowship with so-called kings who are pagan and damned, for the Eternal King reigns in Heaven, while the pagan is damned and laments in Hell. The voices of readers should be heard in your houses, not the crowd of revelers in the streets.

4. West-Saxon Royal Genealogies

a. From Asser,[2] *Life of King Alfred* (893), ch. 1

[Source: *Alfred the Great: Asser's Life of King Alfred and Other Contemporary Sources*, trans. and ed. Simon Keynes and Michael Lapidge (Harmondsworth: Penguin, 1983) 67.]

In the year of the Lord's Incarnation 849 Alfred, king of the Anglo-Saxons, was born at the royal estate called Wantage, in the district known as Berkshire (which is so called from Berroc Wood, where the box-tree grows very abundantly). His genealogy is woven in this way: King Alfred was the son of King Æthelwulf, the son of Egbert, the son of Ealhmund, the son of Eafa, the son of Eoppa, the son of Ingild. Ingild and Ine, the famous king of the West Saxons, were two brothers; Ine journeyed to Rome, and honourably ending this present life there he entered the heavenly land to reign with Christ. They were the sons of Cenred, the son of Ceolwold, the son of Cutha, the son of Cuthwine, the son of Ceawlin, the son of Cynric,

---

1   Alcuin of York (735-804), head of the cathedral school at York and after 782 head of Charlemagne's palace school at Aachen. The recipient of this letter, "Speratus," was formerly identified as Hygebald, Bishop of Lindisfarne (797), but is now thought to be a Mercian bishop. Alcuin's rhetorical question is a Christian commonplace, deriving ultimately from St Paul (2 Corinthians 6:15) by way of Tertullian and Jerome. Ingeld is also mentioned in *Widsith* 45-49 (see below, Appendix A6). See further Levine, and Bullough.

2   Asser, monk, bishop, and biographer of Alfred, king of Wessex. His work begins with the genealogy of the West-Saxon royal house, a list that includes a number of names familiar from *Beowulf*. The *Anglo-Saxon Chronicle*, a record of English history begun in the latter decades of the ninth century, contains a similar genealogy in its entry for the year 855. The genealogy of Æthelwulf of Wessex suggests not only an interest in blending the Danish and English past, but also the conflation of Germanic and biblical stories in the creation of royal authority.

the son of Creoda, the son of Cerdic, the son of Elesa, the son of Gewis (after whom the Welsh call that whole race the Gewisse), the son of Brand, the son of Bældæg, the son of Woden, the son of Frithuwald, the son of Frealaf, the son of Frithuwulf, the son of Finn, [the son of] Godwulf, the son of Geat (whom the pagans worshipped for a long time as a god). The poet Sedulius mentions Geat in his poem *Carmen Paschale*, as follows:

> Since the pagan poets sought in their fictions to swagger either in high-flowing measure, or in the wailing of tragedy's speech, or with comedy's absurd Geta,[1] or by means of any sort of verse whatever to relate the violent crimes of evil deeds and sing of monumental wickedness, and with scholarly application commit these many lies to paper: why should I—a poet accustomed to chanting the measures of the harp in the manner of David, and of taking my place in the holy chorus and hymning heavenly melodies in pleasing diction—be silent concerning the renowned miracles of Christ who brought us salvation?

Geat was the son of Tætwa, the son of Beaw, the son of Sceldwa, the son of Heremod, the son of Itermon, the son of Hathra, the son of Hwala, the son of Bedwig, the son of Seth, the son of Noah, the son of Lamech, the son of Methuselah, the son of Enoch, [the son of Jared], the son of Mahalaleel, the son of Cainan, the son of Enos, the son of Seth, the son of Adam.

b. From Æthelweard,[2] *Chronicle* III.3

[Source: A. Campbell, ed., *The Chronicle of Æthelweard* (London, 1962) 33. Trans. RML.]

... Godwulf, son of Geat, son of Tatwa, son of Beow, son of Scyld, son of Sceaf. This Sceaf, surrounded by weapons, was driven ashore in a ship on an island in the ocean which is called Scani; and he was a very young boy and unknown to the inhabitants of that land. However, he was taken in by them, and they looked after him with tender care as one of their own household, and later chose him as their king. From his line King Æthelwulf traces his descent.

---

1 This "Geta" is in reality a comic character in the plays of Terence, and has nothing to do with any tribe in *Beowulf*.

2 Æthelweard (d. c. 1000), Anglo-Saxon nobleman, descendant of Alfred the Great and Latin historian. His genealogy is largely derived from Asser but contains additional information; the story he tells of Sceaf is told of his son Scyld in *Beowulf*. For more information on Anglo-Saxon royal genealogy, see Sisam, "Anglo-Saxon Royal Genealogies"; Dumville, "Anglian Collection" and "Kingship, Genealogies and Regnal Lists"; Moisl; and Murray.

5. "The Fight at Finnsburh"[1]

[Source: Text in Klaeber, 3rd. ed., 245-49. Trans. RML.]

<pre>
                    ... are burning."
Then Hnæf spoke, the battle-young king:
"This is not the eastern dawn; no dragon flies here,
nor are the gables of this hall aflame,
But they bear forth here ...
                    ... birds are singing,   5
the gray-coated one howls, the war-wood resounds,
shield echoes to shaft. Now this moon shines
wandering under the clouds; now woeful deeds arise
which will make enemies for our people.
But awake now, my warriors!   10
take up your shields, think of valor,
fight in the vanguard, and be resolute!"
Then many a gold-laden thane arose, girded his sword;
then to the door went the noble warriors
Sigeferth and Eaha, drew their swords,   15
and at the other door Ordlaf and Guthlaf,
and Hengest himself was at their heels.
—Meanwhile Garulf exhorted Guthere
that he should not risk so precious a life
at the first attack on the hall-door,   20
since a hardy warrior wished to take it away,
but he asked over all, openly,
the bold-minded hero, who held the door.
"Sigeferth is my name," said he, "I am a prince of the Secgan,
a well-known exile; I have survived many woes,   25
hard battles, and here there is appointed to you
whatever fate you wish to seek from me."
    Then in the hall was the sound of slaughter:
the hollow shield, the body's guard, was to shatter
in the hands of the brave; the rafters rattled,   30
</pre>

---

1   Anonymous and undated Old English poem. The only record of this poem is a tran-
    scription in George Hickes's 1705 *Thesaurus*. Hickes reports that he found the poem
    on a single leaf in the Archbishop of Canterbury's library at Lambeth Palace,
    London, but the leaf has never been found. Hickes's transcript is probably not
    entirely accurate, and the language of the poem is somewhat difficult, but the poem
    appears to recount an episode in the battle between Finn and Hengest alluded to in
    Beowulf 1063-1162. See further Fry; Tolkien, *Finn and Hengest*; and Stanley,
    "Heroic Lay."

until in the battle Garulf fell,
the foremost of all the men of that country,
the son of Guthlaf, and around him a host of good men,
the corpses of the brave. The raven wheeled,
dark and dusky. The gleam of swords shone   35
as if all Finnesburh were on fire.
I have never heard of sixty more worthy warriors
bearing themselves better in the clash of foes;
nor ever was the sweet mead better repaid
than those young companions paid to Hnæf.[1]   40
They fought five days, so that none fell
among those retainers, but they held the door.
    Then a wounded hero took himself away,
said that his mail-coat was broken,
his armor useless and his helmet pierced;   45
then the ruler of the people quickly asked him
how those other warriors endured their wounds,
or which of the two young men ...

6. *Widsith*[2]

[Source: Kemp Malone, *Widsith*, rev. ed. (Copenhagen: Rosenkilde and Bagger, 1962). Trans. RML.]

Widsith spoke, unlocked his word-hoard,
he who had wandered most widely over the earth
among the races of men; often he had received

---

1   The meaning of these lines is disputed and the text corrupt. They seem to refer to the
    idea that warriors who drank at their lord's table incurred an obligation to repay his
    generosity with their loyalty in battle. The mead is sweet, the repayment bitter.
2   Anonymous and undated Old English poem found in the "Exeter Book" of Old
    English poetry, a manuscript written c. 975 and kept since that time in the Cathedral
    Library in Exeter. The Exeter Book is a miscellaneous collection—it begins with a
    group of Advent lyrics and ends with a collection of sometimes obscene riddles—
    and the various origins of its various pieces are unknown. This poem tells of a *scop*
    or poet named Widsith (whose name means "far-traveler") who boasts of the many
    lands he has seen and the generous kings he has entertained. His fabulous journeys
    include some tribes and rulers who are no more than names today, and may not have
    been much more than that to the poem's original audience, but his catalogue also
    mentions a number of characters found in *Beowulf*. See Malone, *Widsith*, for further
    discussion of the obscurer personages in the poem, and Joyce Hill, "*Wīdsīð* and the
    Tenth Century" (*Neuphilologische Mitteilungen* 85 [1984]: 305-15); still useful is
    R.W. Chambers, *Widsith: A Study in Old English Heroic Legend* (Cambridge: Cam-
    bridge UP, 1912).

precious treasures in the hall. His noble blood
sprang from the Myrgings. He was with Ealhhilde, 5
beloved peace-weaver, on her first journey,
when she sought the country of the victorious king
Eormanric, east among the Angles,
the scourge of traitors.[1] He began to speak many things:
  "Much have I heard of men who wield power! 10
Every prince must practice virtue,
each nobleman guide his land like others,
if he wishes his princely throne to prosper.
  For a time Hwala was the best of these,
and Alexander the most powerful of all 15
the race of men, and he prospered the most
of all those I've heard of on the face of the earth.
Attila ruled the Huns, Eormanric the Goths,
Becca the Banings and the Burgundians Gifica.
Caesar ruled the Greeks and Caelic the Finns, 20
Hagen the Holmrygs and Henden the Glomman.
Witta ruled the Swaefe, Wada the Halsings,
Meaca the Myrgings, Mearchealf the Hundings.
Theodric ruled the Franks, Thyle the Rondings,
Breca the Brondings, Billing the Werns. 25
Oswine ruled the Eow and Gefwulf the Jutes,
Finn Folcwalding the race of the Frisians.
Sighere for a long time ruled the Sea-Danes,
Hnæf the Hocings, Helm the Wulfings,
Wald the Woings, Wod the Thuringians, 30
Sæferth the Sycges, the Swedes Ongentheow.
Sceafthere the Ymbers, Sceafa the Langobards,
Hun the Hætwera and Holen the Wrosns.
Hringweald was called the king of the War-farers,
Offa ruled the Angles, Alewih the Danes; 35
he was the bravest of all these men,
yet he did not surpass the valor of Offa,
for Offa won, while still a boy
in his first manly fight, the greatest of kingdoms.
No one in his day could equal him in valor 40
on the field of battle. With a single sword
he redrew the map of the Myrgings
around Fifeldore; afterwards the Angles
and Swedes held their land just as Offa had won it.

---

1 Or "the cruel oath-breaker," an allusion to Eormanric's future slaying of his wife.
   The reading here is that of Kemp Malone.

Hrothulf and Hrothgar held peace together 45
for a long time, uncle and nephew,
after they had driven off the race of vikings
and humbled Ingeld's battle-array,
hacked down at Heorot the pride of the Heathobards.

Since I have sojourned in many strange lands 50
across the wide world, where I have come to know
good and evil, cut off from my home,
wandered wide, far away from my kinsmen,
therefore I can sing and tell a tale,
make known before the crowd in the mead-hall 55
how my noble patrons chose to reward me.
I was with the Huns and with the Hreth-Goths,
with the Swedes and the Geats and the South-Danes.
With the Wendels I was, and the Wærns and the vikings,
with the Gifthas I was, and the Wineda and the Gefflegas, 60
With the Angles I was, and the Swedes and the Ænenas,
with the Saxons I was, and the Sycges and the Swordsmen.
With the Hrones I was, and the Deans and the Heathoreams,
With the Thuringians I was and the Throwends,
and with the Burgundians, where I received a ring; 65
Guth-here gave me a gracious treasure there
as a reward for my song—that was no miserly king!
With the Franks I was, and the Frisians and the Frumtings,
with the Rugians I was, and the Glomman and the Romans.
I was also in Italy with Ælfwine, 70
who had, to my knowledge, the readiest hand
of any man for earning praise,
the most generous heart for giving our rings,
bright circlets, the son of Eadwine.

With the Sercings I was and with the Serings, 75
with the Greeks I was, with the Finns and with Caesar,
who had possession of the cities of wine,
riches and beauty and the realms of the Walas.
I was with the Scots and the Picts and the Scride-finns,
with the Lid-vikings and the Leons and the Langobards, 80
with heathens and heroes and Hundings.
I was with the Israelites and the Assyrians,
the Hebrews and Hindus and Egyptians;
I was with the Medes and the Persians and the Myrgings,
and the Ongen-Myrgings and the Mofdings, 85
and with the Amothings. With the East-Thuringians I was
and with the Eols and the Ists and the Idumings.
And I was with Eormanric all the while,

where the king of the Goths did good for me; 90
he gave me a ring, that prince of city-dwellers,
whose worth was reckoned at six hundred *smœts*
of brightest gold, counted out in shillings;
I gave it over to Eadgils,
my lord and protector, when I came to my home, 95
a reward for the dear one because he gave me land,
the lord of the Myrgings, my father's homeland.
And then Ealhhild gave me another,
noble queen, daughter of Eadwin.
Her praise spread far and wide in many lands,
when I could tell in my songs 100
where I knew under the skies the best
gold-laden queen for giving of gifts,
when Scilling and I raised up a song
with a clear voice for our victorious lord,
loud with the harp the joyful noise rang, 105
when many men, proud of heart,
said in words what they knew well,
that they had never heard a better song.
    Afterwards I passed through all the land of the Goths,
always seeking the best companions: 110
such was the household of Eormanric.
I sought Hehca and Beadeca and the Herelings,
I sought Emerca and Frindla and East-Goth,
the wise and good father of Unwen.
I sought Secca and Becca, Seafola and Theodoric, 115
Heathoric and Sifeca, Hlitha and Incgentheow;
I sought Eadwin and Elsa, Ægelmund and Hungar,
and the proud troop of the With-Myrgings.
I sought Wulfhere and Wyrmhere, where war seldom ceased,
when the army of Hræd with hard swords 120
had to defend around Vistula-wood
the old ancestral home from the people of Attila.
I sought Rædhere and Rondere, Rumstan and Gislhere,
Withergild and Frederic, Wudga and Hama;
that band of comrades was by no means the worst, 125
though I must name them last in my song.
Often from that throng flew hissing
the singing spear among an angry people;
those exiles, Wudga and Hama, there commanded
the twisted gold of men and women. 130
Thus I have always found in my journeys
that he is most beloved to land-dwellers

to whom God gives power over men
into his hands while he lives here."

    And so, wandering as their fate unfolds,   135
the bards of men among many lands,
speaking of necessity, saying words of thanks,
always south or north where, wise in songs,
they meet one who is not stingy with gifts,
who would raise up his fame in the presence of his men,   140
do noble deeds until it all fades away,
light and life together; he earns glory,
and has towering fame under the heavens.

Appendix B: Analogues to the Themes and Events in Beowulf

1. From *Grettissaga*[1] (c. 1300)

[Source: The translation is that of G.A. Hight, first published in 1913; it is reprinted in *The Saga of Grettir the Strong*, ed. Peter Foote (London: J.R. Dent, 1965).]

a. The Fight in the Hall, ch. 32-35

[A farmer named Thorhall hires a strong man named Glam to work as a shepherd on his haunted farmstead. Glam is killed on Christmas Day (after mocking the Christian customs of the holiday); his body, too foul and heavy to move, is buried under a cairn.]

It was not long before men became aware that Glam was not easy in his grave. Many men suffered severe injuries; some who saw him were struck senseless and some lost their wits. Soon after the festival was over, men began to think they saw him about their houses. The panic was great and many left the neighborhood. Next he began to ride on the house-tops by night, and nearly broke them to pieces. Almost night and day he walked, and people would scarcely venture up the valley, however pressing their business. The district was in a grievous condition.

[The situation grows worse over time; eventually the hero Grettir learns of Glam's predations, and resolves to see things for himself.]

Grettir rode to Thorhallsstad where he was welcomed by the bondi [farmer]. He asked Grettir whither he was bound, and Grettir said he wished to spend the night there if the bondi permitted. Thorhall said he would indeed be thankful to him for staying there.

"Few," he said, "think it a gain to stay here for any time. You must have heard tell of the trouble that is here, and I do not want you to be inconvenienced on my account. Even if you escape unhurt yourself, I know for certain that you will lose your horse, for no one can keep his beast in safety who comes here."

---

1 Anonymous Norse prose saga. Parallels between *Beowulf* and *Grettir's Saga* were noted as early as 1878 (Guðbrandur Vigfússon, "Prolegomena," *Sturlunga saga*, 2 vols. [Oxford: Clarendon, 1878]), though scholars disagreed over which work had influenced the other. *Grettir's Saga* is a long tale, and only the episodes that are parallel to episodes of *Beowulf* are presented here. See further Chambers; Benson, "Originality of *Beowulf*"; Turville-Petre; Liberman; Scowcroft; and Stitt.

Grettir said there were plenty more horses to be had if anything happened to this one.

Thorhall was delighted at Grettir's wishing to remain, and received him with both hands. Grettir's horse was placed securely under lock and key and they both went to bed. The night passed without Glam showing himself.

"Your being here has already done some good," said Thorhall. "Glam has always been in the habit of riding on the roof or breaking open the doors every night, as you can see from the marks."

"Then," Grettir said, "either he will not keep quiet much longer, or he will remain so more than one night. I will stay another night and see what happens."

Then they went to Grettir's horse and found it had not been touched. The bondi thought that all pointed to the same thing. Grettir stayed a second night and again the thrall did not appear. The bondi became hopeful and went to see the horse. There he found the stable broken open, the horse dragged outside and every bone in his body broken. Thorhall told Grettir what had occurred and advised him to look to himself, for he was a dead man if he waited for Glam.

Grettir answered: "I must not have less for my horse than a sight of the thrall."

The bondi said there was no pleasure to be had from seeing him: "He is not like any man. I count every hour a gain that you are here."

The day passed, and when the hour came for going to bed Grettir said he would not take off his clothes, and lay down on a seat opposite to Thorkell's sleeping apartment. He had a shaggy cloak covering him with one end of it fastened under his feet and the other drawn over his head so that he could see through the neck-hole. He set his feet against a strong bench which was in front of him. The frame-work of the outer door had been all broken away and some bits of wood had been rigged up roughly in its place. The partition which had once divided the hall from the entrance passage was all broken, both above the cross-beam and below, and all the bedding had been upset. The place looked rather desolate. There was a light burning in the hall by night.

When about a third part of the night had passed Grettir heard a loud noise. Something was going up on to the building, riding above the hall and kicking with its heels until the timbers cracked again. This went on for some time, and then it came down towards the door. The door opened and Grettir saw the thrall stretching in an enormously big and ugly head. Glam moved slowly in, and on passing the door stood upright, reaching to the roof. He turned to the hall, resting his arms on the cross-beam and peering along the hall. The bondi uttered no sound, having heard quite enough of what had gone on outside. Grettir lay quite still and did not move. Glam saw a heap of something in the seat, came farther into the hall and seized the cloak tightly with his hand. Grettir pressed his foot against the plank and the cloak held firm. Glam tugged at it again still more violently, but it did not give way. A third time he pulled, this time with both hands and with such force that he pulled Grettir up out of the seat, and between them the cloak was torn in two. Glam looked at the bit which he held in his hand and wondered much who could pull like that against him. Suddenly Grettir sprang under his arms, seized him round the waist and squeezed his back with all his might, intending in that way to bring him down, but the thrall wrenched his arms till he staggered from the violence. Then Grettir fell back to another bench. The benches flew about and everything was shattered around them. Glam wanted to get out, but Grettir tried to prevent him by stemming his foot against anything he could find. Nevertheless Glam succeeded in getting him outside the hall. Then a terrific struggle began, the thrall trying to drag him out of the house, and Grettir saw that however hard he was to deal with in the house, he would be worse outside, so he strove with all his might to keep him from getting out. Then Glam made a desperate effort and gripped Grettir tightly towards him, forcing him to the porch. Grettir saw that he could not put up any resistance, and with a sudden movement he dashed into the thrall's arms and set both his feet against a stone which was fastened in the ground at the door. For that Glam was not prepared, since he had been tugging to drag Grettir towards him; he reeled backwards and tumbled hind-foremost out of the door, tearing away the lintel with his shoulder and shattering the roof, the rafters and the frozen thatch. Head over heels he fell out of the house and Grettir fell on top of him. The moon was shining very brightly outside, with light clouds passing over it and hiding it now and again. At the moment when Glam fell the moon shone forth, and Glam turned his eyes up towards it. Grettir himself has related that that sight was the only one which ever made him tremble. What with fatigue and all else that he had endured, when he saw the horrible rolling of Glam's eyes his heart sank so utterly that he had not strength to draw his sword, but lay there wellnigh betwixt life and death. Glam possessed more malignant power than most fiends, for he now spoke in this wise:

"You have expended much energy, Grettir, in your search for me. Nor is that to be wondered at, if you should have little joy thereof. And now I tell you that you shall possess only half the strength and firmness of heart that were decreed to you if you had not striven with me. The might which was yours till now I am not able to take away, but it is in my power to ordain that never shall you grow stronger than you are now. Nevertheless your might is sufficient, as many shall find to their cost. Hitherto you have earned fame through your deeds, but henceforward there shall fall upon you exile and battle; your deeds shall turn to evil and your guardian-spirit shall forsake you. You will be outlawed and your lot shall be to dwell ever alone. And this I lay upon you, that these eyes of mine shall be ever before your vision. You will find it hard to live alone, and at last it shall drag you to death."

When the thrall had spoken the faintness which had come over Grettir left him. He drew his short sword, cut off Glam's head and laid it between his thighs. Then the bondi came out, having put on his clothes while Glam was speaking, but he did not venture to come near until he was dead. Thorhall praised God and thanked Grettir warmly for having laid this unclean spirit. Then they set to work and burned Glam to cold cinders, bound the ashes in a skin and buried them in a place far away from the haunts of man or beast. Then they went home, the day having nearly broken. Grettir was very stiff and lay down to rest. Thorhall sent for some men from the next farms and let them know how things had fared. They all realized the importance of Grettir's deed when they heard of it; all agreed that in the whole country side for strength and courage and enterprise there was not the equal of Grettir the son of Asmund.

Thorhall bade a kindly farewell to Grettir and dismissed him with a present of a fine horse and proper clothes, for all that he had been wearing were torn to pieces. They parted in friendship. Grettir rode to Ass in Vatnsdal and was welcomed by Thorvald, who asked him all about his encounter with Glam. Grettir told him everything and said that never had his strength been put to trial as it had been in their long struggle. Thorvald told him to conduct himself discreetly; if he did so he might prosper, but otherwise he would surely come to disaster. Grettir said that his temper had not improved, that he had even less discretion than before, and was more impatient of being crossed. In one thing a great change had come over him; he had become so frightened of the dark that he dared not go anywhere alone at night. Apparitions of every kind came before him. It has since passed into an expression, and men speak of "Glam's eyes" or "Glam visions" when things appear otherwise than as they are.

Having accomplished his undertaking Grettir rode back to Bjarg and spent the winter at home.

b. The Fight at the Falls, ch. 64-66

[Grettir, now an outlaw traveling in disguise under the name of Gest, comes to the aid of a woman named Steinvor, mistress of a farmstead at Sandhaugar which is haunted by trolls. Twice at the Yule celebration the farm has been raided by some creature, and a man has disappeared. Grettir hears of this problem and offers his help:]

When he had eaten something he told the servants to go to the other end of the hall. Then he got some boards and loose logs and laid them across the hall to make a great barricade so that none of the servants could get across. No one dared to oppose him or to object to anything. The entrance was in the side wall of the hall under the back gable, and near it was a cross bench upon which Grettir laid himself, keeping on his clothes, with a light burning in the room. So he lay till into the night....

Towards midnight he heard a loud noise outside, and very soon there walked a huge troll-wife into the room. She carried a trough in one hand and a rather large cutlass in the other. She looked round the room as she entered, and on seeing Gest lying there she rushed at him; he started up and attacked her furiously. They fought long together; she was the stronger but he evaded her skillfully. Everything near them and the paneling of the back wall were broken to pieces. She dragged him through the hall door out to the porch, where he resisted vigorously. She wanted to drag him out of the house, but before that was done they had broken up all the fittings of the outer door and borne them away on their shoulders. Then she strove to get to the river and among the rocks. Gest was terribly fatigued, but there was no choice but either to brace himself or be dragged down to the rocks. All night long they struggled together, and he thought he had never met with such a monster for strength. She gripped him so tightly to herself that he could do nothing with either hand but cling to her waist. When at last they reached a rock by the river he swung the monster round and got his right hand loose. Then he quickly seized the short sword which he was wearing, drew it and struck at the troll's right shoulder, cutting off her right arm and releasing himself. She sprang among the rocks and disappeared in the waterfall. Gest, very stiff and tired, lay long by the rock. At daylight he went home and lay down on his bed, blue and swollen all over.

When the lady of the house came home she found the place rather in disorder. She went to Gest and asked him what had happened, and why everything was broken to pieces. He told her everything just as it had happened. She thought it a matter of great moment and asked him who he was. He told her the truth, said that he wished to see a priest and asked her to send for one. She did so; Steinn came to Sandhaugar and soon learnt that it was Grettir the son of Asmund who had come there under the name of Gest. The priest asked him what he thought had become of the men who had disappeared; Grettir said he thought that they must have gone among the rocks. The priest said he could not believe his word unless he gave some evidence of it. Grettir said that later it would be known, and the priest went home. Grettir lay many days in his bed and the lady did all she could for him; thus Yule-tide passed. Grettir himself declared that the trollwoman sprang among the rocks when she was wounded, but the men of Bardardal say that the day dawned upon her while they were wrestling; that when he cut off her arm she broke, and that she is still standing there on the mountain in the likeness of a woman. The dwellers in the valley kept Grettir there in hiding.

One day that winter after Yule Grettir went to Eyjardalsa and met the priest, to whom he said: "I see, priest, that you have little belief in what I say. Now I wish you to come with me to the river and to see what probability there is in it."

The priest did so. When they reached the falls they saw a cave up under the rock. The cliff was there so abrupt that no one could climb it, and nearly ten fathoms down to the water. They had a rope with them. The priest said: "It is quite impossible for any one to get down to that."

Grettir answered: "It is certainly possible; and men of high mettle are those who would feel themselves happiest there. I want to see what there is in the fall. Do you mind the rope."

The priest said he could do so if he chose. He drove a stake into the ground and laid stones against it.

Grettir now fastened a stone in a loop at the end of the rope, and lowered it from above into the water.

"Which way do you mean to go?" asked the priest.

"I don't mean to be bound when I come into the fall," Grettir said. "So my mind tells me."

Then he prepared to go; he had few clothes on and only a short sword; no other arms. He jumped from a rock and got down to the fall. The priest saw the soles of his feet but after that did not know what had become of him. Grettir dived beneath the fall. It was very difficult swimming because of the currents, and he had to dive to the bottom to get behind the fall. There was a rock where he came up, and a great cave under the fall in front of which the water poured. He went into the cave, where there was a large fire burning and a horrible great giant most fearful to behold sitting before it. On Grettir entering the giant sprang up, seized a pike and struck at him, for he could both strike and thrust with it. It had a wooden shaft and was of the kind called "heptisax." Grettir struck back with his sword and cut through the shaft. Then the giant tried to reach up backwards to a sword which was hanging in the cave, and at that moment Grettir struck at him and cut open his lower breast and stomach so that all his entrails fell out into the river and floated down the stream. The priest who was sitting by the rope saw some debris being carried down all covered with blood and lost his head, making sure that Grettir was killed. He left the rope and ran off home, where he arrived in the evening and told them for certain that Grettir was dead, and said it was a great misfortune to them to have lost such a man.

Grettir struck few more blows at the giant before he was dead. He then entered the cave, kindled a light and explored. It is not told how much treasure he found there, but there is supposed to have been some. He stayed there till late into the night and found the bones of two men, which he carried away in a skin. Then he came out of the cave, swam to the rope and shook it, thinking the priest was there; finding him gone he had to swarm up the rope and so reached the top. He went home to Eyjardalsa and carried the skin with the bones in it into the vestibule of the church together with a rune-staff, upon which were most beautifully carved the following lines:

"Into the fall of the torrent I went;
dank its maw towards me gaped.
The floods before the ogress' den
Mighty against my shoulder played";

and then:

"Hideous the friend of troll-wife came.
Hard were the blows I dealt upon him.
The shaft of Heptisax was severed.
My sword has pierced the monster's breast."

There too it was told how Grettir had brought the bones from the cave. The priest when he came to the church on the next morning found the staff and all that was with it and read the runes. Grettir had then returned home to Sandhaugar.

2. From Saxo Grammaticus,[1] *Gesta Danorum* (II.1.1-3)

[Source: Saxo Grammaticus, *The History of the Danes*, 2 vols., trans. Peter Fisher, ed. H. Ellis Davidson (Cambridge: D.S. Brewer, 1979).]

[Frothi son of Hadingus, king of Denmark, in search of adventures and the funds to pay for them, overhears the song of a countryman:]

"Near here, rising in gentle slopes, lies an island
whose hills conceal a rich hoard of treasure.
The guardian of the mount keeps the choice pile,
a dragon intricately twined and curled in multiple
spirals, dragging the sinuous folds of its tail,
lashing its manifold coils and vomiting poison.
To overcome it, stretch the skins of bulls
over your shield and cover your body with oxhides,
so that you do not expose your naked flesh

---

1 Saxo Grammaticus, late-twelfth-century Danish churchman and historian. His *Gesta Danorum* records the early history of Denmark from its legendary founder Dan through a host of fabulous heroes and kings. Its style has not attracted many modern readers, but it is a treasury of legendary history and strange stories, including an early version of the revenge-tale that would become Shakespeare's *Hamlet*. A number of characters in *Beowulf* appear in Saxo's work, though they are often hard to recognize; some scenes in Saxo, such as the one presented here, offer analogues to the action in *Beowulf*.

to the biting venom and be burnt by the slaver it spews.
Though its flickering triple tongue leaps from its gaping
mouth and its grim fangs threaten hideous wounds,
be fearless, nor let the spikes of its teeth, nor its starkness,
nor the virulence shot from its darting jaws dismay you.
Its tough scales scoff at man's weapons, but know there's a place
far beneath its belly to plunge in your blade;
seek this with your sword-point and probe its snaky guts.
Safely then go to the mountain and with a mattock
rake out the hollows; soon you will drench your purse
in treasure, and sail your gold-laden ship to shore."

Frothi believed him and crossed over alone to the island with no more company to attack the monster than when champions fight a duel. The dragon was returning to its cave after quenching its thirst as Frothi's weapon struck, but its hard prickly exterior made light of it. His next attempt was foiled when he launched javelins, which only rebounded idly. When its back proved impenetrably hard he found on closer inspection that the softness of its stomach gave access to his sword. It tried to bite him in retaliation, but its sharp-pointed teeth only fastened on his shield, and with many quick little jabs of its tongue it gasped away its life and poison at the same time.

Enriched by his treasure-trove the king was able to equip himself with a fleet and sail into the area of the Kurlanders.

3. From Snorri Sturluson,[1] *Heimskringla* (c. 1223-35), *Ynglinga saga*

[Source: The English translation is by Samuel Laing (London: Longman, 1844). The text is found in *Heimskringla*, ed. Bjarni Athalbjarnarson, vol. I-III (Reykjavik: Islenzka Fornritafélag, 1946-51).]

[from ch. 8] Odin ... established by law that all dead men should be burned, and their belongings laid with them upon the pile, and the ashes be cast into

---

1   Snorri Sturluson (1179-1241), Icelandic poet, chronicler, and law-speaker of Iceland, roughly the "president" of the Althing or legislature. He is the author of the *Prose Edda* (or *Younger Edda*), a handbook for poets that is also a compendium of Scandinavian mythological lore. His other major work is the *Heimskringla*, a collection of sagas forming a history of the various rulers of Norway from legendary times to 1177 CE. The first saga Snorri includes is *Ynglinga saga* (The Story of the Yngling Family from Odin to Halfdan the Black); it tells among many other things of Odin's institution of the practice of cremation. Odin in Snorri is a lawgiver and founder of customs; the funeral rites described in Snorri are similar to those practiced in *Beowulf*. See further Lee M. Hollander, *Heimskringla* (Austin: U of Texas P, 1964).

the sea or buried in the earth. Thus, said he, every one will come to Valhalla with the riches he had with him upon the pile; and he would also enjoy whatever he himself had buried in the earth. For men of consequence a mound should be raised to their memory, and for all other warriors who had been distinguished for manhood a standing stone; which custom remained long after Odin's time.

[from ch. 10] It is said that ... at his [Odin's] pile there was great splendor. It was their [the Swedes'] faith that the higher the smoke arose in the air, the higher he would be raised whose pile it was; and the richer he would be, the more property that was consumed with him.

[from ch. 27] King Hake [of Sweden] had been so grievously wounded that he saw his days could not be long; so he ordered a warship which he had to be loaded with his dead men and their weapons, and to be taken out to the sea; the tiller to be shipped, and the sails hoisted. Then he set fire to some tar-wood, and ordered a pile to be made over it in the ship. Hake was almost if not quite dead, when he was laid upon this pile of his. The wind was blowing off the land—the ship flew, burning in clear flame, out between the islets, and into the ocean. Great was the fame of this deed in after times.

4. From *The Life of Saint Gildas*[1]

[Source: *Gildae de Excidio Britanniae, Fragmenta, Liber de Paenitentia*, ed. Hugh Williams (Cymmrodorion Record Series 3, London, 1899) 366. Trans. RML.]

[When the saint is about to die, he says to his companions and disciples:]

"I charge you by Christ, my sons, not to quarrel over the remains of my corpse, but as soon as I have sent forth my spirit, carry me down and lay me on a ship, placing under my shoulders the stone on which I used to lie down. Let none of you remain with me in the ship, but push it into the sea and let it go where God wishes. The Lord will provide a place for my burial where it will please Him."

---

1 Anonymous Breton saint's life. The date of composition of this work is not known; its presentation of what is a fairly common motif in the lives of the Celtic saints— the revealing of God's will by the drifting of a rudderless boat—is reminiscent of the funeral of Scyld Scefing in *Beowulf*. See further Cameron, and Meaney.

5. From Blickling Homily[1] 17, Lines 237ff

[Source: R. Morris, *The Blickling Homilies of the Tenth Century* (Early English Text Society [EETS], os 58, 63, 73; Oxford, 1874-80). Trans. RML.]

[The Archangel Michael is giving St Paul a tour of the underworld:]

As Saint Paul was looking toward the northern part of this world, where all waters descend, he also saw over the waters a gray stone. And north of the stone had grown very frosty groves, and there were gloomy mists, and under the stone was the dwelling-place of sea-monsters and evil spirits. And he saw that on the cliff many black souls were hanging in the icy groves, bound by their hands, and devils in the shape of sea-monsters were clutching at them like greedy wolves. And the water was black under the cliff below, and from the cliff to the water was about twelve miles. And when the boughs broke, the souls that hung on the twigs fell down, and the sea-monsters seized them. These were the souls of those who had sinned here in this world, and would not cease from it before their life's end. But let us now eagerly ask St Michael that he lead our souls to bliss, where they might rejoice without end in eternity.

---

1   A collection of anonymous early tenth-century homilies preserved in Princeton University Library, W.H. Scheide Collection 71. The occasion of the sermon is the dedication of St Michael's church; its sources are of questionable orthodoxy but undoubted popularity. See further Malone, "Grendel and His Abode."

Appendix C: Christians and Pagans

1. Gregory the Great[1] (c. 540-604), Letter to Abbot Mellitus (601)

[Source: Pope Gregory the Great, *Epistle XI*, 56, trans. J. Barmby, *A Select Library of Nicene and Post-Nicene Fathers*, Second Series, XIII (Oxford and New York: Christian Literature Company, 1898), 84-85. The letter is also found in Bede's *Ecclesiastical History*, I.30.]

Since the departure of our congregation, which is with you, we have been in a state of great suspense from having heard nothing of the success of your journey. But when Almighty God shall have brought you to our most reverend brother the Bishop Augustine, tell him that I have long been considering with myself about the case of the Angli; to wit, that the temples of idols in that nation should not be destroyed, but that the idols themselves that are in them should be. Let blessed water be prepared, and sprinkled in these temples, and altars constructed, and relics deposited, since, if these same temples are well built, it is needful that they should be transferred from the worship of idols to the service of the true God; that, when the people themselves see that these temples are not destroyed, they may put away error from their heart, and, knowing and adoring the true God, may have recourse with the more familiarity to the places they have been accustomed to. And, since they are wont to kill many oxen in sacrifice to demons, they should have also some solemnity of this kind in a changed form, so that on the day of dedication, or on the anniversaries of the holy martyrs whose relics are deposited there, they may make for themselves tents of the branches of trees around these temples that have been changed into churches, and celebrate the solemnity with religious feasts. Nor let them any longer sacrifice animals to the devil, but slay animals to the praise of God for their own eating, and return thanks to the Giver of all for their fullness, so that, while some joys are reserved to them outwardly, they may be able the more easily to incline their minds to inward joys. For it is undoubtedly impossible to cut away everything at once from hard hearts, since one who strives to ascend to the highest place must needs rise by steps or paces, and not by leaps. Thus to the people of Israel in Egypt the Lord did indeed make Himself known;

---

1   Gregory the Great (c. 540-604), pope from 590 to 604, is regarded as the last of the great Fathers of the Church. His works, well known to the Anglo-Saxons, include the *Pastoral Care* (instructions for bishops), the *Dialogues* (lives of St Benedict and other Italian saints), and a commentary on the biblical book of Job. His long interest in converting the English culminated in his sending Augustine and a number of monks as missionaries there in 597. This letter is addressed to a French abbot (later bishop) on his way to England.

but still He reserved to them in His own worship the use of the sacrifices which they were accustomed to offer to the devil, enjoining them to immolate animals in sacrifice to Himself; to the end that, their hearts being changed, they should omit some things in the sacrifice and retain others, so that, though the animals were the same as what they had been accustomed to offer, nevertheless, as they immolated them to God and not to idols, they should be no longer the same sacrifices. This then it is necessary for Your Love to say to our aforesaid brother, that he, being now in that country, may consider well how he should arrange all things.

2. From Bede the Venerable,[1] *Ecclesiastical History of the English People* II.13 (the Conversion of King Edwin of Northumbria)

[Source: *Bede's Ecclesiastical History of the English People*, ed. and trans. Bertram Colgrave and R.A.B. Mynors (Oxford: Oxford UP, 1969) 182-87.]

[Edwin, already inclined toward Christianity by several miraculous events, submits the question of his conversion to his advisors:]

When the king had heard his words, he answered that he was both willing and bound to accept the faith which Paulinus taught. He said, however, that he would confer about this with his loyal chief men and his counselors so that, if they agreed with him, they might all be consecrated together in the waters of life. Paulinus agreed and the king did as he had said. A meeting of his council was held and each one was asked in turn what he thought of this doctrine hitherto unknown to them and this new worship of God which was being proclaimed.

Coifi, the chief of the priests, answered at once, "Notice carefully, King, this doctrine which is now being expounded to us. I frankly admit that, for my part, I have found that the religion which we have hitherto held has no virtue nor profit in it. None of your followers has devoted himself more earnestly than I have to the worship of our gods, but nevertheless there are many who receive greater benefits and greater honour from you than I do and are more successful in all their undertakings. If the gods had any power they would have helped me more readily, seeing that I have always served them with greater zeal. So it follows that if, on examination, these new doctrines which have now been explained to us are found to be better and more effectual, let us accept them at once without any delay."

---

1 Bede, eighth-century historian, spent most of his life in the monastery of Wearmouth-Jarrow in Northumbria. His *Ecclesiastical History of the English People* tells the story of the conversion of the English, and the struggles between Roman and Irish missionaries in the newly Christian land.

Another of the king's chief men agreed with this advice and with these wise words and then added, "This is how the present life of man on earth, King, appears to me in comparison with that time which is unknown to us. You are sitting feasting with your ealdormen and thegns in winter time; the fire is burning on the hearth in the middle of the hall and all inside is warm, while outside the wintry storms of rain and snow are raging; and a sparrow flies swiftly through the hall. It enters in at one door and quickly flies out through the other. For the few moments it is inside, the storm and wintry tempest cannot touch it, but after the briefest moment of calm, it flits from your sight, out of the wintry storm and into it again. So this life of man appears but for a moment; what follows or indeed what went before, we know not at all. If this new doctrine brings us more certain information, it seems right that we should accept it." Other elders and counselors of the king continued in the same manner, being divinely prompted to do so.

Coifi added that he would like to listen still more carefully to what Paulinus himself had to say about God. The king ordered Paulinus to speak, and when he had said his say, Coifi exclaimed, "For a long time now I have realized that our religion is worthless; for the more diligently I sought the truth in our cult, the less I found it. Now I confess openly that the truth shines out clearly in this teaching which can bestow on us the gift of life, salvation, and eternal happiness. Therefore I advise your Majesty that we should promptly abandon and commit to the flames the temples and the altars which we have held sacred without reaping any benefit." Why need I say more? The king publicly accepted the gospel which Paulinus preached, renounced idolatry, and confessed his faith in Christ. When he asked the high priest of their religion which of them should be the first to profane the altars and the shrines of the idols, together with their precincts, Coifi answered, "I will; for through the wisdom the true God has given me no one can more suitably destroy those things which I once foolishly worshipped, and so set an example to all." And at once, casting aside his vain superstitions, he asked the king to provide him with arms and a stallion; and mounting it he set out to destroy the idols. Now a high priest of their religion was not allowed to carry arms or to ride except on a mare. So, girded with a sword, he took a spear in his hand and mounting the king's stallion he set off to where the idols were. The common people who saw him thought he was mad. But as soon as he approached the shrine, without any hesitation he profaned it by casting the spear which he held into it; and greatly rejoicing in the knowledge of the worship of the true God, he ordered his companions to destroy and set fire to the shrine and all the enclosures. The place where the idols once stood is still shown, not far from York, to the east, over the river Derwent. Today it is called Goodmanham, the place where the high priest, through the inspiration of the true God, profaned and destroyed the altars which he himself had consecrated.

3. From St Boniface,[1] *Letters*

[Source: *The Letters of Saint Boniface*, trans. with an introduction by Ephraim Emerton (New York: Columbia UP, 1940) 74-75, 124-30. The Latin text is found in *Briefe des Bonifatius, Willibalds Leben des Bonifatius*, ed. and trans. (into German) Reinhold Rau (Darmstadt: Wissenschaftliche Buchgesellschaft, 1968) 134, 212-27.]

a. *Letter 46* (c. 738)

To all his reverend fellow bishops, to all those clothed with the grace of priesthood, deacons, canons, clerks, abbots, and abbesses set over the true flock of Christ, monks living in humble submission to God, virgins consecrated by vows to God, and all consecrated handmaids of Christ—and, in general, to all God-fearing catholics of the stock and race of the Angles, Boniface named also Winfred, born of that same race, German legate of the Church Universal, servant of the Apostolic See and called Archbishop for no merit of his own, sends greetings of humble communion and unfeigned love in Christ.

We earnestly beseech your brotherly goodness to be mindful of us, who are worth so little, in your prayers that we may be delivered from the snare of Satan the huntsman and from wicked and cruel men, that the word of God may make its way and be glorified. We beseech you to obtain through your holy prayers, that our Lord and God Jesus Christ, "who will have all men to be saved, and to come unto the knowledge of God," may turn the hearts of the pagan Saxons to the catholic faith, that they may free themselves from the snares of the devil in which they are bound and may be gathered among the children of Mother Church.

Take pity upon them; for they themselves are saying: "We are of one blood and one bone with you." Remember that the way of all the earth is at hand and that in hell no one will confess God, nor will death praise him.

Know also that in making this request I have the approval, the consent, and the blessing of two pontiffs of the Roman Church. Act now upon this our supplication so that your reward may shine with increasing splendor in the heavenly house of the angels.

May the Omnipotent Creator always keep the unity and communion of your affection in power and progress in Christ.

---

1   St Boniface (680-754, named in English Wynfrith), English churchman and martyr. Most of his life was devoted to missionary work on the Continent among the Saxons and Frisians, among whom he was martyred in 754. He is the author of numerous letters; this general letter to the English appeals to their sense of kinship with their continental pagan cousins to encourage support for their conversion.

b. *Letter 73*[1] (c. 746)

To his dearest master, King Ethelbald, cherished in the love of Christ above all other kings and holding glorious sway over the realm of the Anglians [sic], Boniface, archbishop and legate of the Roman Church in Germany, and his fellow bishops, Wera, Burkhardt, Werbert, Abel, and Willibald, send greetings of unfailing love in Christ.

We acknowledge before God and the holy angels, that when we have heard through trustworthy messengers of your prosperity, your faith in God, and your good works before God and man we have returned joyful thanks to God, praying and beseeching the Savior of the world to keep you forever safe and steadfast in faith and works before God and in the leadership of the people of Christ. But when we hear that any harm befalls you, be it in the conditions of your government or the event of war or, worse yet, some peril to your soul's welfare, we are afflicted with pain and sorrow; for by God's will we rejoice with you in your joy and grieve with you in your sorrow.

We have heard that you are very liberal in almsgiving, and congratulate you thereon; for they who give to the least of their needy brethren shall hear at the day of judgment, according to Gospel truth, the gracious word of the Lord: "Inasmuch as ye have done it unto the least of these my brethren, ye have done it unto me. Come, ye blessed of my Father, inherit the kingdom prepared for you from the foundation of the world." We have heard also that you repress robbery and wrongdoing, perjury, and rapine with a strong hand, that you are famed as a defender of widows and of the poor, and that you have established peace within your kingdom. In this also we have rejoiced, because the Truth itself and our Peace, which is Christ, said, "Blessed are the peacemakers, for they shall be called the children of God."

But amidst all this, one evil report as to the manner of life of Your Grace has come to our hearing, which has greatly grieved us and which we could wish were not true. We have learned from many sources that you have never taken to yourself a lawful wife. Now this relation was ordained of the Lord God himself from the very beginning of the world and was repeatedly insisted upon by the Apostle Paul saying: "On account of fornication let every man have his own wife, and every woman have her own husband." If you had willed to do this for the sake of chastity and abstinence, or had refrained from women from the fear and love of God and had given evidence that you were abstinent for God's sake we should rejoice, for that is not worthy of blame but rather of praise. But if, as many say—but which God forbid!—you have neither taken a lawful spouse nor observed chastity

---

1 This letter of advice from Boniface and other bishops to King Ethelbald of Mercia reproves a king whose evil conduct has caused widespread scandal; Boniface notes that even the pagans do not tolerate the kinds of vices Ethelbald is accused of practicing.

for God's sake but, moved by desire, have defiled your good name before God and man by the crime of adulterous lust, then we are greatly grieved because this is a sin in the sight of God and is the ruin of your fair fame among men.

And now, what is worse, our informants say that these atrocious crimes are committed in convents with holy nuns and virgins consecrated to God, and this, beyond all doubt, doubles the offense.... We therefore, beloved son, beseech Your Grace by Christ the son of God and by His coming and by His kingdom, that if it is true that you are continuing in this vice you will amend your life by penitence, purify yourself, and bear in mind how vile a thing it is through lust to change the image of God created in you into the image and likeness of a vicious demon. Remember that you were made king and ruler over many not by your own merits but by the abounding grace of God, and now you are making yourself by your own lust the slave of an evil spirit, since, as the Apostle says, whatever sin a man commits, of that he becomes the slave.

This is held to be a shame and disgrace, not by Christians only but even by pagans. For the pagans themselves, although ignorant of the true God, keep in this matter the substance of the law and the ordinance of God from the beginning inasmuch as they respect their wives with the bond of matrimony and punish fornicators and adulterers. In Old Saxony, if a virgin disgraces her father's house by adultery or if a married woman breaks the bond of wedlock and commits adultery, they sometimes compel her to hang herself with her own hand and then hang the seducer above the pyre on which she has been burned. Sometimes a troop of women get together and flog her through the towns, beating her with rods and stripping her to the waist, cutting her whole body with knives, pricking her with wounds, and sending her on bleeding and torn from town to town; fresh scourgers join in with new zeal for purity, until finally they leave her dead or almost dead, that other women may be made to fear adultery and evil conduct. The Wends, who are the vilest and lowest race of men, have such high regard for the mutual bond of marriage that the wife refuses to survive her husband. Among them a woman is praised who dies by her own hand and is burned upon the same pyre with her husband.

If, then, heathen who know not God and have not the law do, as the Apostle says, by nature the things of the law and have the works of the law written upon their hearts, know you, beloved son, who are called a Christian and a worshipper of the true God—if in your youth you were ensnared in the filth of wantonness and involved in the mire of adultery and sunk in the whirlpool of lust as in an abyss of hell—it is now high time that you should remember your Lord, should rouse yourself from the snares of the devil, and wash your soul clean from the filthiness of lust. It is time for you in fear of your Creator no longer to venture to defile yourself by repeating such sins. It is time for you to have mercy upon the multitude of your people who are perishing by following the example of a sinful prince and are falling into the abyss of death. For, beyond a doubt, we shall receive from the eternal judge rewards for as many as we lead by good example into the life of our heavenly fatherland, and punishment for those whom we guide by evil example into perdition.

If the English people, as is reported here and as is charged against us in France and Italy and even by the heathen themselves, are scorning lawful marriage and living in wanton adultery like the people of Sodom, then we must expect that a degenerate and degraded people with unbridled desires will be produced. At last the whole race will become debased and finally will be neither strong in war nor steadfast in faith, neither honored among men nor pleasing in the sight of God. So it has been with the peoples of Spain and Provence and Burgundy. They turned thus away from God and lived in harlotry until the Almighty Judge let the penalties for such crimes fall upon them through ignorance of the law of God and the coming of the Saracens....

The riches of this world are of no avail in the day of requital if a man comes to the end of his life while still making bad use of them; for after the death of the body he shall fall into eternal punishment of the soul. Take these warnings to heart, my dear son, and, I pray you, yield to the prudent words of God's law and reform your life. Turn away from your vices and make an effort to acquire the sacred virtues; so shall you prosper in this world and receive eternal reward in the world to come.

May Almighty God so turn your life to better things that you may be worthy of the grace of our Lord himself forevermore.

4. Wulfstan,[1] *On False Gods*

[Source: Dorothy Bethurum, *Homilies of Wulfstan* (Oxford: Oxford UP, 1957) 221-24. Trans. RML.]

Alas! Long ago it was that because of the Devil many things went wrong, and that mankind disobeyed God too much, and that heathenism all too widely caused great harm, and still widely causes harm. Yet we do not read anywhere in books that people raised up any heathen altars anywhere in the world during all the time that was before Noah's flood. But after that it came about that Nimrod and the giants made a marvelous tower after Noah's

---

1   Wulfstan (d. 1023), bishop of London 996-1002 and archbishop of York 1002-23, royal counselor and author of vigorous Old English homiletic prose. This brief sermon is an abridgement and adaptation of a piece by another writer, Ælfric, which in turn draws upon a still earlier source, the sixth-century archbishop Martin of Braga. It is found in only one copy, a manuscript in the Bodleian Library at Oxford (MS Hatton 113-14, ff. 58v-61).

flood, and it came to pass that they had as many languages, as the book tells, as they had workmen.[1] Then afterwards they scattered into distant lands, and then mankind soon greatly increased. And then finally they were deceived by the ancient Devil who had betrayed Adam long before, so that perversely and heretically they made heathen gods for themselves, and scorned the true God and their own Creator, who formed them as men and fashioned them.

They also took it as wisdom, through the devil's teaching, that they ought to worship the sun and moon as gods because of their shining brightness; and finally, through the devil's teaching, they offered them sacrifices and abandoned their Lord who had made and fashioned them. Some men also said that the shining stars were gods, and began to zealously worship them, and some also believed in fire for its sudden heat; some in water, and some believed in the earth because it nourishes all things. But they might have readily realized, if they had had discernment, that he is the true God who made all these things for the enjoyment and use of us human beings, which he granted to mankind because of his great goodness. These created things, moreover, act just as their own Creator ordained for them, and can do nothing except by our Lord's consent, because there is no other creator but the one true God in whom we believe, and Him alone above all other things we love and honour with certain faith, saying with our mouth and with the conviction of our heart that He alone is true God, who made and fashioned all things.

Yet the heathens would not be content with as few gods as they had previously, but finally took to worshipping various giants and violent men of the earth who became mighty in worldly power and were terrifying while they lived, and foully followed their own lusts. There was a man in days gone by living on the island that is called Crete, who was called Saturn, and he was so savage that he destroyed his own sons, all but one, and in an unfatherly way destroyed their lives early in their childhood. He uneasily left one alive, though he had destroyed all his brothers, and this one was called Jove, and he became a fierce enemy. He later drove his own father out of the aforesaid island called Crete, and would readily have slain him if he could. This Jove grew so lecherous that he took to wife his own sister, who was called Juno, and she became a very important goddess according to the heathen religion. Their two daughters were Minerva and Venus. These wicked men of whom we speak were considered the greatest gods in those days, and the heathens greatly worshiped them, through the Devil's teaching. And yet the son was worshipped among the heathens even more than

---

1   The story of the Tower of Babel is told in the Bible, Genesis 11:1-9. The Bible does not call the builders of the tower "giants," but apocryphal tradition ascribes incredible size to the generations before the Patriarchs. The Anglo-Saxons sometimes called great ruins *eald enta geweorc*, "the old work of giants."

the father had been, and he is considered most honorable of all those whom the heathens, in their error, took for gods in those days. He is called by another name, Thor, in some nations—the Danish people, in their error, love him greatly and worship him most diligently.[1] His son was called Mars, who always caused strife and trouble, and frequently stirred up conflict and hostility. The heathens also honoured this wretch, after his death, as an important god, and whenever they went to war or battle, they first offered their sacrifices in honour of this false god; and they believed that he would assist them with great strength in battle, because he loved battle and combat when he was alive.

There was also a certain man named Mercury while he was alive, who was very crafty and, though clever in speech, deceitful in his deeds and in falsehoods. The heathens also made him a great god, by their reckoning, and time and again they offered him sacrifices at crossroads through the devil's teaching, and often brought him various sacrifices of praise on high hills. This false god was also honoured among all heathens in those days, and in the Danish fashion he is called by the other name Odin. Now some of these Danish men, in their error, say that this Jove, whom they call Thor, was the son of Mercury, whom they call Odin, but they are not right because we read in books, both heathen and Christian, that the evil Jove is in fact Saturn's son. And a certain woman was called Venus, who was Jove's daughter, and she was very foul and so given over to lust that her own brother lay with her, as is said, through the devil's teaching, and the heathens also honour this evil one as an exalted woman.

Additionally, many other heathen gods were variously invented, and likewise many heathen goddesses held in great honour throughout the world for the ruin of mankind, but these are considered the most important in heathen religion, though they lived foully in the world. And the scheming devil, who always deceives mankind, brought the heathens into such deep error that they chose as gods such filthy people who had made their foul lusts a law for themselves and spent their whole life in uncleanness as long as they lived.

But blessed is he who scorns all this, and loves and honors the true God who formed and fashioned all things. Almighty God is one in three persons, that is, Father and Son and Holy Spirit; all three names enfold one divine power and one eternal God, ruler and maker of all creation. To him always be praise and honor forever and ever, world without end, amen.

---

1   Germanic and Roman pantheons were regarded as equivalent, as is seen in the days of the week: English Wednesday "Woden's Day" for the Latin day of Mercury (cf. French *mercredi*), English Thursday "Thor's Day" = the day of Jove (cf. French *jeudi*), English Friday "Frig's Day" = the day of Venus (cf. French *vendredi*). The Germanic pantheon had no equivalent for Saturn, so they simply called the seventh day *Sæternesdæg*. I am indebted to Peter S. Baker for this footnote.

5. Laws against Paganism

a. From Wulfstan, *Canons of Edgar* no. 16[1]

[Source: Roger Fowler, ed. *Wulfstan's Canons of Edgar* (EETS os 266; London, 1972) 26. Trans. RML; the version of Oxford, Bodleian Lib. Junius 121 is translated here.]

And it is right that every priest eagerly teach Christianity and crush all heathenism; and forbid the worship of springs, and necromancy, and divination and incantations, and the worship of trees and stones, and the devilish trick people perform in which a child is dragged across the earth, and the superstitions practiced with various auguries on New Year's night and at pagan shrines and elder-trees, and a great many other errors which men practice much more than they should.

b. From the Laws of Cnut, 1-5[2]

[Source: Felix Liebermann, *Die Gesetze der Angelsachsen*, 3 vols. (Halle: M. Niemeyer, 1903-16) I.312. Trans. RML.]

0.1 This is the secular law which I wish, with the advice of my counselors, to be held all across England:

1 First, that I wish that proper laws should be raised up and all outlawry should certainly be felled, and that one should weed out and root up all unrightfulness, as best one can, from this land, and raise up God's law.

[...]

3 And we command that Christian men ought not to be sold out of the country so often nor brought to heathen lands; but be on guard lest one's soul be destroyed, which Christ purchased with His own life.

4 And we command that everyone eagerly begin to clean this land in every part, and cease everywhere from sinful deeds.

---

1 The *Canons of Edgar*, a collection of ordinances of the late tenth century, was compiled by Wulfstan; the passage quoted here suggests a more immediate concern with pagan practices than that found in *On the False Gods*.

2 Perhaps drafted by Wulfstan (Liebermann 1903-16, I, 308-70), the laws of Cnut also forbid pagan practices, in the context of general law and order and the establishment of a Christian commonwealth.

4a And if witches or sorcerers, murderers or whores are caught anywhere in this land, drive them out of the country immediately, or put them away, unless they desist and more fervently amend themselves.

4.1 And we command that traitors and outlaws from God and man depart from this land, unless they submit and more readily amend themselves.

4.2 And thieves and public criminals perish, unless they cease.

5. And we strictly forbid all heathenism. Heathenism is the worship of idols, that is, when one worships heathen gods, and the sun or moon, fire or flood, watery springs or stones or any kind of forest tree, or prefers witchcraft or commits murder in any way, either by sacrifices or sorcery, or undertaking any such vain things.

Appendix D: Contexts for Reading Beowulf[1]

1. Wulfstan, *Sermo Lupi ad Anglos* (1014)[2]

[Source: Dorothy Bethurum, *Homilies of Wulfstan* (Oxford: Oxford UP, 1957) 255-60. Trans. RML.]

The Sermon of 'Wolf' to the English, when the Danes were greatly persecuting them, which was in the 1014th year after the Incarnation of our Lord Jesus Christ.

Beloved men, recognize what is true: this world is in haste and it draws near its end. And therefore in this world things get worse and worse, and so it must be that because of the people's sins things will get very much worse before the coming of the Antichrist; and then it will indeed be terrible and grim widely throughout the world. Understand well, too, that the Devil has led this nation too far astray for many years, and there has been little loyalty among men, though they might speak well, and too many wrongs have ruled this land, and there were never many men who sought the remedy as eagerly as they should, but every day they piled evil upon evil, and raised up wrong and injustice too widely throughout this entire land.

And therefore we have also suffered many injuries and insults, and if we are to expect any remedy then we must deserve better of God than we have done previously. For with great demerit we have earned the miseries that oppress us, and with very great merits we must obtain the remedy from God, if things are to improve henceforth. Indeed, we know full well that a great breach requires a great remedy, and a great fire needs no little water, if one

---

1 The following selections were all circulating in manuscript at about the same time the manuscript of *Beowulf* was written. In this sense they may be regarded as "contexts" for the reading of the poem and suggest different elements of the literary milieu in which *Beowulf* was copied and read. Moreover, each comments, in some way, on the central themes of the poem.

2 On Wulfstan, see Appendix C4. In this vigorous sermon, written in a strongly rhythmical prose, Wulfstan considers the Viking attacks as divine retribution for the sins of the English. He adapts the historical attitude of the sixth-century British writer Gildas, whose *De excidio Britanniae* lamented the arrival of the Angles and Saxons as a similar retribution upon the British; in doing so Wulfstan subscribes to a biblical view of history that sees the rise and fall of nations as a reflection of their morality. Even pagans may be instruments of God's justice, and he notes as a rebuke to the English that pagans practice their religion more faithfully and with more morality than Christians do.

would quench that fire at all. And the necessity is great for every man henceforth diligently to heed God's law, and pay God's dues justly. Among heathen peoples no one dares withhold little or much of that which is pledged to the worship of false gods, and everywhere we withhold God's dues all too often. And among heathen people no one dares diminish, inside the temple or out, anything brought to the false gods and given over as an offering; and we have completely stripped the houses of God, inside and out, and the servants of God are everywhere deprived of respect and protection. And among heathen people no one dares abuse the servants of the false gods in any way, just as is now done too widely to the servants of God, where Christians ought to observe God's laws and protect God's servants.

But what I say is true: there is need of a remedy, because God's dues have decreased for too long in this land in every region, and the laws of the people have deteriorated all too much, and sanctuaries are commonly violated, and the houses of God are entirely stripped of ancient dues and are despoiled within of all their dignities. And widows are wrongfully forced to take a husband, and too many are reduced to poverty and greatly humiliated; and poor men are sorely betrayed and cruelly defrauded, and widely sold out of this land into the power of foreigners, even though they are completely innocent; and with cruel injustice children in the cradle are enslaved for petty theft commonly throughout this nation; and the rights of freemen are taken away, and the rights of slaves restricted, and the right to alms curtailed, and to speak briefly, the laws of God are hated and His teachings scorned; therefore through God's anger we all are frequently put to shame, let him know it who can. And although one might not imagine it, the harm will become common to all this nation, unless God protects us.

For it is clear and evident in us all that we have hitherto more often marred than we have amended, and therefore many things have befallen this nation. For a long time now, nothing has prospered either at home or abroad, but there has been plunder and famine, burning and bloodshed in nearly every region time and again. And stealing and slaughter, plague and pestilence, murrain and disease, slander and hatred and the thievery of robbers have harmed us severely. And excessive taxes have greatly afflicted us, and bad weather has often caused a bad harvest; therefore there have been in this land, so it seems, many years now of injustices and unstable loyalties among men everywhere. Now very often a kinsman will not protect his kinsman any more than a foreigner, nor the father his children, nor sometimes the child his own father, nor one brother the other. Nor has any of us ordered his life as he should, neither the cleric according to the rule nor the layman according to the law. But all too frequently we have made lust into our law, and have kept neither the teachings nor the laws of God or men as we should. Neither has anyone had loyal intentions toward others as justly as he should, but almost all men have betrayed and injured others by word and deed; and indeed almost everyone unjustly stabs the other in the back with shameful assaults: and would do even more, if he could.

Therefore there are here in this land great disloyalties towards God and towards the state, and there are also in this country many who betray their lords in various ways, and the greatest of all betrayals of one's lord in the world is that a man betrays his lord's soul. And it is also a great betrayal of one's lord in the world when a man plots against his lord's life, or, living, drive him from the land, and both have happened in this country. They plotted against Edward and then killed and later burned him; and Æthelred was driven out of his country. And too many godparents and godchildren have been destroyed widely throughout this nation, and likewise too many other innocent people have been too commonly slain. And also far too many holy places have fallen down because previously certain men have been placed in them who ought not to have been, if one wished to show respect to God's sanctuary. And too many Christian people have been sold out of this land, all the time now, and all this is hateful to God—let him believe it who will. And it is shameful to speak of what happens too commonly, and dreadful to know what too many often do, who practice a wretched deed: they pool their money together and buy a woman in common as a joint purchase, and with the one woman commit foul sin, one by one and each after the other, like dogs who pay no mind to filth, and then for a price they sell out of the land into the hands of the enemy this creature of God, His own purchase that He bought so dearly.

Also we know well where the crime has occurred that a father has sold his son for a price, and a son his mother, and one brother has sold another into the hands of foreigners; and all those are serious and terrible deeds, let him understand it who will. And yet that which is injuring this nation is still greater and more manifold: many are forsworn and greatly perjured, and vows are broken time and again, and it is evident in this nation that God's anger violently oppresses us, let him know it who can.

And indeed, how can greater shame befall men through the wrath of God than frequently does us for our own deeds? Though a slave should escape from his lord and, leaving Christendom become a Viking, and it afterwards happens that armed combat takes place between thane and slave, if the slave should slay the thane, he will lie without payment to any of his family; but if the thane kills the slave that he had previously owned, he must pay the price of a thane. Utterly shameful laws and disgraceful tributes are common among us, because of God's anger, let him understand it who can; and many misfortunes befall this nation time and again. For a long time now nothing has prospered at home or abroad, but there has been devastation and hatred in every region time and again, and for a long time now the English have been entirely without victory and too much disheartened through God's wrath, and the pirates so strong through God's consent that often in battle one drives away ten, sometimes less and sometimes more, all because of our sins. And often ten or twelve, one after the other, will disgracefully put to shame a thane's wife, and sometimes his daughter or close kinswomen, while he looks on, he who considered himself brave and strong and good enough before that happened. And often a slave will bind fast the thane who had been his lord, and make him a slave through God's anger. Alas the misery, and alas the public shame that the English now suffer, all because of God's anger! Often two seamen, or sometimes three, will drive the droves of Christian men out from this nation from sea to sea, huddled together as a public shame for us all, if indeed we could properly feel any. But all the disgrace we often suffer we repay with honour to those who shame us: we pay them continually, and they humiliate us daily. They ravage and they burn, plunder and rob and carry off to the ship; and indeed, what else is there in all these events than the wrath of God, clear and evident, upon this nation?

It is no wonder that misfortune should befall us, because we know full well that for many years now men have not cared what they did in word or deed. Rather it seems this nation has become thoroughly corrupted through manifold sins and many misdeeds: through acts of murder and evil, through avarice and greed, through theft and thievery, through slavery and pagan abuses, through treachery and trickery, through the breach of law and order, through mayhem upon kinsmen and manslaughter, through crimes against clergy and adulteries, through incest and various fornications. And everywhere, as we said before, by the breaking of oaths and by various lies many more than should be are lost and betrayed, and breaches of feasts and fasts are widely and frequently committed. And here in this land also there are far too many degenerate apostates, hostile enemies of the Church, and cruel tyrants, and widespread scorners of divine law and Christian custom, and everywhere in the nation foolish mockers, most often of those things that the messengers of God command, and especially those things which always by right belong to God's law. And therefore it has now come far and wide to such an evil state that men are nowadays more ashamed of good deeds than of misdeeds; because too often good deeds are dismissed with derision and God-fearing men are reviled all too much, and especially mocked and treated with contempt are those who love justice and fear God to any extent. And because men behave thus, blaming all that they should praise and hating too much all that they ought to love, they bring all too many to evil intentions and wicked deeds, so that they are never ashamed even though they sin greatly and commit wrongs against God himself. But because of idle assaults they are ashamed to atone for their misdeeds as the books teach, like those fools who for pride will not guard themselves against injury, until they could not do so even if they wanted to.

Here, so it seems, too many in this country are sorely injured by the stains of sin. Here there are slayers of men and slayers of kinsmen, and murderers of priests and enemies of monasteries, and here are perjurers and murderers, and here there are whores and child-killers and many foul fornicating adulterers, and here there are wizards and sorceresses, and here there are robbers and thieves and plunderers, and, to be brief, countless numbers of crimes and misdeeds. And we are not ashamed of it at all, but we are greatly ashamed to begin the remedy as the books teach us, and that is obvious in this wretched and sinful nation. Alas, many could easily call to mind much more in addition, which one man could not hastily devise, how wretchedly things have gone all the time now widely throughout this nation. And indeed let each one examine himself well, and not delay it all too long.

But lo!, in God's name, let us do what is necessary for us, defend ourselves as best we may, lest we all perish together. There was a historian in the time of the Britons named Gildas, who wrote about their misdeeds, how they with their sins angered God so exceedingly that He finally allowed the army of the English to conquer their land and completely destroy the nobility of the Britons. And this came about, he said, through robbery by the powerful and the coveting of ill-gotten gains, through the people's lawlessness and evil judgments, through the slackness of bishops and the abject cowardice of God's heralds, who too often kept silent from the truth and mumbled in their jaws when they should have shouted. Likewise, through the foul excesses of the people and through gluttony and manifold sins they destroyed their nation and themselves perished. But let us do what is needful—warn ourselves by such things; and what I say is true, we know of worse deeds among the English than we have ever heard of among the Britons. And therefore it is very necessary that we consider ourselves and earnestly plead with God Himself. And let us do what is necessary for us—bow to justice, and in some measure abandon injustice, and repair carefully what we have broken; and let us love God and follow God's laws, and earnestly practice what we promised when we received baptism, or those who were our sponsors at baptism; and let us arrange our words and deeds rightly, and cleanse our conscience thoroughly, and carefully keep our oaths and pledges, and have some faith between ourselves without deceit. And let us frequently consider the great judgment to which we all must come, and eagerly defend ourselves against the surging fires of the torments of hell, and earn for ourselves the glories and delights which God has prepared for those who do His will in the world. May God help us. Amen.

2. Ælfric,[1] *Life of St Edmund* (c. 995)

[Source: Mitchell and Robinson 195-203 (editing London, BL Cotton Julius E.vii). Trans. RML.]

A certain very learned monk came from the south over the sea from St Benedict's place, in the days of King Æthelred, to Archbishop Dunstan three years before he died; the monk was named Abbo. Then they took to conversation, until Dunstan told the story of St Edmund, just as Edmund's sword-bearer had told it to King Athelstan, when Dunstan was a young man and the sword-bearer was a very old man. Then the monk set down that whole narrative in a book, and later, when the book came to us, within a few years, we translated it into English, just as it appears below. Within two years, the monk Abbo returned home to his monastery, and was immediately appointed abbot in the same monastery.

The blessed Edmund, king of the East Angles, was wise and honorable, and always worshiped the almighty God with noble customs. He was humble and virtuous, and continued so steadfastly that he would not turn to shameful sins, nor did he turn away on either side from his good practices, but was always mindful of that true teaching, "You are appointed ruler? do not exalt yourself, but be among men as one of them."[2] He was generous to the poor and widows like a father, and with benevolence always guided his people to righteousness, restrained the violent, and lived blessedly in the true faith.

It eventually happened that the Danish people went with their fleet, pillaging and killing throughout the land, as their custom is. The principal leaders of the fleet were Ivar and Ubbi, united by the devil, and they landed in Northumbria with warships, and wasted the land and killed the people. Then Ivar turned eastwards with his ships, and Ubbi remained in Northumbria, the victory having been won with savagery. Then Ivar came rowing to the East Angles in the year when Prince Alfred, who later became the famous king of the West Saxons, was twenty-one. And the aforesaid Ivar quickly stalked about the land like a wolf, and slew the people, men and women and innocent children, and shamefully tormented innocent Christians.

---

1   Ælfric (c. 950-c. 1020), abbot of Eynsham, prolific writer of homilies, sermons, and saints' lives. His *Life of St Edmund* commemorates a king of the East Angles who was killed by the Danes in 869. Edmund's martyrdom was celebrated on 20 November. Ælfric's source is the Latin *Passio Sancti Edmundi* by Abbo of Fleury (c. 945-1004), reworked by Ælfric in a more elaborate vernacular style as an example of a Christian ideal of kingship. See further Needham 43-59, Whitelock, "Fact and Fiction." For a discussion of some ways in which the *Vita* of Edmund is a "context" for *Beowulf*, see the Introduction, p. 35.

2   Ecclesiasticus 32:1.

He then immediately sent to the king a boastful message that he must submit to his service, if he cared for his life. Then the messenger came to King Edmund and quickly announced Ivar's message: "Ivar our king, brave and victorious on sea and land, has command of many people, and has now suddenly come to land with an army here so that he might have winter quarters here with his troops. He now commands you to share your hidden treasures and your ancestral wealth with him without delay, and be his under-king, if you wish to live, for you do not have the power to resist him."

Then King Edmund summoned the bishop who was nearest at hand, and considered with him how he should answer the fierce Ivar. The bishop was afraid for this sudden event and for the king's life, and said that it seemed advisable to him that he should submit to what Ivar demanded of him. Then the king fell silent and looked at the ground, and then said regally to him: "Alas, bishop! the wretched people of this land are treated too shamefully, and I would prefer to fall in battle, so long as my people could enjoy their native land." Then the bishop said, "Alas, dear king! your people lie slain, and you do not have the forces to be able to fight, and these pirates will come and bind you alive, unless you save your life with flight or save yourself by submitting to them." Then King Edmund said, very brave as he was: "I desire and wish in my heart that I alone should not remain after my dear thanes, who have been suddenly slain in their beds with their children and wives by these pirates. It has never been my custom to flee, but I would rather die, if I must, for my own land, and the almighty God knows that I will never turn away from his worship nor from his true love, whether I live or die."

After these words he turned to the messenger whom Ivar had sent to him and said to him, undaunted: "Indeed you were now worthy of death, but I will not defile my clean hands with your foul blood, because I follow Christ, who gave us such an example; and I will gladly be slain by you if God so decrees it. Go now very quickly and tell your fierce lord, 'Edmund will never in his life submit to Ivar, a heathen chieftain, unless he first submit with faith in this land to Christ the Savior.'"

Then the messenger went away quickly and met the bloodthirsty Ivar along the way, hastening to Edmund with all his band, and told the dishonorable man how he had been answered. Then Ivar boldly commanded the army that they should seize only the king, who had despised his commands, and immediately bind him. And Lo! then King Edmund, when Ivar came, stood within his hall, mindful of the Savior, and threw away his weapons; he wished to imitate the example of Christ, who forbade Peter to fight with weapons against the bloodthirsty Jews. And Lo! then the dishonorable men bound Edmund and insulted him shamefully and beat him with rods, and afterwards led the faithful king to a tree set fast in the earth and tied him to it with strong bonds, and again beat him with whips for a long time; and he always cried out, between the strokes, with true faith to the Savior Christ. And then the heathens, because of his faith, became madly angry, because he called on Christ to help him. They shot at him with missiles, as if for their sport, until he was entirely covered by their shots like the bristles of a hedgehog, as Sebastian was.[1]

When Ivar, the wicked pirate, saw that the noble king would not forsake Christ, but with steadfast faith continually cried out to him, he commanded him to be beheaded, and the heathens did so. While he was still calling out to Christ, the heathens dragged the holy man to his death, and struck off his head with one blow, and his soul went blessed to Christ. There was a certain man nearby, kept hidden from the heathens by God, who overheard all this and afterwards told it, just as we tell it here.

Lo! then the pirates went back to their ship, and hid the holy Edmund's head in thick brambles, so that it would not be buried. Then after a while, when they had gone away, the people of that land—those who were left— came to the place where their lord's headless body lay, and they were very sorry in their hearts for his death, and moreso because they did not have the head for the body. Then the eyewitness who had seen it said that the pirates took the head with them, and it seemed to him, as indeed was very true, that they had hidden the head somewhere in the woods.

Then they all went together into the woods, searching everywhere through bushes and brambles, to see if they could find the head anywhere. It was indeed a great wonder that a wolf was sent by the guidance of God to guard the head day and night against other wild beasts. Then they went searching and continually crying out, as people who often go into the woods always do, "Where are you now, companion?," and the head answered them: "Here, here, here!" And so it called out frequently, answering them all whenever any of them called, until by means of that shouting they all came to it. The gray wolf that watched over the head lay there, with the head clasped between his two paws, greedy and hungry, and did not dare, for God's sake, to taste the head but guarded it against wild beasts. They were amazed at the wolf's care, and carried the holy head home with them, thanking the Almighty for all his wonders. But the wolf followed along with the head until they came to the village, as if he were tame, and then he turned back to the woods. The people of the land afterwards lay the head beside the holy body and buried it as best they could in such haste, and immediately built a church above it.

Eventually, many years later, when the pillaging stopped and peace was granted to the afflicted people, they banded together and built a church

---

1 St Sebastian, whose feast is celebrated on 20 January, was a Roman soldier martyred under the emperor Diocletian. According to legend he was riddled with arrows by a firing squad—a scene frequently depicted in Renaissance art—but recovered from this ordeal and returned to the Emperor, who then ordered him to be beaten to death with cudgels.

worthy of the saint, because miracles had frequently taken place at his grave in the chapel where he was buried. They wished to transport the holy body with public ceremony and lay it inside the church. It was great wonder then that he was just as whole as if he were alive, with an uncorrupted body, and his neck was healed which had been severed, and there was something like a red silken thread around his neck, to show people how he had been slain. Likewise the wounds which the bloodthirsty heathens had made on his body with their repeated shots had been healed by the heavenly God; and he lies uncorrupted like this until this present day, awaiting the resurrection and eternal glory. His body, which lies undecayed, shows us that he lived here in the world without fornication, and journeyed to Christ with a pure life. A certain widow named Oswyn dwelt at the saint's tomb in prayers and fasting for many years afterwards; she would cut the saint's hair every year and pare his nails carefully with devotion, and keep them in a shrine as relics on the altar. So the people of that region faithfully venerated the saint, and Bishop Theodred richly endowed the church with gifts of gold and silver, in honour of the saint.

Then at a certain time eight unlucky thieves came one night to the venerable saint, wishing to steal the treasures people had brought there, and craftily conniving how they might get in. One struck the hasps hard with a sledgehammer, one of them filed around them with a rasp, one even dug under the door with a spade, one of them with a ladder wanted to unlock the window, but they toiled in vain and fared miserably, for the holy man miraculously bound them, each as he stood there struggling with his tool, so that none of them could commit his crime nor escape, but they stood in that manner until morning. People were amazed at how the criminals were hanging—one on a ladder, one bending down to dig, and each was bound fast in his labor. Then they were all brought to the bishop, and he commanded that they should all hang on a high gallows, but he was not mindful how the merciful God spoke through his prophet these words that stand here, *Eos qui ducuntur ad mortem eruere ne cesses*[1] "do not fail to save those who are led to death";[1] and also the holy canons forbid those in holy orders, both bishops and priests, to concern themselves with thieves, for it is not fitting that those who are chosen to serve God should have a hand in any man's death, if they are the Lord's servants. Then after Bishop Theodred had examined his books, he repented with lamentation that he had passed such a cruel sentence on the unfortunate thieves, and he always regretted it until the end of his life, and earnestly asked the people if they would fast with him fully for three days, asking the Almighty to have mercy on him.

In that region was a certain man named Leofstan, powerful in the world and foolish before God, who rode to the saint's shrine with great arrogance, and very insolently commanded them to reveal to him whether the holy

---

1 Proverbs 24:11.

saint was uncorrupt; but as soon as he saw the saint's body, he immediately went mad and roared savagely, and wretchedly ended with an evil death. This is similar to what the faithful Pope Gregory said in his narrative about Saint Lawrence, who lies in the city of Rome—that men, both good and evil, were always wanting to examine how he lay, but God restrained them, so that once in the examination seven men died there together, and then others stopped examining the martyr with their human foolishness.

We have heard many miracles in popular report concerning the holy Edmund, which we will not set down in writing, but everyone knows them. By this saint and by others like him, it is clear that almighty God is able to raise man again on doomsday uncorrupted from the earth, He who keeps Edmund whole in his body until the great day, though he came from the earth. The place is honored because of that worthy saint, that men should honor it and provide it well with pure servants of God in the service of Christ, because the saint is greater than men may conceive.

The English nation is not lacking in the Lord's saints, since in England there lie such saints as this holy king, and the blessed Cuthbert, and Æthelthryth in Ely,[1] and also her sister, sound in body as a confirmation of the faith. There are also many other saints in the English nation who perform many miracles, as is widely known, for the praise of the Almighty in whom they believed. Christ declares to mankind through His famous saints that He is almighty God who does such miracles, though the wretched Jews completely rejected him, wherefore they are accursed, just as they wished upon themselves.[2] No miracles are performed at their tombs, because they do not believe in the living Christ, but Christ makes clear to mankind where the true faith is, when He works such miracles through His saints widely throughout this earth. Wherefore to Him be glory forever with His heavenly father and the Holy Ghost. Amen.

---

1 Cuthbert (c. 634-687) was an Anglo-Saxon monk, hermit, and bishop of Lindisfarne in Northumbria; Æthelthryth (c. 636-679) was a queen, nun, and abbess of Ely in Cambridgeshire. Their stories, including accounts of the incorruptibility of their bodies after death, are told in Bede's *Ecclesiastical History*. Æthelthryth's sister Seaxburh (d. c. 699) was also queen of Kent, founder of the abbey of Minster-in-Shippey, and abbess of Ely after Æthelthryth's death.

2 Matthew 27:25.

3. *Vainglory*[1] (before c. 975)

[Source: *The Exeter Book*, ed. G.P. Krapp and E.V.K. Dobbie (New York: Columbia UP, 1936). Trans. RML.]

Listen! An old advisor long ago
told me, wise messenger, of many marvels:
he opened his word-hoard of the prophets' wisdom,
the old sayings of the saints, this scholarly man,
so that afterwards I might truly recognize⠀⠀⠀⠀⠀⠀⠀⠀⠀⠀5
by these sayings the true son of God,
a welcome guest, and the weaker one too
I might discern, cut off by his sins.
⠀⠀Every man can easily understand this,
who does not let a lecherous mind⠀⠀⠀⠀⠀⠀⠀⠀⠀⠀⠀⠀10
mar his reason in this fleeting world
or drunkenness drown all his days:
when many men meet in the assembly,
proud warmongers in their cities of wine,
they sit at the feast singing old songs,⠀⠀⠀⠀⠀⠀⠀⠀⠀⠀15
exchanging words, and try to determine
what field of strife may find its dwelling
among the men in the hall, when wine whets
their thoughts. The clamor rises,
a din in the company; in discord⠀⠀⠀⠀⠀⠀⠀⠀⠀⠀⠀⠀20
they shriek their words. So the minds of men
are differently divided; men of honor
are not all alike. One in his arrogance
vaunts his glory, within him swells
an immoderate mind—there are too many like this!⠀⠀25
He is entirely filled with envy,

1⠀⠀Anonymous and undated poem of homiletic instruction, found in the Exeter Book of Old English poetry immediately before *Widsith* (see Appendix A6). The author has drawn heavily upon the wisdom and thought patterns of the Church Fathers, particularly Augustine and Cassiodorus, for his understanding of the workings and consequences of pride, but the poem is also a moral reflection on the boasting and feasting inherent in the heroic life, a Christian condemnation of the life in the hall. Pride, envy, and malice are described as a kind of spiritual combat; compare Hrothgar's similar description in *Beowulf* 1740-46. The vocabulary of heroic verse is turned around, and the world of the hero is seen in the unflattering light of Christian humility. See further Bernard F. Huppé, *The Web of Words* (Albany: SUNY P, 1970) 1-26; Catherine Regan, "Patristic Psychology and the Old English *Vainglory*," *Traditio* 26 (1970): 324-35.

the flying darts and schemes of the devil;
he shouts and belches, boasts of himself
much more than does a better man,
thinks that his ways will seem to everyone   30
utterly unblemished. It will turn out otherwise
when he sees the result of that wickedness.
He shifts and he cheats and imagines deceits,
so many snares, shoots his mental darts,
lets them fly in showers. He feels no guilt   35
for the crimes he has committed, hates the better
man with envy, lets the arrows of malice
break the castle wall which his Maker commanded
him to protect, that place of battle.
He sits proud at the feast, foggy with wine,   40
with wily cunning he lets a word
slip out in provocation, leavened with pride,
inflamed with envy, glutted with vainglory,
malice and treachery. Now you can know,
if you should meet such a thane   45
living in the dwellings, learn from these
few declarations that this is the devil's child
incarnate, with a corrupt life,
his spirit bound for hell, empty of God,
the King of Glory.   50
                   The prophet sang of this,
ready of speech, and spoke this verse:
'He who exalts himself in arrogance,
advances himself in an evil time
in haughty pride, he will be humbled,
brought down after his journey of death   55
to dwell in torments, entangled in serpents.'
It was long ago in the Kingdom of God
that pride arose among the angels,
a notorious struggle; they raised up strife,
a hard campaign, polluted heaven,   60
betrayed their better when they tried with treason
to steal the kingdom and the King of Glory's
royal throne—as was not right—
and then to occupy just as they pleased
the fair land of glory. The Father of creation   65
stopped them in battle—too bitter was the fight for them.
    It will not be the same for the other one,
who lives his life humbly here on earth,
and always keeps with all his neighbors

peace in the land, and loves his enemy,   70
though he has often done him offense
willfully in this world. In wonderful joy
he may ascend hence from the earth
to the land of the angels. Not so the other,
who in his pride and wicked deeds   75
lives in his sins; the reward will not be the same
from the King of Glory. Keep this in mind,
if you meet a modest prince,
a thane in the nation—to him is always
joined as a guest God's own son,   80
delight of the world, if the prophet did not lie.
Therefore always considering the counsel of salvation,
we must remember at every moment
the truest good, the God of victories. Amen.

Appendix E: Translations of Beowulf

Since its rediscovery at the beginning of the nineteenth century, *Beowulf* has attracted scores of translators. The history of the poem in Modern English reflects not only two centuries of progress in linguistic and historical knowledge, but also changes in attitudes toward the poem's meaning and style. The passage below, chosen for its relative lack of textual difficulty or highly-wrought poetic effect, can illustrate the course of this history of translation. Some early translators tried to recreate the poem in an idiom that their contemporaries would recognize as "heroic" (nos. 2, 4, 7, 8); others have tried to reproduce the aural effects of the poem's alliteration and stress (notably nos. 8, 19, 21). Some avoid imitation or archaism and present the poem in a modern idiom (nos. 13, 18, 20); others, beginning with Kemble (no. 3) have foregone verse altogether and presented the poem in prose. In all cases the translation of the poem suggests the interplay, anxious but productive, between early verse and a later ear.

Beowulf 229-57 (Old English text)

Þā of wealle geseah	weard Scildinga,	
sē þe holmclifu	healdan scolde,	230
beran ofer bolcan	beorhte randas,	
fyrdsearu fūslicu;	hine fyrwyt bræc	
mōdgehygdum,	hwæt þā men wæron.	
Gewāt him þā tō waroðe	wicge rīdan	
þegn Hrōðgāres,	þrymmum cwehte	235
mægenwudu mundum,	meþelwordum frægn:	
'Hwæt syndon gē	searohæbbendra,	
byrnum werede,	þē þus brontne cēol	
ofer lagustrǣte	lǣdan cwōmon,	
hider ofer holmas?	[Hwæt, ic hwī]le wæs	240
endesǣta,	ǣgwearde hēold,	
þē on land Dena	lāðra nǣnig	
mid scipherge	sceðþan ne meahte.	
Nō hēr cūðlīcor	cuman ongunnon	
lindhæbbende,	nē gē lēafnesword	245
gūðfremmendra	gearwe ne wisson,	
māga gemēdu.	Nǣfre ic māran geseah	
eorla ofer eorþan,	ðonne is ēower sum,	
secg on searwum;	nis þæt seldguma,	

wǣpnum geweorðad,   næf[n]e him his wlite lēoge,[1]   250
ǣnlīc ansȳn.   Nū ic ēower sceal
frumcyn witan,   ǣr gē fyr heonan
lēasscēaweras   on land Dena
furþur fēran.   Nū gē feorbūend
merelīðende,   mīn[n]e gehȳrað   255
ānfealdne geþōht: ofost is sēlest
tō gecȳðanne,   hwanan ēowre cyme syndon.'

1. Sharon Turner,[2] *The History of the Manners, Landed Property, Government, Laws, Poetry, Literature, Religion and Language of the Anglo-Saxons* (London: Longman, Hurst, Rees & Orme, 1805) 404

Then from the wall
He that the sea-cliff should guard
Beheld the warder of Scyldingi
Bear over the hills
The bright shields,
The instruments of battle.
Instantly he broke the fire vessel
In the doubts of his mind
What these men were.
The Thegn of Hrothgar with his host
Went straight then
To ride to the shore of the conflict.
The powerful wood
He shook in his hands,
He asked counsel by his words.

"What are the designs
of this mail-clad host
That thus have brought this warlike ship
Over the streets of the sea?
Come they hither over the ocean,
Injuring every where the settled people?
The land of the Danes
Holds nothing more odious

---

1   The manuscript actually reads *næfre* "never," which most editors emend to *næfne* "unless." The manuscript reading might be translated "May his looks never belie him."

2   Sharon Turner (1768-1847), English antiquary. His work has the distinction of being the first version of any part of the poem in modern English, but it is highly inaccurate, and was only lightly and partially corrected in subsequent editions.

Than ship-plunderers. —
How I will your origin know
Before that far hence,
Like false spies
On this celebrated land,
You shall further go now,
Band of sea-dwellers.
Hear my simple thought;
It will be best to tell with speed
Why you have come here."

2. John Josias Conybeare,[1] *Illustrations of Anglo-Saxon Poetry* (London: Harding and Lepard, 1826) 39; ellipses in the original

Nor was it long, ere he who held in charge
To guard each inlet of the rocky coast,
The Scylding's warden, from his tower descried
The prompt and well train'd band in fair array
Bearing their bright shields onwards. Then arose
Care in his heart, and question, who might be
That stranger host; and straight he flew to horse
And sought the shore, and high uplifted shook
His herald staff, and thus in solemn guise
Bespoke them: "Whence and what ye are, declare,
Who thus in arms o'er ocean's watery path
Have urged to Denmark's coasts your rapid keel.
'Tis mine, the warden of the seas, to hold
with loyal care these outposts of the Dane,
Lest pirate force assail them. * * *
* * * * * * * * * *

And sure, methinks, mine eyes ne'er yet beheld
A chief of nobler port than him that leads you;
No stranger (if his bright and beauteous aspect
Belies him not) to the proud garb of war,
Nor in its toil unhonour'd. Speak ye then,
Ere yet your further march explore our realm,

---

1   John Josias Conybeare (d. 1824), professor of Anglo-Saxon and Poetry at Oxford from 1809 to 1812. His translations were made around 1820 but not published until two years after his death. His blank-verse rendering is notably Miltonic, to suit the expectations of his age: "Manifestly he feared the roughness, the remoteness of the poem in its natural state. He feared to offend a nation of readers reveling in the medievalism of Scott and Byron. A literal Latin translation was inserted to appease the scholar" (Tinker 31).

Or friend or foe, your names and kindred speak.
Here, ye far-faring tenants of the wave,
My full and clear demand — soonest were best
To give me answer — whence and what ye are."

3. J.M. Kemble,[1] *A Translation of the Anglo-Saxon Poem of Beowulf, with a Copious Glossary, Preface, and Philological Notes* (London: William Pickering, 1835; vol. 2 appeared in 1837)

Then from the wall, the warder of the Scyldings, whose duty it was to keep the sea-cliffs, beheld bear over the balks *their* bright shields, *their* ready implements of war. Curiosity overcame him in the thoughts of his mind, what the men might be. He then set out to ride upon *his* horse to the sea-shore; Hrothgar's thane brandished a mighty spear in his strong hands: he spake with prepared words; "What are ye, of armed men, guarded with mailed coats, that thus have come to lead a foaming keel, over the lake paths, hither over the deeps of the sea? I on this account placed here at the extremity *of the territory* have kept an ocean-watch, that on the land of the Danes no foe might do injury with a sea-force. Hither no shield-bearers have begun to come more openly, who knew not already the password of *our* warriors, the due observances of kinsmen. I never saw throughout the earth a larger champion than one of you is, a warrior in his trappings. That man is not *one* seldom dignified in *feats of* arms, unless his face, his comely countenance, belie him. Now must I know your origin, before ye proceed farther hence into the land of the Danes, false spies *as ye are*. Now ye dwellers afar off; ye sailers over the sea, *ye* hear my simple thought: Speed were best to reveal whence is your coming."

4. From Henry Wadsworth Longfellow, "Anglo-Saxon Literature," *North American Review* 47 (1838): 90-143; rptd. in *Poets and Poetry of Europe* (Philadelphia: Carey and Hart, 1845)

Then from the wall beheld
The warden of the Scyldings,
he who the sea-cliffs
Had in his keeping,
Bear o'er the balks
The bright shields,

---

1 Kemble (1807-57) was the first Anglo-Saxonist in England to embrace the new philological methods of Germans such as Jacob Grimm (1785-1863). His translation accompanied an edition of the poem, indebted in many respects to Thorkelin but notably more accurate. Italics in Kemble's translation indicate words that are not in the original, but are added by the translator to fill out the sense.

The war-weapons speedily.
Him the doubt disturbed
In his mind's thought,
What these men might be.
    Went then to the shore,
On his steed riding,
The Thane of Hrothgar.
Before the host he shook
His warden's-staff in hand,
In measured words demanded:
    "What men are ye
War-gear wearing,
Host in harness,
Who thus the brown keel
Over the water-street
Leading come
Hither over the sea?
I these boundaries
As shore-warden hold;
That in the Land of the Danes
Nothing loathsome
With a ship-crew
Scathe us might....
Ne'er saw I mightier
Earl upon earth
Than is your own,
Hero in harness.
Not seldom this warrior
Is in weapons distinguished;
Never his beauty belies him,
His peerless countenance!
Now would I fain
Your origin know,
Ere ye forth
As false spies
Into the Land of the Danes
Farther fare.
Now, ye dwellers afar-off!
Ye sailors of the sea!
Listen to my
One-fold thought.
Quickest is best
To make known
Whence your coming may be."

5. A. Diedrich Wackerbarth,[1] *Beowulf: An Epic Poem Translated from the Anglo-Saxon into English Verse* (London: William Pickering, 1849) 10-11

Soon from the Wall the Scylding Ward,
Whose duty was the Cliffs to guard,
Beheld them from the Vessel draw
Bright Shields, and Instruments of War,
His Curiosity brake through
In ponderings of his Mind to view
    What Men they e'en might be,
Therefore on horseback rode he to
    The Margin of the Sea.
The Thane of Hróth-gár brandish'd in
Strong Hands, his mighty Javelin
    And thus in Words he spake:
"Who are ye, that, in Armour dight,
And guarded well with Byrnies bright,
Your foaming Keel have hither led
Athwart the Holm, and traversèd
    The Passage of the Lake?
I, as the Border-warden, keep
My Watch upon the Ocean deep,
    Lest with a pirate Band
Some of the Foemen to our State
Should harry, rob, and depredate,
    Upon the Danish Land.
Yet ne'er did shielded Warriours [*sic*] here
More openly before appear,
The Pass-word of our warlike Crew
Unknown, and Rites to Kindred due.
Throughout the Earth I ne'er did see
'Mongst Earls, a Chief in Panoply

---

1   One of the most fascinatingly misguided attempts to translate *Beowulf* surely must be that of Athanasius Diedrich Wackerbarth, professor of English at the Catholic college of St Mary's, Oscott. Wackerbarth translated the poem into a version of Middle English ballad meter, explaining in his Preface that he abandoned the original meter because "I do not think the Taste of the English People would at present bear it" (ix; capitalization in the original). Like Longfellow, Wackerbarth relied on, and worked in the shadow of, Kemble's far more accurate prose version; his translation is, if nothing else, a striking reminder that the pressures exerted upon the translator by popular "Taste" and readerly expectations can at times be stronger than those of the text itself.

Of nobler Form to view
Than one of you appears, and he
In Arms must not unfrequently,
Unless his Countenance's grace
Belie him, and his matchless Face,
　　High Deeds of Worship do.
Now I, ere o'er the Danish Land
　　From hence you farther go,
Like leasing Spies in traitor Band,
　　Your Origin must know.
Now Dwellers of a far Countrey, [*sic*]
Ye, Wanderers o'er the mighty Sea,
　　My simple Thought ye know,
And Speed were wisest, whence may be
Your Coming here to shew."

6. John Earle, *The Deeds of Beowulf* (Oxford: Clarendon, 1892)

Then from his rampart did the Scyldings' warden, he who had to guard the sea-cliffs, espy men bearing over bulwark bright shields, accoutrements ready for action; — curiosity urged him with impassioned thoughts (to learn) who those men were. Off he set then to the shore, riding on horseback, thane of Hrothgar; powerfully he brandished a huge lance in his hands, and he demanded with authoritative words — "Who are ye arm-bearing men, fenced with mail-coats, who have come thus with proud ship over the watery highway, hither over the billows? Long time have I been in fort, stationed on the extremity of the country; I have kept the coast-guard, that on the land of the Danes no enemy with ship-harrying might be able to do hurt: — never have shield-bearing men more openly attempted to land here; nor do ye know beforehand the pass-word of our warriors, the confidential token of kinsmen. I never saw, of eorlas upon ground, a finer figure in harness than is one of yourselves; he is no mere goodman bedizened with armour, unless his look belies him, his unique aspect. Now I am bound to know your nationality, before ye on your way hence as explorers at large proceed any further into the land of the Danes. Now ye foreigners, mariners of the sea, ye hear my plain meaning; haste is best to let me know whence your comings are."

7. William Morris and A.J. Wyatt,[1] *The Tale of Beowulf Sometime King of the Folk of the Weder Geats* (London: Longmans, Green, 1895; originally published Hammersmith: Kelmscott P, 1895) 15-16

But now from the wall saw the Scylding-folks' warder,
E'en he who the holm-cliffs should ever be holding,
Men bear o'er the gangway the bright shields a-shining,
Folk-host gear all ready. Then mind-longing wore him,
And stirr'd up his mood to wot who were the men-folk.
So shoreward down far'd he his fair steed a-riding,
Hrothgar's Thane, and full strongly then set he a-quaking
The stark wood in his hands, and in councilspeech speer'd he:
What men be ye then of them that have war-gear,
With byrnies bewarded, who the keel high upbuilded
Over the Lake-street thus have come leading,
Hither o'er holm-ways hieing in ring-stem?
End-sitter was I, a-holding the sea-ward,
That the land of the Dane-folk none of the loathly
Faring with ship-horde ever might scathe it.
None yet have been seeking more openly hither
Of shield-havers than ye, and ye of the leave-word
Of the framers of war naught at all wotting,
Or the manners of kinsmen. But no man of earls greater
Saw I ever on earth than one of you yonder,
The warrior in war-gear: no hall-man, so ween I,
Is that weapon-beworthy'd, but his visage belie him,
The sight seen once only. Now I must be wotting
The spring of your kindred ere further ye cast ye,
And let loose your false spies in the Dane-land a-faring
Yet further afield. So now, ye far-dwellers,
Ye wenders o'er sea-flood, this word do ye hearken
Of my one-folded thought: and haste is the handiest
To do me to wit of whence is your coming.

8. Francis B. Gummere, *The Oldest English Epic: Beowulf, Finnsburg, Waldere, Deor, Widsith, and the German Hildebrand* (New York: Macmillan, 1909) 3-4

Now saw from the cliff a Scylding clansman,
a warden that watched the water-side,
how they bore o'er the gangway glittering shields,

---

1 In this joint venture Wyatt was responsible for a preliminary prose translation, which Morris then converted to verse.

war-gear in readiness; wonder seized him
to know what manner of men they were.
Straight to the strand his steed he rode,
Hrothgar's henchman; with hand of might
he shook his spear, and spake in parley.
"Who are ye, then, ye armed men,
mailed folk, that yon mighty vessel
have urged thus over the ocean ways,
here o'er the waters? A warden I,
sentinel set o'er the sea-march here,
lest any foe to the folk of Danes
with harrying fleet should harm the land.
No aliens ever at ease thus bore them,
linden-wielders: yet word-of-leave
clearly ye lack from clansmen here,
my folk's agreement. — A greater ne'er saw I
of warriors in world than is one of you, —
yon hero in harness! No henchman he
worthied by weapons, if witness his features,
his peerless presence! I pray you, though, tell
your folk and home, lest hence ye fare
suspect to wander your way as spies
in Danish land. Now, dwellers afar,
ocean-travellers, take from me
simple advice: the sooner the better
I hear of the country whence ye came."

9. William Ellery Leonard, *Beowulf* (New York: Century Co., 1923; Heritage Club, 1939)

Then from the wall the Watchman,   the Scylding set to guard
The water-cliffs, espied them   over the gangway bear
Their glittering shields of linden,   their ready fighting-gear.
His wits were seized with wonder,   what men were these indeed!
Down to the strand he gat him,   riding on a steed;
Henchman, he, of Hrothgar, —   mightily did shake
With his hands his spear-shaft,   and in parlay spake:
"What are ye, ye mail-clad,   what armor-bearing braves,
Who lead a keel so high-prowed   hither o'er the waves,
O'er the ocean causeway?   I've been out-post long,
Long I've held the sea-watch,   lest a pirate throng
In their fleet might sometime   do our Daneland wrong.
Here have strangers never   made them more at home;
Yet to you no word-of-leave   from my kin hath come,

No consent from braves here.   Never did I view
O'er earth a mightier jarlman,   than is one of you, —
That Hero in his harness: yon Man in weapons dight,
He is no mere retainer,   if tells his face aright,
His peerless port and presence!   But know I must your kin,
Your home, before from hence ye   (as if some spies ye bin)
Farther fare on Daneland.   Ye boatmen of the brine,
Ye far-off dwellers, hear now   this simple thought of mine:
'T'were best forthwith ye tell me   whence your coming be!"

10. R.K. Gordon, *The Song of Beowulf* (London: Dent, 1923)

Then the watchman of the Scyldings whose duty it was to guard the sea-
cliffs saw from the height bright shields and battle-equipment ready for use
borne over the gangway. A desire to know who the men were pressed on his
thoughts. The thane of Hrothgar went to the shore riding his steed; mightily
he brandished his spear in his hands, spoke forth a question: "What warriors
are ye, clad in corslets, who have come thus bringing the high ship over the
way of waters, hither over the floods? Lo! for a time I have been guardian
of our coasts, I have kept watch by the sea lest any enemies should make
ravage with their sea-raiders on the land of the Danes. No shield-bearing
warriors have ventured here more openly; nor do ye know at all that ye have
the permission of warriors, the consent of kinsmen. I never saw in the world
a greater earl than one of your band is, a hero in his harness. He is no mere
retainer decked out with weapons, unless his face belies him, his excellent
front. Now I must know your race rather than ye should go further hence
and be thought spies in the land of the Danes. Now, ye far-dwellers, trav-
ellers of the sea, hearken to my frank thought. It is best to tell forth quickly
whence ye are come."

11. Charles W. Kennedy, *Beowulf: The Oldest English Epic* (New York: Oxford UP, 1940)

Then the Scylding coast-guard watched from the sea-cliff
Warriors bearing their shining shields,
Their gleaming war-gear, ashore from the ship.
His mind was puzzled, he wondered much
What men they were. On his good horse mounted,
Hrothgar's thane made haste to the beach,
Boldly brandished his mighty spear
With manful challenge: 'What men are you,
Carrying weapons and clad in steel,
Who thus come driving across the deep
On the ocean-lanes in your lofty ship?

Long have I served as the Scylding outpost,
Held watch and ward at the ocean's edge
Lest foreign foemen with hostile fleet
Should come to harry our Danish home,
And never more openly sailed to these shores
Men without password, or leave to land.
I have never laid eyes upon earl on earth
More stalwart and sturdy than one of your troop,
A hero in armor; no hall-thane he
Tricked out with weapons, unless looks belie him,
And noble bearing. But now I must know
Your birth and breeding, nor may you come
In cunning stealth upon Danish soil.
You distant-dwellers, you far sea-farers,
Hearken, and ponder words that are plain:
'Tis best you hasten to have me know
Who your kindred and whence you come.'

12. Edwin Morgan, *Beowulf: A Verse Translation into Modern English* (Aldington, Kent: Hand and Flower, 1952; rptd. Berkeley: U of California P, 1962)

But the Scyldings' coastguard gazing from his rock,
He whose duty was to watch the sea-cliffs,
Saw shining shields borne across the gangplank,
Saw bared battle-gear; and his thoughts were pricked
With desire to discover the strangers' business.
So he came to the shore, mounted on horseback,
Hrothgar's man, brandishing with force
A formidable spear, and uttered these words:
'What men would you be, here in your armour,
Mail-coat-protected, in that tall ship
Brought through the paths and acres of ocean
Here, to our land? Long have I been
A watcher on these coasts, my vigil the sea,
Lest any enemy with warship-convoy
Should come to plunder the country of the Danes.
Never more openly have shield-armed men
Made harbour here, yet where is your permission,
Pass of any kind from our commanders,
Consent from the court? I never looked on
A finer man living than one of you seems,
He there in his armour: no mere retainer
Tricked out with weapons, unless looks belie him,

Looks without equal. Now I must know
Who you are, and from where, in case from this point
You push forward into Denmark and are taken as spies
As you move on inland. So now far-sailers
From homes sea-hidden, bend your attentiveness
To my plain request: promptly to tell me
Where you have come from, in courtesy is best.'

13. Burton Raffel, *Beowulf* (New York: New American Library, 1963)

       High on a wall a Danish watcher
Patrolling along the cliffs saw
The travelers crossing to the shore, their shields
Raised and shining; he came riding down,
Hrothgar's lieutenant, spurring his horse,
Needing to know why they'd landed, these men
In armor. Shaking his heavy spear
In their faces he spoke:
                "Whose soldiers are you,
You who've been carried in your deep-keeled ship
Across the sea-road to this country of mine?
Listen! I've stood on these cliffs longer
Than you know, keeping our coast free
Of pirates, raiders sneaking ashore
From their ships, seeking our lives and our gold.
None have ever come more openly —
And yet you've offered no password, no sign
From my prince, no permission from my people for your landing
Here. Nor have I ever seen,
Out of all the men on earth, one greater
Than has come with you; no commoner carries
Such weapons, unless his appearance, and his beauty,
Are both lies. You! Tell me your name,
And your father's; no spies go further onto Danish
Soil than you've come already. Strangers,
From wherever it was you sailed, tell it,
And tell it quickly, the quicker the better,
I say, for us all. Speak, say
Exactly who you are, and from where, and why."

14. E. Talbot Donaldson, *Beowulf* (New York: W.W. Norton, 1966, 1975)

Then from the wall the Scylding's guard who should watch over the seacliffs, saw bright shields borne over the gangway, armor ready for battle; strong desire stirred him in mind to learn what the men were. He went riding on his horse to the shore, thane of Hrothgar, forcefully brandished a great spear in his hands, with formal words questioned them: "What are you, bearers of armor, dressed in mail-coats, who thus have come bringing a tall ship over the sea-road, over the water to this place? Lo, for a long time I have been guard of the coast, held watch by the sea so that no foe with a force of ships might work harm on the Danes' land: never have shield-bearers more openly undertaken to come ashore here; nor did you know for sure of a word of leave from our warriors, consent from my kinsmen. I have never seen a mightier warrior on earth than is one of you, a man in battle-dress. That is no retainer made to seem good by his weapons — unless his appearance belies him, his unequalled form. Now I must learn your lineage before you go any farther from here, spies on the Danes' land. Now you far-dwellers, sea-voyagers, hear what I think: you must straightway say where you have come from."

15. Kevin Crossley-Holland, *Beowulf* (London: Macmillan, 1968; rptd. Cambridge: Brewer, 1977)

Then, on the cliff-top, the Danish watchman
(whose duty it was to stand guard by the shore)
saw that the Geats carried flashing shields
and gleaming war-gear down the gangway,
and his mind was riddled with curiosity.
Then Hrothgar's thane leaped onto his horse
And, brandishing a spear, galloped
down to the shore; there, he asked at once:
'Warriors! Who are you, in your coats of mail,
who have steered your tall ship over the sea-lanes
to these shores? I've been a coastguard here
for many years, kept watch by the sea,
so that no enemy band should encroach
upon this Danish land and do us injury.
Never have warriors, carrying their shields,
come to this country in a more open manner.
Nor were you assured of my leaders' approval,
my kinsmen's consent. I've never set eyes
on a more noble man, a warrior in armour,
than one among your band; he's no mere retainer,
so ennobled by his weapons. May his looks never belie him,

and his lordly bearing. But now, before you step
one foot further on Danish land
like faithless spies, I must know
your lineage. Bold seafarers,
strangers from afar, mark my words
carefully: you would be best advised
quickly to tell me the cause of your coming.'

16. Michael Alexander, *Beowulf: A Verse Translation* (Harmondsworth: Penguin, 1973)

The watchman saw them. From the wall where he stood,
posted by the Scyldings to patrol the cliffs,
he saw the polished lindens pass along the gangway
and the clean equipment. Curiosity
moved him to know who these men might be.

Hrothgar's thane, when his horse had picked
its way down to the shore, shook his spear
fiercely at arm's length, framed the challenge:
"Strangers, you have steered this steep craft
through the sea-ways, sought our coast.
I see you are warriors; you wear that dress now.
I must ask who you are.

                    In all the years
I have lived as look-out at land's end here
— so that no foreigners with a fleet-army
might land in Denmark and do us harm —
shield-carriers have never come ashore
more openly. You had no assurance
of welcome here, word of leave
from Hrothgar and *Hrothulf*!

                    I have not in my life
set eyes on a man with more might in his frame
than this helmed lord. He's no hall-fellow
dressed in fine armour, or his face belies him;
he has the head of a hero.
                    I'll have your names now
and the names of your fathers; or further you shall not go
as undeclared spies in the Danish land.
Stay where you are, strangers, hear
what I have to say! Seas crossed,

it is best and simplest straightaway to acknowledge
where you are from, why you have come."

17. Howell D. Chickering, Jr., *Beowulf: A Dual-Language Edition* (Garden City, NY: Anchor Books, 1977)

From high on a wall   the Scylding watchman
whose duty it was   to guard the sea-cliffs
saw glinting shield-bosses   passed hand to hand
down the gangplank,   an army's war-gear.
His mind was afire   to know who they were.
He rode his horse   straight down to the shore,
retainer of Hrothgar,   brandished his spear,
shook the strong wood,   mighty in his hand,
spoke out stiffly: "Who are you armored men,
protected by mail,   who thus come sailing
your high ship   on the sliding wave-roads,
overseas to this shore?   [Long have I] held
the sea-watch in season,   as the king's coast-guard,
that none of our enemies   might come into Denmark,
do us harm with an army,   their fleet of ships.
Never more openly   have warriors landed
when carrying shields,   and you have no leave
from our men of battle,   agreement with kinsmen.
Never have I seen   a mightier noble,
a larger man,   than that one among you,
a warrior in armor.   That's no mere retainer
so honored in weapons —   may that noble bearing
never belie him!   I must know your lineage,
now, right away,   before you go further,
spies scouting out   the land of the Danes.
Now, you far strangers   from across the sea,
ocean-travelers,   hear my simple thought:
haste is needed,   and the sooner the better
it is best to be quick   and say whence you come."

18. S.A.J. Bradley, *Anglo-Saxon Poetry* (London: Dent, 1982) 417-18

Then the sentinel of the Scyldings, who was required to keep guard over the sea-cliffs, observed them carrying gleaming shields and serviceable fighting-gear down the gangplank. An urgency to know what men these might be obsessed his thoughts. Hrothgar's thane, then, went riding down to the shore on horseback, forcefully brandished the sturdy wooden shaft in his hands and demanded with formal words:

'What sort of armour-bearing men are you, protected by corselets, who have come here in this manner, steering your tall ship over the seaways and over the deeps? I have long been the installed custodian of the land's extremity and maintained the coast-guardianship so that no enemy with a ship-borne army might cause damage within the land of the Danes. No shield-bearing warriors have ever arrived here more openly. Yet you were not absolutely sure of the permission and consent of the warrior-kinsmen. Never have I seen a greater nobleman on earth than is that notable person in your midst, that man in his accoutrements. He is no ordinary member of the hall enhanced by his weapons: may his face, a peerless countenance, never belie him.

'Now I must know your extraction before you go any further beyond this point into the land of the Danes as dissembling spies. Now, you inhabitants of far-off places, you voyagers of ocean, listen to my straightforward mind: haste is best in declaring what lies behind your coming here.'

19. Stanley B. Greenfield, *A Readable Beowulf: The Old English Epic Newly Translated* (Carbondale: Southern Illinois UP, 1982)

Then from the wall the Scyldings' warden,
whose task was to keep the sea-cliffs safe,
saw bright shields, battle-ready armor,
carried down the gangway. Curious,
he wondered who and what those men were.
So, riding his horse, right to the shore
went Hrothgar's thane; in his hand he shook
his great spear, spoke to them formally:
"What kind of men are you, armor-clad
in your coats of mail, who have thus come
hither in so tall a ship, taking
the sea-paths in your stride? For some time
have I guarded this land's end, held sea-watch
so that no foes with a force of ships
could launch a raid in our Danish land.
No other band has come so openly
with shields, yet you have no leave to land,
have not received consent of kinsmen,
our noble leaders. Never have I seen
such greatness as one of you suggests:
that warrior so worthily armed
is no plain hall-thane, else peerless looks

deceive. Come now: I must know the source
of your coming, and why, so that you'll
not be held as spies hastening further
into Denmark. Now mark well my thought,
you who dwell afar and dare the sea:
it were best for you to be in haste
to make quite clear whence you've come, and why."

20. Ruth P.M. Lehmann, *Beowulf: An Imitative Translation* (Austin: U of Texas P, 1988)

Then the Scyldings' watch,   who on shore kept guard
along the coastal wall,   saw from the cliffsummit
bucklers on the bulwarks,   bright shields hanging,
casques and mail ready.   Questions assailed him,
tormented his mind,   who these men might be.
Hrothgar's watchman   rode to the seastrand,
his steed striding;   stoutly he brandished
a weighty war-spear   and, well-mannered, asked:
"Who may ye be,   having armor,
defensive corslets,   who have fared hither
over the waterways,   the windswept vessel
guided across ocean?   Guard of the seashore
for a time am I,   trusted watchman,
so that on Danish lands   no dreaded foemen
could inflict damage   with a fleet of ships.
Targe-bearing men   have not touched this land
more openly,   nor have you met, surely,
leave of warriors,   license of kinsmen.
Never have I noted   among noble men
a greater on ground   than that grand fellow,
a warrior in war-gear.   He is no waiting-man,
honored by his armor,   unless his aspect lies,
his peerless appearance.   Now I propose to know
your ancestry   before you enter here,
faring further   as informers hence
on the strand of Danes.   For you strangers all,
seavoyagers,   a simple question:
whence come you now?   I call for answer.
Recount to us clearly,   for quickest is best."

21. Marc Hudson, *Beowulf: A Translation and Commentary* (London: Associated University Presses, 1990)

Then the Scylding guard gazed out from the wall,
he who must patrol the sea-beaten cliffs
saw bright shields, cunning war-gear
borne over the gang-plank; he was feverish
with desire to know who the men were.
Spurring his horse, he rode down to the shore,
Hrothgar's man, brandishing a spear
fiercely in his hand, and spoke these formal words:
"Who are you, in your steel harness,
your coats of mail, that have dared steer
your tall ship over the sea-ways,
hither on uncertain currents. Listen well:
I've kept sea-watch for a long time now,
making sure no raiders come ashore
to pillage and plunder the Danish land.
None have beached their ships more brazenly
than you men-at-arms and yet you await
no word of leave from our warriors,
consent from my kinsmen. Never have I seen
a greater man than that one there,
a champion in war-gear: nor is he someone's servant,
possessed of such weapons, unless his face belies him,
that singular visage. Now I must know
your lineage before you take another step —
spies that you may be — onto Danish soil.
You seafarers, strangers from afar,
hear now my naked thought:
you'd best make known straightway
whence you are come."

22. Frederick Rebsamen, *Beowulf: A New Verse Translation* (San Francisco: HarperCollins, 1991)

Watching above them   the warden of the shores
glimpsed from the cliff-top   a glinting of armor
as they bore from their boat   bright shields and spears
rich with war-weapons.   He wrenched his thoughts
groped within his mind   who these men might be.
He roused his horse then   rode to the seashore —
Hrothgar's cliff-guardian   heaved up his spear
shook it to the sky   and spoke this question:

"Who might you be   in your burnished mailcoats
shining with weapons?   Who steered this warboat
deep-running keel   across the waveswells
here against this shore?   I assure you now
I've held this guard-post   hard against sailors
watched over Denmark   down through the years
that no hateful shipband   might harbor unfought.
Never have boatmen   beached more openly
shield-bearing thanes   unsure of your welcome
hoisting no signal   to hail peace-tokens
friendship to the Danes.   I doubt that I've challenged
a loftier shieldman   than your leader there
hale in his war-gear —   no hall-lounger that
worthied with weapons —   may his wit not belie
so handsome a swordman.   I will hear quickly
first where you came from   before you move on
you possible pirates   pushing further
into Danish land.   Now let me advise you
horseless sailors   hear my counsel
my heartfelt words: Haste will be best
in letting me know   the land you came from."

23. R.M. Liuzza, *Beowulf* (Peterborough, ON: Broadview, 1999)

When from the wall the Scyldings' watchman,
whose duty it was to watch the sea-cliffs,
saw them bear down the gangplank bright shields,
ready battle-gear, he was bursting with curiosity
in his mind to know who these men were.
This thane of Hrothgar rode his horse
down to the shore, and shook mightily
his strong spear, and spoke a challenge:
"What are you, warriors in armor, wearing
coats of mail, who have come thus sailing
over the sea-road in a tall ship,
hither over the waves? Long have I been
the coast-warden, and kept sea-watch
so that no enemies with fleets and armies
should ever attack the land of the Danes.
Never more openly have there ever come
shield-bearers here, nor have you heard
any word of leave from our warriors
or consent of kinsmen. I have never seen
a greater earl on earth than that one among you,

a man in war-gear; that is no mere courtier,
honored only in weapons — unless his looks belie him,
his noble appearance! Now I must know
your lineage, lest you go hence
as false spies, travel further
into Danish territory. Now, you sea-travelers
from a far-off land, listen to my
simple thought — the sooner the better,
you must make clear from whence you have come."

24. Seamus Heaney, *Beowulf* (New York: Farrar, Straus, and Giroux, 2000)

When the watchman on the wall, the Shieldings' lookout
whose job it was to guard the sea-cliffs,
saw shields glittering on the gangplank
and battle-equipment being unloaded
he had to find out who and what
the arrivals were. So he rode to the shore,
this horseman of Hrothgar's, and challenged them
in formal terms, flourishing his spear:

"What kind of men are you who arrive
rigged out for combat in coats of mail,
sailing here over the sea-lanes
in your steep-hulled boat? I have been stationed
as lookout on this coast for a long time.
My job is to watch the waves for raiders,
any danger to the Danish shore.
never before has a force under arms
disembarked so openly — not bothering to ask
if the sentries allowed them safe passage
or the clan had consented. Nor have I seen
a mightier man-at-arms on this earth
than the one standing here: unless I am mistaken,
he is truly noble. This is no mere
hanger-on in a hero's armour.
So now, before you fare inland
as interlopers, I have to be informed
about who you are and where you hail from.
Outsiders from across the water,
I say it again: the sooner you tell
where you come from and why, the better."

Works Cited and Recommended Reading

***Beowulf*: Editions and Translations**

Alexander, Michael. *Beowulf: A Verse Translation*. Harmondsworth: Penguin, 1973.

——. *Beowulf.* London: Penguin, 1995.

Bradley, S.A.J. *Anglo-Saxon Poetry*. London: Dent, 1982.

Chickering, Howell D. *Beowulf: A Dual-Language Edition*. Garden City, NY: Anchor Books, 1977. Rev. ed. 2006.

Conybeare, John Josias. *Illustrations of Anglo-Saxon Poetry*. London: Harding and Lepard, 1826.

Crossley-Holland, Kevin. *Beowulf.* London: Macmillan, 1968.

Donaldson, E. Talbot. *Beowulf.* Ed. Joseph F. Tuso. New York: W.W. Norton, 1966, 1975.

Earle, John. *The Deeds of Beowulf: An English Epic of the Eighth Century Done into Modern Prose*. Oxford: Clarendon, 1892.

Fulk, R.D., Robert E. Bjork, and John D. Niles, eds. *Klaeber's Beowulf and the Fight at Finnsburg*. 4th ed. Toronto: U of Toronto P, 2008.

Gordon, R.K. *The Song of Beowulf.* London: Dent, 1923.

Greenfield, Stanley B. *A Readable Beowulf: The Old English Epic Newly Translated*. Carbondale: Southern Illinois UP, 1982.

Gummere, Francis B. *The Oldest English Epic: Beowulf, Finnsburg, Waldere, Deor, Widsith, and the German Hildebrand*. New York: Macmillan, 1909.

Heaney, Seamus. *Beowulf.* New York: Farrar, Straus, and Giroux, 2000.

Hudson, Marc. *Beowulf: A Translation and Commentary*. London: Associated University Presses, 1990.

Jack, George. *Beowulf: A Student Edition*. Oxford: Oxford UP, 1994.

Kemble, John M. *A Translation of the Anglo-Saxon Poem of Beowulf, with a Copious Glossary, Preface, and Philological Notes*. Vol. 2. London: William Pickering, 1837.

Kennedy, Charles W. *Beowulf: The Oldest English Epic*. New York: Oxford UP, 1940.

Klaeber, F. *Beowulf and the Fight at Finnsburg*. 3rd. ed., with First and Second Supplements. Boston: D.C. Heath, 1950.

Lehmann, Ruth P.M. *Beowulf: An Imitative Translation*. Austin: U of Texas P, 1988.

Leonard, William Ellery. *Beowulf.* New York: Century Co., 1923.

Longfellow, Henry Wadsworth. *Poets and Poetry of Europe*. Philadelphia: Carey and Hart, 1845.

Mitchell, Bruce, and Fred C. Robinson. *Beowulf: An Edition*. Oxford: Blackwell, 1998.

Morgan, Edwin. *Beowulf: A Verse Translation into Modern English*. Aldington, Kent: Hand and Flower, 1952. Rptd. Berkeley: U of California P, 1962.

Morris, William, and A.J. Wyatt. *The Tale of Beowulf Sometime King of the Folk of the Weder Geats*. Hammersmith: Kelmscott P, 1895.

Raffel, Burton. *Beowulf*. New York: New American Library, 1963.

Rebsamen, Frederick. *Beowulf: A New Verse Translation*. San Francisco: HarperCollins, 1991.

Turner, Sharon. *The History of the Manners, Landed Property, Government, Laws, Poetry, Literature, Religion and Language of the Anglo-Saxons*. London: Longman, Hurst, Rees & Orme, 1805.

Wackerbarth, A. Diedrich. *Beowulf: An Epic Poem Translated from the Anglo-Saxon into English Verse*. London: William Pickering, 1849.

Other Primary Sources

Dobbie, E.V.K., ed. *The Anglo Saxon Minor Poems*. Anglo-Saxon Poetic Records VI. New York: Columbia UP, 1942.

Dümmler, E., ed. *Alcuini Epistolae*. Monumenta Germaniae Historica, Epistolae Aevi Carolini, vol. 2. Berlin, 1895.

Fry, D.K. *Finnsburh: Fragment and Episode*. London: Methuen, 1974.

Needham, G.I. *Lives of Three English Saints*. London: Methuen, 1966.

Beowulf: Critical Studies

Amodio, Mark. "Affective Criticism, Oral Poetics, and Beowulf's Fight with the Dragon." *Oral Tradition* 10 (1995): 54-90.

Amos, Ashley Crandell. *Linguistic Means for Determining the Dates of Old English Literary Texts*. Cambridge: Medieval Academy of America, 1981.

Baker, Peter S. *Beowulf: Basic Readings*. Basic Readings in Anglo-Saxon England I. New York: Garland, 1995.

Barnes, Daniel. "Folktale Morphology and the Structure of 'Beowulf.'" *Speculum* 45 (1970): 416-34.

Bately, Janet. "Linguistic Evidence as a Guide to the Authorship of Old English Verse: A Reappraisal, with Special Reference to *Beowulf*." *Learning and Literature in Anglo-Saxon England: Studies Presented to Peter Clemoes on the Occasion of his Sixty-Fifth Birthday*. Ed. Michael Lapidge and Helmut Gneuss. Cambridge: Cambridge UP, 1985. 409-32.

Benson, Larry D. "The Literary Character of Anglo-Saxon Formulaic Poetry." *PMLA* 81 (1966): 334-41.

———. "The Originality of *Beowulf*." *The Interpretation of Narrative: Theory and Practice*. Ed. Morton W. Bloomfield. Harvard English Studies 1. Cambridge, MA: Harvard UP, 1970. 1-43. Rprt. L.D. Benson, *Contradictions: From Beowulf to Chaucer*. Ed. Theodore M. Andersson and Stephen A. Barney. Aldershot, Hants: Scolar P, 1995. 32-69.

———. "The Pagan Coloring of *Beowulf*." *Old English Poetry: 15 Essays*. Ed. Robert Creed. Providence, RI: Brown UP, 1967. Rptd. Baker 35-50.

Bjork, Robert. "Digressions and Episodes." Bjork and Niles 193-212.

———. "Grímur Jónsson Thorkelin's Preface to the First Edition of *Beowulf*, 1815." *Scandinavian Studies* 68 (1996): 291-323.

———, and John D. Niles, eds. *A Beowulf Handbook*. Lincoln: U of Nebraska P, 1997.

Bonjour, Adrien. *The Digressions in Beowulf*. Oxford: Blackwell, 1950.

Brodeur, Arthur. "Variation." *The Art of Beowulf*. Berkeley: U of California P, 1959. Rptd. Fulk, *Interpretations* 66-87.

Bruce, Alexander M. *Scyld and Scef: Expanding the Analogues*. Foreword by Paul E. Szarmach. London and New York: Routledge, 2002.

Bruce-Mitford, R.L.S. *The Sutton Hoo Ship Burial: A Handbook*. 3rd ed. London: British Museum, 1979.

Bullough, Donald A. "What Has Ingeld to Do with Lindisfarne?" *Anglo-Saxon England* 22 (1993): 93-125.

Cabaniss, Alan. "*Beowulf* and the Liturgy." *Journal of English and Germanic Philology* 54 (1955): 195-201.

Calder, Daniel G. "The Study of Style in Old English Poetry: A Historical Introduction." *Old English Poetry: Essays on Style*. Ed. Daniel G. Calder. Berkeley: U of California P, 1979. 1-65.

Cameron, Angus. "Saint Gildas and Scyld Scefing." *Neuphilologische Mitteilungen* 70 (1969): 240-46.

Campbell, Joseph. *The Hero with a Thousand Faces*. 2nd ed. Princeton: Princeton UP, 1968.

Carver, Martin. *Sutton Hoo: Burial Ground of Kings?* Philadelphia: U of Pennsylvania P, 1998.

Chambers, R.W. *Beowulf: An Introduction to the Study of the Poem with a Discussion of the Stories of Offa and Finn*. 3rd ed. with a Supplement by C.L. Wrenn. Cambridge: Cambridge UP, 1959.

Chase, Colin, ed. *The Dating of Beowulf*. Toronto: U of Toronto P, 1981.

Cherniss, Michael. *Ingeld and Christ: Heroic Concepts and Values in Old English Christian Poetry*. The Hague: Mouton, 1972.

Clark, Francelia Mason. *Theme in Oral Epic and in 'Beowulf.'* New York: Garland, 1995.

Creed, Robert P. "The Making of an Anglo-Saxon Poem." *Journal of English Literary History* 26 (1959): 445-54.

Damico, Helen. *Beowulf's Wealhtheow and the Valkyrie Tradition*. Madison: U of Wisconsin Press, 1984.

Davis, Craig. *'Beowulf' and the Demise of Germanic Legend in England.* New York: Garland, 1996.

——. "An Ethnic Dating of *Beowulf*." *Anglo-Saxon England* 35 (2006): 111-29.

Dean, Paul. "*Beowulf* and the Passing of Time." *English Studies* 75 (1994): 193-209, 293-302.

Deskis, Susan. *'Beowulf' and the Medieval Proverb Tradition.* Tempe, AZ: Medieval and Renaissance Texts and Studies, 1996.

Donahue, Charles. "*Beowulf*, Ireland, and the Natural Good." *Traditio* 7 (1949-51): 263-77.

Dronke, Ursula. "Beowulf and Ragnarok." *Saga-Book* 17 (1969): 302-25.

Dumville, David. "The Anglian Collection of Royal Genealogies and Regnal Lists." *Anglo-Saxon England* 5 (1976): 23-50.

——. "Kingship, Genealogies and Regnal Lists." *Early Medieval Kingship.* Ed. P.H. Sawyer and I.N. Wood. Leeds: Leeds UP, 1977. 72-104.

Duncan, Ian. "Epitaphs for Æglæcan: Narrative Strife in *Beowulf*." *Beowulf.* Ed. Harold Bloom. New York: Chelsea House, 1987. 111-30.

Earl, James W. *Thinking about 'Beowulf.'* Stanford, CA: Stanford UP, 1994.

Ettmüller, Ludwig. *Beowulf: Heldengedicht des achten Jahrhunderts.* Zurich: Meyer und Zeller, 1840.

Evans, A.C. *The Sutton Hoo Ship Burial.* London: British Museum Publications, 1986.

Evans, Jonathan D. "Episodes in Analysis of Medieval Narrative." *Style* 20 (1986): 126-41.

Farrell, Robert, and C. Neuman de Vegvar, eds. *Sutton Hoo: Fifty Years After.* Kalamazoo, MI: Medieval Institute, 1992.

Farrell, Robert T. "Beowulf, Swedes, and Geats." *Saga-Book* 18 (1972): 225-86.

Fell, Christine. "Paganism in Beowulf: A Semantic Fairy-Tale." *Pagans and Christians: The Interplay between Christian Latin and Traditional Germanic Cultures in Early Medieval Europe.* Ed. T. Hofstra et al. *Mediaevalia Groningana* 16 (1995): 9-34.

Foley, John Miles. *Immanent Art: From Structure to Meaning in Traditional Oral Epic.* Bloomington: Indiana UP, 1991.

——. *Oral-Formulaic Theory and Research: An Introduction and Annotated Bibliography.* New York: Garland, 1985.

——. "Texts That Speak to Readers Who Hear: Old English Poetry and the Languages of Oral Tradition." *Speaking Two Languages: Traditional Disciplines and Contemporary Theory in Medieval Studies.* Ed. Allen J. Frantzen. Albany: SUNY P, 1991. 141-56.

——. *The Theory of Oral Composition: History and Methodology.* Bloomington: Indiana UP, 1988.

———. "Tradition and the Collective Talent: Oral Epic, Textual Meaning, and Receptionalist Theory." *Cultural Anthropology* 1 (1986): 203-22.

Fontenrose, Joseph. *Python: A Study of Delphic Myth and Its Origins.* Berkeley: U of California P, 1959.

Frank, Roberta. "*Beowulf* and Sutton Hoo: The Odd Couple." *Voyage to the Other World: The Legacy of Sutton Hoo.* Ed. Calvin B. Kendall and Peter S. Wells. Minneapolis: U of Minnesota P, 1992. 47-64.

———. "The *Beowulf* Poet's Sense of History." *The Wisdom of Poetry: Essays in Early English Literature in Honor of Morton W. Bloomfield.* Ed. Larry D. Benson and Sigfried Wenzel. Kalamazoo, MI: Medieval Institute Publications, 1982. 53-65.

Fulk, R.D. *A History of Old English Meter.* Philadelphia: U of Pennsylvania P, 1992.

———, ed. *Interpretations of Beowulf: A Critical Anthology.* Bloomington: Indiana UP, 1991.

Georgianna, Linda. "Hrethel's Sorrow and the Limits of Heroic Action in *Beowulf.*" *Speculum* 62 (1987): 829-50.

Glosecki, Stephen O. *Shamanism and Old English Poetry.* New York: Garland, 1989.

Goldsmith, Margaret. *The Mode and Meaning of Beowulf.* London: Athlone, 1970.

Greenfield, Stanley. "The Formulaic Expression of the Theme of 'Exile' in Anglo-Saxon Poetry." *Speculum* 30 (1955): 200-06.

———. "Geatish History: Poetic Art and Epic Quality in *Beowulf.*" *Neophil* 47 (1963): 211-17. Rptd. Fulk, *Interpretations* 120-26.

Hanning, Robert W. "Beowulf as Heroic History." *Medievalia et Humanistica* 5 (1974): 77-102.

Helterman, Jeffrey. "*Beowulf*: The Archetype Enters History." *Journal of English Literary History* 35 (1968): 1-20.

Hill, John M. *The Cultural World in 'Beowulf.'* Toronto: U of Toronto P, 1995.

Hill, Thomas. "The Christian Language and Theme of *Beowulf.*" *Companion to Old English Poetry.* Ed. H. Aertsen and R. Bremmer. Amsterdam: Vrije UP, 1994. 63-77.

Hills, Catherine M. "*Beowulf* and Archaeology." Bjork and Niles 291-310.

Hobsbawm, Eric J., and Terence Ranger, eds. *The Invention of Tradition.* Cambridge: Cambridge UP, 1983.

Howe, Nicholas. *Migration and Mythmaking in Anglo-Saxon England.* New Haven, CT: Yale UP, 1989.

Irving, Edward B. *A Reading of Beowulf.* New Haven, CT: Yale UP, 1968.

Joy, Eileen A., and Mary K. Ramsey, eds. *The Postmodern 'Beowulf': A Critical Casebook.* With the assistance of Bruce D. Gilchrist. Morgantown: West Virginia UP, 2006.

Jurasinski, Stefan. *Ancient Privileges: 'Beowulf,' Law, and the Making of Germanic Antiquity.* Medieval European Studies 6. Morgantown: West Virginia UP, 2006.

Kaske, Robert E. "*Sapientia et Fortitudo* as the Controlling Theme of *Beowulf.*" *Studies in Philology* 55 (1958): 423-56. Rptd. *An Anthology of Beowulf Criticism.* Ed. Lewis Nicholson and D.W. Frese. Notre Dame, IN: Notre Dame UP, 1963. 269-310.

Kelly, Birte. "The Formative Stages of *Beowulf* Textual Scholarship." Part One: *Anglo-Saxon England* 11 (1983): 247-74; Part Two: *Anglo-Saxon England* 12 (1984): 239-75.

Kiernan, Kevin. *"Beowulf" and the "Beowulf" Manuscript.* 1981. Rev. ed. Ann Arbor: U of Michigan P, 1996.

———. *The Thorkelin Transcripts of 'Beowulf.'* Anglistica 25. Copenhagen: Rosenkilde and Bagger, 1986.

Leake, Jane. *The Geats of Beowulf: A Study in the Geographical Mythology of the Middle Ages.* Madison: U of Wisconsin P, 1967.

Lerer, Seth. "Grendel's Glove." *Journal of English Literary History* 61 (1994): 721-51.

Levine, Robert. "Ingeld and Christ: A Medieval Problem." *Viator* 2 (1971): 105-28.

Leyerle, John. "The Interlace Structure of Beowulf." *University of Toronto Quarterly* 37 (1967): 1-17. Rptd. Fulk, *Interpretations* 146-67.

Liberman, Anatoly. "Beowulf—Grettir." *Germanic Dialects: Linguistic and Philological Investigations.* Ed. Bela Brogyanyi and Thomas Krömmelbein. Amsterdam Studies in the Theory and History of Linguistic Science 38. Amsterdam: John Benjamins, 1986. 353-401.

Lionarons, Joyce. "*Beowulf*: Myth and Monsters." *English Studies* 77 (1996): 1-14.

Liuzza, R.M. "On the Dating of *Beowulf.*" Baker 281-302.

Lord, Albert B. *The Singer of Tales.* Cambridge, MA: Harvard UP, 1960.

Magoun, F.P. "*Beowulf A*: A Folk Variant." *Arv: Journal of Scandinavian Folklore* 14 (1958): 95-101.

———. "*Beowulf B*: A Folk-poem on Beowulf's Death." *Early English and Norse Studies Presented to Hugh Smith in Honour of His Sixtieth Birthday.* Ed. Arthur Brown and Peter Foote. London: Methuen, 1963. 127-40.

———. "The Oral-Formulaic Character of Anglo-Saxon Narrative Poetry." *Speculum* 28 (1953): 446-67. Rptd. Fulk, *Interpretations* 45-65.

———. "The Theme of the Beasts of Battle in Anglo-Saxon Poetry." *Neuphilologische Mitteilungen* 56 (1955): 81-90.

Malone, Kemp. "Grendel and His Abode." *Studia Philologica et Litteraria in Honorem L. Spitzer.* Ed. A.G. Hatcher and K.L. Selig. Bern: Francke, 1958. 297-308.

———. "King Alfred's Geatas." *Modern Language Review* 20 (1925): 1-11.

McNamee, M.B. "*Beowulf*: An Allegory of Salvation?" *Journal of English and Germanic Philology* 59 (1960): 190-207. Rptd. Fulk, *Interpretations* 88-102.

Meaney, Audrey. "Scyld Scefing and the Dating of *Beowulf*—Again." *Bulletin of the John Rylands Library* 75 (1989): 7-40.

Mellinkoff, Ruth. "Cain's Monstrous Progeny in *Beowulf*: Part I, Noachic Tradition." *Anglo-Saxon England* 8 (1979): 143-62; "Part II: Post Diluvian Survival." *Anglo-Saxon England* 9 (1981): 183-97.

Mitchell, Bruce. "*Beowulf*, line 1020b: *brand* or *bearn*?" *Studi sulla cultura germanica* (*Romanobarbarica* 10). Ed. M.A. D'Aronco et al. Rome: Herder, 1988-89. 283-92.

——, and Fred C. Robinson. *A Guide to Old English*. 5th ed. Oxford: Blackwell, 1997.

Moffat, Douglas. "Anglo-Saxon Scribes and Old English Verse." *Speculum* 67 (1992): 805-27.

Moisl, H. "Anglo-Saxon Royal Genealogies and Germanic Oral Tradition." *Journal of Medieval History* 7 (1981): 215-48.

Moorman, Charles. "The Essential Paganism of *Beowulf*." *Modern Language Quarterly* 28 (1967): 3-18.

Müllenhoff, Karl. "Der Mythus von *Beovulf*." *Zeitschrift für deutsches Altertum* 7 (1849): 419-41.

——. "Die innere Geschichte des *Beovulfs*." *Zeitschrift für deutsches Altertum* 14 (1869): 193-244.

Murray, Alexander Callander. "*Beowulf*, the Danish Invasions, and Royal Genealogy." Chase 101-12.

Nagler, Michael. "*Beowulf* in the Context of Myth." *Old English Literature in Context*. Ed. John Niles. Cambridge: D.S. Brewer, 1980. 143-56.

Newton, Sam. *The Origins of 'Beowulf' and the Pre-Viking Kingdom of East Anglia*. Woodbridge, Suffolk: D.S. Brewer, 1993.

Niles, John. *Beowulf and Lejre*. With contributions by Tom Christensen and Marijane Osborn. Foreword by John Hines, afterword by Tom Shippey. Tempe: Arizona Center for Medieval and Renaissance Studies, 2007.

——. "Locating *Beowulf* in Literary History." *Exemplaria* 5 (1993): 79-109.

——. "Myth and History." Bjork and Niles 213-32.

——. "Understanding *Beowulf*: Oral Poetry Acts." *Journal of American Folklore* 106 (1993): 131-55.

O'Brien O'Keeffe, Katherine. "Diction, Variation, and the Formula." Bjork and Niles 85-104.

——. *Visible Song: Transitional Literacy in Old English Verse*. Cambridge: Cambridge UP, 1990.

Orchard, Andy. *Pride and Prodigies: Studies in the Monsters of the Beowulf Manuscript*. Cambridge: D.S. Brewer, 1995.

——. *A Critical Companion to 'Beowulf.'* Cambridge: D.S. Brewer, 2003.

Page, Amy, and V.H. Cassidy. "*Beowulf*: The Christologers and the Mythic." *Orbis Litterarum* 24 (1969): 101-11.

Page, R.I. "The Audience of *Beowulf* and the Vikings." Chase 113-22.

Panzer, Friedrich. *Studien zur germanischen Sagengeschichte, I: Beowulf.* Munich: Beck, 1910.

Pasternak, Carol Braun. *The Textuality of Old English Poetry.* Cambridge: Cambridge UP, 1995.

Prescott, Andrew. "The Ghost of Asser." *Anglo-Saxon Manuscripts and their Heritage.* Ed. P. Pulsiano and E. Treharne. Aldershot: Ashgate Publishing, 1998. 255-91.

——. "'Their Present Miserable State of Cremation': The Restoration of the Cotton Library." *Sir Robert Cotton as Collector: Essays on an Early Stuart Courtier and his Legacy.* Ed. C.J. Wright. London: British Library Publications, 1997. 391-454.

Robinson, Fred C. "Beowulf." *The Cambridge Companion to Old English Literature.* Ed. Malcolm Godden and Michael Lapidge. Cambridge: Cambridge UP, 1991. 142-43.

——. *'Beowulf' and the Appositive Style.* Knoxville: U of Tennessee P, 1985.

——. "Why is Grendel's Not Greeting the *gifstol* a *wræc micel*?" *Words, Texts, and Manuscripts.* Ed. Michael Korhammer. Cambridge: D.S. Brewer, 1992. 257-62.

Rosenberg, Bruce. "Folktale Morphology and the Structure of 'Beowulf': A Counterproposal." *Journal of the Folklore Institute* 11 (1975): 199-202.

Russom, Geoffrey. "Artful Avoidance of the Useful Phrase in *Beowulf, The Battle of Maldon*, and *Fates of the Apostles.*" *Studies in Philology* 75 (1978): 371-90.

Schaefer, Ursula. "Rhetoric and Style." Bjork and Niles 105-24.

Schrader, Richard. "Succession and Glory in *Beowulf.*" *Journal of English and Germanic Philology* 90 (1991): 491-504.

Scowcroft, R. Mark, "The Irish Analogues to *Beowulf.*" *Speculum* 74 (1999): 22-64.

Shippey, Thomas A. "Structure and Unity." Bjork and Niles 149-74.

Sisam, Kenneth. "Anglo-Saxon Royal Genealogies." *Proceedings of the British Academy* 39 (1953): 287-348.

——. "Notes on Old English Poetry: The Authority of Old English Poetical Manuscripts." *Studies in the History of Old English Literature.* Oxford: Clarendon, 1953. 148-98.

——. *The Structure of Beowulf.* Oxford: Clarendon, 1965.

Stanley, Eric G. "*Beowulf.*" *Continuations and Beginnings.* London: Thomas Nelson, 1966. Rptd. Baker 3-34.

———. "The Germanic 'Heroic Lay' of Finnesburg." *A Collection of Papers with Emphasis on Old English*. Publications of the Dictionary of Old English 3. Toronto: Pontifical Institute of Medieval Studies, 1987. 281-97.

Stitt, J. Michael. *Beowulf and the Bear's Son: Epic, Saga, and Fairytale in Northern Germanic Tradition*. New York: Garland, 1992.

Tinker, Chauncey B. *The Translations of Beowulf: A Critical Bibliography*. Yale Studies in English XVI. New York: Henry Holt, 1903.

Tolkien, J.R.R. "*Beowulf*: The Monsters and the Critics." *Proceedings of the British Academy* 22 (1936): 245-95. Rptd. Fulk, *Interpretations* 14-44.

———. *Finn and Hengest: The Fragment and the Episode*. Ed. Alan Bliss. London: Allen and Unwin, 1982.

Turville-Petre, J. "*Beowulf* and *Grettis Saga*: An Excursion." *Sagabook* 19 (1977): 347-57.

Whitelock, Dorothy. *The Audience of Beowulf*. Oxford: Clarendon, 1951.

———. "Fact and Fiction in the Legend of St Edmund." *Proceedings of the Suffolk Institute of Archaeology* 31 (1970): 217-33.

Wormald, Patrick. "Bede, *Beowulf*, and the Conversion of the Anglo-Saxon Aristocracy." *Bede and Anglo-Saxon England: Papers in Honour of the 1300th Anniversary of the Birth of Bede, Given at Cornell University in 1973 and 1974*. Ed. Robert T. Farrell. London: British Archaeological Reports, 1978. 32-95.

from the publisher

A name never says it all, but the word "broadview" expresses a good deal of the philosophy behind our company. We are open to a broad range of academic approaches and political viewpoints. We pay attention to the broad impact book publishing and book printing has in the wider world; we began using recycled stock more than a decade ago, and for some years now we have used 100% recycled paper for most titles. As a Canadian-based company we naturally publish a number of titles with a Canadian emphasis, but our publishing program overall is internationally oriented and broad-ranging. Our individual titles often appeal to a broad readership too; many are of interest as much to general readers as to academics and students.

Founded in 1985, Broadview remains a fully independent company owned by its shareholders—not an imprint or subsidiary of a larger multinational.

If you would like to find out more about Broadview and about the books we publish, please visit us at **www.broadviewpress.com**. And if you'd like to place an order through the site, we'd like to show our appreciation by extending a special discount to you: by entering the code below you will receive a 20% discount on purchases made through the Broadview website.

Discount code: **broadview20%**

Thank you for choosing Broadview.